I keep telling myself that the beauty of hiking and climbing is discovery, pure and simple. How hard is the next hill, what's the trail really like from Low Divide to Elip Creek? Climbers have developed a system to rate and grade climbs, and they are now into a veritable foreign language about it all . . . Rather than demystify climbing it has bred unholy competition. Climbing magazines routinely diagram a pitch or climb with all sorts of little symbols. It's all become too clinical, techno-climbing. Are we going to publish scale side views of hikes, so you can visually see the ups and downs? No, leave that to me, the hiker, for those dark winter nights at home.

—William E. Hoke, after a trek through
the Olympic Mountains

Mount Olympus

Storm Damage

Each year winter storms produce flooding, rockslides, avalanches, washouts, and downed trees that impact trail passability. Backcountry storm damage from record-breaking storms in late October 2003 had yet to be assessed by land managers within Olympic National Park and Olympic National Forest when this printing went to press. To determine the most up-to-date conditions, readers are encouraged to either call the agency that manages a trail that interests them or review trail conditions on the agency's website.

TABLE OF CONTENTS

An asterisk preceding the listing of a trail indicates that it is a wholly or partially abandoned trail or a way path with limited or no maintenance.

PART I LEEWARD OLYMPICS

PART II WINDWARD OLYMPICS

PREFACE TO THE THIRD EDITION

Like its predecessors in 1984 and 1991, this third edition of *Olympic Mountains Trail Guide* is intended to serve not only as a field guide to hiking the trails of the Olympic Mountains but also as a reference work to consult at home. Although written primarily for hikers and backpackers who are not well acquainted with the Olympics and are therefore seeking ideas about where and when to go, the book can be used by persons familiar with the region and also by armchair adventurers who desire to explore the country the easy way—by reading about it when lounging beside the fireplace on a cold winter evening. I have attempted to describe the roads and trails in helpful language; I have also endeavored to answer the questions invariably expressed by hikers or backpackers: Why go there? Why hike a particular trail?

Essentially, the book has been distilled from my intimate acquaintance with the Olympics during the last half-century. I do not know how many miles I have walked in these mountains, but they number in the thousands. I went on my first hike in 1948, and a year later made my initial backpacking trip. Since then I have hiked, backpacked, and climbed in the Olympics every year, during all seasons, and in all kinds of weather. I have often repeated trips a number of times because I find that hiking familiar trails is much like wearing a comfortable pair of old shoes.

I have also walked many miles—often alone, but usually with companions—beyond the trails, traveling cross-country through forested valleys and canyons, along windswept ridges, and across pathless meadows. I have stood upon the summits of many of the higher peaks a number of times. During the period 1954–85, I participated in twenty-seven climbers' expeditions to Mount Olympus, during which I ascended West Peak, its highest pinnacle, sixteen times. On several of these climbs I camped overnight on the summit of Five Fingers Peak (West Peak's slightly lower companion), and as far as I am concerned this experience was the ne plus ultra of my Olympic adventures.

Only in this way, I felt, could I really get to know the Olympics, and when writing about them capture the essence and feel of the country. I have attempted to include all the trails, both in the national park and the national forest, but I am not so naïve as to contend that I have described every footpath created by man. Not long after the first edition appeared, a young man who prided himself on his knowledge of the high Olympics wailed in heartbroken dismay: "Why, you don't even have the P J Lake Trail in your book!" If I have overlooked others, I have not been made aware of them, and they would necessarily have to be either seldom-used way paths or perhaps fragments of long-abandoned trails that have vanished. Nearly all trails of consequence have been included in this book.

I have not, of course, walked *every* trail during *all* four seasons of the year; the descriptions therefore depict the country traversed as I observed it during particular seasons in certain years. But conditions vary from year to year, and from one season to another. Hikers are thus likely to note change, because it is inevitable and constant. Few things, if any, are truly permanent. Man-made features such as bridges, paths, and shelters can be destroyed virtually overnight by a fierce storm or more slowly by the insidious processes of erosion. The reader should therefore keep in mind that the text of this book reflects the conditions as they appeared when the writer or his trail checkers were personally on the scene observing the country. But to adopt an old phrase, the bridge that is here today may be gone tomorrow, and visitors to the wilderness should come prepared for change.

During the half-century that has swept by since I began seeking the solitude of the Olympics, considerable change has occurred in other aspects of the wilderness experience. In the good old days fifty years ago, regulations were few, gasoline inexpensive, and backcountry permits, although required, were seldom checked by the rangers. One could camp just about anywhere he or she wished, and fires could be built in any established campsite. One could also drink the water straight from the mountain streams without fear that it might be polluted and cause illness.

Some time along about the mid-1970s, the size of overnight parties going into the Olympics was limited, both by the National Park Service and the U.S. Forest Service, to a dozen persons. Fires were forbidden in most subalpine areas, and a reservation system was adopted for popular areas in an attempt to give everyone an equal opportunity to enjoy this wilderness. The ban on fires was instituted chiefly to save the picturesque "ghost forests" left by natural fires—forests that were becoming increasingly depleted because campers chopped them down for firewood.

When I wrote what became the first edition of *Olympic Mountains Trail Guide*, I included detailed descriptions of several trails or parts of trails that had been abandoned by the National Park Service and the Forest Service and were no longer maintained. I included them not only to preserve their historical value but also with the hope that putting them in the guidebook would encourage the government agencies involved to reopen these once-excellent trails. Unfortunately, it did not—perhaps not because of disinterest by the agencies but due to limited funds budgeted for trail maintenance and restoration. Be that as it may, abandoning these trails and not showing them on current maps (and letting nature return them to the wild) makes the areas traversed by such trails essentially inaccessible—and thus presents a good argument for deleting these lands from either the national park or the Forest Service's wilderness areas and again making them available to logging or other commercial activities. If they cannot be visited due to the absence of reasonably maintained trails, why retain these lands in a national park or wilderness area?

By describing all the trails in the Olympic Mountains, it is my hope this guidebook will help disperse visitors and lessen the natural tendency for hikers to congregate on the well-known, popular routes. Many trails that are obscure and seldom used have just as much to offer as do those that are tramped regularly.

It is also my hope that this book will help preserve the Olympic wilderness for hikers and backpackers—not just for the present generation but for future ones as well. I once heard a government official say, with regard to older people who wouldn't, or couldn't, or thought they couldn't hike or backpack anymore: "These people come to us and tell us they are glad we are building logging roads into the backcountry because the roads make it possible for them to visit again the places they hiked to when they were young." He made the statement to bolster his argument for road building into the remote corners of the wilderness, but of course he was placing a premium on one generation, with little regard for the young men and women of the future. So, too, were the former hikers who expressed their thanks to him for building the roads.

The Olympic Mountains are not as wild today as they were during the pioneer years of settlement in the Pacific Northwest or, for that matter, as they were fifty years ago. Nevertheless, they constitute one of the finest primitive regions remaining in the United States. Most of the area enclosed within the Olympic National Park, plus part of the adjoining national forest, can be accurately defined as wilderness. Thus, when hikers shoulder their packs and start up the trail, the magic of the wild closes around them, invoking its spell of magnetic enchantment.

ACKNOWLEDGMENTS

In acknowledging the assistance of others in the creation of this book, I find it difficult to divorce the third edition from its relationship as successor to the first and second editions. Although it is virtually impossible to acknowledge everyone who has been helpful with respect to the three editions, it is even more difficult to separate those who helped on the second edition from those who made contributions to the first. Certainly anyone who was mentioned in the acknowledgments of either one or both of the first two books can rightfully consider that they are credited here with making significant contributions, and I again wish to thank them for their past assistance.

The major problem I faced in researching and writing this edition of *Olympic Mountains Trail Guide* was how to deal with my increasing disability due to Parkinson's disease, which has greatly limited my ability to make field trips into the mountains. I realize that my climbing days are over, and most of my hiking ones as well. As a result, I have had to rely on close friends to become, so to speak, my arms and legs, my eyes and ears, insofar as noting and writing about changes that have occurred along the trails in recent years.

With respect to this new edition, I wish to express my special thanks to the members of what I call the "Committee of the Three Bills"—William Fleming, William E. Hoke, and William G. Sipple—who, together with my good friend Kent Heathershaw, instructor of mountaineering and backpacking at Olympic College, volunteered to assist with the rigorous field work needed in order to update the book. I owe these four, together with their hiking companions, a deep debt of gratitude because they did this out of kindness and dedication to the task and not for material gain. My thanks go to Jim Benton, Frank Chapin, John Fleming, Arthur Jacobsen, Dick McConaughy, Robert Scribner, Curt Steeb, John Stiever, Nancy Trask, Robert Van Pelt, and Barry G. White. If I have left out the name of anyone who should be acknowledged, it has been unintentional, and I extend my sincere apologies.

I am also grateful to Bill Sipple for convincing me I should get a personal computer and then teaching me how to use it, so that I am still able to keep up my correspondence and type manuscripts. Putting such a lengthy manuscript as this one on computer disk is, however, still somewhat beyond my capabilities. For her efforts in this regard, I thank my good friend Jessica Tonne.

For their assistance in the preparation of the 2004 update, Terry Wood would like to thank Bryan Bell of Olympic National Park, plus Susie Graham, Pete Erben, Ken Eldredge, Marji Dunmyer and Molly Erickson of Olympic National Forest.

INTRODUCTION

The Olympic Peninsula is located on the western coast of North America, approximately midway between the North Pole and the Equator, and marks the southern end of a fiorded coastline extending southeasterly from Cook Inlet, Alaska. The peninsula forms the northwestern corner of the conterminous United States and is bordered by saltwater on three sides—by the Pacific Ocean on the west, Puget Sound to the east, and the Strait of Juan de Fuca on the north. Only on the south is it connected to the mainland.

About half of the peninsula's 6500 square miles is occupied by the Olympic Mountains. They dominate the interior and are surrounded by lowlands that seldom rise more than 500 feet above sea level. The point where the mountains begin is not a distinct line because they blend gradually into the lowlands.

Once covered with vast stands of virgin forest, the country surrounding the mountains has been greatly altered since the arrival of Europeans in the latter part of the eighteenth century. As a consequence of the impact created by the white man, the area still in its natural state has been reduced to about 50 percent of what it was prior to the coming of Europeans to the Pacific Northwest.

Although the peninsula is located at a fairly high latitude, the nearby Pacific Ocean gives the land a mild marine climate. Extreme temperatures are unknown and precipitation is heavy, particularly on the windward side which faces the ocean. Here the rainfall often exceeds 140 inches a year, with still greater amounts deposited as snow at the higher elevations during the winter and spring. The summer and fall months are comparatively dry. The annual precipitation dwindles to about 20 inches in the northwest corner of the mountains' leeward side, where the slopes stand as a barrier to storms that move inland from the sea.

THE OLYMPIC MOUNTAINS

Because they comprise a complex cluster of ridges, canyons, and peaks, the Olympic Mountains cannot be called a range in the normal sense. This cluster is somewhat steeper on the north and east than it is on the south and west. Although the terrain is rugged and precipitous, it is not lofty as mountains go, rising less than 8000 feet above the bordering seas. This fact can be misleading, however, because the Olympics stand almost as high above the Pacific Ocean as do the Rocky Mountains above the Great Plains.

This domelike cluster does not have a central divide, but a number of ridges and so-called ranges separate the various watersheds. Some ridges are long and unbroken, but others have been eroded into sharp peaks and hanging valleys, truncated spurs and glacial cirques.

The creation of the Olympic Mountains occurred about 120 million years ago, when the land that now constitutes the Olympic Peninsula lay under a shallow sea. The peninsula has been alternately submerged beneath the sea or uplifted above it on at least five occasions, with erosion following each of the uplifts. The final rise occurred when the Puget Trough was depressed, leaving the mountains bordered by lowlands. The present-day mountains are composed of rocks that range in age from 15 million to 55 million years, thus in geologic terms the mountains are young. This uplift is chiefly composed of sandstones and shales that are closely folded and have been increasingly altered toward the interior. However, a horseshoe-shaped band of basalt encloses the mountains on all sides except the western. This band is thickest and widest in the east. Both the sedimentary rocks and the basalt were formed beneath the ocean—the former by deposits on the ocean floor, the latter by undersea lava flows. The only granite found in the Olympics, despite the reports of pioneer prospectors, is in the form of glacial erratics—boulders carried down from Canada by the Cordilleran Ice Sheet.

According to the currently popular theory of plate tectonics, the Olympics were uplifted by the movement of oceanic plates against and beneath the continent, which is not in agreement with an earlier theory that the mountains are the remnants of an upthrusted dome. Nevertheless, they do have a discernible domelike appearance. Although the Olympics are related to the coastal chain of mountains found along the western margin of North America, they are not part of it, having been uplifted at a separate time.

The Olympics were sculpted by alpine glaciers during the last Ice Age. The ice carved its way down the precipitous slopes, transporting debris which was deposited at lower elevations. Subsequently, the Cordilleran Ice Sheet from Canada pushed into the basin between the Cascades and the Olympics. One ice lobe moved westward along the Strait of Juan de Fuca, another thrust southward down the Puget Trough. The ice sheet then retreated, but large alpine glaciers remained on the higher peaks.

The climate following the Ice Age was mild for about three thousand years, and subtropical conditions extended as far north as Canada. During this warm period—which occurred about ten thousand years ago—the alpine glaciers retreated, postglacial erosion took place, and forests began to invade the country where the ice had prevailed.

The largest glaciers existing today in the Olympics—chiefly the ones on Mount Olympus and Mount Anderson—are believed by some geologists to be survivors of the Ice Age, but the smaller ones found throughout the Olympics are thought to have been formed during a subsequent cooling period—the so-called Little Ice Age of historic time, three thousand to five thousand years ago. Glaciers still exist on the higher peaks today, and the Olympics are noteworthy for having the lowest snow line in the United States (excluding Alaska). This line is the elevation above which snow can be found the year around. The largest glaciers today vary from 1 to 3 miles in length. Although glacial carving is most pronounced on the northern and eastern sides of the mountains, all the larger valleys and canyons have been deepened and steepened by glacial erosion.

STREAMS AND LAKES

The rounded, domelike configuration of the Olympic Mountains has resulted in a pattern of rivers that spiral outward from the central heights. These rivers, numbering perhaps a dozen having major significance, flow in all directions—west to the Pacific Ocean, east to Hood Canal (an arm of Puget Sound), north to the Strait of Juan de Fuca, and south into the Chehalis River drainage. Beginning in the north and proceeding clockwise around the mountain uplift, the major rivers are the Elwha, Dungeness, Quilcene, Dosewallips, Duckabush, Hamma Hamma, Skokomish, Wynoochee, Humptulips, Quinault, Queets, Hoh, Bogachiel, and Soleduck.

The rivers are all short, but they rapidly carry enormous quantities of water to the sea because the precipitation on most of the peninsula is excessive. When the streams are in flood, they lose their normal clarity and roll along at high speed. At this time they are dangerous to cross, and they should at all times be treated with respect. Flooding occurs after heavy, sustained rains and when the snowmelt reaches its maximum in late spring and early summer. At this time the tributary creeks, unrestrained and brawling, as they flow through deep, narrow canyons, clatter like freight trains racing across the country.

The Olympic Mountains have many lakes, most of them located in the higher elevations. With the exception of four at low elevation—Crescent, Quinault, Sutherland, and Cushman (which technically is a reservoir)—they are small and were created in various ways, including by glacial activity and dam building at the hand of man. Most of the lakes are cold, but a few are warm enough to permit bathing. The lakes in the high country, at timberline or above, generally are thawed out and open by mid-July, but after winters of excessively heavy snowfall, if followed by a cool spring or summer, they sometimes remain frozen until mid-August. At this time the adjacent meadows—particularly on northern, shaded exposures—are still covered by a foot or two of winter's snow while flowers bloom on southern slopes facing the sun.

VEGETATION ZONES

In mountainous regions, a phenomenon known as altitudinal zonation is present, caused by climatic changes that occur with an increase or decrease in elevation. As the elevation increases, the temperature decreases, and the climate becomes harsher. This has resulted in a classification called vegetation zones. Four such zones are present on the Olympic Peninsula—the Lowland Forest Zone, the Montane Forest Zone, the Subalpine Zone, and the Alpine Zone.

The Lowland Forest Zone ranges from sea level upward to elevations varying from 1500 to 2000 feet. This zone not only covers the lowlands surrounding the Olympics but also extends deep into the mountains by following the major rivers, gradually phasing into the Montane Forest Zone, which extends from the upper limits of the Lowland Forest Zone to an elevation about 3500 feet above sea level. The Subalpine Zone occupies the territory between the upper limits of the Montane Forest Zone and approximately the 5000 foot level. Above it, the Alpine Zone extends upward to the summits of the highest peaks.

Like everything in nature, the vegetation zones do not have distinct boundaries; instead, they blend into one another in an irregular manner. On cold northern slopes, for example, the Subalpine Zone at times extends well below 3500 feet. On the other hand, mountainsides with southern exposure often exhibit Montane Forest Zone conditions above 3500 feet. At times the Alpine Zone occurs at elevations below 5000 feet, particularly in the vicinity of glaciers.

On the peninsula, the Lowland Forest Zone has a mild marine climate, one typical of sea level at this latitude (45° to 50° north of the Equator). Within the mountains, this zone dominates the river bottoms and the lower foothills. The principal conifers are Douglas-fir, western hemlock, western red cedar, and Sitka spruce. Deciduous trees include red alder, bigleaf maple, black cottonwood, and Pacific dogwood. The luxuriant forest floor exhibits green mosses, flowering plants, and bushy shrubs. Included among the latter are willow, red elderberry, salmonberry, salal, huckleberry, devil's club, and rhododendron. Low-growing plants include Oregon grape, skunk cabbage, fireweed, and many kinds of ferns. The luxuriance of this zone contrasts markedly with the dark, gloomy stands of the Montane Forest Zone on the slopes directly above. Elk herds live here the year around but particularly in the winter. Deer, bear, and cougar are also present. The bird life is varied—kingfishers and dippers on the streams, wrens and varied thrushes in the deep forests.

The Montane Forest Zone is largely confined to steep mountainsides, and the temperature is usually somewhat cooler than on the lowlands. This is a realm of dense, somber forests, mostly thick stands of tall conifers. The common trees are Pacific silver fir, western hemlock, and Douglas-fir, with a sprinkling of western white pine and western red cedar. Because the trees grow in heavy stands, and their crowns interlock, the sunlight that reaches the ground is soft and indirect, the air cool, fragrant, and moist. In fact, this canopy is so dense it intercepts the first winter snows, which often melt on warm succeeding days, never having reached the earth. On the steeper mountainsides, pistol-butted trees may be observed. Occasionally this results from ground creep, but the phenomenon is more often caused by heavy snow that bent the trees when they were young and pliable. Undergrowth in this zone is sparser than on the lowlands, but it encompasses a wide variety of shrubs and saprophytes. Vine maple, alder, and devil's club border the streams; huckleberry, salal, and rhododendron clothe the drier slopes. The conditions in this zone are less favorable to wildlife than in the other zones, thus animals are not abundant, but the chattering of chipmunks and Douglas squirrels may often be heard. Bird life is also less varied than in the other zones, but it does include the gray jay, varied thrush, and several species of owls, including the controversial spotted owl.

The climate is still cooler in the Subalpine Zone. This zone exhibits great variety—a mixture of subalpine trees, meadows, glacial lakes, swamps, and bogs. The forests in this zone's lower levels blend gradually into the denser stands in the Montane Forest Zone below. In sharp contrast, in the upper levels open meadowland appears as the forest gives way to the treeless Alpine Zone.

The continuity of the Subalpine Zone forests is broken by the meadows. As in the Montane Forest Zone, the trees are chiefly conifers, but the dominant species are different—subalpine fir, mountain hemlock, and Alaska cedar. The trees are tenacious, having adapted themselves well to the harsh environment. Little groves are scattered over the grassy slopes and rises, and the ubiquitous low-growing juniper sprawls over the rocky ridges. Shrubs common to this zone include willow and slide alder on the stream banks, huckleberry and heather on the mountainsides.

Largest known western red cedar

Despite the difficult living conditions, a large variety of plants, animals, and birds are present in this zone. The meadows are snowbound for seven or eight months, but when the snow melts the low-growing plants bloom with a sudden rush. Although wildflowers are present in all zones, at all elevations, they reach their climax in these high meadowlands. The floral display attains its peak in late July or early August, flooding the mountainsides with color. Among the flowers are avalanche and glacier lilies in July, which bloom alongside receding snowbanks, and lupine, beargrass, and scarlet paintbrush in August. Of the ninety-five genera of flowering plants growing in this zone, all but one consist of perennials.

Weather conditions in the Alpine Zone—the highest in the Olympics—are the harshest to be found on the peninsula. Lying above timberline, this is a region of tundralike meadows intermingled with snowfields, glaciers, and barren country. Much of the year this zone lies under deep snow. Plant growth is sparse because the soil is poor and the growing season abbreviated. Cold and constant wind are the rule, and night frosts sometimes occur during the summer. Because the climate is rigorous and the growing season brief, the plants have a tendency to be dwarfed, compact, and dense. Less plentiful in kind and number than the ones in the Subalpine Zone, they are all low-growing perennials, and include grasses, sedges, rushes, and a few shrubs and flowers. They blossom hurriedly, and their seeds are scattered by the autumn winds. Among them are phlox, goldenrod, bluebell, alpine lupine, and pleated gentian. Arctic willows hug the ground; anemones and Douglasia add touches of color to glacial moraines. At the extreme limits of plant growth are found grasses such as bent, timothy, and squirrel-tail, with mosses and lichens thriving in protected spots among the rocks.

Several endemic plants occur in the Alpine Zone, chiefly in areas that were not glaciated during the Ice Age. They include Henderson's spiraea, Flett's violet, and Piper's harebell, all bearing the names of pioneer botanists who collected in the Olympics. Occurring nowhere else, these species have been adversely affected by the depredations of mountain goats, which are not native to the area.

THE OLYMPIC FORESTS

The Olympic Mountains are renowned for the stands of fir, hemlock, cedar, and spruce that clothe their flanks on all sides but attain their climax in the rain forests of the western valleys. The Olympic trees are part of the great conifer forest that parallels the Pacific coast of North America from southern Alaska to central California. Except for the high mountain district, the entire peninsula was once covered by unbroken stands of virgin forest, but most of the trees have been destroyed by logging operations since the coming of the white man. The best of the remaining old growth is found on the river bottoms and the lower slopes within Olympic National Park.

Douglas-fir grows everywhere in the mountains, but it is most abundant on the northern, eastern, and southern sides up to about 3000 feet altitude. Fire creates conditions favorable to the reproduction of this species, which requires sunlight and mineral soil. Thus one finds Douglas-fir flourishing where fires have raged in the past. Conversely, western red cedar occurs principally on wet flatlands and valley bottoms, and Sitka spruce is confined almost exclusively to the west-side lowlands, which receive excessive rainfall and summer fogs. The fir, cedar, and spruce are the largest trees in the Olympics, frequently surpassing 250 feet in height and 10 feet in diameter. Western hemlock, a smaller tree, is probably the most abundant species because it thrives in dense shade. Of the true firs, Pacific silver fir is common throughout intermediate elevations, but grand fir is comparatively rare.

The high-altitude conifers—subalpine fir, mountain hemlock, and Alaska yellow cedar—display varied characteristics. The fir and hemlock are spire shaped, with stiff trunks that resist breakage caused by the heavy burden of snow. Alaska yellow cedar has a different pattern of growth. The foliage droops, and the limber trunk bends readily under the weight of snow without breaking. Pacific madrona, a broadleaf evergreen, grows at lower elevations throughout the Olympics, but it is most common on the drier northern and eastern slopes.

Deciduous trees include red alder, bigleaf and vine maples, and black cottonwood. They thrive on river bottoms, particularly alongside streams, but occasionally grow elsewhere. Red alder, which prepares new ground for conifers, is the most abundant broad-leaved tree. Bigleaf maple is a large tree with a sturdy trunk and huge leaves that turn yellow in the autumn, but vine maple is a small, sprawling tree that could almost be characterized as a large shrub. The largest deciduous tree is the black cottonwood, but it is not numerous. Almost invariably found along streams, it frequently attains a diameter of 4 to 6 feet and heights of 180 feet.

The Olympic forests contain several trees recognized by the American Forestry Association as the largest known examples of their species. However, tree champions wear uneasy crowns—they have to face not only the prospect of destruction by nature (wind, fire, or flood) or by man (fire, logging, or road building) but also the possibility that a larger specimen may be discovered elsewhere. Consequently, the champions change from time to time.

On occasion, in the past, as many as six or eight record-size trees in the Olympic Mountains have been recognized simultaneously by the association. Most of the champions have been conifers, located within the boundaries of the national park, but occasionally a deciduous tree has held the crown. Because the trees having championship status vary from one decade to another, even from year to year, no listing is given here of the current title holders inasmuch as such a list would, in all probability, become obsolete in the near future.

Snags and hollow trees are common in the virgin forest, in marked contrast to their absence in second-growth stands. Such trees were once considered useless, but they are now recognized as having great value because they provide both food and shelter for many woodland creatures. For example, woodpeckers carve holes in standing dead trees, either to make cavities for nesting purposes or to search for insects. After the holes have been abandoned, they provide homes for other birds and small woodland creatures.

THE RAIN FOREST

The Olympic rain forest, one of the few temperate-zone rain forests in the world, is confined to the windward slopes of the Olympic Mountains between sea level and approximately 2000 feet elevation. Rainfall exceeds 12 feet a year, occurring mostly during the winter months. Because this forest is located on the windward side of the mountains, where it is exposed to rain and fog and protected from cold east winds, the luxuriance of vegetation is comparable to that of equatorial rain forests.

The rain forest is a complex community of plants and animals that are interdependent—living and dying together, competing and cooperating with one another. Elk browse in the mingled sunlight and shadow, squirrels and chipmunks scurry over the forest floor, and salmon leap the cascades in the creeks and rivers. Standing over all are the big trees. The most common ones are Douglas-fir, western hemlock, western red cedar, and Sitka spruce. They overshadow the bigleaf maples and black cottonwoods, and the still lower understory of red alder, vine maple, devil's club, and low-growing shrubs. Occasionally, rain-forest conditions extend to higher altitudes, into the zone of silver fir, yew, and grand fir.

The strange appearance of the rain forest is due to thick growths of mosses, liverworts, ferns, and lichens. The mosses that live upon the ground are sustained by nutrients obtained from the soil; those that cling to the trees are dependent upon nourishment transported by the wind. Selaginella, the most common growth, is not a true moss but a club moss, with sprigs that resemble reindeer antlers. This plant festoons almost every branch of the maple trees. Equally abundant are the tropical-looking ferns which grow in profusion—on the ground, on fallen trees, and on limbs a hundred feet overhead. In addition to the mosses and ferns, the forest floor supports many kinds of flowering plants and shrubs, including huckleberry and devil's club. In fact, the varieties number in the hundreds. The old logs lying on the ground are covered with mosses, oxalis, and conifer seedlings. Thus the death of large trees in this forest does not end their usefulness. As they slowly decay, the prostrate trees serve as seedbeds or nurse logs, providing sustenance for thousands of plants and the little trees that compete with each other for the limited space available; consequently, only a few of the latter—the strongest, healthiest, most favorably situated—survive to become large trees.

Here is a landscape that cannot be appreciated at a glance from an automobile window. One must linger a while and walk among the trees—alone, if possible— because the moods are variable, changing from hour to hour, day to day, season to season. Shafts of subdued green-gold sunlight pierce the treetops to create a twilight effect, with dapples of sun and shadow; cushions of moss, illumined by vagrant rays of light, glow among the ferns on tree limbs above the trail, adding a mystic, eerie touch. One seems transported to an unreal, magical realm, a place where one would not be surprised to find elves and goblins lurking in the shadows. The visitor may walk for hours here, enchanted and humbled by the giant trees that rise silently toward the sky.

Most people see this forest in the dry season, when the weather is pleasant, the sky sunny. But to really capture the region's mood, one should come during the winter, when clouds cling to the timbered mountainsides and the wind surges through ancient treetops. Often it will be raining, perhaps lightly, and the moisture dripping from the fog-shrouded spruce and fir adds still another dimension to this brooding forest, which is quiet except during storms because the thick foliage muffles sounds. On wind-free days one becomes acutely aware of the distant murmur of the river, the humming of an insect, or perhaps the call of a lone bird.

But the rain forest is probably at its best in early spring, when the new shoots, delicate green in color, come forth on the trees and shrubs, the grasses spring forth on the forest floor, and the sun shining through the vine maples creates a fairyland. Later, during the summer, the views are more restricted because the dense foliage not only screens out distant vistas but also tends to hide the mosses and lichens.

MAMMALS

Almost half the territory covered by the Olympic Mountains lies within Olympic National Park, where wildlife is protected, thus making the park one of the nation's finest refuges because it is large enough to include the annual migratory range of several species. Good habitat is also provided in the adjoining Olympic National Forest and on state lands that border the park on the west.

One is more apt to see wildlife when hiking alone than when traveling with companions. This rule applies to the smaller animals as well as the large mammals.

The Roosevelt elk, native to the Pacific coast, is the largest mammal inhabiting the Olympics, the bulls sometimes attaining 1000 pounds. Wildlife experts estimate that the elk population on the peninsula varies from five thousand to seven thousand animals. How many live within the mountains is debatable, but it is a considerable number. The elk winter in the lowlands, where some herds remain throughout the year, while others (less than 50 percent) move to the higher altitudes during the summer and fall months. Apparently, the elk do not engage in true seasonal migration. Although they are found throughout the Olympics, most of them inhabit the windward side of the mountains.

Elk frequent the rain forests, but the animals tend to be wary, and they are not observed—particularly in large herds—as often as they were a half-century ago. This is probably due to the greatly increased visitation by humans in the valleys—the elk seek seclusion by retreating to wilderness cul-de-sacs seldom visited by man. The elk trails are well defined, however, and the tracks of the animals are often visible in the mud or snow. Were it not for the elk, the rain forest would be an impenetrable jungle. As the bands wander about, the animals not only graze on grasses and sedges but also browse on the tender shoots, leaves, and twigs of willow, alder, huckleberry, vine maple, and salmonberry—thus creating a landscaped effect. The elk population is determined chiefly by the availability of browse, secondarily by the number of animals that perish during the winter. Apparently, predators are not numerous enough to have much effect upon their numbers.

Hikers are more likely to see deer. Both the Columbia black-tailed deer and the mule deer are present in the Olympics. The former, the native variety, is the one most often observed. The mule deer was introduced into the area many years ago and is comparatively rare. When deer run, they actually bound, jumping high into the air. Apparently, this is a defense mechanism—they leap high in order to obtain a better view of their surroundings when attempting to elude pursuit.

Mountain goats are not native to the Olympics; they were introduced into the area in the 1920s. Their numbers increased slowly at first, but accelerated greatly during the 1970s and 1980s. This was probably due to two factors—lack of natural enemies and the prohibition on hunting in the national park. They have, in fact, become so numerous that they are, in some locations, severely damaging the native vegetation, particularly endemic, low-growing plants in the subalpine meadows. During recent years, biologists have studied the habits and movements of the goats. As a consequence, the National Park Service has removed some goats from districts that were overpopulated. The final solution to the mountain goat problem in the Olympics remains to be decided.

Predators in the Olympics include the black bear, mountain lion, wildcat, and coyote. The Olympic wolf once roamed the mountains, but it is believed to be extinct, having been exterminated by hunters and ranchers. None have been observed since the mid-1920s.

At the present time, a movement to reintroduce the gray wolf in the Olympics has numerous adherents, who are encouraged by the successful reintroduction of the animal in Yellowstone National Park. Like the goat question, however, reintroduction remains controversial and undecided, and proponents and opponents are equally vociferous in stating their opinions on the issue.

Of all the national parks, Olympic is believed to have the largest number of mountain lions, but this does not mean they are numerous. Because the big cats are elusive, they are seldom observed, although sightings have become more common the last few years. This is true also of wildcats and coyotes, which are comparatively rare; black bears, however, are fairly numerous. They are found throughout the Olympics, and almost every hiker has encountered them. The black bear has several color phases, but the black phase is the only one that occurs in the Olympics.

Among the smaller animals, the most common are the Olympic marmot, Douglas squirrel, Townsend's chipmunk, raccoon, snowshoe rabbit, and mountain beaver. Fur bearers are rare, but include the otter, weasel, fisher, marten, and mink.

Marmots generally inhabit the high meadows, and they seem to be everywhere, whistling continuously whenever their realm is invaded. They often frolic on the snow, playing with one another. Two will stand nose to nose, facing each other, then rise upon their hind legs, appearing to shake hands or touch noses. One cannot but wonder what this maneuver means. Then they drop to all fours, flip their tails, and race away across the snow, only to repeat the performance.

Significant by their absence in the Olympics are several animals native to the Pacific Northwest. When the Cordilleran Ice Sheet overwhelmed the Puget Sound basin during the Ice Age, the animals fled south ahead of the advancing ice. When the glaciers retreated, the wildlife gradually returned, but some species are now extinct and others have never made their way back to the peninsula. Still missing are the red fox, wolverine, pika, and golden-mantled ground squirrel.

BIRDS

According to ornithologists, 261 species of birds have been noted on the Olympic Peninsula and two dozen others are believed to be casual visitors, although no specimens have been taken. The coastal zones provide a suitable habitat for marine birds, but about half the species live inland—along rivers, on cut-over uplands, in the mountain forests, and in the high meadows. No definite figures are available on the number of species that inhabit or visit the Olympic Mountains per se.

Bird life in the forests bordering the mountain streams is varied and includes wrens, sparrows, crows, woodpeckers, kingfishers, and dippers. Other species will be noted in the deep conifer forests on the lower slopes—hawks, owls, grouse, swifts, warblers, and jays.

The open country near timberline provides better viewing conditions. Here one is likely to see sparrows, finches, larks, bluebirds, and ravens. Hawks soar over the meadows, searching for small animals, because they are easier to find here than in the dense forests below. The perching birds are present in great variety. Most commonly one will see flycatchers, kinglets, chickadees, bluebirds, robins, and juncos.

One of the friendliest birds, the gray jay can be found at almost any altitude except, perhaps, the heights above timberline. Hardly has one set up camp—or merely stopped to rest by the trail a few minutes—than a flock of these "camp robbers" makes its appearance, looking for handouts. The more venturesome birds will take food from the hand, while others keep their beady eyes alert to the possibilities of larceny. Then, as suddenly as they came, the jays will depart.

Throughout the Olympic forests, one is likely to first hear, then see, the "Mozart of the woods," otherwise known as the winter wren. This little bit of feathered fluff with the big, happy voice flits about—along the trail, in the campgrounds, wherever the hiker happens to be—constantly trilling a lovely aria.

Other common birds include juncos and chickadees around campsites, salvaging scraps of food; crows cawing by the rivers before dawn; grouse drumming in the forest; pileated woodpeckers making a loud racket as they attack dead snags; and, at high lakes, ducks swooping over with a whooshing sound as they circle and come in to land upon the water.

Golden eagles are occasionally seen in the Olympics, gliding above the meadows while searching for dinner. Bald eagles frequent the coast of the peninsula, but they are rare in the mountains, although sometimes noted along the west-side rivers.

FISH

The rivers, creeks, and lakes in the Olympic Mountains contain many kinds of fish. Each fall and winter, salmon and steelhead (an ocean-going rainbow trout) fight their way up the rivers to spawn, forcing passage through rapids and cascades in accordance with their instincts. The Indians and the pioneer settlers depended upon the fish for food. The rich red flesh was eaten fresh when the salmon were running, and great quantities were dried and smoked for use at a later time.

Several rivers on the peninsula have been dammed, either to generate electricity or for flood control. As a consequence, salmon and steelhead are no longer found in the streams above the obstructions. The most notable examples are the Elwha River and the North Fork Skokomish, but dams are also located on the Big Quilcene and the Wynoochee. At the present time, a strong movement is under way to have the government remove the two dams on the Elwha River, so that this once great salmon stream can be restored to its natural state as a splendid breeding ground for fish.

Trout are found in the mountain streams and lakes. The varieties include cutthroat, rainbow, Eastern brook, and steelhead. The regulations regarding fishing change from time to time; therefore, anglers should check with the National Park Service or the U.S. Forest Service—whichever agency is the appropriate one for the particular occasion—before indulging in this sport.

During the pioneer years the rivers and creeks had an abundance of fish, far more than they have today, and it was a simple matter to catch large quantities. Many of the mountain lakes were barren, however, until fish were planted in them.

THE HUMAN IMPACT

The first humans who lived on the Olympic Peninsula were Pacific Coast Indians, whose ancestors had migrated to the region from Asia by way of Alaska. No one knows how long they were present before the white people came, but archaeological evidence indicates they had lived along the coast for centuries. They developed a complex social system based on hunting, fishing, and gathering. Their settlements were limited to the coastal perimeter. Most of the food supply was taken from the beaches, the ocean, and the rivers, but the women went into the forest to gather berries and roots, and the men occasionally ventured into the interior to hunt elk and deer.

According to Indian legends, before the time of the Quileutes the peaks of Mount Olympus were one big mountain—the abode of the Thunderbird. This was their god—an immense creature capable of darkening the heavens and responsible for lightning and thunder.

European seafarers sailing along the western coast of North America in the latter part of the eighteenth century were the first white men to view the Olympics. One of them sighted and named Mount Olympus in 1788. Eventually the mariners became daring enough to sail into Puget Sound, and a British captain named just about everything in sight. With the advent of the nineteenth century, the sailors departed the Pacific Northwest coast. During the next fifty years the peninsula was more or less ignored by Europeans, but after the boundary between the United States and Canada was agreed upon in 1846, settlement accelerated, and the native inhabitants were forced to cede most of their lands to the United States, reserving only small tracts for themselves. About this time prospectors and hunters began roaming through the Olympics, but they left no records or trails.

The first organized attempt to explore the Olympic Mountains occurred in 1882, when the U.S. Army cut a trail from Fort Townsend, on the northeastern tip of the Olympic Peninsula, to the Dungeness River. The soldiers were followed, three years later, by an expedition commanded by Lieutenant Joseph P. O'Neil that explored the northeastern Olympics.

During the severe winter of 1889–90, a small party of civilians known as the Press Expedition succeeded in crossing the mountains, but the explorers suffered severely from the hardships and almost perished. In the summer of 1890, Lieutenant O'Neil returned with a much larger party and thoroughly explored the country. As a result of his explorations, he recommended the creation of a national park in the Olympics, as did James Wickersham, a civilian who spent some time wandering through the Olympics.

Mountaineers began scaling the peaks in the early 1900s. The first ascent of Mount Olympus occurred in 1907, and by 1931, when US 101 was completed around the mountains, the major peaks had been climbed. Such exploits made people aware of the outstanding qualities of the peninsula and brought into focus the need for a national park. The new highway made the Olympics accessible and not only resulted in a large increase in visitors but also meant that the region could be commercially exploited more readily. Thus it soon became apparent that the scenic resources of the Olympics needed permanent protection.

The story of conservation in the Olympics began with the establishment of the Olympic Forest Reserve in 1897. The reserve originally contained about 2 million acres and included not only the Olympic Mountains but also the extensive territory between them and the Pacific Ocean. However, commercial interests quickly succeeded in having large areas deleted from the reserve. The reserve was surveyed at the turn of the century, and in 1907 its name was changed to Olympic National Forest.

In 1909 President Theodore Roosevelt signed a proclamation creating the Mount Olympus National Monument, which consisted of 615,000 acres in the heart of the national forest. During World War I, however, President Woodrow

Wilson reduced the monument's size by 50 percent because of pressure from the timber interests. The monument was transferred to the jurisdiction of the National Park Service in 1933. Five years later, after much debate, Congress created Olympic National Park. Included in its 648,000 acres was the core of the Olympic Mountains, consisting of the higher and more rugged peaks. Additions made in subsequent years, including the ocean beaches in 1953, increased the park's size to almost 900,000 acres. The main area of the park is bordered on the north, east, and south by the Olympic National Forest, with state-owned lands lying adjacent to the park's western border. Generally speaking, the national forest and state lands are more heavily forested than the park, because much of the latter consists of high-altitude forest, meadowland, and barren peaks and ridges. Excluding the ocean beaches, the park as it exists today extends roughly 40 miles in each direction—north to south and east to west—with most of the area still in its natural state. Because commercial activities are barred, the park is a wilderness providing homes to a large variety of wildlife.

In 1984 five wilderness areas, totaling 92,966 acres, were created in the Olympic National Forest. They adjoin the national park on the east and south. All but one are located in the eastern Olympics, the rugged peaks and ridges visible from Puget Sound. Fifty years ago these areas were slated for inclusion in the national park, but this was never done because the allotted acreage was used instead to add to the park the ocean beaches and a river corridor.

ROADS AND CAMPGROUNDS

During the early days of settlement in the Pacific Northwest, the Olympic Mountains had few visitors because they were virtually inaccessible due to lack of trails and roads. Today, however, one can reach the Olympics with comparative ease. Although still wild, the region is no longer unknown. The Olympic Highway, US 101, together with the highway connecting Grays Harbor with Puget Sound, encircles the Olympics. Numerous spur roads extend inward into the mountains from the encircling highways like the broken spokes of a wheel. Most of the roads follow river valleys and end at low elevations, but several climb the ridges to the high country. Although some of the roads are paved, most of these secondary routes are graveled two-lane tracks, at times so narrow as to require turnouts for vehicles to pass each other. Forest Service roads are identified throughout by the abbreviation FS.

Olympic National Park is essentially a wilderness crisscrossed by trails, with roads penetrating only short distances. Although the park is unmarred by a network of highways, the spur roads permit automobile travelers to see representative portions of its major features. The west-side roads provide access to the rain forests, where deer and elk are often observed. On the northern side the roads to Hurricane Ridge and Deer Park climb above 5000 feet, and travelers see a succession of snowfields and meadows, as well as the higher peaks.

At various times a proposal has been made to build a highway across the Olympics, but this would destroy the park's wilderness character, which is its greatest asset. Moreover, the park's unique features—the rain forests, the elk herds, the mountain-and-sea vistas—are already accessible to motorists.

The park exhibits, more by accident than design, a natural zoning. The primitive core, a true wilderness without trails, is surrounded by two concentric belts. The inner, broader belt contains the bulk of the trail system; the outer band is penetrated by both roads and trails.

Because the Olympic National Forest borders the national park on three sides, it forms, with state lands on the west, still another band in the concentric arrangement. Until recent years the national forest and state lands were, like the national park, almost roadless. Today, however, they are cut up by hundreds of miles of logging roads, and the road pattern is constantly changing. Consequently, such wilderness as remains in the national forest is primarily found in the high country that borders the national park on the east.

Both the National Park Service and the Forest Service maintain public campgrounds along the major roads. These have individual camping units with cooking facilities and picnic tables, but not all of them are equipped with piped water and comfort stations with flush toilets. The developed sites usually charge a fee for staying overnight.

Hikers who elect to begin or end their backpacking trips by staying in automobile campgrounds should not expect them to be as quiet and peaceful as they were thirty years ago. Today the campgrounds are inclined to be noisy, but perhaps this is merely a reflection of the present age. Usually, however, the campground stay is an enjoyable one, albeit not a wilderness experience—because dogs bark, children cry and shriek, radios blare, and motor vehicles break the stillness. The best locations are invariably selected by those who arrive early; thus riverside camps are usually occupied. Here, despite the noise and the cawing of crows before dawn, one can sleep well, lulled into dreamland by the mesmeric sound of the river.

THE TRAIL SYSTEM

At the present time, the Olympics have nearly 900 miles of trails, of which approximately 66 percent are in the national park. In times past, several paths within the park received such infrequent maintenance (or none at all) that they acquired the status of abandoned trails. Recently, though, park officials have adopted a policy that ensures some degree of maintenance for every trail within park boundaries. The bulk of the trails in this 600-mile network are in reasonably good shape, however, and receive some maintenance—although not as much as might be desirable because of cuts in the National Park Service's budget.

The network of usable trails—approximately 85 percent of the total mileage— is heavily used by backpackers and equestrians. Beginning at various points on the spur roads, the paths follow the valleys through virgin forests, climb the foothills and ridges, then traverse high meadowlands to the barren rock, snow, and ice of the higher peaks and ridges. Although many routes are steep, the trails are safe, and healthy persons should experience no difficulty. Most trails have moderate grades, but they are narrow, varying from 18 to 24 inches in width.

How did this trail system originate? Obviously, it has not always existed, but it is probable that most of today's backpackers do not understand or appreciate the difficulties the pioneer explorers faced a hundred years ago, when game trails were the only routes in the Olympics. The first trails were the paths made by elk and deer during their wanderings, and most of them have been worn deep through centuries of use. They form a complex network which may still be in the process of creation. Usually they are best developed in rough terrain, where they collect together to follow one route—often the only possible way. However, where the landscape becomes more gentle, game paths tend to branch out and lose their continuity. This explains the "disappearing elk trail" so prevalent in the Olympics.

The first trails that resulted from human activity might be considered the equivalent of game trails. The paths were not built; they were tramped out, either by Indians hunting in the foothills or by white men hunting and prospecting. The first trails actually constructed by men were the ones made by expeditions during the late nineteenth century. When reconnoitering the country, the explorers quickly discovered that every river bottom had its game trails and that such routes were the best ones to travel. Accordingly, they improved and combined them with bits of trail they made themselves.

Most of the trails in the Olympics were constructed by the Forest Service when it had jurisdiction not only of the present national forest but also of what is now Olympic National Park. When the Forest Service built the trails, it followed the example set by the explorers and utilized elk trails whenever possible, linking them together for continuity. During the 1930s the Civilian Conservation Corps constructed a number of trails for the Forest Service.

When Olympic National Park was created in 1938, the National Park Service inherited a large percentage of the existing trail system. The agency then added several new trails, but the mileage was not extensive.

The trail mileage in the Olympics is less today than it was sixty years ago. This mileage has been lost because trails have been destroyed by the building of logging roads, by being abandoned, or by lack of maintenance. As roads have proliferated, the mileage available to users of recreational vehicles has steadily increased, but the trail mileage has significantly decreased. In addition to the hundreds of miles of roads where recreational vehicles may be driven, about half of the national forest's trail mileage is also open to motorbike travel as well as to mountain bikes.

Numerous fragments of what once were trunk trails can be found today in the national forest. Logging roads frequently paralleled trunk trails and often severed their branches, separating one portion of a trail from another. Despite little or no maintenance, the fragments are often in surprisingly good condition. Although they provide an enjoyable hiking experience, they do not traverse wilderness terrain.

Trail mileage has been lost in both the national forest and the national park through lack of maintenance. Trails have become choked with brush, windfalls have not been cut out, the paths not regraded where they have been badly eroded or obliterated by slides. This has been due, at least in part, to lack of funds. Other trails have been lost because they have been abandoned or relocated.

In addition to constructed trails, the Olympics have numerous paths which came into existence simply because people walked that way, following routes that offered the least resistance. Such way trails, as they are called, can be found throughout the mountains wherever hunters, fishermen, prospectors, climbers, and sightseers have followed streams and ridges or wandered from one makeshift camp to another. Although exceptions occur, such footpaths are generally inferior to constructed routes, having steeper gradients that provide rougher, less secure footing. The majority are not well defined, date from years ago, and often coincide in part with game trails. Many are unknown except to the locals, the people living in adjacent communities. Others have become lost to everyone because they have been hidden by the undergrowth, which quickly conceals a path that is not used regularly.

Both the national park and the national forest have a few nature trails built especially for casual visitors. Usually located near ranger stations or campgrounds, they are the antithesis of way trails—broad, well marked, with easy grades, often graveled, at times paved.

When it built the trails years ago, the Forest Service constructed log-and-shake shelters at intervals of 8 to 10 miles, in both the low and high country, as housing for trail-maintenance crews. When not occupied, the shelters were open to the public and frequently used by backpackers. After the creation of Olympic National Park, the National Park Service maintained the shelters that were under its jurisdiction, repairing or replacing broken-down ones. However, use of the wilderness increased greatly after World War II, and several decades later the areas near the shelters revealed signs of overuse and deterioration. In fact, the shelters themselves have, for years, been considered fair game by the people who have stayed in them. On cold, rainy days they have torn shakes from the sides and roofs for fuel or, finding nothing else to do, have laboriously inscribed their names and initials on the logs, plus the dates of their visits.

After studying the matter, the National Park Service decided to remove the shelters because they tended to concentrate people in particular locations. Many backpackers objected, however, with the result that the agency modified its policy, removing or relocating certain shelters but retaining others (primarily in the forested valleys) as emergency huts where hikers can hole up during severe storms.

HIKING

The Olympic Mountains exhibit splendid forest and alpine scenery which can be visited with comparative ease. Mount Olympus, the culminating point, is not quite 8000 feet high, yet it is similar in appearance, though miniature in comparison, to the world's great peaks. Because the elevation is low, its effects are negligible and hikers or climbers are quickly conditioned. They do not suffer from altitude sickness and are spared the rigors of combating fierce winds and extreme cold, of pitting their strength against the thin air of high altitudes. This fact is appreciated by most backpackers or climbers, although it may diminish the challenge sought by dedicated alpinists. However, the latter can test themselves in the Olympics, if they wish—by climbing Mount Olympus with 60-pound packs during a midwinter blizzard.

Occasionally they do, but not many years ago the Olympics were virtually isolated during the winter. Most people restricted their visits to the summer and fall months, as they still do, with lesser numbers going in the spring. Many found the Indian summer weather of the autumn months the best time of the year to go on long trips in the backcountry. With the increasing popularity of cross-country skiing and winter mountaineering, however, people now visit the Olympics throughout the year. In fact, winter ascents of the peaks are no longer unusual, although they cannot be said to have become commonplace.

Basically, however, the Olympics are trail country, and the opportunities for walking are almost unlimited. When hikers start up the trail with their packs, leaving roads and civilization behind, they enter another world, one where living is reduced to primitive, elemental terms despite the sophisticated equipment and trail foods available today. Although the delights of the wilderness include comparative freedom from regulations, visitors should keep in mind the basic rules of conduct. For example, horses have the right of way on trails, but livestock are not permitted in camping areas. People who use horses, burros, or llamas as pack animals should realize that grazing may be inadequate and therefore carry feed for their livestock. Except where walking cross-country is necessary to reach specific destinations, hikers should stay on the trails, and should not cut switchbacks because this leads to erosion that disfigures the slopes. Hunting is prohibited in the national park but permitted in season in the national forest. Likewise, motorbikes are not allowed on the national park trails, but they are permitted on some national forest trails, not on others. The riders are required to stay on the trails, yield the right of way to both hikers and horses, and equip their machines with spark arresters approved by the Forest Service. When traveling on national forest trails, hikers should bear these facts in mind and at all times should watch out for trail bikes (even though hikers have the right of way). During the hunting season hikers should wear red hats and be alert for hunters.

When traveling in the Olympic Mountains, every hiker should cary the "Ten Essentials," which consist of extra clothing, extra food, sunglasses, knife, firestarter, first-aid kit, matches in a waterproof container, flashlight, map, and a compass that is in good working order.

The time required to hike the trails varies greatly with different people, depending upon numerous factors, including one's age, physical condition, stamina, motivation, degree of freshness or fatigue, weight of pack, the weather, and the condition of the trail. A psychological factor is also involved: when the pack is heavy and the path is rough, the trail will seem to be much longer, and this may retard one's rate of progress. Generally speaking, however, backpackers can expect to travel level trails at the rate of 2.0 to 2.5 miles/3.2 to 4.0 kilometers per hour; 3.0 mph/4.8 kph, if they are exceptionally fast. On the uphill stretches, 1.5 to 2.0 mph/2.4 to 3.2 kph, is a good rate, and the average hiker will cover 2.0 to 3.0 mph/ 3.2 to 4.8 kph, when traveling downhill.

The prudent hiker in the Olympics keeps one eye on the sky and always packs wet weather gear—parka or poncho, rain pants or chaps, pack cover, and tent. Quite often, of course, one can successfully violate this rule—at least for a day or two—but the weather changes rapidly in the Olympics, and cloudless skies at sunset are no guarantee that the next day will be clear. Perhaps a front will move inland during the night, the stars disappear, and the backpacker awaken to the gentle patter of raindrops striking the tent. The weather can thus shift within a few hours, skies with unlimited visibility giving way to fog and clouds so thick one can see scarcely a hundred yards; or sunshine may be replaced by steady rain.

The weather does not always change quickly, however, particularly during late summer and fall, when a high-pressure cell often settles over the Pacific Northwest. At such times skies may remain blue for a month or more, and people have gone on outings lasting a week or two when every day was clear, with no rain. Conversely, they have also gone on trips that began coincident with the onset of stormy weather and thus experienced dismal gray skies and rainfall on a daily basis. However, both instances cited are unusual; during late summer and fall, rain can be expected to occur on two or three days during an outing lasting about two weeks. The hiker should therefore be prepared—not only in camp but also along the trail—with rain gear and warm clothing.

The Olympics are inclined to have cool temperatures, but the afternoons are warm during occasional spells of hot weather, and at such times the nights may have just a slight breeze or perhaps none at all. When this condition prevails, practical backpackers will arise at dawn, break camp quickly, and accomplish their day's march during the morning, thus avoiding travel during the heat of the day. They can then enjoy the afternoon warmth instead of arduously toiling up the trail. If the day's hike is long or involves considerable elevation gain, they may wish to split it, doing the first half in the morning, resting over during the midday hours, then completing the walk in the evening. If, however, their schedule demands that they backpack on a hot afternoon, their rate of travel (particularly uphill) will necessarily be slow. They will need lots of liquid and should halt from time to time and prepare one of the various drinks used by runners.

Generally speaking, one need not carry water when hiking in the Olympics because it is readily available. Exceptions occur, however, and trails that follow ridges are likely to be dry. Accordingly, everyone's pack should include a water bottle.

The hiker is never far from running water in the Olympics, and rushing streams are legion, but is the water safe to drink? The National Park Service and the U.S. Forest Service advise one to boil or filter the water in order to prevent contracting giardiasis. Numerous hikers will swear they have drunk untreated water from the Olympic streams for many years without ill effects, but giardiasis has become a serious health problem in recent years. Accordingly, both the National Park Service and the Forest Service recommend boiling or filtering the water to make it safe to drink. Although it is often impractical to boil the water, one can always filter it.

Most Olympic streams and lakes are cold, but the water can be used for bathing. However, hikers should avoid bathing in streams and lakes because this could result in pollution. The method adopted by the U.S. Army in Korea is practical—taking a sponge bath with water scooped up in a wash basin. Although the streams are icy, the small tarns and ponds that have no inlets or outlets may be utilized as bath tubs, because one would not use the water for drinking purposes in any event. Many such pools are located in the high meadows, and they are often warm, particularly on hot afternoons.

Many excellent campsites are located along the trails, both in the forests and the high meadowlands. Responsible hikers avoid camping within 200 feet of lakes, and they do not disturb the soil and vegetation by ditching around their shelters. They leave a clean camp and an extinguished fire and also pack out all trash that cannot be destroyed by burning. This includes aluminum foil. Good campers also use ground cloths beneath or inside tent bottoms to provide protection from the dampness so notorious in the Olympics. Unless the trip is entirely in the lowlands, hikers should carry lightweight backpack stoves and fuel because fires are prohibited in high-country areas. Moreover, in the forest, where they are allowed, fires can be difficult to build and maintain during wet weather, when dry wood is scarce.

CROSS-COUNTRY TRAVEL

When hiking in the Olympics, one should stay on the trails whenever possible. At times, however, certain objectives can be reached only by traveling cross-country—picking out the best route possible, based upon one's prior experience. This may be in deep forest, in canyons, across meadowland, or upon ridges, peaks, snowfields, or glaciers. On such occasions an ice ax is helpful, provided one knows how to use it. The hiker should also be prepared to travel in all kinds of weather.

The first explorers in the Olympics traveled cross-country because man-made trails were nonexistent. They quickly learned that the best way to traverse rugged terrain was to follow elk trails, and today's hiker finds this still to be true. The conditions encountered in cross-country travel vary greatly, ranging from easy to difficult. At timberline it is often just a matter of walking across meadowland and through groves of subalpine trees. When attempting to reach a river below, it is usually better to follow down a spur ridge because the streams are likely to be in box canyons. On the ridges the ground is often open beneath the trees, although at lower elevations it is likely to be brushy.

One needs clear, sunny weather when traveling cross-country through rough terrain because route finding is all important. Often, it seems, the fog has a tendency to gather, obscuring the view, just when one needs to see the way ahead. The uncertainties of such travel sometimes make it necessary to bivouac. This can be disconcerting when one is on what was intended to be a day trip and is hiking without tent and sleeping bag. When an unexpected bivouac occurs at high elevation, the hiker is likely to face a long, cold night; if in a place where a campfire is permitted, one can keep reasonably warm but will have to sit around the fire all night. On the other hand, a scheduled bivouac is usually a pleasant experience. Perhaps one wishes to reach a certain destination—a peak or lake—without carrying a full pack, but the distance is too great for a one-day trek. On these occasions the hiker should take along a sleeping bag, ground cloth, bivvy sack, stove, and fuel, in addition to the Ten Essentials listed earlier.

HAZARDS

Occasionally, one is amazed at the temerity exhibited by inexperienced hikers with regard to traveling in the Olympics. With little knowledge of what they face, they will start out—often alone and ill-equipped—to walk across the mountains or to seek solitude in remote, almost inaccessible areas. Often they do not understand that it is still winter in the high mountains although on the lowlands the warm sunshine may indicate that spring has arrived. Hardly a year goes by that we do not read or hear of someone getting lost in the mountains and either suffering death or severe injury. As a consequence, most hikers would be well-advised not to travel alone in the Olympics.

Nevertheless, in all honesty I cannot say that it is dangerous to do so—at least during the summer and early fall months when one is less likely to be caught by sudden, unexpected storms. I have done a great deal of hiking alone, and on such occasions I am doubly cautious. However, my personal experience should not be taken by readers as a recommendation that they go on solitary hikes. In this respect, it might be well to point out that during the summer months the main trails—and sometimes the secondary ones—are heavily traveled by lone individuals as well as by parties numbering up to the maximum allowed. At such a time the person who hikes without companions is not really alone.

Wilderness is deceptive, its dangers largely hidden so far as the uninitiated are concerned. Consequently, the hiker who exercises poor judgment—whether through inexperience or imprudence—may suffer serious injury or death due to a mishap. At times even the seasoned backpacker is the victim of carelessness, and lack of knowledge is often responsible for the neophyte wandering into terrain avoided by the sophisticated hiker.

The dangers in the Olympics are numerous. The rivers that flow swift and cold over boulder-strewn beds are often unsafe to cross. Caution should be exercised when wading or crossing on slippery logs. Other hazards include the tangled windfalls in the forests, impassable canyons, slippery heather, scree slopes, and of course glaciers. The latter are broken by deep crevasses, which are often hidden beneath snow. No one should venture upon them except mountaineers equipped with climbing paraphernalia. Many snowfields are dangerous because they are undermined by streams or lie in avalanche paths. However, the greatest hazard in the Olympics is uncertain weather. Fogs move in rapidly, confusing one's sense of direction, and sudden storms may bring snow and freezing temperatures to the higher peaks, even in the middle of summer. On clear nights, fog often forms in the river bottoms, covering the lowlands under a dense blanket, but the sun usually breaks through during the morning; thus the afternoons are likely to be clear and warm. But sometimes the fog comes and goes all day, the peaks seldom revealing themselves.

One warning signal should always be heeded. When a well-developed storm moves in from the ocean and dark clouds begin to cascade like waterfalls through the gaps in the ridges, one can expect heavy rain within an hour or two, preceded by strong winds. On the glaciers, where no barriers exist to block the wind, the gusts may be so strong that climbers have to lean against the charge of rain or sleet. Quite often the passage of the front will be followed by several days of unsettled weather, with low clouds drifting about, patches of blue sky, and intermittent precipitation.

THE SEASONS

Most of the hikers and backpackers who go to the Olympic Mountains do so during the warm months, from May through September, when the days are long because of the high latitude. But to really know the Olympics, one must visit them throughout the year because they have moods that vary with the changing seasons. Viewing the peaks when they are softened by summer haze is not enough, because they are equally interesting when shrouded in autumn's fog banks and winter's mists, or during the springtime, when they hide behind dark, wind-driven clouds.

Spring comes early to the lowlands, arriving in April when the dogwoods splash white against the evergreens, and climbs the mountainsides as the snow line recedes, to culminate at higher elevations when the rhododendrons blossom in early July. This season is uncertain and tentative in the Olympics, with damp, chilly weather, and fog lingering in the deep canyons. A noisy time, it contrasts vividly with the white silence of winter and the lazy somnolence of summer. The squawking of the ravens and jays and the booming of streams that carry the melting snow to the sea are accented by the rumble of avalanches. In the lowlands the forest comes alive, exhibiting many shades of green.

Spring fades into the lovely summer, which is brief in the high country—a succession of sunny days, cool in the morning, warm in the afternoons. Clouds often gather during the day, when cumulus masses float around the higher peaks, only to dissipate with the approach of night. Occasionally they develop into thunderheads accompanied by lightning and heavy showers, but this is unusual.

The balmy days of autumn, known as Indian summer, add a delightful touch to the close of summer, and with regard to pleasant hiking weather, the Olympics are at their best during this season. This is a beautiful time in the high country, often heralded by a definite chill in the air. The days are warm, seldom hot, with an abundance of sunshine mellowed by cool breezes. The atmosphere has an almost indescribable quality—an essence akin, perhaps, to that of an exotic wine, intensified by the stillness, the buzzing of bees, the murmur of distant brooks. The vagrant winds rustle the brown grasses and remind one that winter is lurking in the wings, soon to rush onstage.

Down in the lowland forests the maples turn scarlet and gold, brilliant against the dark green of the conifers, and the slim trunks of the alders stand starkly white beside the streams. On high, exposed meadows huckleberry bushes glow like purple beacons, and the hiker is likely to see bears gorging on the fruit. Nights become longer and crisper, and the stage is set for snowfall when the first storms arrive.

At this time of year the sun dips behind the western ridges early, and the nights are cold enough to kill most of the insects; thus one may not have to contend with mosquitoes, flies, gnats, and yellow-jackets. The fish are hungry because they have few bugs upon which to feed. Consequently, anglers are usually successful during this season. On cloudless nights the stars shine brightly above the dark silhouettes of the mountains, heavy frost sparkles on the grass and heather, and before dawn skims of ice edge the pools and lakes.

Backpackers who delight in hiking through the high country at this season should bear in mind that the days are shorter than they are in midsummer, and that darkness arrives early. They should also be prepared for lengthy sessions in their sleeping bags. Not only are the nights longer, they are also colder, and the chilly morning air is not conducive to early rising. Well-equipped hikers illuminate their tents with candle lanterns and have reading material available. They also take plenty of warm clothes. They will meet fewer people on the trails—in fact, at times no one—and thus are strictly on their own and should be prepared to cope with sudden storms, which might leave the trail covered with snow.

The Olympics are not blessed with Indian summer every year, and sometimes the high country undergoes a sudden transition from summer to winter. Usually, however, one can expect several weeks of fine autumn weather, perhaps broken now and then by an early storm. In fact, during this seasonal transition the weather pattern is variable and changes quickly. One day the skies are sunny, the air redolent with the odors of fall; the next, the sun has disappeared and ragged clouds scud across the skies, trailing rain as they move inland.

Snow usually begins to fall in the high country in October, the autumn storms drenching the lowlands with rain and whitening the peaks and ridges left barren by the summer sun. Although the snow often melts on warm succeeding days, especially on exposed southern slopes, this frosting of the mountaintops signals the approach of winter, when gray clouds roll in relentlessly from the Pacific, releasing

Winter scene, Hurricane Ridge

heavy rain on the lowlands and snow at the higher elevations. As the weather becomes colder, the snow line descends the mountainsides. The high peaks now stand isolated, seldom disturbed by man. On clear mornings the peaks appear to have been chiseled from marble; thus they contrast vividly with the green forests and the blue skies. But during the storms, when the wind howls through the canyons, the peaks are hidden behind a veil of clouds.

The snowpack usually reaches its maximum depth in late winter. On the windward side of the mountains, this may be 30 to 40 feet on the higher peaks, an accumulation that leads to heavy avalanches in the springtime.

HOW TO USE THIS TRAIL GUIDE

This is not a formula guidebook featuring prepackaged hikes that require little input from hikers who are planning an outing. Hiking guides can prescribe too much as well as not enough when recommending itineraries involving various combinations of trails. As my good friend William E. Hoke expressed it succinctly, "The beauty of hiking and climbing is discovery, pure and simple," and part of the thrill of discovery stems from having made one's own plans and choices.

The book does, however, describe all the trails in the Olympic Mountains (or at any rate all that the writer is aware of), including the ones that are not maintained. Thus, *Olympic Mountains Trail Guide* is, so to speak, a dictionary or encyclopedia, offering assistance when it is needed but remaining silent when it is not.

The text describes 177 trails in the Olympic Mountains that have a total length of almost 900 miles. Of this total, 104 trails, or 59 percent, are in the Leeward Olympics, the sheltered side of the mountains. The trails in the Windward Olympics, the side exposed to winter storms, number 73, or 41 percent of the grand total. Total trail mileage, however, is almost evenly divided between the two sections. While there are fewer trails in the Windward Olympics, they tend to be somewhat longer than those in the leeward mountains.

About 140 miles, or 15 percent of the total trail mileage, represent either unmaintained way trails or abandoned trails, indicating that the situation with respect to maintenance is not as bad as one might suspect. The mileage of unmaintained trails is almost evenly divided between the leeward and the windward sides, although one would have suspected that most of the abandoned trails and unmaintained way trails would be on the wet west side of the mountains.

The trails are described beginning at Lake Crescent and proceeding clockwise around the more or less circular uplift of peaks and ridges. The mountains are divided into sixteen major watersheds, eight of them in the Leeward Olympics, also eight in the Windward Olympics. The trails in the Leeward Olympics—the slopes facing north and east—are described first because they are closer to the centers of population and in general have the best weather. The Windward Olympics—the slopes oriented to the south and west—demand that one drive considerably farther to reach the trailheads, and one has to gamble on the weather because this district, although having milder temperatures, has much greater precipitation. The trails are grouped into chapters according to the watersheds in which each trail is found (in whole, or in major extent). For convenience in identifying routes on the maps in this book, each trail has been given a specific number according to its listing in the Table of Contents. The numbers have been placed on the maps at relevant points so that one may identify the trails depicted.

The eight watersheds which comprise the Leeward Olympics, are the Lyre, Elwha, North Slope, Dungeness-Graywolf, Quilcene, Dosewallips, Duckabush, and Hamma Hamma. The eight watersheds of the Windward Olympics are the North Fork Skokomish, South Flank, East Fork Quinault, North Fork Quinault, Queets, Hoh, Bogachiel-Calawah, and Soleduck.

Each chapter begins with a general, overall description of the watershed, followed by a detailed description of the roads that provide access to the trails in that area.

A WORD ABOUT NAMES

The names of geographic features change over the course of time for various and sundry reasons, but I am convinced that many of them are due to cartographers' mistakes and the subsequent perpetuation of, or attempts to correct, such errors. The map makers frequently misspell names; or, worse yet, transpose names to other locations. For example, the name of a creek may be shifted onto an adjacent stream; that of a peak or lake placed on a nearby, usually unnamed, feature. Because new maps gradually replace old ones, errors due to carelessness become fixed or accepted as time goes by, with the result that eventually few people realize that a name or its location has been changed. Numerous examples of cartographers' errors—or, more charitably, variations in designation—can be cited. Heart Lake, near the headwaters of the Duckabush, has been changed to Hart Lake on most maps, and another Heart Lake, on the High Divide, may experience the same fate. Crazy Creek has been moved to the next upstream tributary of the Duckabush. Blizzard Pass on Mount Olympus was incorrectly designated on the 15-minute USGS quadrangle for years, but it is correctly placed in the new 7.5-minute quadrangle. One of the most interesting errors appeared on an early edition of the USGS quadrangle titled Hurricane Hill. The quadrangle showed a trail, labeled Upper Lillian War Trail, climbing from the Elwha Trail to Lost Cabin Mountain. I was not aware of any trail ascending from the Elwha to this peak, and a later version of the map shows the trail following the Lillian River and not going to Lost Cabin Mountain (although both maps indicated the trail started at the same spot on the Elwha Trail). The name had been changed later, on a revised map, to Lillian River Trail. I had been puzzled by the designation of War Trail, thinking perhaps the path had some relationship to a World War II aircraft spotting station, when the truth suddenly dawned upon me—that somewhere along the line a cartographer had mistaken the word *war* for *way*. The reference was to a way trail, not a war path.

In the trail descriptions that follow, I have attempted to be as accurate as possible with regard to place names, and at times have cited the historical basis for using a certain name.

At the beginning of each individual trail description there is a capsular listing of information designed to give the hiker a quick overview of the essay that follows. If the trail is an abandoned route or an unmaintained way trail, this fact is noted. Anyone attempting to follow these abandoned, unmaintained pathways, should be a self-reliant person well-versed in cross-country travel, not a neophyte in the art of hiking. Next, the trail's length is stated both in miles and kilometers, followed by the name of the principal access road to the trailhead or, if the starting point is another trail, the name of that trail. For a detailed description of the access road/s readers should refer back to the "Roads" section at the beginning of the chapter. Also provided is the name or names of the U.S. Geological Survey's 7.5-minute quadrangle that includes the territory traversed by the trail. Although other good maps, particularly the 15-minute quadrangles, are available, the 7.5-minute quadrangles are the most recent and up-to-date. Lastly, the name of the entity responsible for the trail, whether Olympic National Park, Olympic National Forest, or another body, is given. Telephone numbers for these entities are provided in Appendix 2.

Within the trail descriptions accumulated mileage, as well as the elevation at pertinent points, is given parenthetically. As an aid to trip planning, the names of connecting trails that have their own entry elsewhere in the book appear in boldface type.

MEASURING MILEAGE

The reader may note that road and trail distances given in this book do not always agree with the official figures adopted by the National Park Service and the U.S. Forest Service. In fact, both agencies revise their official figures from time to time. In addition, the official figures are not always in agreement with the ones posted at trailheads and route intersections, and the trail signs themselves at times conflict with one another. Where the figures in this book differ from the official ones currently in use, it is because I am convinced that the latter are erroneous. I have therefore stated distances that I feel are most reasonable, based not only upon the official figures but also the time required to hike the trails under varying conditions. I have not attempted to run an engineer's measuring wheel over the trails because I believe the results of wheel measurement—while perhaps of value as a confirmatory aid—are not as accurate as one might suppose, considering all the little ups and downs and other imperfections in the mountain paths, as well as their general roughness, which tend to magnify mechanical errors. A mountain trail is, of course, considerably different from a level, smoothly paved sidewalk in the city.

At this point the reader may note that figures for elevation gain and loss are not given. One cannot, of course, determine gain or loss by simply subtracting the starting altitude from the ending one, because gains and losses (both large and small) occur along the way. The fact that such trails are uneven means that any given path is characterized by numerous little rises and falls, which cannot be readily calculated and taken into account when figuring the route's net gain or loss. One would have to know the precise elevation at every point where the trail starts to ascend or descend.

Hikers soon come to realize that some trails are almost continuously uphill, while others are primarily level or even predominately downhill. The average trail is a mixture of ups and downs and level stretches, and it gains or loses elevation gradually. Accordingly, no attempt has been made to label trails as having specific elevation gains or losses. The best way to deal with this subject when a hiker is planning a trip is to read the trail description and note the elevation figures given for various points along the way. This will give an overall impression of the difficulty of the route, without considering all the incomputable little ups and downs that characterize almost every trail.

The trails described in this book have not been rated as to their degree of difficulty because such characterization is neither practical nor fair. What is easy for one hiker may well be average for others. Such judgment calls are highly subjective matters and depend largely upon one's personal opinion. It almost goes without saying that what is easy for most people (including neophytes) might be moderately strenuous for someone with physical problems. One's stamina, age, and general state of health play large roles in determining how we personally rate the degree of difficulty.

Another factor that can and often does affect a hike's degree of difficulty is the weather prevalent at the time. A trail rated average in benign weather may easily be reclassified as strenuous when one hikes the route during inclement weather, or severe if the hike is undertaken during a violent storm.

Not only is the weather per se a critical factor in determining how difficult one should consider a trail to be but so is the season of the year. Because it is obvious, it hardly seems necessary to mention that an ascent of Mount Olympus in midwinter would be rated by almost anyone cognizant of the conditions in the field as being more difficult than a summer climb. The same criterion is true for the trails. A hike to Lake Constance is tough enough for most people in the summer, let alone attempting the route during the winter months.

Still another element which can affect the difficulty rating of trails: Is the scheduled hike of a certain trail going to be a day hike or an overnight one? The inference is clear. If it is to be a day hike, where the participants carry only lightweight rucksacks, the rating is more likely to be in the easy or average class, as opposed to the rating for the same trail if the trip is to be an overnight one with the participants carrying backpacks loaded with overnight gear—including cooking equipment, tent or tarp, and sleeping bags. Obviously, the overnight trip will receive a greater degree of difficulty rating than will the day hike.

When and where to go? This question is often asked, and it is a good one, not to be taken lightly. The simplest, most direct answer is: Go when you feel like going, go where you want to go—provided, that is, that you have the necessary skill and knowledge to attempt the route. If you are strictly a hiker and not trained in the art of climbing, don't try to scale Mount Olympus; leave it for a later day when your skills have improved. The guidebook writer can make suggestions as to destinations, but they are only that; the final choice is yours. If the description of a trail raises the suspicion in your mind that it may be beyond your skill level, don't go. Try an easier trail first.

The answer is much the same for when to go. Obviously, summer is a better time than winter to spend on mountain trails. Spring and fall are seasonal transition times, when the weather can quickly change from summer to winter, or vice versa. The weather is therefore the critical factor in determining when to go into the remote backcountry areas. The best times for backpacking trips are summer and fall—especially the delightful Indian summer in the fall, which is usually all-too-brief. In fact, backpacking is generally restricted by most of its devotees to the summer and fall months. Not many care to go camping during the winter—the nights are too long, the temperature too low, the threat of incoming storms ever present. It just is not the time when most people want to camp out, although some do and apparently find it rewarding. Spring, on the other hand, is touch and go. Often in the high country it is no more than a lingering winter, and the snowpack in the Olympics is usually deep at that time of year. Down in the low valleys, the winter's sometimes heavy accumulation of snow is slow to melt, and the river bottoms usually aren't compatible with camping out until mid-April or May, although exceptions occur in some years. Above 2500 feet it is still winter in the spring.

So, as a rule of thumb, if you must camp out in the winter, limit yourself to areas below 1500 feet elevation. In the spring months you can go as high as you feel inclined to posthole your way up slopes covered with deep snow, being always mindful of the risk of being caught in the path of an avalanche. Think of mid-July as the time to begin your high-country backpacks—from mid-July to late October. And constantly keep the weather in mind. Whenever a severe storm is forecast, don't go—unless your goal is to experience such a phenomenon. Wait until another day when the weather is benign.

One last matter before we go into the realm of the trail descriptions, which are designed, admittedly, to lure you into the sanctuary of the inner Olympics. Both Olympic National Park and Olympic National Forest have implemented new user fees (as of 1997). The purpose of these fees is to obtain funds to enable crews to restore eroded trails, rebuild bridges, and remove fallen trees, following years of neglect because of budget cuts. The fees charged by the National Park Service and the U.S. Forest Service are basically the same.

In Olympic National Park, new fees include those for parking at most trailheads, and the backpacker's entrance fee has been raised. The fees for the Olympic National Forest are a set rate to park in the national forest, plus an additional charge if one backpacks into the neighboring national park, which also charges an additional fee per person.

The fees vary considerably, depending upon the age of the participants, the length of time they intend to spend in the wilderness, and the size of the party, etcetera. Because the fees are almost certain to change, if not from one year to the next perhaps every two or three years, the various fees charged when this book was published are not listed here. For current fees, hikers should contact the national park's Wilderness Information Center (see Appendix 2).

Legend

(26)	US Highway	★	Point of Interest
(22)	State Highway	▲	Automobile Campground
FS 25	Forest Service Road	△	Major Backcountry Camp
113	Trail Numbers	△	Off-Trail Backcountry Camp
═══	Road	⌂	Ranger Station
-----	Trail	⌂	Ranch
··········	Primitive Route	☆	General Store
────	River or Stream	⋀	Peak
──·──	Boundary Line of Olympic National Park	)(	Pass
──·──	Boundary Line of Olympic National Forest	⊙	Glacier

A NOTE ABOUT SAFETY

Safety is an important concern in all outdoor activities. No guidebook can alert you to every hazard or anticipate the limitations of every reader. Therefore, the descriptions of roads, trails, routes, and natural features in this book are not representations that a particular place or excursion will be safe for your party. When you follow any of the routes described in this book, you assume responsibility for your own safety. Under normal conditions, such excursions require the usual attention to traffic, road and trail conditions, weather, terrain, the capabilities of your party, and other factors. Because many of the lands in this book are subject to development and/or change of ownership, conditions may have changed since this book was written that make your use of some of these routes unwise. Always check for current conditions, obey posted private property signs, and avoid confrontations with property owners or managers. Keeping informed on current conditions and exercising common sense are the keys to a safe, enjoyable outing.

— The Mountaineers

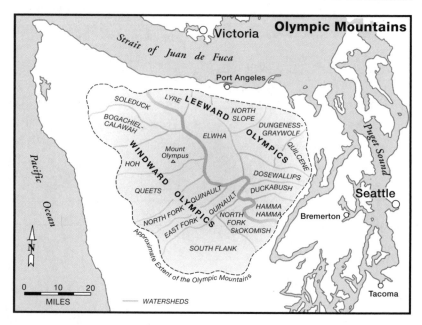

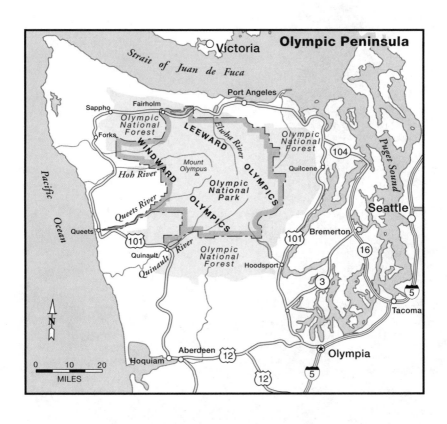

PART I

LEEWARD OLYMPICS

The northern and eastern slopes of the Olympic Mountains constitute the leeward side because the prevailing winter winds at this latitude in the northern hemisphere come from the southwest. Accordingly, the leeward side is sheltered from storms by the Windward Olympics, the mass of peaks to the south and west. As a consequence, the northern and eastern slopes receive much less precipitation because they occupy what is called the rain shadow of the mountains. The northeastern Olympics—or the Jupiter Hills as they were once called—have the lightest precipitation, from 20 to 30 inches yearly. As one goes west or south from the northeastern apex, the annual precipitation gradually increases (at the rate of about an inch per mile). Although these slopes lie within the bounds of the Leeward Olympics, they gradually phase, at the western and southern extremities, into the windward belt. Of course no sudden break occurs; one cannot draw a line and call one side the windward, the other the leeward. The boundary is approximate.

Because the northern and eastern sides of the Olympics are steeper than the southern and western slopes, the Leeward Olympics constitute only 40 percent of the total area included in the mountains. However, the peaks are generally higher in this section, and therefore the area contains as much, or perhaps more, of the high country as do the Windward Olympics.

Mount Anderson from Hayden Pass Trail (Photo by Frank O. Shaw)

LYRE
(LAKE CRESCENT)

Lake Crescent, the source of the Lyre River, lies 579 feet above sea level and forms a narrow arc at the northern edge of the Olympics. Almost 9 miles long and generally about a mile wide, the lake covers slightly more than 5000 acres, making it the third largest natural lake in western Washington. Originally called Lake Everett, in honor of John Everett, a Hudson's Bay Company trapper who sought furs along its wooded shores, the lake was renamed because its form roughly resembles a crescent. The largest lake in the Olympic Mountains, it occupies a trough deepened during the Ice Age by the Cordilleran Ice Sheet, which moved westward down the Strait of Juan de Fuca. Except at its two ends, the lake has a precipitous shoreline, and it is bordered by steep, forest-clad mountains. On clear winter days, the snowy slopes cast silvery reflections in the intensely blue waters.

The lake is suited to various activities, including swimming, boating, fishing, and water skiing. At one time fishermen trolled its waters for the Beardslee trout, a variety of rainbow. This fish, named for Leslie A. Beardslee, its discoverer, was declared by ichthyologist David S. Jordan to be a new species. However, it no longer exists in a pure state because it has crossbred with hatchery-raised fish. The lake also contained the *crescenti* trout, a unique type of cutthroat, but it, too, has been hybridized.

Lake Crescent is paralleled on the south by Aurora Ridge, the divide between two rivers, the Lyre and the Soleduck; on the north by a lower ridge that culminates in Pyramid Mountain. Near the lake's eastern end, Mount Storm King rises 4000 feet above the water. Mountain goats clamber on its cliffs, and it was here in the 1920s that the animals were introduced in the Olympics. Since then they have spread throughout the mountains.

About a dozen creeks flow into the lake from the bordering ridges and keep the water level constant. Barnes Creek, the largest, has built a small delta at its mouth. The lake has its outlet in the Lyre River, which flows from the northernmost point to the Strait of Juan de Fuca, only 5 miles distant.

Geologists believe that the lake originally drained to the Elwha, via Indian Creek, but that a slide pinched off the eastern part (thus creating Lake Sutherland) and the drainage was then diverted to the north, via the Lyre River.

Among the first settlers on Lake Crescent were Sarah Barnes and Paul Barnes, mother and brother of Charles A. Barnes, who was second in command of the Press Expedition. They settled on the delta of Barnes Creek in the 1890s, and in later years other members of the family established homesteads at various points on the lake.

ROADS

Several roads provide access to the trails near Lake Crescent. At one time ferries plied up and down the lake, but they disappeared with the building of the Olympic Highway along the south shore. Trails begin at various points and climb to the nearby peaks and ridges. (Several of the trails are also accessible from roads

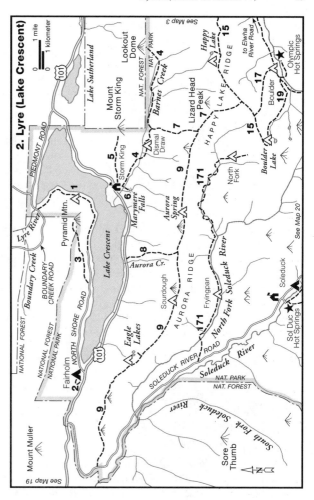

leading to Olympic Hot Springs and Sol Duc Hot Springs. See road descriptions in the Elwha and Soleduck chapters.)

Olympic Highway (US 101). This highway loops around the Olympic Mountains on the three seaward sides—Hood Canal, the Strait of Juan de Fuca, and the Pacific Ocean. The road cuts through the northern edge of the mountains at Lake Crescent, making that district—together with Hurricane Ridge—the most accessible part of Olympic National Park.

Within the park the highway parallels the lake's southern shore. Numerous turnouts are provided where one can stop and look at the vistas. At various times in the past, conservationists proposed building an alternate route outside the national park for commercial traffic, thus reserving the road along the lake as a scenic parkway, where people could drive slowly and enjoy the views. Unfortunately, the proposals came to naught, and in 1982 the State Highway Department began widening and straightening the highway in order that commercial vehicles and logging trucks could travel at a higher rate of speed.

Distances on US 101 from downtown Port Angeles to the Lake Crescent area are as follows: Elwha River, 8.5 mi/13.7 km; Piedmont Road, 15.9 mi/25.6 km; Storm King Ranger Station, 19.6 mi/31.6 km; Aurora Creek Trail, 22.4 mi/36.1 km; La Poel Picnic Area, 23.9 mi/38.5 km; Fairholm Resort, at the western end of the lake, 26.6 mi/42.8 km; North Shore Road, 26.8 mi/43.1 km; Soleduck River Road, 28.5 mi/45.9 km.

Piedmont Road. This road begins on the Olympic Highway, 15.9 mi/25.6 km west of Port Angeles, climbs slightly, then descends to the eastern end of Lake Crescent, where it crosses into the national park. The road winds along the lake's northern shore to Piedmont (3.1 mi/5.0 km) and the Log Cabin Resort. At 3.3 mi/5.3 km the road forks: the Boundary Creek Road branches to the left; the Piedmont Road continues to the right.

Boundary Creek Road. The road begins at Piedmont, 3.3 mi/5.3 km from US 101, and crosses the Lyre River to a spur road (0.7 mi/1.1 km), then angles right and enters the national forest. The spur road leads left (0.2 mi/0.3 km) to a parking area at the eastern terminus of the Spruce Railroad Trail.

North Shore Road. This road begins at a junction with the Olympic Highway, just beyond Fairholm Resort, near the western end of Lake Crescent. The road provides access to Fairholm Campground and its nature trail, the Pyramid Mountain Trail, and the Spruce Railroad Trail. The road ends at a turnaround (4.8 mi/7.7 km).

1   SPRUCE RAILROAD TRAIL

Length 4.0 mi/6.4 km
Access North Shore Road; Boundary Creek Road
USGS Map Lake Crescent
Agency Olympic National Park

This is a good trail to hike during the winter, and it is unique in the Olympics because it follows an old railroad grade, that of the Spruce Railroad, about 600 feet above sea level, along the north shore of Lake Crescent. During World War I, the government built the railroad from Port Angeles to the west side of the Olympic Peninsula in order to obtain spruce to use in airplane construction.

Snow often covers the peaks and ridges in the winter, and on cloudy days the lake is slate-colored, but the views are excellent, and the friendly ducks—hungry now that the tourists have departed—will approach you and engage in a bit of panhandling. (Officially, the park does not encourage the feeding of any wild animals.) During the summer, ticks are abundant and can be a problem. So too, the poison oak. In fact, this is one of the few places in the Olympics where both ticks and poison oak are encountered.

The trail starts just off the Boundary Creek Road near the lake's outlet and climbs away from the water, going by the remnants of an old orchard. The path turns onto an abandoned logging road and follows it briefly, then descends to the grade of the Spruce Railroad. The trail now keeps close to the shore, where it provides frequent views of the lake and the forested peaks, including Mount Storm

Spruce Railroad Trail

King. On the trail's uphill side the slopes are clad with dark, somber conifers. After rounding Harrigan Point, the trail goes by the north end of a tunnel, the first of two on the route. Because the tunnel has collapsed, it is choked with debris, and the entrance can be easily overlooked.

As it traverses the cliffs to avoid the tunnel, the trail climbs slightly to round Devils Point (1.1 mi/1.8 km), which has splendid views up, down, and across the lake, and is deeply indented by a little bay or cove called Devils Punch Bowl. This is the most picturesque spot on the route. The cliffs of pillow basalt come down precipitously to the water, and the lake is deep near the shore. The trail crosses the cove via a steel and wood bridge that arches over the water to the next jutting headland. The rock walls bordering the bay are decorated with mosses, ferns, and stonecrop.

Beyond the bridge, the trail skirts basalt cliffs at the lake's edge, then passes the tunnel's south entrance and returns to the railroad grade. A little creek (1.5 mi/2.4 km) that cascades down the slopes of Pyramid Mountain is the only stream of consequence on the trail. At various places the path goes by basalt cliffs 150 to 200 feet high, where madronas cling to the barren rocks. All along this section the trail has numerous "windows" among the trees. The views they provide across the lake are better during the winter and spring, before the leaves develop on the deciduous trees.

One can see through the second tunnel (2.9 mi/4.7 km), but the floor is blocked by large timbers, and warning signs indicate it is dangerous to walk through because rocks fall from the roof. At any rate, the hiker should not miss the view from the trail around this point, which is directly opposite the delta of Barnes Creek. Here the lake is narrow—not more than a half mile wide—and one can see Lake Crescent Lodge and the cabins on the far shore.

Beyond the second tunnel the trail once again follows the railroad grade, going through a mixture of second-growth and virgin timber, mostly stands of Douglas-fir, where more windows are present. The trail then leaves the railroad grade and descends to the end of the North Shore Road (4.0 mi/6.4 km).

2   FAIRHOLM CAMPGROUND TRAIL

Length 0.8 mi/1.1 km
Access North Shore Road
USGS Map Mount Muller
Agency Olympic National Park

This nature trail provides a good evening walk when one is staying at Fairholm Campground. The path begins opposite the campground's entrance (ca. 700 ft/213 m) on the North Shore Road (0.2 mi/0.3 km from US 101) and makes a horseshoe-shaped loop, coming back out to the road at a point about 200 yards to the north (0.7 mi/1.1 km).

Although the trail traverses an area close to the Olympic Highway, the forest is quiet and peaceful. Here the path meanders through an impressive stand of tall, old-growth Douglas-fir. The undergrowth is luxuriant, and smaller trees are mixed among the big firs.

3   PYRAMID MOUNTAIN TRAIL

Length 3.5 mi/5.6 km
Access North Shore Road
USGS Map Lake Crescent
Agency Olympic National Park

The trailhead (700 ft/213 m) is reached by driving 3.1 mi/5.0 km on the North Shore Road from the Olympic Highway. The path is continuously uphill, ending at the top of Pyramid Mountain, thus making it a 2400-ft/732-m climb. On this trail you can hear the noise of vehicles traveling on US 101 along the lake's south shore.

At first the trail ascends a bench covered with large second-growth fir, but it soon enters the virgin forest and contours the steep mountainside above Lake Crescent.

The trunks of the tall, slender firs have been blackened by a fire that swept these slopes in the past. Numerous madronas grow among the conifers, and the ground cover consists largely of salal and Oregon grape. Sunlight streams through the trees, and one has glimpses of the lake and the ridges beyond.

Climbing steadily, the trail crosses a rocky watercourse, where a stream flows underground in late summer and fall. Usually water can be heard issuing from rocks above the trail at a point where the stream comes to the surface. This is June Creek (1.4 mi/2.3 km; 1070 ft/326 m). The stream probably received its name because it flows during June but disappears in July.

The trail then crosses a brook in a rocky ravine and presently comes out to an open spot having a good view of the lake. Beyond this point the route steepens, rounds a spur, then switchbacks sharply upward to the divide west of Pyramid Mountain. Here the hiker will see on the north slope a big clearcut that comes right up to the ridge crest; the contrast with past memory is striking, because the forest that formerly stood here was dense and shaded. The ridge marks the boundary between the national park and the national forest, and the trees were cut right to the line. The clearcut does have one virtue—it provides a view of the Strait of Juan de Fuca.

After climbing a bit, the trail leaves the ridge and works its way up the north slope of Pyramid Mountain. The trees are remarkably large for this elevation, and the undergrowth is sparse. The trail begins to switchback again, then descends slightly before emerging from the deep shadows into the bright sunlight on the ridge. Much of Lake Crescent is visible from the open, sunny spot here. Directly ahead stands the summit lookout, which was used during World War II as an aircraft spotting station.

The trail follows the narrow ridge to the cabin, which sits upon an airy perch (3.5 mi/5.6 km; 3100 ft/945 m). The vista is outstanding—an excellent view of Lake Crescent and the hills beyond, with Lake Sutherland glimmering in the distance. However, the scene is dominated by Mount Storm King and complemented by the blue-green slopes of Aurora Ridge to the south. One has only to glance downward to see the delta of Barnes Creek far below, protruding into the lake.

Hikers should use care when moving around outside the cabin to check the different viewpoints because the slopes of the peak drop sharply on the north and east sides.

4   BARNES CREEK TRAIL

Length 9.4 mi/15.1 km (last 5.5 mi/8.8 km not maintained)
Access US 101
USGS Maps Lake Crescent; Lake Sutherland
Agency Olympic National Park

The Barnes Creek Trail begins near the Storm King Ranger Station and Visitor Center on the delta of Barnes Creek, close to the south shore of Lake Crescent. This trail follows the stream almost 10 miles to its headwaters on Baldy Ridge. Only the first half is maintained; the latter part has more or less been abandoned. Together with a short side path leading to Marymere Falls, the first half mile of the Barnes Creek Trail forms a self-guiding nature walk that is popular with travelers who drive along the shores of Lake Crescent. This section of the path is paved, and it is broad and smooth as it parallels Barnes Creek and meanders among giant firs and cedars. When hikers on the trail approach US 101, they will hear the noise made by vehicular traffic and regret the broken solitude. The trail crosses beneath the highway where a bridge spans the creek, and the traffic sounds are soon left behind and quickly forgotten. This valley is especially beautiful during the fall when the enormous leaves of the maples and devil's clubs turn golden yellow.

Beyond junctions with the **Mount Storm King Trail** (0.4 mi/0.6 km) and the **Marymere Falls Trail** (0.5 mi/0.8 km), the way narrows, becoming a typical Olympic footpath about 18 inches wide. The route parallels Barnes Creek through a narrow valley where the forest is primarily Douglas-fir and western hemlock, with a ground cover of ferns. Here the chatter of the stream is always present. During the first few miles, the undergrowth is luxuriant, and the path crosses numerous little brooks; thus water is always available.

The trail is not level; it goes up and down, but ascends more than it descends, crossing Barnes Creek via foot logs at the low points. The path then crosses a large tributary. Here it penetrates dense thickets of salmonberry and devil's club.

The trail now begins to switchback up the mountain, and the creek roars lustily far below. Upon reaching a point opposite a slope where slides have occurred, the trail veers away from Barnes Creek, then levels out as it approaches Dismal Draw Camp (3.5 mi/5.6 km; 1700 ft/518 m), where a little brook flows down a dark and gloomy defile.

Despite its name, this is a pleasant camp. The silence of the deep woods is broken by the subdued murmur of the brook, the croaking of ravens, and the wind whispering in the hemlocks and cedars. The campsite is a tiny shelf below the trail, barely large enough for two small tents.

As it ascends Dismal Draw, which is almost always in the shade, the trail crosses the brook and returns to the Barnes Creek side of the spur. Once again the stream can be heard, but it is muffled now and sounds like the clatter of a distant train. The forest is so dense that virtually nothing grows upon the ground except moss. The trees are small, the stands cluttered with dead broomsticks—saplings that perished in the struggle for sunlight. Scattered among them are many snags and a few large firs that were blackened near the ground by the fire which destroyed the virgin timber.

The trail climbs steadily as it makes a long traverse—where Mount Storm King is visible through the trees—then crosses an avalanche path. Barnes Creek is now hidden in the depths of its canyon, but the hiker can look across and up the valley to Baldy Ridge. Upon entering the forest again, the trail comes to a junction with the **Aurora Divide Trail** (3.9 mi/6.3 km; 1500 ft/457 m).

Beyond this point the upper Barnes Creek Trail, which continues to the left, has not been maintained, and the path—almost obliterated by young trees and windfalls—is often covered with moss. The experienced hiker will have no difficulty following the route, but it should be avoided by the novice. Many logs lie across the trail, and one is constantly climbing over or crawling under them. All through this section the route traverses splendid stands of Douglas-fir. The path then crosses Lizard Head Creek (6.1 mi/9.8 km; 1830 ft/558 m). Beyond this stream the forest is mostly western hemlock, but as the trail approaches Happy Lake Creek, which flows in a deep ravine, the route again goes through stands of Douglas-fir. The trail crosses the creek at the site of an old camp (6.8 mi/10.9 km; 2075 ft/632 m). Four logs arranged in a square mark the spot where a cabin once stood.

The trail ascends a spur, then parallels the upper reaches of Barnes Creek. After crossing the stream, the path climbs sharply upward, then forks (9.1 mi/14.7 km; 4800 ft/1463 m). The right branch ends about a hundred yards distant in a stand of stunted western hemlock, approximately at the national park boundary on the divide between Barnes Creek and Hughes Creek. The left branch, commonly called Lookout Dome Way, climbs to Lookout Dome (9.4 mi/15.1 km; 5090 ft/1551 m). The trail switchbacks sharply upward to the base of the domelike rock, where one can look down Hughes Creek toward the Elwha River. Baldy Ridge, to the northeast, exhibits outcrops of barren basalt.

The trail goes left, around the rock's base, then up the easy back side to the summit. Here a few sprawling juniper bushes have managed to survive, as well as a lone subalpine fir that stands like a sentinel, buffeted by the wind. The east side of the dome is a vertical wall about 300 feet high, and hikers not subject to vertigo can look almost straight down into the tops of tall trees growing directly below. The view includes the vista down Barnes Creek toward Lake Crescent, and the ridge to the south, but the eye is drawn to the rough cliffs of Baldy Ridge, where hawks ride the wind as they search for prey in the timber below.

5 MOUNT STORM KING TRAIL

Length 2.8 mi/4.5 km
Access Barnes Creek Trail
USGS Maps Lake Crescent; Lake Sutherland
Agency Olympic National Park

One of the most popular paths in the northern Olympics, this trail overlooks Lake Crescent as it climbs about two-thirds of the way up the west ridge of Mount Storm King, a peak composed of basalt.

The trail begins at a junction (700 ft/213 m) with the **Barnes Creek Trail,** 0.4 mi/0.6 km from Storm King Ranger Station. The path doesn't fiddle around with tentative uphill starts but climbs sharply through stands of tall Douglas-fir, where the ground is covered with ferns and moss. As it switchbacks up the mountainside, the trail ascends to successive vantage points that provide ever-changing vistas of Lake Crescent, Aurora Ridge, and the valley of Barnes Creek. Fog often lies over the lake in the morning, but when the afternoon sun slants low, softening the shadows, the water loses its vivid blue color, changing to slate gray. Log trucks roar along the lake's southern shore, their grinding motors breaking the otherwise somber stillness.

Upon gaining the western spurs of Mount Storm King, the trail ascends a steep "hogback," switchbacking to several overlooks. The noise made by the logging trucks becomes pronounced, seemingly magnified rather than lessened by the increased altitude.

At one viewpoint a warning sign indicates it is dangerous to go farther. The trail does not end here, but inexperienced hikers should not proceed beyond this

Lake Crescent from US 101

point. Beyond the viewpoint the ascent of Mount Storm King involves scrambling up rotten rock on a narrow ridge. The path becomes progressively steeper, then vanishes at a jutting promontory (2.8 mi/4.5 km; ca. 4265 ft/1300 m). Bordered by steep, forest-clad mountains, Lake Crescent sweeps across the line of sight. Pyramid Mountain stands to the northwest, Aurora Ridge to the southwest, with the valley of Barnes Creek lying at the foot of the mountain. Across the valley the mountainside is a series of uniform spurs between creeks that flow parallel to one another and at right angles to Barnes Creek. This is an excellent example of a trellis drainage pattern.

6   MARYMERE FALLS TRAIL

Length 0.2 mi/0.3 km
Access Barnes Creek Trail
USGS Map Lake Crescent
Agency Olympic National Park

The Marymere Falls Trail leaves the **Barnes Creek Trail** 0.5 mi/0.8 km from the Storm King Ranger Station. Together with the first part of the Barnes Creek path, it forms a self-guiding nature trail that is popular during the summer with casual visitors.

The path first crosses Barnes Creek and Falls Creek, then ascends the opposite slope to Marymere Falls (0.2 mi/0.3 km), forming a loop at the end that leads to two vantage points. The vistas overlook a saucer-shaped basin at the foot of an abrupt wall. At this point Falls Creek plunges through a notch in the cliff to form the 90-foot-high falls. The water drops vertically about half the distance; then, striking a slanting ledge, ribbons down the rock face to a small hollow at the bottom. Ferns and mosses decorate the rock walls on either side.

This attraction was originally called Meremere Falls, but the name was changed many years ago to honor Mary Alice Barnes, sister of Charles A. Barnes, a member of the Press Expedition.

7   AURORA DIVIDE TRAIL

Length 5.6 mi/9.0 km
Access Barnes Creek Trail; Aurora Ridge Trail; Happy Lake Ridge Trail
USGS Maps Lake Sutherland; Mount Carrie
Agency Olympic National Park

This trail connects a lowland path, the **Barnes Creek Trail**, with two upland ones, the **Aurora Ridge Trail** and the **Happy Lake Ridge Trail**. The path begins 3.9 mi/6.3 km up the Barnes Creek Trail from Lake Crescent, at 1500 ft/457 m elevation.

The route parallels an unnamed creek that flows in a deep ravine, the trail at first ascending through stands of Douglas-fir and western hemlock having little or no undergrowth. The forest is quiet, the silence broken now and then by the hoarse croaking of ravens. One can see, across the ravine to the left, where avalanches have knocked down a number of trees.

The climb is gradual, but steady, via long switchbacks, and as elevation is gained the Douglas-fir is replaced by silver fir. Near the ridge crest the terrain becomes less precipitous, and a dense undergrowth is present.

As it switchbacks upward, the trail crosses an avalanche track several times. The slide zone is covered with thick growths of salmonberry, willow, huckleberry, devil's club, and baneberry. The trail then climbs to a campsite (3.2 mi/5.0 km; 4200 ft/ 1280 m) where water is available. The forest is thinner here, and huckleberry bushes grow beneath the trees. The path goes by a couple of ponds, then meanders through moss-covered boulders and crosses the divide—Aurora Ridge or Happy Lake Ridge, whichever one chooses to call it. (This is near the indefinite point where one ridge becomes the other.) The trail then intersects the Aurora Ridge Trail (3.6 mi/5.8 km; 4750 ft/1448 m).

The trail climbs up and down as it follows Happy Lake Ridge, either traversing along the crest or on one side or the other. Here it alternates between forest and meadowland. The trees consist of subalpine fir, mountain hemlock, and silver fir; the wildflowers include lupines, gentians, mountain azalea, daisies, and thistles. Hikers should keep alert because the tread deteriorates and often disappears in the meadows. One should watch for signs of the trail or note on the tree trunks bits of orange-colored tape which indicate the way.

On this exposed divide, one can hear the wind in the trees—murmuring softly on quiet summer days, howling during wild autumn storms. At one point the trail dips a bit, and one can see, to the left, the steep pyramid of Lizard Head Peak (5370 ft/

1637 m). The trail then enters a dense stand of subalpine fir. The tall trunks rise to a considerable height without limbs, and the crowns are festooned with lichen.

Eventually the trail comes out on a slope where the sound of a stream—a tributary of the North Fork Soleduck—rises faintly from below. The path continues down the ridge, and one can look to the right into the headwaters of the North Fork Soleduck or to the left across the Barnes Creek watershed and the valley of Lizard Head Creek. During late September, *Boletus edulis,* a prized mushroom, can sometimes be gathered here.

Again the trail follows the narrow spine, at times through stands of subalpine fir and mountain hemlock, where gentians bloom beneath the contorted trees. Then, coming out into another meadow, the trail ends at a junction with the Happy Lake Ridge Trail (5.6 mi/9.0 km; 4950 ft/1509 m), where the latter departs its namesake ridge to follow an unnamed divide to Boulder Lake. This is not only confusing but also illogical, but the trails in the Olympics do not always follow a logical course.

8   AURORA CREEK TRAIL

Length 2.5 mi/4.0 km
Access US 101
USGS Map Lake Crescent
Agency Olympic National Park

One of the steepest paths in the Olympics, this trail begins on US 101 on the south side of Lake Crescent, 2.8 mi/4.5 km west of the Storm King Ranger Station. Although parking space has not been provided at the trailhead, one can use the nearby turnouts along the highway.

The trail ascends the spur between Aurora Creek and Smith Creek, climbing above the lake through Douglas-fir forest. At first the noise of traffic is pronounced, but with increasing elevation the sound diminishes. Occasionally the hiker can glimpse Lake Crescent through the trees.

The path climbs unrelentingly along the narrow spine. The trees gradually become smaller, and western hemlock is dominant at the higher altitudes. One can hear Aurora Creek flowing in a deep draw to the right, and a sign at a branch trail (1.7 mi/2.7 km) indicates water is available. The side path drops to the creek, the only place on this route where water can be obtained.

Beyond this point silver fir gradually replaces Douglas-fir, and the hemlocks stand so thick on the mountainside that little direct sunlight penetrates the forest canopy; consequently, undergrowth is sparse, in many places nonexistent. The gloom is unrelieved, even on the brightest days, and the darkness is depressing.

Higher up, the trail goes through dense stands of mountain hemlock and silver fir as it more or less follows the narrow ridge, shifting back and forth from one side to the other, like a lost dog looking for its master, and occasionally going along the crest. Here the mountain hemlocks often form clusters of six to ten trees.

After skirting a rock outcrop, the trail crosses Aurora Ridge, then descends slightly on the south side to a junction with the **Aurora Ridge Trail** (2.5 mi/4.0 km; 4100 ft/1250 m).

9   AURORA RIDGE TRAIL

Length 16.0 mi/25.8 km
Access US 101
USGS Maps Lake Crescent; Lake Sutherland
Agency Olympic National Park

This trail follows the divide between the Soleduck and Lyre Rivers. Although it begins on the Soleduck, it is more closely allied to the Lyre and therefore has been included in this section.

Beginning 2.5 mi/4.0 km south of US 101 on the Soleduck River Road (see Soleduck chapter for road description), the trail climbs to Aurora Ridge, then follows the watershed until the path merges with the **Aurora Divide Trail**, where Aurora Ridge becomes Happy Lake Ridge. (The change in terminology is arbitrary because the ridge is unbroken; thus it reflects man's penchant for classifying geographic features into ever smaller units.) The ridge does not rise above timberline, but the route crosses meadows that provide excellent views. Because this trail is not one of the popular "beaten paths," the hiker is more apt to find solitude here than on most trails that are close to roads.

Beyond the parking area (1150 ft/351 m), the trail follows an abandoned logging road bordered by colonnades of tall alders. This area, logged before the national park was created, is now covered with second-growth forest. The trail crosses several brooks here, then leaves the logging road and enters virgin forest, consisting mostly of Douglas-fir. When the ridge crest is attained, one can see, through the trees, sky below on either side and hear logging trucks operating in the nearby Olympic National Forest. The trail now follows the rounded crest of Aurora Ridge, through dense stands of western hemlock and silver fir, to a junction (5.5 mi/8.9 km; 3700 ft/1128 m) with a path that leads left to the Eagle Lakes, the source of Eagle Creek.

The spur trail climbs a bit, then drops sharply, ending at the largest lake (0.6 mi/1.0 km; 3075 ft/937 m). Bordered by tall conifers, it lies on a bench, and a stream flows into it from the south. The second lake, slightly lower in elevation and to the north, is little more than a long, narrow pothole half-filled with silt and aquatic plants. The third and smallest lake is located still farther down the slope.

Beyond the Eagle Lakes, the Aurora Ridge Trail meanders through stands of silver fir, western hemlock, and Douglas-fir, then makes a gradual ascent, no longer on the ridge top but traversing the steep south side. Once again the hiker may hear trucks and, through openings, view logging operations in the national forest. The trail then returns to the ridge, where one can look to either side. Here the forest consists mostly of true firs, and the undergrowth is sparse. On the south slope of Sourdough Mountain, the trail crosses a big meadow overgrown with juniper, ferns, lupine, huckleberry, and wild strawberry. The beautiful view here includes Mount Olympus, Mount Tom, and intervening forested ridges, as well as the vista up the North Fork Soleduck.

Sourdough Camp (8.5 mi/13.7 km; 4550 ft/1387 m) is located north of the trail in a little meadow just beyond the big one. The shelter that once stood here is nothing but a heap of ruins today. This camp is not inviting because the terrain is not level and water is scarce, although a nearby path leads to a ravine where it can be found in early summer.

The trail now begins a long, ascending traverse of a steep sidehill, then switchbacks down to a brackish pond and a meadow marked by snags with bleached trunks. A tiny stream crosses the trail here.

Beyond the junction with **Aurora Creek Trail** (11.0 mi/17.7 km; 4100 ft/ 1250 m), located in a thick stand of silver fir, the trail descends a bit, crosses a little meadow, where Mount Olympus is once again visible, then climbs toward Aurora Peak. Skirting just below the summit, the trail contours to Aurora Spring (12.0 mi/ 19.3 km; 4450 ft/1357 m). The tiny rivulet emerges from the bottom of a slope covered by meadowland and subalpine firs. The spot is too swampy for camping, but tents can be pitched on the ridge above.

East of Aurora Spring, patches of forest, which extend to the ridge crest, alternate with a succession of ever larger meadows, from where one can see for miles. Most of the time the trail traverses the south slope of Aurora Ridge, but now and then it follows the narrow divide or drops into the mountain hemlock forest on the north slope. At various points one can look up and down the North Fork Soleduck and glimpse, beyond intervening timbered ridges, the snowy peaks of Olympus, Tom, Carrie, and Appleton. The view to the north includes the valley of Barnes Creek. Occasionally, part of Lake Crescent is visible, but generally it is hidden by Mount Storm King.

One is most impressed, however, by the vista of the North Fork Soleduck. The river is not visible, hidden in the dense forest, but the beautiful scene down the valley includes truncated spurs that appear to alternately overlap each other, like shingles, as they extend toward the stream from the bordering ridges, thus creating through the forest a zigzag line that marks the river's course. The valley is heavily timbered, and the view of virgin forest, unmarred by fire, logging, or road building, is one of the finest in the national park, comparable on a lesser scale to what a more famous vista was like before it was impaired by logging—the view from Kloochman Rock, overlooking the Queets Valley (see **Kloochman Rock Trail**).

This stretch of trail is particularly delightful during Indian summer in late September and October. The ice on Mount Olympus glitters in the soft, pale sunlight, the wind whispers in the clumps of subalpine firs on the ridge, and the tall meadow grasses undulate restlessly with every vagrant breeze.

Beyond the last meadow the trail traverses dense forests of silver fir to a junction with the Aurora Divide Trail (16.0 mi/25.8 km; 4750 ft/1448 m).

The Elwha often floods during the winter. (Photo by Frank O. Shaw)

ELWHA

The Olympic Mountains were first sighted by Europeans when mariners sailed along the Pacific coast in the late 1700s, but the first part of the Olympics visited by white men was the northern slopes facing the Strait of Juan de Fuca. Here the Elwha Valley provides a natural pathway into the interior, and during the latter part of the nineteenth century explorers used it as a route of entry. In 1885 Lieutenant Joseph P. O'Neil sent part of a military expedition up

the river, possibly beyond the Lillian River, perhaps as far as the lower end of Press Valley. Then, during the winter of 1889–90, the Press Expedition plodded up the Elwha, and this party's route, where it followed the river, became the Elwha Trail of later years. The men named many geographic features in the valley, including Mount Christie, Mount Barnes, and Hayes River.

The upper Elwha lies in the heart of the Olympics. The valley is flanked on the west by the Bailey Range, Cat Creek Ridge, Happy Lake Ridge, and Baldy Ridge. On the east the valley is bordered by the Elwha River Range, Hurricane Ridge, and the mountains extending southward to Mount Anderson. The Burke Range and the Elwha Basin peaks enclose the valley on the south. The gap between Mount Seattle and Mount Christie, known as Low Divide (3662 ft/1116 m), is the lowest trans-Olympic pass. Beyond it lies the Quinault River.

Because it cuts through rocks of varying hardness, the Elwha River has eroded a valley of variable width as it has modified the U shape that resulted from glaciation during the Ice Age. The bottomlands are broader near the river's headwaters than they are downstream, where the valley floor narrows to deep gorges, only to widen again. Throughout the river's course, the bottoms and canyons are bordered by steep mountainsides.

The river has its source in the Elwha Snowfinger, near the center of the mountains, where the Bailey Range, the Mount Olympus Range, and the Elwha Basin peaks are knotted together. This snowfield extends down from Dodwell-Rixon Pass, the low point between Mount Queets and Mount Barnes. The river first flows to the southeast through Elwha Basin, then curves around until its direction is northerly; thus it forms a fishhook pattern.

The Elwha is swift but often deceptively smooth. At times it plunges through wild gorges, booming and thundering, with a show of white rapids, then flows quietly into deep pools. Upon leaving the mountains, the river goes through broken country, then discharges into the Strait of Juan de Fuca. The principal tributaries are the Lillian, Lost, Goldie, and Hayes. Many creeks also flow into the Elwha. The largest ones are Delabarre, Buckinghorse, Boulder, Long, Cat, and Godkin.

Once a good salmon stream, the Elwha can now be fished only for trout because two dams built during the early 1900s effectively prevent salmon from going up the river to spawn. The reservoir impounded behind the Elwha Dam is known as Lake Aldwell, in honor of Thomas T. Aldwell, who worked hard for the development; the reservoir behind the Glines Canyon Dam (named for George A. Glines) is called Lake Mills (for E. M. Mills). The dams were built many years prior to establishment of the national park.

ROADS

The Elwha Valley is essentially roadless. The Elwha River Road, together with its two branches—to Boulder Creek and Whiskey Bend—is the only route penetrating the district. Accordingly, access to most of the valley is via the trails.

Elwha River Road. This road leaves US 101 at the Elwha River, 8.5 mi/13.7 km west of downtown Port Angeles, and follows the river through cutover land dotted with stump ranches, where rustic buildings mingle with old and new homes. After entering Olympic National Park, the road follows the river to Elwha Campground (3.0 mi/4.8 km), at the base of the Elwha River Range. An amphitheater,

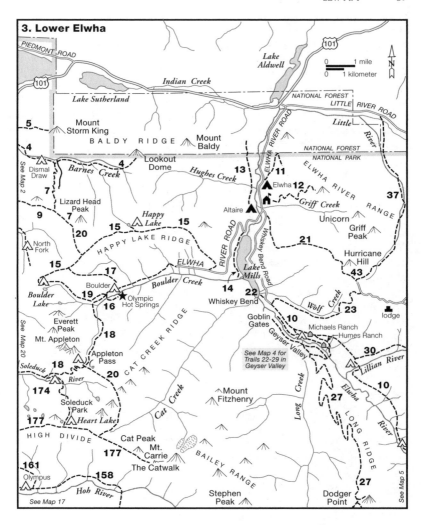

3. Lower Elwha

where park naturalists give illustrated talks during the summer, is located in a grove of firs west of the road.

Wilderness camping permits can be obtained at the Elwha Ranger Station (3.9 mi/6.3 km; 300 ft/91 m). The Whiskey Bend Road branches to the left just beyond the station. The river road (now sometimes known as the Boulder Creek Road) leads straight ahead, up the east side of the Elwha, then crosses the river. The entrance to Altaire Campground (4.4 mi/7.1 km) is just beyond the bridge. The campground has tent sites, picnic tables, and rest rooms along the west bank of the Elwha.

The road ascends forested foothills to the Glines Canyon Dam (5.5 mi/8.9 km), the upper of two power dams on the Elwha. This dam was constructed in the 1920s and, together with the Elwha Dam outside the national park, it is slated to be removed in an attempt to restore the once fabled salmon runs in the Elwha River.

Past the dam the road twists and turns as it climbs high above Lake Mills to Observation Point (8.0 mi/12.9 km; 1492 ft/455 m), which overlooks the Elwha Valley. The road then follows the course of Boulder Creek through stands of Douglas-fir. The last section of the road, beginning at 9.9 mi/15.9 km, was permanently closed in 1982, the last 2.2 mi/3.5 km having become too difficult to maintain due to slides and extensive erosion. This closed section, now part of the trail system, leads to what was formerly an automobile campground.

Whiskey Bend Road. This road begins 4.0 mi/6.4 km from US 101 on the Elwha River Road, near the Elwha Ranger Station, and goes up the east side of the Elwha. The unpaved road is narrow and winding, with turnouts for passing, and one should keep alert for vehicles approaching from the opposite direction. Built in the 1930s by the Forest Service, it was part of a road that climbed with steep grades to Hurricane Ridge. However, the section above Whiskey Bend was closed to automobile traffic after construction of a new road to the ridge and is now known as the Wolf Creek Trail. The road ascends through stands of second-growth Douglas-fir, and as it climbs over the Devils Backbone, where the Press Expedition lost a mule, the vista of the Elwha River is impressive. Twisting and turning as it gains altitude, the road goes by Glines Canyon Dam, rounds Windy Arm, and crosses three creeks—Sege, Hurricane, and Wolf. The road ends at Whiskey Bend (4.3 mi/6.9 km; 1198 ft/365 m), where ample parking space has been provided for hikers, backpackers, and horseback riders.

10 ELWHA TRAIL

Length 28.8 mi/46.4 km
Access Whiskey Bend Road
USGS Maps Hurricane Hill; Mount Angeles; McCartney Peak; Chimney Peak; Mount Christie; Mount Queets
Agency Olympic National Park

During the late 1880s the settlers on the Elwha River cut a primitive trail upstream as far as they had taken claims. The Press Expedition extended this route, and today the Elwha Trail more or less coincides with the path the party blazed, except where the route was obliterated by the creation of Lake Mills. The well-kept trail, the main route leading into the mountains from the north, lies entirely within Olympic National Park and follows the river to the Elwha Basin, in the center of the Olympics.

Near its point of origin at Whiskey Bend (1198 ft/365 m), the trail passes Winslow Spring, where a pioneer family by that name once had a cabin. Although normally a perpetual source of water, the spring sometimes disappears in late summer, particularly in dry years.

The first 4 miles of the Elwha Trail, from Whiskey Bend almost to the junction with the Lillian River Trail, are virtually a pedestrian's boulevard—a broad, smooth path that may well be the most-used trail in the Olympic Mountains. All kinds of people walk the trail, and it is exceptionally popular with equestrians, senior citizens, and families with small children. On the other hand, in recent years cougars have become more numerous in this area, and on several occasions have attacked people as well as a pack train.

For several miles the trail goes through stands of second-growth fir, at times entering patches of virgin forest. During the early 1900s settlers' fires swept up the mountainsides and destroyed much of the old-growth timber. The bits of original forest that escaped appear, when viewed from a distance, as dark green areas among the lighter-hued second growth.

As the trail contours high above the Elwha to avoid Rica Canyon, the river can be heard roaring in the depths, but it is not visible. A spur trail (0.8 mi/1.3 km) descends to the right about 250 yards to Elk Overlook. This rock outcrop was the "Eagle's Nest" used by the Press Expedition as an observation post, and it provides a vista across the Elwha to the meadow that was formerly the Billy Anderson Ranch. Elk often graze here, and the hiker intent on a good view should carry binoculars.

At Benchmark Rock (1.0 mi/1.6 km; 1300 ft/396 m), the Elwha Trail enters an area devastated by fire in 1977. The heat apparently damaged the rock, which has started to slide down the mountainside. Near the center of the blackened district, the trail intersects the **Rica Canyon Trail** (1.1 mi/1.8 km).

The trail now contours above Geyser Valley, the bottomland bordering the Elwha between what are now known as Rica Canyon and the Grand Canyon. The Press Expedition gave both gorges more picturesque names. The former they called Goblin Canyon because it began at Goblin Gates. The latter they named Convulsion Canyon inasmuch as the gorge reminded them of an Indian legend in which the Spirit of the Mountains shook the earth, opening up great chasms that swallowed bands of Indians.

The trail leaves the burn at a junction with the **Krause Bottom Trail** (1.5 mi/ 2.4 km) and continues through second-growth forest to a junction with the **Long Ridge Trail** (1.8 mi/2.9 km; 1150 ft/351 m). The Michaels Ranch cabin stands nearby at the edge of the clearing. Originally the home of Addison "Doc" Ludden, who settled here about 1906, the cabin was later occupied by E. O. Michaels, a predator hunter known as Cougar Mike. The cabin has been given historical status by the National Park Service and was restored in 1980. Ludden also built a lodge, which he called Geyser House, but it was destroyed in 1958.

The Elwha Trail ascends a bench above Geyser Valley, then again enters the virgin forest. The trunks of the old firs are covered with lichen, and now and then a yew tree clings to the slope below the trail. Between Antelope Creek and Idaho Creek, where the trail contours high above the latter's canyon, one should watch for Press Party blazes because several well-preserved ones are present on the older trees. They consist of three ax cuts, one above the other.

Beyond Idaho Creek the trail follows a glacier-cut terrace as it contours toward Lillian River through stands of second-growth fir. Many trees are not much larger than broomsticks, but a few fire-scarred veterans are scattered among them. The trail then traverses a section where the soil is apparently poor or does not retain water. The trees are stunted, the ferns tiny, the salal only a few inches high.

After intersecting the **Lillian River Trail** (4.1 mi/6.6 km; 1580 ft/482 m) on the brink of Lillian Canyon, the trail descends sharply to Camp Lillian (4.6 mi/7.7 km; 1273 ft/388 m), located in a setting of tall firs and cedars on the bank of the Lillian River. The deep shade is unrelieved, and it is always dark, damp, and gloomy in the canyon, even on warm, sunny days. Several campsites are located on the flats, in the midst of a luxuriant growth of sword ferns.

The trail crosses the river, goes by additional camps, then ascends Difficulty Hill, so named by the Press Expedition because the men anticipated their mule would have trouble negotiating the steep grade. The path climbs steadily, occasionally switchbacking, through a forest of stunted firs and madronas, then traverses high above the Grand Canyon of the Elwha. The river roars loudly, but the stream is not visible, although occasionally one can view, through the trees, the heavily forested Elwha Valley.

Upon reaching the high point (5.8 mi/9.3 km; 2000 ft/610 m), the trail begins a long, gradual descent to the Elwha, during which it crosses several creeks. The trees are now much larger, the undergrowth more luxuriant. Beyond Prescott Creek, the trail comes out onto the banks of the Elwha (ca. 1200 ft/366 m), where big firs tower above a riverside camp. The trail then climbs over a small rise to Marys Falls Camp (8.8 mi/14.2 km) and Camp Baltimore (9.0 mi/ 14.5 km). The falls which give the first camp its name are located across the river on a creek that tumbles down the eastern slopes of Long Ridge. Of considerable height, the cascade is impressive during the spring and early summer, when the volume of water is large.

The trail now has a more or less level grade as it winds through river bottoms, traverses alder and maple glades, and crosses little streams. The path then approaches what the Press Party called Thunder Canyon. The river booms noisily here as it follows a serpentine course between rocky walls.

Canyon Camp (10.4 mi/16.7 km; 1400 ft/427 m), located on the river just above the canyon, has a number of excellent sites. The trail then climbs high above a deep pool in the Elwha. Numerous brooks are present here, and the river runs deep and smooth at this point.

At Little Elkhorn Camp (11.5 mi/18.5 km; 1450 ft/442 m) the trail enters a grassy meadow bordered by firs and cottonwoods, where one has a view of the river and the timbered mountainsides to the west. Elkhorn Ranger Station is staffed only in the summer months. On the right, toward the river, stands a hikers' shelter and a little barn for pack animals. A campsite where tents may be pitched is located in a grove of trees opposite the ranger's cabin.

The trail goes through a grove of large firs at Stony Point. The spot is well-named because the forest grows upon what appears to be an ancient rock slide. After crossing Stony Creek, the trail meanders over flats, then ascends and descends as it traverses steep hillsides covered with heavy stands of Douglas-fir. The path then enters an area where winds have wrecked the forest for about a mile. More than half the trees have been uprooted or broken. Almost every tree was bowled over in places, and here the logs are often piled up three and four deep; but in nearby spots many trees were left standing. The scene is unsightly. However, it vividly demonstrates not only the power exhibited by nature in a destructive mood but also the rapidity of forest regeneration. Although full recovery will take years, young hemlocks are already springing up.

The trail crosses Lost River (12.5 mi/20.1 km), then rounds a bend, where an old family hideaway, the Remann Cabin, comes into view. The building stands near the edge of the devastated area. Beyond it is the ford (13.0 mi/20.9 km) on the Elwha leading to the **Dodger Point Trail.**

The trail now parallels Semple Plateau, which lies just across the river, then passes the confluence of the Elwha and Goldie Rivers and enters Press Valley (15.0 mi/24.2 km; 1600 ft/488 m). All three geographic features were named by the Press Expedition: the plateau for Eugene Semple, former governor of Washington Territory; Goldie River for R. H. Goldie of Seattle; and Press Valley for the expedition's sponsoring newspaper. Today's maps restrict the name Press Valley to the flats along the Elwha between the Goldie and Hayes Rivers, but the name was originally applied to the upper Elwha Valley extending from the Goldie to Elwha Basin.

The bottomlands broaden in Press Valley, and the trail meanders southward past Tipperary Camp and Chateau Camp to Hayes River Ranger Station (16.7 mi/26.9 km; 1680 ft/512 m). At this point the Elwha Trail makes a sharp turn to the east and parallels Hayes River to an important junction with the **Hayden Pass Trail** (17.0 mi/27.4 km; 1780 ft/543 m), which ascends the east side of the Elwha Valley to Hayden Pass, thus providing access to the eastern Olympics. The Elwha Trail then crosses the Hayes River—which was named for Christopher Hayes, a member of the Press Expedition—and resumes its southerly course.

Above the Hayes River the Elwha Trail penetrates wild, isolated country beyond the reach of the casual hiker, and the trout fishing is excellent. At irregular intervals the booming of the river resounds through the forest. Towering firs line the trail, their dark crowns outlined against the sky. On the forest floor dense growths of vanilla leaf mingle with thick pads of moss. Lupine grows abundantly in little openings, its bright blue blossoms adding still another contrast.

The trail now climbs high above the rushing Elwha, traversing terraces, then descends to flats along the river, where it meanders among giant firs. In this idyllic setting, cool breezes sweep down from the snowfields above, and the thunderous roar of the river is always present.

Beyond Camp Wilder, also called Crackerville (20.9 mi/33.6 km; 1885 ft/575 m) the trail trends westward, following the curve of the Elwha, and crosses Godkin Creek, one of the river's larger tributaries, which has its source in the Burke Range, near Bretherton Pass.

The route then traverses stands of old Douglas-fir as far as Buckinghorse Creek. The trees are huge, and mixed among them are many smaller ones, chiefly silver fir and western hemlock. The trail then crosses to the Elwha's west bank and enters a forest composed almost exclusively of the latter species.

Chicago Camp (25.8 mi/41.5 km; 2185 ft/666 m) is located in the midst of dense, damp forest. Nearby is a junction with the **Low Divide Trail.** Beyond this camp the Elwha Trail follows the river through stands of hemlock, fir, and cedar, and has been rerouted in places due to heavy damage wrought by high winds and flooding caused by severe winter storms. Happy Hollow (27.0 mi/43.5 km; 2400 ft/732 m), the last trail shelter in the valley, is located in an area having few level spaces where one can pitch a tent. Not far beyond, a cavelike recess beneath an overhanging rock wall has provided hikers with emergency shelter on more than one occasion.

Goblin Gates on the Elwha River

Emerging from the deep forest, the trail crosses the Elwha to the southwest side. Several decades ago Mother Nature bridged the river at this point in the form of a small foot log high above the swift, rushing water. Eventually, floods swept the foot log away, and today one must either wade across or remain on the northeast side where travel is more difficult. If the party elects to cross the Elwha, a fixed rope should be set up so that the people who are crossing can grasp it firmly for support should they lose their footing. On the far side the trail meanders through thick growths of willow and alder near the river, then breaks out into the subalpine meadows of Elwha Basin (28.8 mi/46.4 km; 2700 ft/823 m), where it ends.

The basin is a deep cleft bordered by snow-clad peaks, cliffs, and cascades. The lower slopes are clothed with conifers, slide alder, and little meadows where elk often graze. Mount Meany and Mount Noyes stand to the southwest; Mount Queets rises to the west.

Beyond the open meadows, one can follow an elk path to the basin's upper end, then descend a steep, brushy slope, returning to the river again near the terminus of the Elwha Snowfinger. Hikers not skilled in cross-country travel should not venture beyond this point. One must cross the Elwha, which may be difficult to do, in order to reach the snowfield, and the latter is often honeycombed with ice caverns, particularly in late summer, making travel upon it hazardous.

Experienced and well-prepared hikers consider the long, gradual climb up to historic Dodwell-Rixon Pass (31.5 mi/50.7 km; 4750 ft/1448 m) a pleasant hike in good weather, a miserable one when it is cold and raining. Snow and sleet sometimes fall in midsummer, but on hot days hikers welcome the cool breezes that descend from the snowy peaks. A number of cascades film down the mountainsides enclosing the narrow trough. Near the top the snowfields become steeper, and the wind blows almost continuously. The snow is often marked by elk tracks, made by the animals during their wanderings between the Elwha Basin and Queets Basin. Occasionally hikers are fortunate and see a band crossing the broad snowfields in Queets Basin.

The men that Lieutenant O'Neil sent to climb Mount Olympus were probably the first to cross this pass. They did so on September 19, 1890, then camped near Plutos Gulch in the Queets Basin. The Dodwell-Rixon party, which surveyed the Olympics at the turn of the century, used the pass about a decade later. Then, in 1907, while on their way to Mount Olympus, men from the Explorers Club traversed the pass. Because they believed the surveyors had been the first to cross the gap, they named it for them.

The pass is the low point on the divide between the Queets and Elwha Basins, and the panorama is varied. The Elwha Basin, encircled by rugged peaks, lies to the southeast; the Queets Basin, a vast, snowy area, is to the west. Here the winter snowfall is so heavy that cornices often remain until midsummer. Mount Olympus stands directly west, its pinnacles rising above the Humes Glacier. North of the glacier a sharp-pointed ridge extends to Bear Pass (5500 ft/1676 m) and walls in the Queets Basin on the north.

11   CASCADE ROCK TRAIL

Length 2.0 mi/3.2 km
Access Elwha River Road
USGS Map Elwha
Agency Olympic National Park

One of two routes that climb spurs to the western end of the Elwha River Range, this trail starts near the north end of the Elwha Campground. At first it parallels a stream flowing alongside the campground, then it divides. The correct route goes left, uphill; the right branch leads to the community kitchen and a network of confusing paths that people have made in the adjacent forest.

The trail switchbacks upward through a stand of large Douglas-fir. The understory consists largely of vine and bigleaf maple; the ground cover is primarily sword fern. This area is attractive in the fall, when the maple leaves turn color and come down in showers of gold with every passing breeze. Often the trail is hidden beneath the accumulation. As one ascends, the sound of the Elwha River comes up from below.

The trail again divides—one path goes up, the other down. The hiker should follow the downhill path, although the natural inclination is to take the uphill trail. The latter is worth a side trip, however, because it climbs to an open slope that provides a good view (better than the vista from Cascade Rock) of the Elwha Valley, including the forested slopes on the opposite side, broken by outcrops of barren basalt. Mount Fitzhenry and the tip of Mount Carrie are also visible. The valley is colorful in the fall because the forest is a mixture of conifers and deciduous trees.

The left branch goes downhill about 200 yards, then begins to climb again and briefly follows the obscure grade of an old road. Here it penetrates second growth, the original forest having been logged. After more switchbacks, the route returns to the virgin forest (chiefly Douglas-fir, with an understory of vine maple) and makes a more or less level traverse northward.

Angling away from the Elwha, the trail climbs gradually. Among the attractions are hillsides clothed with sword ferns, outcrops of moss-covered rock, and crooked madronas. At one point the trail follows a rock ledge to a viewpoint overlooking the Elwha Valley. Apparently, this is Cascade Rock (1.5 mi/2.4 km; 1000 ft/305 m), but it is not impressive. However, one can look across the river and observe the slopes beyond, where rounded domes of basalt protrude from the forest.

The trail zigzags up a spur through young trees and fire-scarred veterans of the old growth as it climbs to another rock outcrop where contorted madronas are clad with lichen. The view looks north over the valley of Madison Creek, beyond the national park, and one sometimes hears dogs barking down below. The trail ends at this point (2.0 mi/3.2 km; ca. 1800 ft/549 m).

12   GRIFF CREEK TRAIL

Length 2.8 mi/4.5 km
Access Elwha River Road
USGS Map Elwha
Agency Olympic National Park

Hikers should park their cars at the Elwha Ranger Station (390 ft/119 m), then go to the trailhead in the rear. They should carry water; it is not available on this route, which starts near Griff Creek, then switchbacks up a spur of the Elwha River Range. The creek was named for a pioneer family that homesteaded the site now occupied by the ranger station. The family name was Griffin, which somehow became shortened with reference to the creek.

After crossing the river flats, the trail makes a grueling, unrelenting climb, gaining almost 3000 feet, via thirty-five switchbacks, in less than 3 miles. The route switchbacks through old-growth forests, where the ground is covered with moss,

Oregon grape, and sword ferns. Here and there madronas enliven the scene. As the trail climbs higher, the trees become much smaller, and the undergrowth remains sparse but now includes ocean spray.

Gradually the country becomes more open, with a number of rock outcrops. Manzanita flourishes here, and madronas covered with lichen stand alongside. The vista up Griff Creek reveals a narrow, V-shaped canyon. Beyond the twenty-first switchback, a side trail leads left to a rounded knoll decorated with mosses and lichen. Here the hiker can see the river below, look out across the Elwha Valley, and gaze up Hughes Creek, as well as observe Lake Mills in the distance. The promontory also provides a vista of forested mountains up Griff Creek.

The grade now eases as the route traverses to a mossy rock that rises perhaps 100 feet above the trail. The path follows a ledge around it, then goes alongside another monolith. Again madronas are present because the trees have an affinity on this, the drier side of the mountains, for rock outcroppings.

Circling around the rocks, the trail goes back into the dense timber, then deteriorates (2.0 mi/3.2 km). Many windfalls bar the way, and the path is stony and in generally poor condition. Beyond fire-scarred firs on a rocky slope, the trail climbs via a series of short, steep switchbacks as it skirts beneath pillow basalt. The path then crosses over the ridge to the south side, where it terminates abruptly among cliffs and pinnacles (2.8 mi/4.5 km; 3300 ft/1006 m). Here one has a view of the valley of Griff Creek. Ahead, to the southeast, rise two peaks of the Elwha River Range. The sharp rock horn is Unicorn Peak (5100 ft/1555 m); to its right stands Griff Peak (5120 ft/1561 m).

13 WEST ELWHA TRAIL

Length 3.0 mi/4.8 km
Access Elwha River Road
USGS Map Elwha
Agency Olympic National Park

The trail begins at the north end of Altaire Campground (400 ft/122 m). This route was once part of the Olympic Hot Springs Trail, most of which was destroyed by extension of the Elwha River Road up Boulder Creek.

As it parallels the river, the trail goes through stands of Douglas-fir, a mix of virgin forest and second growth but primarily the latter. After about a half mile, the trail veers away from the Elwha and crosses a maple-and-fern glen, then returns to the conifer forest. The latter now consists mostly of young trees, with a scattering of big firs blackened near the ground by fire.

The trail contours a steep hillside, and the river can be heard below. This is a good point (1.0 mi/1.6 km) for families to stop; otherwise the adults might have to carry their children up the hill on the return trip. The path descends to a flat where a few old firs still stand, but most of the big trees were cut years ago. One can still see the springboard cuts in the rotted stumps. The trail then crosses Hughes Creek (1.5 mi/2.4 km). The forest beyond is dense second growth.

The trail climbs around a bluff overlooking the Elwha. Here one has a splendid view upriver, with the Elwha River Range rising beyond. After crossing Freeman

Creek, the trail climbs to the national park boundary at the top of the hill (2.6 mi/ 4.2 km), then continues through private land to the Herrick Road (3.0 mi/4.8 km).

14 WEST LAKE MILLS TRAIL

Length 2.0 mi/3.2 km
Access Elwha River Road
USGS Maps Elwha; Hurricane Hill
Agency Olympic National Park

This trail is reached by leaving the Elwha River Road just beyond the Glines Canyon Dam and following the boat launch road to Lake Mills (0.2 mi/0.3 km; 600 ft/183 m).

Although the trail more or less follows the lake's west shore, it is one of those up-and-down routes that hikers find disconcerting. One moment the trail is at lake level, close to the shore; then it climbs high above the water, only to return to the shore, crossing several streams en route. Nevertheless, it is an interesting route to walk, particularly in the fall, when the maple leaves turn golden yellow. The trail also makes an excellent "owl hike" during the evening. A few old-growth firs, scarred by fire, are scattered through the stands of second-growth timber.

Beginning in a stand of alder and bigleaf maple, the trail climbs to an old road-bed and follows it a short distance. The path then descends to lake level and crosses Stubey Creek near an old fir that has an osprey's nest in its top.

The route climbs over a couple of spurs that extend down to the lake. Madrona trees add artistic touches, and at the second spur the hiker can see the upper end of Lake Mills and the mountains beyond. The trail then descends to a little stream and a good viewpoint, where one can look down the length of the lake. The buildings near the dam are visible; so, too, are the heavily timbered spurs that rise from the lake's eastern shore. At night the lights twinkle on the lake's surface, making the scene romantic.

Beyond this point a short path leads left to a campsite on the shore. The main trail goes right, and one can hear Boulder Creek just ahead. The trail ends abruptly (2.0 mi/3.2 km) at the edge of a precipice overlooking the arm of the lake that leads to the creek. Caution is advised. The hiker who walks too fast, without paying attention, may take an involuntary header in the lake. However, the scene at the brink is picturesque—the lake lies at one's feet, and the cascades made by Boulder Creek are visible.

15 HAPPY LAKE RIDGE TRAIL

Length 10.0 mi/16.1 km
Access Elwha River Road
USGS Maps Lake Sutherland; Mount Carrie; Lake Crescent
Agency Olympic National Park

Happy Lake Ridge Trail begins on the Boulder Creek section of the Elwha River Road, 8.6 mi/13.8 km from US 101, and climbs to Happy Lake Ridge.

The path then follows the divide in a westerly direction, ending near Boulder Lake. The country traversed is somewhat drier than one would expect, probably because it is sheltered by the Bailey Range from the full effect of winter storms.

The trailhead (1750 ft/533 m) is located in a stand of fir. Madronas and vine maples are scattered among the conifers, and the ground cover consists of thick growths of salal, Oregon grape, manzanita, kinnikinnick, and red huckleberry. Other plants include vanilla leaf, rattlesnake plantain, pipsissewa, lupine, and twisted stalk, with its orange berries.

A side path (0.2 mi/0.3 km) leads to the first of two places where water can be obtained between the road and Happy Lake. The route then contours a steep slope, and openings permit one to look across the valley of Boulder Creek to Mount Carrie and its glaciers, which rise above the timbered foothills. As the trail climbs higher, the route steepens and the undergrowth becomes sparse. The trunks of the firs have been blackened by fire, and a few western white pines mingle among them. A tiny stream (2.6 mi/4.2 km), one of the rivulets forming the headwaters of Deep Creek, is the last source of water until one reaches Happy Lake.

The route now crosses grassy glades dotted with old, rough-barked firs. A bunch of switchbacks then climb a fairly open slope, although huckleberry brush becomes predominant near the crest of Happy Lake Ridge (3.0 mi/4.8 km; 4500 ft/1372 m).

At this point the trail turns westward and traverses along the ridge. One can see to the left and right, respectively, the valleys of Boulder Creek and Hughes Creek. As it follows the narrow divide, the path levels out, at times descending a bit, and Mount Olympus and Mount Carrie appear to rise side by side in the distance. The Elwha Valley lies to the southeast, with Mount Anderson beyond. The trees include silver and subalpine fir, mountain hemlock, and Alaska cedar, with a growth of juniper upon the ground. The meadows nearby are made colorful by wildflowers, particularly daisies, thistles, and beargrass.

The trail drops to the northern side, where it traverses dense stands of mountain hemlock and a silver forest—a grove of fire-killed trees—where thick brush has sprung up, chiefly mountain ash, azalea, and huckleberry. Two peaks stand to the north and the view to the northeast includes the lower Elwha, Port Angeles, Ediz Hook, and the Strait of Juan de Fuca, with Mount Baker on the horizon. As the path climbs higher, little meadows alternate with subalpine forest. The trail then enters a large meadow, where a transverse north–south ridge—the divide between Hughes Creek and Barnes Creek—connects Happy Lake Ridge with Baldy Ridge. An old sign (5.0 mi/8.0 km) indicates this is the summit or the highest point on the trail. Actually the summit is the mile-high saddle where the north–south ridge contacts Happy Lake Ridge.

At this point a spur trail descends through meadowland and groves of mountain hemlock to Happy Lake (0.5 mi/0.8 km from the junction; 4875 ft/1486 m). The tarn, which contains Eastern brook trout, is more or less round, ringed by trees, and edged along the north and south shores by patches of meadow. A campsite is located at the lake's south end.

Beyond the saddle the trail follows Happy Lake Ridge as it curves to the southwest, alternately traversing meadowland and subalpine forest. Like most ridge trails in the Olympics, the path climbs up and down, with views of valleys on both sides:

to the left, or south, the gash made by Boulder Creek; to the right, or north, the tributaries of Barnes Creek as well as ridges and the Strait of Juan de Fuca. The trail then goes through another silver forest, where the undergrowth is heavy.

The route intersects the **Aurora Divide Trail** (7.5 mi/12.1 km; 5000 ft/1524 m), where the northern end of Crystal Ridge joins Happy Lake Ridge. Beyond this junction the trail abandons its namesake ridge and follows the northern spur of Crystal Ridge, which wraps around the headwaters of Crystal Creek like a horseshoe. (The long-abandoned **Crystal Ridge Trail** ascends the ridge directly from the Boulder Creek Campground near Olympic Hot Springs.) The route goes through fairly open country, then crosses to the south side of the crest, where it enters still another silver forest.

As the trail follows Crystal Ridge, it alternately traverses meadowland and dense subalpine forest. Here one often hears the wind murmuring in the trees. The view to the east looks down the valley of Boulder Creek.

Like an airplane coming in to land, the trail now begins a long, steady descent toward Boulder Lake, which sparkles in the distance. The trail ends at a junction (10.0 mi/16.1 km; 4400 ft/1341 m) with the **Boulder Lake Trail,** just north of the lake.

16 OLYMPIC HOT SPRINGS TRAIL

Length 2.7 mi/4.4 km
Access Elwha River Road
USGS Map Mount Carrie
Agency Olympic National Park

This path leads to the hot springs from the end of the Boulder Creek section of the Elwha River Road. Before the road was built, the trail was about 15 miles long and followed the Elwha River and Boulder Creek.

The trail begins where the Elwha River Road now ends (1700 ft/518 m) and follows the closed portion of the old road to what was formerly an automobile parking lot. Nearby is the walk-in Boulder Creek Campground (2.2 mi/3.5 km; 2200 ft/671 m), which is unique because it is the only walk-in campground in the park. Beyond the former parking area the path follows the north side of Boulder Creek a short distance before crossing the stream, where it reverses its direction 180 degrees in order to go down the south bank to the hot springs (2.7 mi/4.3 km; 2100 ft/ 640 m), where several pools of warm water are located.

Olympic Hot Springs were discovered in 1892 by Andrew Jacobsen, but they were almost inaccessible for many years because no trails or roads penetrated the country. In the early 1900s William Everett acquired the location rights and blazed a trail to the springs. With the assistance of the Forest Service, the county built a road to the site in the 1930s. Everett and Harry Schoeffel developed a resort, and it became the most popular one in Clallam County. Eventually it declined, and everything is gone now. Only the hot pools are left.

Geologists are uncertain of the mechanism that has produced the Olympic Hot Springs. They do lie on a fault, and it is probable that breaks in the rock structure permit the water—which chemically resembles surface water—to circulate down toward the hot interior of the earth.

17 CRYSTAL RIDGE TRAIL

Abandoned trail, no longer maintained
Length 3.0 mi/4.8 km
Access Elwha River Road
USGS Map Mount Carrie
Agency Olympic National Park

The abandoned Crystal Ridge Trail—which is steep, dry, and waterless— begins (2300 ft/701 m) on the northeast side of Boulder Creek Campground in the fir forest. The first half of the trail is in fair condition, but the second half is much poorer. In fact, the path virtually disappears at the higher elevations.

The route follows the narrow, spinelike ridge. The forest is mostly fir and hemlock at the lower elevations, but higher up it includes the typical mountain hemlock and Alaska cedar. Brush is more or less nonexistent on the lower part, but thick and troublesome on the upper section. Rocks sprinkled with tiny crystals, like grains of sugar, apparently gave rise to the name Crystal Ridge.

Eventually, the ridge broadens and flattens somewhat; the trail disappears, but one can walk across the open stretches. Here the hiker can look to the left across the valley of Boulder Creek and to the right to Happy Lake Ridge. The route goes first on one side of the ridge, then the other, whichever affords the best footing, then strikes the **Happy Lake Ridge Trail** (3.0 mi/4.8 km; 5000 ft/1524 m) about 1.5 mi/2.4 km east of that trail's junction with the **Boulder Lake Trail**.

18 APPLETON PASS TRAIL

Length 7.8 mi/12.6 km
Access Elwha River Road; Soleduck Trail
USGS Map Mount Carrie
Agency Olympic National Park

This route links Olympic Hot Springs with the **Soleduck Trail.** The pass lies on the divide between the Soleduck and Elwha watersheds, and the trail follows the valley of Boulder Creek. Obtaining water is not a problem because streams cross the trail at frequent intervals.

Beginning 2.2 mi/3.5 km from the end of the Boulder Creek section of the Elwha River Road, at a junction with the **Olympic Hot Springs Trail** near Boulder Creek Campground (2200 ft/671 m), the trail winds through the shaded coolness of Douglas-fir and western hemlock to a junction with the **Boulder Lake Trail** (0.6 mi/ 1.0 km; 2350 ft/716 m). The ground beneath the trees is open in many places, with skunk cabbage growing in the swampy spots. About a half mile beyond this junction, the forest changes abruptly, and silver fir competes with the other species. The ground cover consists of huckleberry and vanilla leaf, with devil's club near the streams.

After crossing the North Fork of Boulder Creek, the trail contours near the picturesque falls in the South Fork. At this point (1.5 mi/2.4 km) a side path descends to Lower Boulder Creek Falls, where the South Fork leaps about 30 feet into a large bowl, then makes a series of cascades. This spot is cool on the hottest days, and the windblown spray is refreshing. A small campsite is located nearby.

The trail now begins to climb, switchbacking as it parallels the South Fork. A second side path (1.7 mi/2.7 km) leads to Upper Boulder Creek Falls and another little campsite. The falls are narrower than the ones below, and it is more difficult to obtain a good view. The creek cascades perhaps 60 feet, first jumping 30 feet to a ledge, then angling back to the right, thus more or less forming a crescent.

The trail crosses the South Fork, and the murmuring of little brooks can be heard around bends in the path. At one point the trail overlooks an avalanche track, where slides have swept down the flanks of Mount Appleton. The path then makes a long, ascending traverse to another camp (2.4 mi/3.9 km), crosses several avalanche tracks as it climbs through subalpine forest, and switchbacks up through a jungle of slide alder. The creek, not far below, chatters constantly.

Breaking out into open country, the now stony trail enters a large meadow where big boulders are strewn around. Marmots sit upon the rocks and stare at the bipeds who dare to intrude upon their domain. A huge rock near the meadow's edge is a favorite perch, probably because it is high and offers a good lookout. Wildflowers are abundant in midsummer. The display includes azalea, Sitka valerian, broadleaf arnica, common bistort, false hellebore, lupine, spiraea, paintbrush, and avalanche lily. Huckleberry, mountain ash, slide alder, and willow are the predominant bushy plants.

The trail switchbacks a couple of times, then crosses the South Fork of Boulder Creek twice. Beyond this point the switchbacks end for a while, then the trail makes a half dozen as it climbs to a basin. Tarn Camp is located here, beside a little pond which often disappears in late summer.

The path now makes nine short, steep switchbacks as it climbs to Appleton Pass (5.2 mi/8.4 km; 5050 ft/1539 m), the low point in the divide between Boulder Creek and the Soleduck River. The **Cat Creek Way Trail** begins here, and several campsites are located near the pass, where the high-country views are outstanding. Mount Appleton looms to the north. One can obtain water from Oyster Lake or a nearby stream.

Beyond Appleton Pass the trail descends sharply, via switchbacks and long traverses, to the Soleduck River. The forest consists of subalpine fir and mountain hemlock at the higher elevations; otherwise it is mostly western hemlock, with scattered Douglas-fir, western white pine, Alaska cedar, and silver fir.

Upon leaving the pass, the route at first traverses a mixture of heather meadows and stands of subalpine firs, with views across the upper Soleduck to Soleduck Park and the High Divide. Mount Olympus and Mount Tom rise above the latter. Flowers include spiraea, Columbia lily, paintbrush, beargrass, and penstemons. As the trail switchbacks down the slope, the forest becomes thicker, but windows appear now and then where one can look out to Mount Olympus.

Below the meadowland, the trail goes by two potholes (6.0 mi/9.7 km; 4600 ft/ 1402 m). The stagnant tarns are unattractive, and although the water can be used, it should be boiled. Beargrass, lupine, and huckleberry are abundant in this area. So, too, are mosquitoes.

About a half mile beyond the potholes the views disappear, but the sound of the Soleduck River can be heard coming up from below. As the trail switchbacks down the steep slope, the undergrowth becomes sparse. The trail then traverses a slide zone grown up with bracken fern and vine maple and crosses Rocky Creek at the far end (7.4 mi/11.9 km; 3400 ft/1036 m). This is the only source of water between the pass and the river. Hikers going up the trail should fill their water bottles here.

As the trail descends, one can both see and hear the creek, which flows noisily below on the left. After crossing a slide where the rocks are covered with lichen, the trail ends at a junction with the Soleduck Trail (7.8 mi/12.6 km; 3100 ft/ 945 m) in a forest of tall conifers.

19   BOULDER LAKE TRAIL

Length 2.8 mi/4.5 km
Access Appleton Pass Trail
USGS Map Mount Carrie
Agency Olympic National Park

The trail begins at 2350 ft/716 m on the **Appleton Pass Trail**, 0.6 mi/1.0 km west of Boulder Creek Campground. The path does not switchback but makes a long, ascending traverse as it climbs steadily above the North Fork of Boulder Creek through dense stands of Douglas-fir. The stream is hidden in its canyon, but its booming breaks the stillness. As the trail ascends, the forest changes to western hemlock, and little openings exhibit displays of beargrass during the summer. Here one has glimpses of Mount Appleton across the valley.

Halfway Creek (1.1 mi/1.8 km; 3200 ft/975 m) marks the midpoint between the campground and Boulder Lake, not the halfway point on this trail.

After crossing a rock slide where devil's club and vine maple flourish, the trail goes through stands of silver fir, Alaska cedar, and western hemlock. Here the route traverses a flood slide (an area of finely broken shale, boulders, gravel, and detritus that has slid among the trees), then enters a grove of Alaska cedar, where many trees are adorned with burls. An oddity—five large trunks rising from a single root system—stands beside the trail at one point.

Two creeks that cascade down this slope become raging torrents on hot days when the snowpack is melting. After crossing them, the route flattens at the canyon's head, at this point entering the subalpine forest and meadow country. The ground is swampy. Marsh marigolds, daisies, and asters bloom among the heather, adding touches of color. Huckleberry bushes grow everywhere, clustering thickly around the subalpine firs.

Beyond the **Happy Lake Ridge Trail** junction (2.7 mi/4.3 km), the trail turns south, tops a small rise, and ends at Boulder Lake (2.8 mi/4.5 km; 4350 ft/1326 m). Cupped on the northeast side of Boulder Peak, the more or less round lake is almost encircled by a forested ridge, with cliffs and snowfields to the southwest. Along the lake's north side, where a camp is located, the land is fairly level, and a peninsula juts into the water. The lake is the source of the North Fork of Boulder Creek and is stocked with Eastern brook and rainbow trout.

Boulder Peak rises above the ridge to the southwest. The walk to the summit (5600 ft/1707 m) is steep but not difficult and rewards the hiker with views in all directions. Mount Appleton stands nearby to the south. A dozen miles distant, Mount Olympus rises to the right of the northern spurs of the Bailey Range, which are topped by Mount Carrie. Heavily forested ridges and valleys extend westward, with the ocean in the distance. The Strait of Juan de Fuca is to the north. Beyond the timbered ridges to the east, the snow-flecked peaks of the eastern Olympics extend to the horizon. Directly below lie the Three Horse Lakes. The rounded upper lake occupies a dish-shaped cirque. The triangular lower one is located on a timbered bench.

20 CAT CREEK WAY TRAIL

Way trail, not maintained
Length 4.5 mi/7.2 km
Access Appleton Pass Trail; High Divide–Bailey Range Trail
USGS Map Mount Carrie
Agency Olympic National Park

This splendid high-country route, noted for rugged terrain and glorious views, extends from Appleton Pass to the High Divide, thus making a semicircle around the headwaters of the Soleduck River. The path was not constructed but tramped out by the feet of trekkers approaching the Bailey Range from the north, following elk trails whenever possible. The trail goes alternately through meadowland and groves of subalpine trees. Wildflowers are abundant in the meadows, including buttercups, daisies, bistort, lupine, and avalanche lilies. One is also apt to see elk and perhaps an occasional bear.

Beginning at Appleton Pass (5050 ft/1539 m) on the **Appleton Pass Trail**, the trail follows the ridge in a southerly direction, bordered by open meadow on the left, subalpine forest on the right. Oyster Lake (0.2 mi/0.3 km; 5170 ft/1576 m), so called because it is shaped like an oyster shell, is little more than a snow pool lying in a slump or depression near the ridge crest. A campsite is located here among the trees, and water can be obtained from a brook that gushes from a hillside adjacent to a nearby snowfield.

The trail steepens as it follows the ridge to a large meadow, then the grade moderates. To the left, or north, a rocky point (5450 ft/1661 m) overlooks Appleton Pass, and the walk to its top is well worth the time. The view is impressive, particularly at sunset. Oyster Lake glimmers like a pool of molten silver, and one can see the switchbacks in the trail leading up to the pass. Beyond them the bulk of Mount Appleton looms over the valleys. The Strait of Juan de Fuca and the San Juan Islands are visible to the northeast. Ten miles directly south, the crest of Mount Olympus rises above Cat Creek Ridge and the meadows of Soleduck Park and the High Divide.

Mount Olympus from Cat Creek Way Trail

The trail disappears in the big meadow, but the route meanders to a high point (5500 ft/1676 m), then descends to a saddle at the head of Schoeffel Creek, where the trail again becomes distinct. The path now makes a descending traverse along a timbered sidehill to a low point (5150 ft/1570 m), where it crosses a brook. Normally this is the only place where water can be obtained between Oyster Lake and Cat Creek Basin. Here one looks down the headwaters of the Soleduck River.

The path then climbs toward Cat Creek Ridge through knee-high grass on steep slopes. The route crosses the divide at Spread Eagle Pass (2.0 mi/3.2 km; 5400 ft/1646 m), so named because a snowfield on the north slope resembles such a figure. On the south side, the path contours the upper levels of a cirque, the third in a line of seven on the southeast slope of Cat Creek Ridge. At the bottom an oval-shaped tarn glitters in the sunlight.

Along the cirque's upper rim, the views of Mount Carrie and Cat Peak are splendid. Mount Olympus is also visible, but it is mostly hidden by the west rim of the cirque. The trail then crosses a lateral ridge into the second cirque, which is larger. Here the view of Mount Olympus and the Blue Glacier is unobstructed. One can also see Mount Tom, Mount Carrie, and Cat Peak.

The traverse of the second cirque entails crossing heather slopes, then boulder fields, where the hiker must step from rock to rock. The trail disappears but begins again, high on the slope beyond. At this point one should be careful not to be misled into taking a game trail lower down the slope.

After crossing the next cirque—the third when going south, the first when coming from the High Divide—the trail breaks out into meadows on the northeast slope of Cat Creek Basin, which lies at the head of Cat Creek. The view of Mount Olympus is dramatic, with the basin spread out below. The trail now disappears but one can either circle around to Cat Lake, high on the western slope, or descend to good campsites on the basin floor (4.0 mi/6.4 km; ca. 4250 ft/1295 m), where the trail can be found again. Cat Lake is also known as Swimming Bear Lake (or Swimming Bare Lake, as some would have it) because the motion picture *The Olympic Elk,* filmed by Herb and Lois Crisler, had a sequence that featured a bear swimming in the tarn.

Cat Creek Basin covers about 250 acres and varies in elevation from 4250 to 5400 ft/1295 to 1646 m. The basin consists of meadows, heather-covered slopes, and groves of subalpine trees, and it is crisscrossed by a multitude of elk trails and man-made paths. In fact, they seem to be everywhere. Wildflowers are abundant, and the displays of beargrass in August are remarkable. The floor of the basin is virtually level—a large meadow covered with heather and grass, surrounded by beautiful stands of subalpine fir and mountain hemlock. Big boulders are scattered about, and dwarf huckleberry is abundant. A creek runs through the middle, and a round pond is located at the western end.

Alas, a well-known landmark that stood in the basin for years, the Castle-in-the-Cat, has collapsed. The "castle" was a nondescript shelter built by Herb Crisler in 1944, which he used when photographing elk on the Bailey Range. A way trail leads from the basin floor, first climbing a bit, then descending to the shelter, which is located in a clump of trees overlooking the canyon. The structure is unkempt, littered with impedimenta, including fruit jars filled with notebooks and sheets of paper upon which visitors have scribbled their names, addresses, and comments.

The Civilian Conservation Corps, which built many trails in the Olympics during the 1930s, had a camp in Cat Creek Basin. Consequently, near the pond the route again becomes well defined. A good path climbs out of the basin, alternately going through meadows and groves of subalpine trees. The trail then crosses a big meadow to an intersection with the **High Divide–Bailey Range Trail** (4.5 mi/ 7.2 km; 4500 ft/1372 m).

21 HURRICANE HILL TRAIL

Length 7.1 mi/9.8 km
Access Whiskey Bend Road
USGS Maps Elwha; Hurricane Hill
Agency Olympic National Park

One of the most interesting trails leading from low to high country, this route is seldom used today because Hurricane Ridge is readily accessible by automobile (see Hurricane Ridge Road description in North Slope chapter). Before the Forest Service built a road to the ridge in the 1930s, the trail was one of several paths used by hikers to reach the meadowland. In fact, a glorious high-country traverse was possible—one could ascend this trail, then follow the ridge many miles, descending via another route.

Most people think the trail merely gives access to the ridge, and why hike up when they can drive? How misinformed they are! The trail provides outstanding views, and it is particularly attractive during Indian summer. Of course, it is a grueling ascent, gaining more than a mile in altitude. Therefore, if the party has two vehicles at its disposal, it may savor the trail but avoid the climb by first leaving one car at the lower trailhead, driving in the other to Hurricane Ridge, hiking the paved **Hurricane Hill Trail**, then walking this trail down to the Elwha.

The trail begins (400 ft/122 m) on the Whiskey Bend Road, just beyond the Elwha Ranger Station. At first one can hear the Elwha River, but the sound gradually fades. The forest is primarily Douglas-fir and western red cedar, the ground an unbroken carpet of sword ferns, with devil's club and maidenhair ferns growing in the damper places.

The trail crosses a fairly large stream (ca. 1.0 mi/1.6 km), then another (ca. 2.0 mi/3.2 km), the last one on this route. Above this point the dense undergrowth disappears, but the tree trunks are covered with staghorn lichen.

As the trail climbs higher, the forest appears to have been manicured by nature. The firs are old, with a rough appearance. Only a few fallen trees lie upon the ground, which is fairly open, covered with vanilla leaf, and a specimen now and then of baneberry and twisted stalk. Along the edge of the forest are displays of cow parsnip and ocean spray.

The route breaks out into the first meadow (3.8 mi/6.1 km), then zigzags upward, climbing a forested ridge. The path makes sweeping switchbacks across steep slopes, through a big, grassy meadow where all is quiet and peaceful, and most hikers will pause here to enjoy the panorama. The valleys of several creeks—Cat, Boulder, and Long—are in sight, and Lake Mills shimmers in the afternoon sunshine. The path then traverses a stand of subalpine firs.

Beyond this point the views of the interior Olympics are remarkable from various spots and include Mount Anderson and the Eel Glacier. The trail traverses meadowland on the south side of the northwest ridge of Hurricane Hill, then the terrain levels somewhat at a large meadow (5.0 mi/8.1 km), where one can look out across to the Bailey Range. Boulders composed of hard basalt lie scattered about.

The hiker is rewarded with a superlative vista, in this country of splendid views, at a point (5.4 mi/8.7 km) that overlooks the lower Elwha, with the Strait of Juan de Fuca and Vancouver Island beyond. The scene in the opposite direction is equally striking and includes the tip of Mount Olympus poking above the Bailey Range.

After traversing open slopes on the south side of the ridge, where the ground is matted with juniper, the trail ascends a narrow ridge overgrown with subalpine firs. Here the terrain drops sharply on the north to a little cirque choked with boulders. Griff Creek is down below, and the Elwha River Range rises beyond.

The trail leaves the ridge again, crossing a meadow on the south side, and presently comes to a junction with the Hurricane Hill Lookout Trail (6.1 mi/9.8 km; 5640 ft/1719 m). Beyond this point the two trails merge and climb to the summit of Hurricane Hill (6.3 mi/10.1 km; 5757 ft/1755 m). (See Hurricane Hill Lookout Trail for a description of the summit panorama.)

22 UPPER LAKE MILLS TRAIL

Length 0.4 mi/0.6 km
Access Whiskey Bend Road
USGS Map Hurricane Hill
Agency Olympic National Park

This path is a remnant of the lower section of the old Elwha Trail, which was obliterated by construction of the Elwha River Road, the Whiskey Bend Road, and the Glines Canyon Dam. The section that climbed from Wolf Creek to Whiskey Bend (of which this fragment is a part) was known as the Old Smoky Hill Trail.

The trail begins on the Whiskey Bend Road, 4.0 mi/6.4 km beyond the Elwha Ranger Station, at 1000 ft/305 m elevation, and descends Smoky Hill to the head of Lake Mills. Half the distance it is a downhill traverse, followed by four switchbacks. The route goes through stands of second-growth fir, the virgin forest having been destroyed by fire. The undergrowth is mostly salal.

At the head of Lake Mills, the trail ends at a campsite (0.4 mi/0.6 km; 600 ft/183 m), and Wolf Creek enters the lake just beyond. The Press Expedition's 1890 camp, where Wolf Creek flowed into the Elwha opposite Cat Creek, now lies beneath the lake. The explorers named the streams in honor of a wolf and a wildcat they had killed.

Slightly upstream from the lake shore, Wolf Creek plunges over a cliff, with still another falls above it. The lower one cascades into a bowl having vertical walls about 40 feet high, lined with ferns. When the water is high, after heavy rains, the falls thunder loudly. The view of Wolf Creek Falls alone makes the hike down from the road worthwhile.

23 WOLF CREEK TRAIL

Length 8.0 mi/12.9 km
Access Whiskey Bend Road
USGS Map Hurricane Hill
Agency Olympic National Park

This trail, which roughly parallels Wolf Creek, follows part of the old road that led from the Elwha River to Hurricane Ridge. Beginning at Whiskey Bend (1198 ft/365 m) it climbs Salal Ridge to Hurricane Ridge (8.0 mi/12.9 km; 4970 ft/1515 m)—coming to a junction with the Hurricane Ridge Road (see North Slope chapter for description) at a point west of the lodge. Before the road was built, the Salal Ridge Trail, dating back to the early 1900s, connected Whiskey Bend with Hurricane Ridge.

The lower part of this trail is an excellent route to walk almost any time, but the upper section is likely to be snowbound from November to June. During cold weather, when the snow line is low, skiers sometimes use the trail for touring because it provides a long downhill run from Hurricane Ridge.

This section of the old road was closed to automobile traffic in the late 1950s with the completion of the new Hurricane Ridge Road. Since then nature has slowly reclaimed the right of way, and little conifers now grow thickly in the old roadbed for several miles above Whiskey Bend. Higher up, however, where the climate is harsher and the soil is stony, the seedlings are fewer in number, the land having been much slower to recover.

The first few miles of this trail are in the deep forest, primarily stands of Douglas-fir, but as the route gains altitude—climbing steeply with many switchbacks—the country becomes more open and the views better and better. They include the peaks of the Bailey Range across the Elwha. When the trail attains the ridge, one has an excellent panorama of the interior Olympics and the Elwha Valley.

24 RICA CANYON TRAIL

Length 0.5 mi/0.8 km
Access Elwha Trail
USGS Map Hurricane Hill
Agency Olympic National Park

Also known as the Goblin Gates Trail, this path leaves the **Elwha Trail** 1.1 mi/1.8 km from Whiskey Bend, in an area burned in 1977, and descends through fire-killed forest to the head of Rica, or Goblin, Canyon. Most of the trees destroyed were large second-growth fir. The fire, caused by a careless camper, apparently started along this trail and swept up the mountainside. The ground cover includes thistle, currant, Oregon grape, ocean spray, bracken fern, and a vine belonging to the pea family.

The trail drops sharply at first, but flattens as it follows a bench covered with broomstick-size trees. Leaving the devastated area, the trail descends steeply to the Elwha River, coming to a junction with the **Geyser Valley Trail** about 75 yards above Goblin Gates. The trail then turns to the right and follows the river, ending on the brink of the canyon by a large yew tree (0.5 mi/0.8 km; 700 ft/213 m).

The Press Expedition named the head of the canyon Goblin Gates. At this point the Elwha River, flowing alongside a steep cliff, comes to a sudden standstill in a deep basin, where the water whirls furiously, then makes a right angle turn and glides through a break in the rock wall. The strata, consisting of alternate layers of slate and sandstone, are tilted on edge, and the sandstone has eroded faster than the slate, thus leaving the latter projecting from the canyon walls. The broken rocks, resembling faces with varied expressions—at least to the imaginative person—line the canyon walls and inspired the name.

Goblin Gates can be viewed to much better advantage from the other side of the Elwha—the point where Charles A. Barnes made the discovery on March 4, 1890—which can be reached by taking the **Long Ridge Trail** to a point about 200 yards beyond the Elwha bridge, then traveling cross-country by following (or attempting to follow) bits and pieces of the now essentially defunct **Anderson Ranch Trail**. Here one can look directly down the gorge through the rock portals and see the various "faces" near the water's edge. Unfortunately, the best-defined profile—that of a goblin with upturned nose—broke away during the winter of 1973–74.

William "Billy" Anderson homesteaded the meadow opposite Goblin Gates in the early 1900s. The claim was later acquired by J. Lloyd Aldwell as a real estate

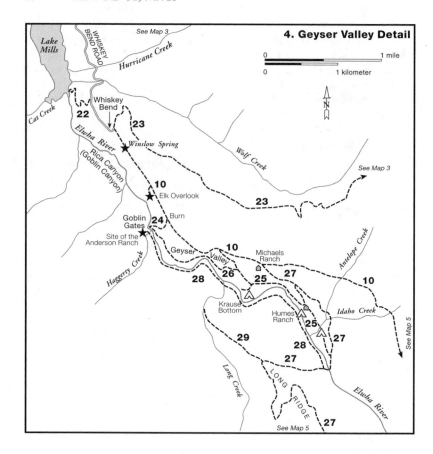

speculation because it included Goblin Gates, a potential hydroelectric site. He renamed the canyon for his daughter, Rica, and held the property for a number of years, then sold it to Crown Zellerbach for $75,000. This company owned the old homestead for many years, but it was later acquired by the National Park Service. This acquisition removes the threat that a dam might be built here that would not only destroy Goblin Gates but also flood historic Geyser Valley.

25 KRAUSE BOTTOM TRAIL

Length 1.3 mi/2.1 km
Access Elwha Trail; Long Ridge Trail
USGS Map Hurricane Hill
Agency Olympic National Park

The Krause Bottom Trail begins 1.5 mi/2.4 km south of Whiskey Bend, on the **Elwha Trail,** and crosses Geyser Valley, going by Humes Ranch.

The trail descends steeply through the forest to a small clearing, where gnarled fruit trees, struggling to exist, are the sole reminders that this was once a pioneer homestead. The trail forks (0.4 mi/0.6 km) on a bench just below the clearing. The right branch is the **Geyser Valley Trail**, which leads to Goblin Gates; the left one, a continuation of the Krause Bottom Trail, which descends to Krause Bottom (0.7 mi/ 1.1 km), on the floor of Geyser Valley, where it forks. The right branch leads to a campsite by the Elwha River, but the Krause Bottom Trail turns left, or south, and traverses the river flats, which are noted for a splendid grove of huge vine maples. This area is well worth a visit in the spring, when the leaves are just emerging on the maples.

The trail then climbs to a bench, the site of the Humes Ranch (1.1 mi/1.8 km). Excellent campsites, reached by a side path, are located below the cabin, by the river. The ranch was homesteaded by Will Humes about the turn of the century, but his brother, Grant, joined him later. Together, the men—who were from New York—planted an orchard and cultivated crops. They also guided hunters and alpinists, including summer outings of The Mountaineers. Will Humes returned to the East Coast in 1914, but Grant continued to reside on the Elwha until his death in 1934. The cabin is the only structure still standing on the ranch, and the National Park Service has restored and preserved it as an example of pioneer settlement. Aged fruit trees accent the isolation and make one wonder what living was like here in the early 1900s.

Beyond the cabin the trail climbs to a junction with the **Long Ridge Trail** (1.3 mi/ 2.1 km) west of Michaels Ranch. An alternate route from the cabin—really a way path—crosses the old hayfield, then reenters the forest. Beyond Idaho Creek, this path goes by a campsite—possibly the best one in Geyser Valley—and ascends to an intersection with the Long Ridge Trail near the bridge over the Elwha.

26 GEYSER VALLEY TRAIL

Length 0.8 mi/1.3 km
Access Krause Bottom Trail; Rica Canyon Trail
USGS Map Hurricane Hill
Agency Olympic National Park

The trail crosses the floor of historic Geyser Valley, which was first explored by the Press Expedition in 1890. One of its members, John H. Crumback, was so impressed he decided to stake a claim, and the party laid the foundation for his cabin opposite the point where Long Creek enters the Elwha River. However, after the exploration concluded, Crumback never returned to perfect his homestead. He settled in the Grays Harbor district instead.

The valley lies between Rica, or Goblin, Canyon and the Grand, or Convulsion, Canyon. Both gorges are cut through sandstone and slate. Because the Press explorers mistook the drumming of grouse (or so it is believed) for the sound of geysers, they named the place Geyser Valley.

At the turn of the century, pioneers began to settle in the valley, carving out homes in the wilderness. Indians may have preceded them—not as residents but as wanderers through the country, perhaps in pursuit of elk—but the first known-for-sure visitors were the men of the Press Expedition.

The ghosts are now gone and the feet of the pioneers no longer tread here. Geyser Valley is silent today except for the babble of hikers and the "river voices" made by the Elwha. But a century ago, men and women were active, cutting trees and digging out stumps, hacking away at underbrush, and building cabins and barns, all in preparation for the good life away from the turmoil of civilization.

The route connects the **Rica Canyon Trail** with the **Krause Bottom Trail**, beginning at a junction with the former near Goblin Gates. At first the trail crosses bottomland covered with large grand firs, cottonwoods, and bigleaf maples. The ground cover consists largely of vanilla leaf and nettles. A campsite is located by the river.

The trail comes out to the river's edge (0.5 mi/0.8 km) and climbs up and down along the face of a bluff, then ascends to a level bench that supports a stand of scrubby fir but no undergrowth other than a few ocean spray bushes. The ground is covered with moss. The trail ends on this bench at an intersection with the Krause Bottom Trail (0.8 mi/1.3 km).

27 LONG RIDGE TRAIL

Length 13.0 mi/20.9 km
Access Elwha Trail
USGS Maps Hurricane Hill; Mount Queets
Agency Olympic National Park

This route replaced the old Long Creek Trail, which has been abandoned for years. Although bits of the latter remain, often one can find no indication of a path at all, then at times discern a faint trace that indicates where the trail may have been. Because the route is choked with countless windfalls, it is not worthwhile to attempt to follow the old trail.

The Long Ridge Trail, its successor, climbs from Geyser Valley to Ludden Peak, most of the way ascending aptly named Long Ridge, which extends north from Dodger Point. The hiker should carry water because it is not available (at least after midsummer) until one approaches the tarns below Dodger Basin.

Beginning at Michaels Ranch on the **Elwha Trail**, the path goes by the intersection with the **Krause Bottom Trail** (0.2 mi/0.3 km), which leads to Humes Ranch, then contours the mountainside. Beyond Idaho Creek, it turns directly south and descends to the Elwha, crossing the river where it emerges from Convulsion Canyon (1.2 mi/1.9 km; 875 ft/267 m). The Elwha formerly broadened below this point and flowed quietly through the bottomlands. However, in 1967 a slide in the canyon dammed the stream temporarily, and when the river broke through, the impounded water swept away the old footbridge and tore out huge chunks of land, thus changing the stream's course. On the west side, tons of gravel and other debris were deposited among the trees, killing most of them; thus a ghost forest now borders the river on that side. The present suspension bridge was built subsequent to the flood.

The trail angles left at an unmarked junction with the **Anderson Ranch Trail** (1.3 mi/2.1 km), then climbs to the northern end of Long Ridge through stands of

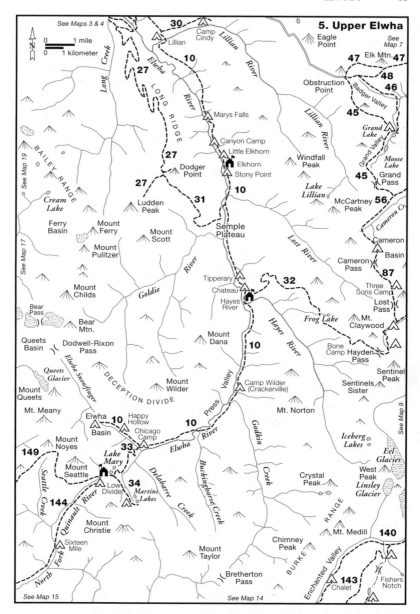

See Maps 3 & 4

5. Upper Elwha

See Map 7

See Map 19

See Map 17

See Map 9

See Map 15

See Map 14

second-growth fir. The virgin forest was destroyed by fire years ago, but a few large trees survived. Beneath the trees the ground is padded with moss, and all is silent except for the trills of winter wrens. The little birds flit through the bushes and peer with curious, friendly eyes at the intruder. Other birds likely to be observed include the varied thrush and the blue grouse.

Upon gaining the ridge, at a junction with the **Seek Way Trail** (2.0 mi/3.2 km; 1600 ft/488 m), the path turns southward. The terrain flattens but the trail climbs steadily, almost imperceptibly, through stands of old Douglas-fir festooned with lichen. The ground is covered by dense thickets of salal. The trail then leaves the ridge and switchbacks through forests on the Elwha side. Here one has views of the Elwha Valley and can look across to Hurricane Ridge.

Again the trail climbs toward the ridge crest—a gradual ascent by means of several long, sweeping switchbacks. Upon crossing over to the west side, where the terrain is more gentle, the trail traverses above Long Creek. The Bailey Range—dominated by Mount Carrie and Stephen Peak—stands to the west. The trail then enters subalpine forest and shortly afterward breaks out into meadowland flecked with mountain hemlocks. The timbered ridges fade away to the horizon, and Lake Mills is visible through a gap formed by the Elwha. Directly north is Hurricane Hill, and the hiker can see the lodge on Hurricane Ridge.

As the trail contours the western slope, Mount Olympus comes into view, partially hidden by the Bailey Range. Mount Carrie and Stephen Peak still dominate the scene, but Ludden Peak now looms to the south. This dark dome, named for Addison Ludden, a Geyser Valley pioneer, was originally called Mount Squire by the Press Expedition to honor Senator Watson C. Squire. Behind the peak rises the bulk of Mount Ferry—named by the Press Party for Elisha P. Ferry, the state's first governor.

The trail crosses rock slides, then edges a meadow above the Dodger Lakes (10.0 mi/16.1 km; 4900 ft/1494 m). One can camp by the tarns which, after midsummer, are usually the only source of water beyond the Elwha. This is not running water, of course, and if used for drinking or food preparation, it should be either boiled or filtered. West of the lakes, away from the trail, spelunkers can find a cave to explore. Nobody should enter the cavern without the security provided by using a fixed rope when making the descent. (Each party must provide its own rope.)

Beyond the lakes the country opens into broad, grassy expanses swept by cool breezes from the nearby snowfields. The wind murmurs in the mountain hemlocks on the bordering ridges, and one may hear the squawking of gray jays. Otherwise silence prevails, accenting the solitude, for this is getting into the remote interior of the Olympics, beyond the reach of the casual hiker. The trail meanders across Dodger Basin—which is strewn with sandstone boulders and is snow-covered until midsummer—and climbs to a low, forested ridge, where it intersects the **Dodger Point Trail** (11.0 mi/17.7 km; 5200 ft/1585 m). (One can go left here 0.5 mi/0.8 km to Dodger Point Lookout.)

Beginning at this intersection the Long Ridge Trail and the Dodger Point Trail share the path briefly. The section where they overlap traverses slopes covered with mountain hemlock and subalpine fir, descending gradually to the second intersection (11.4 mi/18.4 km; 5000 ft/1524 m), on the ridge that connects Dodger Point and Ludden Peak. Here, beside a dark pond, the trails part company. The Long Ridge Trail continues to the right; the Dodger Point Trail goes left.

The trail heads westerly as it follows the divide between Long Creek and Goldie River through meadows and groves of subalpine fir. Stephen Peak stands directly ahead. Turning to the southwest, the path contours the slope that overlooks

Louise Creek, a tributary of the Goldie, then rounds a bend, where Mount Scott comes into view. At this point the route crosses meadows luxuriant with spiraea, mountain ash, and huckleberry, from which there is a beautiful view, across the Goldie, of Mount Claywood and Mount Anderson in the distance.

The ridge ascends, but the trail traverses the south side through stands of mountain hemlock, then breaks out of the dense forest. Here the hiker will notice a faint path descending from the trail to a lower level. This is the beginning of the route to the Bailey Range. The backpacker adept at cross-country travel can leave the trail here and traverse steep mountainsides to the pass (4750 ft/1448 m) between Ludden Peak and Mount Scott, then follow an elk trail to the base of Mount Ferry.

Beyond the way path, the Long Ridge Trail traverses the precipitous face of Ludden Peak, where the trail was blasted through ribs of slate. The route crosses several steep ravines, which in early summer are snow-filled chutes. At that time they are dangerous, and one should not attempt to cross without an ice ax. However, it is pointless to go farther because the trail does not go anywhere but ends abruptly (13.0 mi/20.9 km; 5000 ft/1524 m) on a sheer cliff that supports a dense growth of scrubby Alaska cedar.

After the creation of Olympic National Park in 1938, the government planned to connect this route with the Bailey Range Trail extending from the High Divide. Because the National Park Service ran short of funds with which to complete the project, both trails now end on cliffs where ledges had to be blasted. However, many backpackers and climbers do not regret this, because it leaves the Bailey Range "forever wild," a realm to be explored by the cross-country traveler.

28 ANDERSON RANCH WAY TRAIL

Abandoned trail, no longer maintained
Length 2.0 mi/3.2 km
Access Long Ridge Trail
USGS Map Hurricane Hill
Agency Olympic National Park

The Anderson Ranch Trail starts about 200 yards beyond the Elwha bridge on the **Long Ridge Trail**. The path goes only a few feet before coming to the point where the 1967 flood in Convulsion Canyon eroded the hillside, destroying a section of the trail. At this point hikers have created a scramble route by clambering down the steep, muddy bank almost to the river bottom, then climbing back up to the trail again beyond the ghost forest of flood-killed trees.

The crossing of Long Creek (1.1 mi/1.8 km; 750 ft/229 m) would be difficult during periods of high water had not a huge fir fallen across the stream, thus creating a perfect hiker's bridge, one that the most timid person can walk upon without fear or trepidation.

Beyond the creek the trail meanders through the forest (largely second growth, the virgin trees having been destroyed by fire), occasionally climbing up and down. The path then descends to the site of the William "Billy" Anderson Ranch, the meadow that faces the whirlpool at Goblin Gates (2.0 mi/3.2 km; 680 ft/207 m).

The gates can be viewed to advantage from this point, where Charles A. Barnes discovered them in 1890. When the river is low, in late fall, it forms a picturesque series of steplike cascades just above the whirlpool. (See **Rica Canyon Trail** for a more detailed description of Goblin Gates.)

A good campsite is located slightly upstream from Goblin Gates in the fringe of maples and huge cottonwoods that grow between the meadow and the river. The camp is just distant enough from the stream that the water's sound, although readily heard, is not intrusive.

29 SEEK WAY TRAIL

Abandoned trail, no longer maintained
Length 0.7 mi/1.1 km
Access Long Ridge Trail
USGS Map Hurricane Hill
Agency Olympic National Park

After part of the Anderson Ranch Trail was destroyed by the Convulsion Canyon slide and flood in 1967, the National Park Service authorized a party of volunteers to build an alternate route. The result was this path, as announced by a sign tacked to a tree at the trailhead: "SEEK Way Trail, May 6, 1973." Using this route involves considerable elevation gain and loss, both on the way to Goblin Gates and on the return.

The trail begins where the **Long Ridge Trail** strikes the crest of Long Ridge, 0.8 mi/1.3 km beyond the Elwha bridge, at 1700 ft/518 m elevation—more than 800 feet above the river. The trail descends the steep spur to the flats adjacent to Long Creek, where it ends (0.7 mi/1.1 km; 800 ft/244 m), but one can follow down the creek and make the usual crossing, then find the old **Anderson Ranch Trail** beyond. Or, for a more interesting side trip, one can go up the creek to the point where the stream emerges from its canyon.

This route avoids the swampy, debris-strewn areas where the Anderson Ranch Trail was destroyed by the flood, but the elevation gain and loss is a disadvantage.

30 LILLIAN RIVER TRAIL

Abandoned trail, no longer maintained
Length 3.1 mi/5.0 km
Access Elwha Trail
USGS Maps Hurricane Hill; Mount Angeles
Agency Olympic National Park

The trailhead (1580 ft/482 m) is located 4.1 mi/6.6 km up the **Elwha Trail** from Whiskey Bend. The route follows the Lillian River, ending just below the point where the stream emerges from a canyon.

The trail begins in old-growth Douglas-fir forest, but the stunted trees are only 12 to 18 inches in diameter, their trunks bearded with lichen. An understory of little hemlocks grows beneath the firs, and the ground cover is largely salal. As the trail ascends a ridge on Lost Cabin Mountain, it climbs at a moderate grade. Here one can look back and see the Carrie Glacier on Mount Carrie in the Bailey Range. The trail then makes a long traverse, and the sound of the Lillian River rises from its canyon.

This is dry country, lying in the rain shadow of the Bailey Range. As a consequence, madrona, manzanita, cascara, western white pine, and kinnikinnick are abundant. Other plants include ocean spray, honeysuckle, pipsissewa, and rattlesnake orchid. Many of the madronas have been damaged by elk or bears. Beneath the trees the undergrowth is sparse but includes a great deal of vanilla leaf.

Beyond a point (1.3 mi/2.1 km) where one can look up and down the valley, the trail makes a couple of false starts, then begins a long descent to the Lillian. The trunks of the old firs are scarred by fire, and the brush is thicker here. The trees are also larger—up to 4 feet in diameter—perhaps indicating richer soil or a better supply of moisture.

The trail crosses a stream (2.0 mi/3.2 km), the first source of water on this route. A knoll just beyond provides a good spot for a rest break or perhaps a bit of lunch. The now large trees are mostly fir, but red cedar and hemlock are also present. Thick carpets of moss cover the ground. As the trail descends, one hears a stream roaring lustily, but it is a large creek, not the river. Here the forest is luxuriant; the logs and stumps are thickly padded with deep, soft cushions of moss.

After crossing a level area, the trail descends to another creek, then to a campsite on the north bank of the Lillian. The campsite is subject to washout and may be hard to locate. The trail ends in a tangle of down logs just beyond the camp (3.1 mi/5.0 km; ca. 2000 ft/610 m).

31   DODGER POINT TRAIL

Abandoned trail, no longer maintained
Length 6.0 mi/9.7 km
Access Elwha Trail
USGS Maps McCartney Peak; Mount Queets
Agency Olympic National Park

The trail begins on the Elwha River's west bank, 1.5 mi/2.4 km above Elkhorn Ranger Station on the **Elwha Trail,** and climbs to Dodger Point. One must cross the Elwha in order to reach the trail. The river changes yearly, thus varying the nature of the ford (1450 ft/442 m), which is just beyond the Remann Cabin. Occasionally, one can find a log spanning the stream. More likely, however, the hiker will have to wade. This does not pose a problem in late summer and fall, when the river is shallow, but it can be difficult or impossible when the water is high. One should check with the National Park Service as to the river's condition at any particular time.

After making a steep ascent to the edge of Semple Plateau, which consists of level terraces, the grade eases and the path winds through stands of hemlock and huge Douglas-fir. The route then steepens again as the trail climbs to the plateau's main level. Early in the summer, after the snow has melted out, this area is often quite boggy, and the trail becomes faint and indistinct. Hikers should bear to the far right as they pass through a variety of small, grassy spaces.

The Press Party explorers named this bench Semple Plateau for Eugene Semple, former governor of Washington Territory. The men did so because they believed (probably mistakenly) that the place was the site of an ancient Indian village that could have furnished the basis for the legends of Indian camps and conventions that the governor had related. This bench, which covers about 200 acres on the west side of the Elwha north of the Goldie River, is mantled with gravels that are grown up with stunted pines, which contrast with the large firs and hemlocks on the adjacent slopes. According to geologist Rowland W. Tabor, the gravels were probably the outwash delta of the Goldie, where the stream entered ancient Lake Elwha—the water impounded in the Elwha Valley when the outlet was blocked by the Cordilleran Ice Sheet during the Ice Age.

The trail crosses the flat plateau, then switchbacks as it climbs above Goldie Canyon and The Gallery—the jutting rock from which the Press Party made observations and took photographs. However, The Gallery is not visible from the trail. The path ascends steadily, always up with almost never a step down, and the roar of the Goldie comes up from below. The hiker can see Mount Norton through the trees and glimpse the deep canyon, bordered by heavily forested slopes, with snowclad peaks rising beyond.

As the trail climbs higher, the firs become larger, and the ground cover is almost exclusively salal, with a scattering of little pines. At 2.0 mi/3.2 km one can see Ludden Peak and the Long Ridge Trail on its face—the part that was blasted from the cliff. The hiker's first impression is that it is a road, not a trail, cutting across the mountain.

Beyond this point the trees, now predominantly western hemlock, are festooned with lichen. The trail then makes a long traverse to the eastward, and the sound of the Goldie is reduced to a subdued murmur. Occasionally the silence is broken by the harsh croaking of ravens. The path switchbacks up to a spur, then the grade moderates, only to climb steeply again through dense stands of Douglas-fir. Surprisingly, the trees are larger here. The forest gradually becomes less dense, however, and other species appear—silver fir, mountain hemlock, and Alaska cedar. The undergrowth is largely huckleberry.

The path now enters a bit of open country (3.7 mi/6.0 km; 4200 ft/1280 m), a narrow, grassy finger that extends down from a large meadow above. A little rivulet flows here, the first water beyond the Elwha—at least in late summer and fall. Wildflowers are abundant, especially thistle and elephant's head. The meadow is quiet and peaceful; no sound is heard except the gurgling of the tiny stream. Many snags on the hillside above have created a ghost forest. The pointed summit of Mount Scott is visible to the southwest; Mount Wilder is to the south.

The trail crosses into a larger meadow, where the slope above is covered with both snags and living trees, the silvery trunks of the former contrasting with the green foliage of the latter. Numerous subalpine firs having the traditional Christmas-tree shape are scattered over the meadow, where tags attached to the trees mark the way because the trail is indistinct.

The path goes into more or less open stands of subalpine trees, then breaks out into a spot having a view of mountains all around, thus giving one a taste of what the summit panorama will be like. Again wildflowers make a display, prominent among them the pearly everlasting and lupine. Huckleberries are abundant in late summer, and another little brook in a willow patch provides water for the thirsty hiker.

The trail makes a long, almost level traverse to the west, crosses a rock slide, then intersects, beside a small pond, the **Long Ridge Trail** (5.1 mi/8.2 km; 5000 ft/ 1524 m). The view here is dominated by the Bailey Range—particularly Stephen Peak and Mount Carrie.

Beyond this point the two routes merge briefly as the trail ascends the ridge that leads to the summit. One can look down to the Elwha on the right and see Mount Anderson on the skyline. The river appears to be bordered by groves of deciduous trees. The trail then forks (5.5 mi/8.9 km; 5200 ft/1585 m). The left branch is a continuation of the Long Ridge Trail north through Dodger Basin; the right branch, the Dodger Point Trail, climbs to Dodger Point.

The trail now follows the watershed between the Goldie and Long Creek. The ridge's south side is timbered. The barren northern slope drops sharply to Dodger Basin, a glacial cirque shaped like a half-moon or amphitheater, with the ridge that leads to the summit forming the curved side. As it circles the head of the basin, the trail leaves the ridge crest, and with almost every upward step the view improves, many snow-flecked peaks rising to the east and southeast. The path ends at Dodger Point (6.0 mi/9.7 km; 5753 ft/1754 m).

The old cabin on the summit is no longer used as a fire lookout, but it should be preserved as an example of structures that were once numerous. Anchored by cables to withstand winter storms, the building sits atop the rounded, grassy knoll, surrounded by meadowland, with cone-shaped subalpine firs clustered below.

Due to its central location, Dodger Point is one of the superlative viewpoints in the Olympics, and the 360-degree panorama is outstanding. Most of the major peaks are visible, including, of course, the ones in the nearby Bailey Range. Mount Rainier tops the far horizon. Olympus dominates, however, looming above all. Southward is the Elwha Valley, with snowy peaks standing in the distance. Beyond the Elwha, to the left, the cliffs of Mount Anderson rise above the dark, shadowy canyon of the Hayes River. The view to the north and east includes meadow-crested ridges that are almost barren in late summer. Beyond them lies the Strait of Juan de Fuca.

Overnight camping is prohibited at Dodger Point, but hikers can pitch their tents in Dodger Basin, only a half-mile distant, then spend an evening in the lookout, which provides a grandstand seat from which to observe the stars, and to watch the northern lights when they are present. Hikers should carry flashlights with fresh batteries as the descent from the lookout to Dodger Basin will probably occur during the hours of darkness.

32 HAYDEN PASS TRAIL

Length 8.4 mi/13.5 km
Access Elwha Trail; Dosewallips Trail
USGS Maps McCartney Peak; Wellesley Peak
Agency Olympic National Park

This route, which connects the **Elwha Trail** with the **Dosewallips Trail** at Hayden Pass, is used chiefly on trans-Olympic hikes by backpackers crossing

Hayden Pass Trail

from one valley to the other. Usually one elects to go down this trail rather than up; but, in any event, the ascent from the Elwha should be avoided after July because water is often not available on this route in late summer.

The path begins on the Elwha Trail near Hayes River Ranger Station (1650 ft/ 503 m) and ascends the ridge between Hayes River and Lost River. The climb is arduous, and made more so by the monotony of traversing several miles through somber evergreen forest having but little undergrowth. Apparently, the soil is of poor quality on this mountainside because the old-growth trees are not large; in fact, many are stunted. Although water is scarce, it can sometimes be obtained at Frog Lake Creek (5.0 mi/8.0 km; 4700 ft/1433 m), the intermittent stream that has its source in Frog Lake (5100 ft/1554 m).

Eventually, the trail breaks out of the forest into more or less open country and goes by Bone Camp at a little stream (6.5 mi/10.5 km; 5300 ft/1615 m). Beyond this point the hiker is treated to views of distant peaks and ridges. Mount Olympus and the Bailey Range are visible from several points along the trail; so also are the summits surrounding the head of the Elwha. Near Hayden Pass, where the trail contours along the southwestern side of Mount Fromme, following a shallow swale, the midsummer scene southward is exceptionally picturesque—a vista across receding snowdrifts and fields of nodding avalanche lilies. On the horizon, Mount Anderson—the highest peak in this part of the Olympics—rises above the snow-covered Eel Glacier, the largest icefield in the eastern Olympics.

Hayden Pass (8.4 mi/13.5 km; 5847 ft/1782 m) is the low point in the knife-edge ridge that connects Mount Claywood and Mount Fromme with Sentinel Peak and Sentinels Sister. This ridge is the watershed between the Dosewallips and the streams draining to the Elwha. All four peaks are simple climbs and well worth the effort. Between Claywood and Fromme, scenic Claywood Lake—usually half-full of snow—lies cupped in a glacial hollow.

Beyond the pass the route becomes the Dosewallips Trail.

33 LOW DIVIDE TRAIL

Length 2.6 mi/4.2 km
Access Elwha Trail; North Fork Quinault Trail
USGS Map Mount Christie
Agency Olympic National Park

This route begins on the **Elwha Trail** at Chicago Camp (2185 ft/666 m), near the head of Press Valley, and more or less follows the Press Expedition's route to Low Divide.

The trail crosses the Elwha River, then traverses stands of dense forest on the river bottom to the base of Mount Seattle. At this point the path climbs sharply as it switchbacks up the lower flanks of the peak. At times one can look back across the Elwha to the forested slopes beyond and also view Elizabeth Falls in a branch of Delabarre Creek. The cascades, so named by the Press Expedition, but also called Delabarre Falls, plunge noisily down the side of Mount Christie.

At the base of Mount Christie, the trail angles to the west, following a narrow ledge below the sandstone cliffs climbed by the Press Expedition. As it approaches Low Divide, the path edges by two lakes discovered and named by the expedition. The first one, Lake Mary (3350 ft/1082 m), is relatively warm for a subalpine pool—a good place to swim on a hot day. A vantage point here provides a view down the upper Elwha or Press Valley for many miles. Lake Margaret (3600 ft/1097 m), about double the size of Lake Mary, supports a thick growth of water lilies, a plant usually found at lower altitudes. Mount Seattle is visible from this lake. The broad, massive peak culminates in two sharp pinnacles connected by a snow-crowned ridge.

Both lakes are encircled by dense stands of mountain hemlock and Alaska cedar. The tracks of elk, bear, and an occasional cougar may be observed imprinted in the soft mud near the shorelines.

Beyond the junction with the **Martins Park Trail** (2.3 mi/3.7 km; 3600 ft/1097 m), on the south shore of Lake Margaret, the trail climbs over a low hump—the high point of Low Divide (3662 ft/1116 m)—then descends to Low Divide Ranger Station (2.6 mi/4.2 km; 3602 ft/1099 m), where the route becomes the **North Fork Quinault Trail**.

34 MARTINS PARK TRAIL

Length 2.3 mi/3.7 km
Access Low Divide Trail; North Fork Quinault Trail
USGS Map Mount Christie
Agency Olympic National Park

This trail begins at the south end of Lake Margaret (3600 ft/1097 m), at a junction with the **Low Divide Trail**. The path climbs to the lower and upper basins of Martins Park on the northern slopes of Mount Christie.

Ascending forested slopes, the trail first goes through a marshy area where the vegetation is luxuriant, then follows a deep ravine or gorge, and along the way Mount Seattle can be glimpsed through the trees. Beyond the ravine the path climbs over a little spur into the lower basin of Martins Park (1.0 mi/1.6 km; 4000 ft/1219 m). Although not large, this is one of the loveliest mountain meadows in the Olympics—a flat, grassy garden enclosed on three sides by rugged spurs of Mount Christie. Behind the glossy, burnished cliffs that overlook the basin on the east are the Martins Lakes, hidden from view here. On the basin's south side a snow chute leads up the mountainside. During the winter and spring, avalanches thunder down this track, depositing vast amounts of snow upon the meadow. Consequently, it is usually not free of snow until late summer. After the snow has melted, the path becomes muddy and at times disappears between tree-covered areas.

Wildflowers bloom profusely here beside the clear, rock-bottomed brooks that meander among large, angular blocks of sandstone scattered through the heather and dwarf huckleberry. The basin is well-watered, not dry like many meadows, and the rippling streams reflect glints of sunlight. The wildflowers include the Jeffrey shooting star, mountain meadow buckwheat, alpine yellow monkeyflower, red mountain heather, subalpine buttercup, marsh marigold, pioneer violet, and elephant's head. Clumps of the large-leaved false hellebore add artistic touches.

Although the view higher up is better, this lower basin is an ideal place to relax. One can sprawl beside a big boulder and sunbathe while listening to the gurgle of the brooks, the murmur of the wind, and the humming of bees collecting nectar from the flowers. One should keep an eye out for wildlife—marmots and deer may be observed here; bears, too, on occasion.

The trail across the meadow is often covered by avalanche snow. After crossing the creek that comes down from the upper basin, the path climbs the slope above the stream, traversing thick growths of slide alder and marshy spots noted for displays of elephant's head and Jeffrey shooting star. The trail then emerges onto the lower edge of the upper basin (1.9 mi/3.1 km; 4300 ft/1311 m), which lies below the Christie Glacier. This basin is a large expanse of rocks, heather, and snowfields. The route climbs toward Christie Col, on the mountain's eastern flanks, but angles back to the north, crossing heather slopes. The trail ends at Martins Lakes (2.3 mi/ 3.7 km; 4650 ft/1417 m), also known as Surprise Lakes.

Both lakes are deep and aquamarine in color, the north one more or less round and bluer, the south lake long and narrow and tending toward green. On warm days a multitude of tiny frogs sun themselves on the shores, jumping into the water if disturbed. The lakes are bordered on the west by the crest of the polished cliffs that are visible from the lower basin. A good campsite is located between the lakes.

The tarns are located on a spur that extends north toward the Elwha River. Here the views are splendid—the vista includes the peaks surrounding Elwha Basin (Christie, Seattle, Queets, Meany, and Barnes) as well as such points of historic interest as the Elwha Snowfinger and Dodwell-Rixon Pass. One notes that the Elwha makes a beeline from the pass to the Elwha Basin, in sharp contrast to its usual sinuous course. According to geologist Rowland W. Tabor, at this point the valley was probably eroded along a fault line, although this cannot be determined with certainty because much of the rock is hidden by snow.

NORTH SLOPE

The northern slopes of the Olympics east of the Elwha River are drained chiefly by creeks that flow directly to the Strait of Juan de Fuca, but also by the Little River (a tributary of the Elwha) at the west end, and by Canyon Creek (a tributary of the Dungeness) at the east end. This area, referred to in this book as the North Slope, for want of a better term, was explored in 1885 by an expedition led by Lieutenant Joseph P. O'Neil.

The watersheds that make up this district and separate it from the Elwha and the Dungeness-Graywolf are the Elwha River Range, Klahhane Ridge, Hurricane Ridge, and Grand Ridge. These ridges roughly parallel the strait and are the best-known high country in the Olympics. Because it is easily accessible, Hurricane Ridge is the one most familiar to visitors.

Only 4 miles long, the Elwha River Range trends from northwest to southeast and lies between the South Branch Little River and the Elwha. The range is approached from the west via the Cascade Rock Trail and the Griff Creek Trail. (See descriptions in the Elwha chapter.) The highest elevations are Griff Peak (5120 ft/1561 m) and Unicorn Peak (5100 ft/1554 m).

Klahhane Ridge is higher than the Elwha River Range but more readily accessible because it is penetrated by trails from the Hurricane Ridge Road. Mount Angeles (6454 ft/1967 m) is the culminating point.

Hurricane Ridge extends about 10 miles from Hurricane Hill to Obstruction Point, where it abuts Grand Ridge and Lillian Ridge. The elevation varies (5000 to 6000 ft/1524 to 1829 m), with the highest altitudes at the ends, the lowest at approximately the midpoint. The ridge trends northwest to southeast.

About 6 miles long, Grand Ridge lies at right angles to Hurricane Ridge and extends northeastward from Obstruction Point to Blue Mountain. Grand Creek is south of the ridge, the Maiden Creek drainage to the north. Elk Mountain (6764 ft/2062 m) is the highest point on Grand Ridge.

The Elwha River Range is forested to its crest, but the other ridges rise above the timberline. This high meadowland, flecked by subalpine firs, commands splendid combinations of mountain and marine scenery because it not only looks out over the strait, which is only 10 to 12 miles distant, but also back into the snow-clad peaks of the Olympics, which are broken by deep canyons. Most of the North Slope is contained within Olympic National Park, and all the park's high-altitude roads are in this section, a factor that has some impact on the wilderness characteristics of this district. Access to the trails is via a number of roads.

ROADS

Little River Road. This road connects the Elwha River Road with the Hurricane Ridge Road. Beginning 0.2 mi/0.3 km south of US 101 on the Elwha River Road, it climbs through the foothills as it parallels the Little River. The pavement ends at the junction with the Black Diamond Road (3.4 mi/5.4 km). Beyond this point the road narrows to little more than a one-track lane and climbs steeply to Heart o' the Hills, where it intersects the Hurricane Ridge Road (7.4 mi/11.9 km; 1800 ft/549 m).

Hurricane Ridge Road. During the 1930s, before creation of the national park, the Civilian Conservation Corps built a road for the Forest Service from the Elwha River to Hurricane Ridge, then along the ridge from the lookout on Hurricane Hill to Obstruction Point. Because this road was steep and narrow, the National Park Service constructed a new road from Heart o' the Hills to Hurricane Ridge in the late 1950s and built a lodge at Big Meadow. The section of the old road between Whiskey Bend and Idaho Camp, just west of the lodge, was then closed (becoming the Wolf Creek Trail), and the last part going up Hurricane Hill was converted into the Hurricane Hill Lookout Trail.

Several years later the National Park Service built a new highway from Port Angeles to Heart o' the Hills to replace the old Heart o' the Hills Road. As a result, a modern highway now extends all the way from Port Angeles to Hurricane Ridge. The section from Port Angeles to Heart o' the Hills, together with a strip of land on either side, is now part of the national park.

The new road begins just beyond the Pioneer Memorial Museum in Port Angeles and climbs through the foothills to a junction with the Little River Road at Heart o' the Hills (4.9 mi/7.9 km; 1840 ft/561 m). The road then goes into the main body of the park at an entrance station (5.2 mi/8.4 km). Heart o' the Hills Campground (5.3 mi/8.5 km) is located in a stand of fir, hemlock, and cedar and has the usual facilities, including a forest theater.

Beyond the campground the road climbs to Lookout Rock (8.8 mi/14.2 km; ca. 2800 ft/853 m). This vantage point overlooks the Strait of Juan de Fuca and Dungeness Spit. Visible in the distance are Vancouver Island, Mount Baker, and the San Juan Islands. A paved path here leads to a promontory, where one can look back into the Olympics. Mountain goats clamber on the basalt cliffs above and may be observed at times.

The road goes through three tunnels, then traverses the south face of Burnt Mountain and Klahhane Ridge. At one point it cuts through deposits of pillow lava (10.7 mi/17.2 km) that are nicely exhibited.

Beyond the Switchback Trail (14.6 mi/23.5 km), the road climbs to a junction with the Obstruction Point Road (17.3 mi/27.9 km), where the view of the Olympics is dramatic, then crosses Big Meadow to Hurricane Ridge Lodge (17.5 mi/28.2 km; 5225 ft/1593 m). West of the lodge, part of the old Hurricane Ridge Road leads to the parking area for the Hurricane Hill Lookout Trail (18.6 mi/29.9 km; 5000 ft/1524 m).

Obstruction Point Road. This section of the old Hurricane Ridge Road extends from Big Meadow to Obstruction Point. The road first descends and traverses to the low point at the head of Morse Creek, where the Cox Valley Trail begins (0.6 mi/1.0 km). The road then climbs as it goes beneath Steeple Rock, which resembles a church spire when viewed from the west. The pinnacle, composed of basalt, rises to an elevation of 5567 ft/1697 m.

Waterhole Camp (3.7 mi/6.0 km; 5000 ft/1524 m) was formerly an automobile campground, but it was closed due to an inadequate water supply. Beyond this picnic area the road climbs higher, cutting across rolling meadowland and through

Author Bob Wood on Steeple Rock

groves of subalpine forest. The trees, thick-branched to the ground, have spirelike tops. Snow remains on the ridge well into summer; when it disappears, fields of colorful wildflowers blanket the slopes, where deer and an occasional black bear roam.

The road ends at Obstruction Point (7.5 mi/12.1 km; 6150 ft/1875 m), where trails radiate into the high country.

Deer Park Road. This road begins on US 101, the Olympic Highway, 4.8 mi/ 7.7 km east of downtown Port Angeles and gains more than a mile of altitude as it climbs into the northeastern Olympics. The road, which dates back to the days when the area was in the national forest, originally led to a fire lookout on Blue Mountain.

When the pavement ends (5.4 mi/8.7 km) the road becomes a narrow, unsigned,

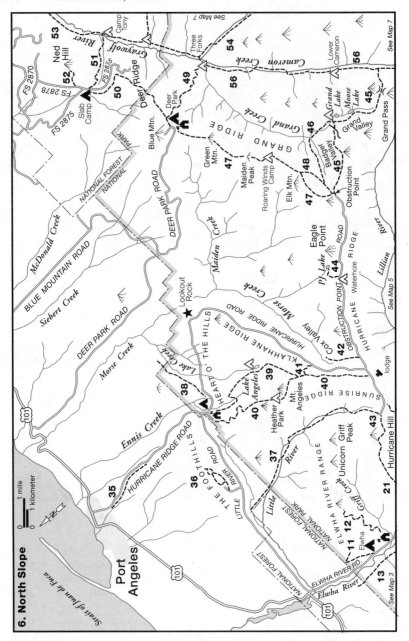

primitive track. After crossing into the national park (8.6 mi/13.8 km), the road climbs the northwest ridge of Blue Mountain, winding and twisting as it follows the topography. With increasing altitude, the road steepens and, where it traverses hard sandstone beds, gets rough. The forest becomes thinner, the trees smaller, and one can look across the valley of Morse Creek to Hurricane Ridge.

A side road (15.7 mi/25.3 km) leads to the Deer Park Ranger Station, then loops back and rejoins the Deer Park Road. The next junction (16.0 mi/25.8 km; 5411 ft/1649 m) provides access to the trails, the picnic area, and the Deer Park Campground.

The meadows of Deer Park, surrounded by groves of subalpine firs, were formerly a winter sports area. Although the weather is good because of the leeward location, the snowfall is light, and the wind often sweeps the snow from exposed slopes. The road has not been kept open during the winter since the development of skiing facilities at Hurricane Ridge.

Beyond Deer Park the road ascends through stands of tall subalpine fir, then crosses open country with views. The road is closed at a parking area on the north side of the peak (16.8 mi/27.0 km; 5850 ft/1783 m). The summit (6007 ft/1831 m) can be reached via a path up the north ridge or by walking the closed portion of the road. The fire lookout, built in 1931, has been gone for years. The vista includes the timbered valley of Morse Creek to the west, snow-clad mountains to the south. Among them are Mount Cameron, The Needles, Baldy, and Graywolf Ridge. Mount Olympus is visible to the southwest. North and east the view overlooks the Strait of Juan de Fuca and Puget Sound. Beyond them are Vancouver Island, the San Juan Islands, and the Cascades. Closer at hand are Port Townsend and the foothills of the Olympics.

Blue Mountain exhibits a showy display of wildflowers during the summer, including numerous examples of Flett's violet. The Olympic onion is also abundant. Generally the snow disappears by early July because this mountain is located in the rain shadow of the Olympics and thus has light precipitation, but after winters of heavy snowfall a few patches may last into August.

Slab Camp Route. This route, a combination of parts of three roads, begins 0.2 mi/0.3 km west of the Dungeness River, on US 101. The first road is called the Taylor Cutoff. After following it 2.6 mi/4.2 km, the route turns right onto the Lost Mountain Road, and at 5.1 mi/8.2 km it turns left onto FS Road 2875, which leads to Slab Camp in the Olympic National Forest (9.5 mi/15.3 km).

Slab Camp (2550 ft/777 m), located in a stand of second-growth fir, consists of a few picnic tables and tent sites. Canyon Creek flows alongside, just outside the entrance road, and water can be obtained from the stream. Hikers need not go into the camp unless they plan to stay overnight. They can park their automobiles on the road at the trailheads.

Nearby is a junction with FS Road 2878, which leads to the Ned Hill Trail.

35 PEABODY CREEK TRAIL

Length 3.0 mi/4.8 km
Access Hurricane Ridge Road
USGS Map Port Angeles
Agency Olympic National Park

This trail is not really in the Olympic Mountains. Beginning at the Olympic National Park Visitor Center in Port Angeles, it parallels the Hurricane Ridge Road about halfway to Heart o' the Hills. Eventually it may be extended the rest of the distance.

The trail first goes through the Thomas T. Aldwell Environmental Study Area, a pocket of natural land within the city, where it descends to Peabody Creek, then crosses to the other side, climbs above the stream, and forks. The right branch is an alternate way back to the museum.

As it follows the creek's little canyon, the trail goes through stands of second-growth fir, then descends to the stream again, where the trees are mostly maples and alders, plus a few cedars. After crossing the creek four more times, the trail follows a ridge between two ravines. The sound of Peabody Creek can be heard to the right, the noise of traffic on the Hurricane Ridge Road to the left.

Leaving the creek, the trail traverses stands of fir and crosses a dirt road (2.0 mi/3.2 km), then veers westerly and returns to the canyon, where it crosses the creek once again. Beyond this point the trail winds through the forest, and many logs lie across the path. The trail comes out into a clearing overgrown with grass, then goes back into the trees and ends in a tangled blowdown (3.0 mi/4.8 km).

The Hurricane Ridge Road is only a few yards away, thus it is a simple matter to crash through the brush, then walk down the road to the museum (2.3 mi/3.7 km by the road).

36 THE FOOTHILLS TRAIL

Length 7.3 mi/11.8 km
Access Little River Road
USGS Map Port Angeles
Agency Department of Natural Resources

The Foothills Trail, built on state land by the Department of Natural Resources, can be reached via the Little River Road—either by driving 3.0 mi/4.8 km from Heart o' the Hills or 4.2 mi/6.8 km from the Elwha River Road, then going north on an unmarked road 0.4 mi/0.6 km to the western trailhead or 1.4 mi/2.3 km to a second trailhead. A third trailhead, accessible only by motorbikes, is located at the eastern end of the trail.

The trail forms a figure eight with two extensions or legs, one at either end. The trail's length is 7.3 mi/11.8 km, but in order to walk it all at one time it is necessary to repeat part of the route, thus making the total 8.7 mi/14.0 km. The trail is monotonous but walking it is good exercise, and the Department of Natural Resources should be commended for having built it. The trail was designed primarily for bike riders, and hikers would be well-advised to avoid it on weekends. However, at other times foot travelers are likely to have the trail all to themselves. This is a good hike in late fall, when the mountains to the south are frosted with fresh snow.

Although it has many ups and downs, the trail makes what is basically a level traverse. No water is available along the route, which varies in elevation from 1750 to 2300 ft/533 to 701 m, and goes through stands of second-growth Douglas-fir. Most of the time views are nonexistent, but occasionally one has glimpses, through the trees, of ridges and mountains to the south, the Strait of Juan de Fuca to the north. One section of the figure eight, along the north side, follows an old road, and after heavy rains it is likely to be a series of ponds that must be detoured.

An information post with a trail map is located at every intersection, but a couple of them have been riddled with bullet holes.

The eastern leg of the trail, leading to the motorbike trailhead, is muddy and covered with puncheon (slabs of wood or logs) in many places.

Birds are the only wildlife one is apt to see. Camp robbers sometimes flit about, and grouse are present, but they are less trusting here than they are in the national park.

37 LITTLE RIVER TRAIL

Length 8.1 mi/13.0 km
Access Little River Road; Hurricane Hill Lookout Trail
USGS Maps Mount Angeles; Port Angeles; Hurricane Hill
Agency Olympic National Park

One of several trails that lead from the lowlands to Hurricane Ridge, this route follows the South Branch Little River, which is bordered on the left by Wildcat Mountain and Mount Angeles and on the right by the Elwha River Range. The elevation gain is considerable (more than 4000 ft/1219 m); therefore, if a party has two vehicles at its disposal, it is better to leave a car at the lower trailhead, then drive to the upper one on Hurricane Ridge and hike down.

The trail begins (990 ft/302 m) on the Little River Road, 0.1 mi/0.2 km east of the junction with the Black Diamond Road, and descends to the Little River, which it crosses on a log bridge, then meanders to the South Branch. Between the trailhead and the national park boundary (1.3 mi/2.1 km; 1200 ft/366 m) the trail traverses stands of large second-growth fir on state land. The virgin forest was logged years ago, and rotted stumps with springboard cuts are all that is left of the old trees.

Within the park the forest consists chiefly of old-growth fir, cedar, and hemlock. Here the route passes the initial trailside attraction—a vertical stone wall, followed by the first Gnome Rock (one of three). The sheer sides of the huge basalt boulder are covered with ferns, both maidenhair and sword. The trail then makes the first of ten crossings of the South Branch. All but the last three are spanned by foot logs of varying size, several of them made more interesting by a luxuriant growth of devil's club alongside.

The trail forks as it approaches a campsite and the second crossing, where the far side of the stream is bordered by lava cliffs. The right branch leads to an old, abandoned mine.

After the third and fourth crossings, the trail goes by the second and third Gnome Rocks. Like the first one, they are enormous piles of basalt covered with ferns. Once again the trail crosses the river—the fifth time in slightly more than a mile. The sixth crossing is the most picturesque—the log spans a deep, clear pool. Beyond the seventh crossing the trail climbs steeply, switchbacking up the mountainside, where it crosses several small streams. The character of the forest changes—the Douglas-firs disappear, and the trees are now mostly western hemlock and silver fir.

The last three crossings are insignificant because the stream is shallow, little more than a brook, and one can step across on rocks. An old campsite is located near the eighth crossing (ca. 6.6 mi/10.6 km).

As the trail ascends higher, the country becomes more open, with views across a little valley to meadowland and slopes covered with cone-shaped evergreens and with brush that turns color in the fall. The trail now climbs sharply, switchbacking through stands of subalpine fir, and the meadows are larger. The trail ends in meadowland at a junction (8.1 mi/13.0 km; 5125 ft/1562 m) with the **Hurricane Hill Lookout Trail**, at the head of the South Branch between Hurricane Hill and Big Meadow, 0.2 mi/0.3 km from the Hurricane Hill Lookout Trail parking area. (Before construction of the old Hurricane Ridge Road, the trail went on to the summit of Hurricane Hill, but the road obliterated the trail. The Hurricane Hill Lookout Trail then replaced the road, thus in effect restoring the old Little River Trail.)

38   HEART O' THE FOREST TRAIL (LAKE CREEK TRAIL)

Length 3.0 mi/4.8 km
Access Hurricane Ridge Road
USGS Map Port Angeles
Agency Olympic National Park

This trail begins at Heart o' the Hills Campground (ca. 1850 ft/564 m) and more or less contours the base of Burnt Mountain, about half the distance paralleling Lake Creek. The stream, a tributary of Morse Creek, has its source in Lake Angeles. Although basically level, the trail has many little ups and downs, and crosses several small brooks.

At first the forest consists of second-growth fir, but it soon changes to old growth, and the path winds through an impressive stand of fir, cedar, and hemlock. The largest firs and cedars near the trail exceed 8 feet in diameter, but the average measurement is 4 to 5 feet. The undergrowth is typical of this altitude—salal, deer fern, bunchberry, and huckleberry.

Leaving the Ennis Creek watershed and the best of the virgin forest, the trail traverses a sidehill above the deep, narrow valley of a tributary of Lake Creek. The latter, flowing below and parallel to the trail, can be heard before it is visible. The forest is now a mixture of young and old conifers, and most of the big trees have been scarred by fire.

A sign marks the national park boundary (2.5 mi/4.0 km; 1350 ft/411 m), and another one nearby notes that this is the end of the maintained trail. The sign means what it says. The route, now through private land, becomes a poor way trail that can be followed for perhaps a half mile, but it is not worthwhile to do so because one has to climb over and under logs and plow through salmonberry thickets. The path leads through second-growth fir and stands of alder, then descends steeply into the canyon of Lake Creek, where it disappears in a tangled jungle (ca. 3.0 mi/4.8 km).

39 KLAHHANE RIDGE TRAIL (LAKE ANGELES TRAIL)

Length 6.5 mi/10.5 km
Access Hurricane Ridge Road
USGS Map Port Angeles
Agency Olympic National Park

This route, also known as the Lake Angeles Trail, connects Heart o' the Hills, on the Hurricane Ridge Road, with the **Mount Angeles Trail** at Victor Pass, the low point between Klahhane Ridge and Mount Angeles. The trailhead (1840 ft/ 561 m) is located near the national park entrance station.

The trail climbs the north slope of Klahhane Ridge, going through second-growth forest and patches of virgin forest. After crossing Ennis Creek, the trail switchbacks upward through extremely dense stands of second-growth fir to Lake Angeles (3.7 mi/6.0 km; 4196 ft/1279 m). The broad, smooth trail is virtually an arterial footpath, and large numbers of people visit the lake, particularly on weekends. Several campsites are located at the northern end.

With an area of 20 acres, Lake Angeles is one of the largest high-country lakes in the Olympics, but it is located on the perimeter of the mountains, only 8 miles south of Port Angeles. The lake is shaped like a teardrop and occupies a deep glacial cirque; thus it is almost surrounded by steep slopes, with a waterfall plunging down the headwall at the upper end. Near the north or outlet end a round, tree-studded isle that resembles a pincushion accents the picturesque quality of the setting. The lake is the source of Lake Creek, which flows to the Strait of Juan de Fuca via Morse Creek, and is stocked with Eastern brook and cutthroat trout.

Beyond the lake the trail becomes a way path that twists and turns to avoid cliffs and chasms as it ascends rocky slopes and works its way back and forth—first on the east side of Ennis Ridge, then on the west, above the head of Ennis Creek, then back to the east side overlooking the lake. The country is now a mix of meadows and subalpine forest, with good views of the lake, Port Angeles, and the strait.

Camp Freezeout (5.0 mi/8.0 km; ca. 5850 ft/1783 m), located on a bench just below and to the right of the point where the path attains Klahhane Ridge, is an excellent place to stay overnight. The tiny brook here usually disappears after late July, but water can be carried from the lake. The views are marvelous—at night the lights of Port Angeles and Victoria flicker mysteriously; and one can watch ships sailing up and down the strait. Because of its easy accessibility, this is a good place to camp in late fall, but hikers should be prepared for sudden storms accompanied by wind, snow, poor visibility, and freezing temperatures.

Beyond this camp the trail follows Klahhane Ridge westward. The terrain is precipitous, and the path has been blasted in the rock. The views are splendid— left, the interior Olympics; right, the lowlands and the strait. Mountain goats can usually be viewed along this trail, often at close range. They should be given the right of way, especially where the ridge is steep and narrow.

The path ends in a junction with the Mount Angeles Trail at Victor Pass (6.5 mi/ 10.5 km; 5880 ft/1792 m). The bulk of Mount Angeles rises to the west.

40 MOUNT ANGELES TRAIL

Length 10.0 mi/16.1 km
Access Hurricane Ridge Road
USGS Maps Mount Angeles; Port Angeles
Agency Olympic National Park

This popular trail climbs from Heart o' the Hills to Mount Angeles, half-circles the peak, then follows Sunrise Ridge to Big Meadow on Hurricane Ridge. Much of the distance the route traverses subalpine country that attracts the casual hiker because the views are good and the access is easy from Hurricane Ridge.

Beginning on the Hurricane Ridge Road near the park entrance station (1840 ft/ 561 m), the trail first winds through stands of second-growth fir and hemlock as it

Mount Angeles Trail on Sunrise Ridge (Photo by Frank O. Shaw)

ascends a spur of Mount Angeles. The forest on the peak's northern slopes was burned a century ago, when fires set by homesteaders swept up the mountainsides, and one can still see blackened stumps and rocks. Halfway Rock (2.5 mi/3.5 km; ca. 3000 ft/914 m) marks the midpoint between the road and Heather Park. This glacial erratic was pushed up the slope by the ice sheet that moved down the strait during the Ice Age. A shelter is located nearby.

Trilliums brighten the somber forest in early summer. Higher up, near timber-line, the ribbed leaves of false hellebore are conspicuous, and violets lurk among the rocks.

Emerging from the trees, the trail enters the open country of Heather Park (4.1 mi/6.6 km; 5300 ft/1615 m), a meadowland splotched with subalpine firs and colorful displays of lupine. The park occupies the basin lying between First Peak and Second Peak. The snowfields, jutting cliffs, and pillow lavas of the latter rise directly above the meadow; Heather Falls are nearby.

The trail then climbs sharply to Heather Pass (4.6 mi/7.4 km; 5650 ft/1722 m), the windswept gap between the two peaks, where a stand of fire-killed subalpine trees grimly remind one of nature's harshness. Two way trails lead from the pass—one to each peak.

Everyone should take the short walk to First Peak (5740 ft/1750 m), which is noted for wildflowers blooming in the splintered shale. Many dwarf plants live here, among them phlox, violets, and subalpine lupine. On all sides basalt pinnacles stand like dark-robed goblins. The summit is a good place to spend the evening when one is camped at Heather Park. As the setting sun approaches the horizon, it appears to flatten, due to atmospheric refraction. The northern coastline of the peninsula becomes a silhouette, and with the darkness the stars appear, and land and water turn purplish gray, then black. When the evening chill becomes pronounced, the lights appear in Port Angeles, at the mountain's base, as well as in Victoria, 30 miles across the strait.

Hardier souls scramble up Second Peak (6025 ft/1836 m) or cross over Heather Pass and make the long trek to Third Peak (6454 ft/1967 m), the highest point of Mount Angeles. The views from these vantage points include the entire length of the strait, with Vancouver Island lying darkly to the north. The distant San Juan Islands and Mount Baker form a scenic backdrop. Southward is the snowy wilderness of the Olympics, with Hurricane Ridge in the foreground.

Beyond Heather Pass the trail descends scree slopes, then traverses beneath pinnacles on the west side of Second Peak. Thumb Rock (5485 ft/1672 m), to the right, rises sheer above Little River Valley. (One can leave the trail here and climb a snowfield that leads to the summit of Third Peak.) The trail then climbs to the notch (5.5 mi/8.9 km; 5760 ft/1756 m) between Second Peak and Third Peak. The latter is composed of sedimentary and volcanic rock. The northeast shoulder of the mountain consists of alternate layers tilted beyond the vertical (that is, leaning over), so that what originally was the upper layer is now underneath. Differential erosion has created chimneys, ledges, ribs, flutes, and pinnacles. The shale slides and scree slopes below are colorful in summer with displays of Douglasia and erysimum.

Crossing over to the northeast side of Third Peak, the trail traverses south, descending scree slopes below cliffs, then climbs to a junction with the **Klahhane**

Ridge Trail at Victor Pass (6.4 mi/10.3 km; 5880 ft/1792 m), where goats are likely to be observed. This gap was used in 1885 by Lieutenant Joseph P. O'Neil's expedition in the northeastern Olympics. O'Neil named it for Victor Smith, prominent Port Angeles pioneer and father of Norman R. Smith, a member of the expedition.

Below the pass the trail descends steep, rocky slopes to a junction with the **Switchback Trail** (7.4 mi/11.9 km; 5100 ft/1554 m), then contours westward to another junction, this time with a climbers' way path that goes about 1.5 mi/2.4 km up the south ridge of Mount Angeles. At this junction the trail turns in a more southerly direction and climbs to Sunrise Ridge (5500 ft/1676 m), which it follows through meadowland and subalpine forest to Big Meadow on Hurricane Ridge (10.0 mi/16.1 km; 5230 ft/1594 m). Sunrise Ridge is a popular snowshoe and ski-touring route during the winter and spring months.

41 SWITCHBACK TRAIL

Length 0.6 mi/1.0 km
Access Hurricane Ridge Road
USGS Map Mount Angeles
Agency Olympic National Park

This route, which is short and steep, provides the quickest, most direct access to Mount Angeles and Klahhane Ridge. The trailhead (ca. 4400 ft/1341 m) is located on the Hurricane Ridge Road, 5.8 mi/9.3 km beyond Lookout Rock.

True to its name, the trail switchbacks as it climbs through meadowland and stands of subalpine forest beneath the frowning basalt of Mount Angeles. The path ends at a junction with the **Mount Angeles Trail** (0.6 mi/1.0 km; 5100 ft/1554 m) on the peak's south slope, below Victor Pass. (Left here to Hurricane Ridge; right to Victor Pass and Klahhane Ridge.).

The views from the Switchback Trail are rewarding, looking out across Morse Creek Valley to Hurricane Ridge. Mountain goats often stand on nearby crags. The display of wildflowers during the summer is excellent, but many low-growing plants have suffered severe damage because the goat population is excessive. Consequently, the National Park Service has established study plots, enclosed by fences, near the trail's upper end. Here biologists study vegetation that has not been disturbed by the animals to determine the impact they have had upon the land.

42 COX VALLEY TRAIL

Abandoned trail, no longer maintained
Length 2.0 mi/3.2 km
Access Obstruction Point Road
USGS Map Mount Angeles
Agency Olympic National Park

All that is left of the old Morse Creek Trail, this route leads down into Cox Valley, the upper part of the valley of Morse Creek. In the early 1900s, A. E. Cox homesteaded one of the "grass parks" on the south side of Mount Angeles, and a friend took a claim on a similar opening in the forest. The men first used the old "government" trail (the route of Lieutenant O'Neil's 1885 reconnaissance), but they later built a trail up Morse Creek—a path that "climbed to greater heights and more of them than any other ever built in the county." Cox used the trail in connection with his duties as county game warden.

The trail begins on the Obstruction Point Road, 0.6 mi/1.0 km east of Big Meadow. The trailhead (4870 ft/1484 m) is not marked, but the path starts on the north side of the road, opposite a board nailed to a tree.

As it switchbacks down the mountainside, the trail goes through a stand of large subalpine fir, then crosses a meadow where the hiker can look down the valley and see the Cascades in the distance. The route now alternately traverses forests and a succession of meadows, where the path is indistinct, marked in places by pieces of tin tacked to posts. The trees are mostly silver fir, Alaska cedar, and subalpine fir. The trail crosses a stream twice, then just beyond a campsite (1.0 mi/1.6 km) crosses another and comes out into a large meadow. The slope to the left is overgrown with dense, impenetrable thickets of slide alder. Burnt Mountain looms ahead; Klahhane Ridge is visible to the northeast. The careful observer may spot mountain goats on the cliffs, and one can hear automobiles driving up the Hurricane Ridge Road.

The trail goes through a fringe of forest, then out into another large meadow (2.0 mi/3.2 km; ca. 3600 ft/1097 m) where, for all practical purposes, it ends. Of course it once traversed the length of Morse Creek Valley as far as the national park boundary before it was rendered obsolete by the new Hurricane Ridge Road. Now, however, the seldom-used route—marked by an occasional ribbon—is virtually nonexistent beyond this meadow. In fact, it does not rise to the dignity of a way trail, although now and then one can find a tag on a tree.

43 HURRICANE HILL LOOKOUT TRAIL

Length 1.4 mi/2.3 km
Access Hurricane Ridge Road
USGS Map Hurricane Hill
Agency Olympic National Park

Hurricane Ridge extends in a northwest–southeast direction from Hurricane Hill to Obstruction Peak and has an average elevation exceeding 5000 ft/ 1524 m. The first road to the ridge, built by the Forest Service in the 1930s, climbed from the Elwha River via Wolf Creek. Upon attaining the ridge, the road forked. The right or main branch went southeasterly along the ridge to Obstruction Point; the left branch followed the ridge in a northwesterly direction to a lookout cabin on Hurricane Hill.

The last 1.4 mi/2.3 km of the left branch was closed to automobile traffic in the late 1950s and converted into a footpath. This is an easy but scenically rewarding hike for persons who drive up to Hurricane Ridge. In fact, it is an excellent walk for both the beginner and the experienced hiker, and it is not unusual for people to picnic near the summit while they enjoy the views. The trail does not cross any streams; therefore one should carry water—or perhaps some kind of beverage. A grove of trees just below the summit can be used for protection when the wind is blowing, but on warm, sunny days almost any spot in the meadows is suitable.

The trail begins at the parking area (5000 ft/1524 m) and follows the old right of way, which cuts through deposits of sandstone and shale. Here the country is mostly meadowland with groves of subalpine fir. The route climbs steadily, with continuous views in all directions, especially up the Elwha.

Beyond the junction with the **Little River Trail** (0.2 mi/0.3 km; 5125 ft/1562 m), the trail ascends the south slopes of Hurricane Hill through open meadows dotted with clusters of hoop-skirted subalpine firs. Near the summit, the path intersects the **Hurricane Hill Trail** (1.2 mi/1.9 km; 5640 ft/1719 m), the old route that ascends from the Elwha River. The merged trails then climb to the top of Hurricane Hill (1.4 mi/2.3 km; 5757 ft/1755 m). The fire lookout cabin that stood on the summit has been gone for years; only the concrete footings remain. Nearby, the National Park Service has laid out a little nature trail through the meadows.

Because Hurricane Hill lies on the edge of the mountains, it provides a superlative vista not only of the interior Olympics but also of the Strait of Juan de Fuca and Vancouver Island. The mountain panorama is splendid—snow-capped peaks slashed by the deep canyons of the Elwha and its tributaries. Although Mount Olympus can be seen to better advantage elsewhere, the Bailey Range stands in full view. Mount Constance and Mount Anderson dominate the southeastern skyline; The Needles tower above the snow-flecked peaks of the northeastern Olympics. Mount Angeles and Klahhane Ridge are nearby; beyond them, Port Angeles lies virtually at the hiker's feet, only 10 miles distant. The city resembles a toy town, and one's hand held at arm's length covers it. The sharp-eyed observer can discern Victoria, 30 miles away, across the strait. Ships sailing the Inside Passage to Alaska are often visible. The San Juan Islands, little more than hazy purple splotches, lie far to the northeast; beyond them, the Cascades, topped by Mount Baker, mark the horizon.

An "owl hike" to Hurricane Hill is recommended, especially when the moon is full. One should carry a flashlight, but in all probability it will not be needed. The snow-clad peaks cast silvery reflections, and the lights of Port Angeles and Victoria flicker faintly, adding an aura of mystery to the loneliness and quiet charm of this high lookout.

44 P J LAKE TRAIL

Length 1.0 mi/1.6 km
Access Obstruction Point Road
USGS Map Mount Angeles
Agency Olympic National Park

This mile-long trail takes its name from the small lakelet named for P. J. Williams, a Port Angeles pioneer who liked to fish its wind-whipped waters. The signed path begins at the old Waterhole Camp, 3.8 mi/6.1 km from the

Hurricane Ridge visitor center

beginning of the Obstruction Point Road. The path, which has a good tread, begins in a stand of subalpine fir containing numerous dead trees.

The trail descends sharply, then comes to a point (0.2 mi/0.3 km) that overlooks a grassland, with a view across a valley to the slope beyond. Emerging at the edge of an open slope, below a rock outcrop, the path looks down the valley of Morse Creek, and one can see the Hurricane Ridge Road cutting across a distant mountainside. The trail switchbacks into a dense stand of trees, then crosses an open slope where pearly everlasting is abundant.

The murmur of a brook comes up from below, as the trail alternates back and forth, through the trees, then across more open slopes. The path crosses several small streams (ca. 0.6 mi/1.0 km) where water still flows in late summer. Here the trees are much larger. The path next crosses below a mossy cliff (0.8 mi/1.3 km) where a waterfall cascades down about 30 feet. This is apparently the outlet stream of P J Lake. Switchbacking as it climbs upward, paralleling the waterfall stream, the trail comes out to the north shore of the lake (1.0 mi/1.6 km; 4540 ft/1384 m).

P J Lake is almost round, its surface broken by ripples from the almost continuous breeze that sweeps across its waters. Double-eared Owl Rock overlooks the lake on the southwest; another Owl Rock, much more distant, can be seen to the southeast, on the crest high above the lake.

The tarn is surrounded by subalpine firs. A campsite is located on the north shore, back about 50 feet, and sheltered by large subalpine firs.

45 GRAND PASS TRAIL

Length 8.0 mi/12.9 km
Access Obstruction Point Road
USGS Maps Wellesley Peak; Mount Angeles; Maiden Peak
Agency Olympic National Park

This up-and-down trail follows Lillian Ridge southward from Obstruction Point, descends to Grand Valley, climbs over Grand Pass, then descends again to a junction with the **Cameron Creek Trail**. Most of the route lies near or above timberline.

The trail begins at Obstruction Point (6150 ft/1875 m), where it traverses barren, almost treeless, tundralike country. This area lies in the rain shadow of the Olympics, and the light snowfall it receives usually disappears by midsummer. The semiarid land resembles the Far North, and it is eerie and mysterious when shrouded in fog.

As it follows Lillian Ridge, the trail climbs, and here the wind often blows fiercely, making the subalpine firs dance. The ridge then flattens, and the trail, after crossing a level expanse, switchbacks down through a rock slide and traverses meadows where grasses wave in the wind. The slopes are matted in many places with low-growing juniper bushes; bluebells and pearly everlasting bloom among chunks of black sandstone covered with lichen.

Because the ridge rises higher, the trail climbs again, crossing shale slides, to its highest point (2.1 mi/3.4 km; 6450 ft/1966 m), where it turns easterly to go down a spur of Lillian Ridge. During the long descent to Grand Valley, the path makes about twenty switchbacks through scree slopes, meadowland, and stands of subalpine fir. The undergrowth among the firs consists of huckleberry, azalea, mountain ash, and numerous kinds of wildflowers. Amalia Falls can be observed from an opening among the trees; beyond the viewpoint, the trail descends to a junction (3.8 mi/6.1 km; 4950 ft/1509 m) with the **Badger Valley Trail** near Grand Lake.

Grand Valley contains three lakes—Grand, Moose, and Gladys—that are linked to each other by Grand Creek. The lakes contain rainbow and naturalized Eastern brook trout. Grand Lake, the lowest and largest of the trio, was formerly known as Etta Lake and lies at 4740 ft/1445 m. More or less triangular in shape, it is fringed by subalpine forest. On both sides the mountains sweep upward to high peaks, and nearby is an added attraction—beautiful Amalia Falls.

As it traverses southward above Grand Lake, the trail goes through stands of subalpine fir and meadowland to Moose Lake (4.3 mi/6.9 km; 5075 ft/1547 m), which lies cupped between rocky, forest-clad slopes. The lake is long, narrow, and deep, and it, too, contains Eastern brook trout. The name is odd, because moose are not found in the Olympics; supposedly, the lake was named for Frank Moose by Amos B. Cameron in the early 1900s.

Beyond Moose Lake the trail climbs through meadows near the headwaters of Grand Creek to tiny Gladys Lake, then ascends barren country, occasionally crossing shale slides and snowfields, to Grand Pass (6.3 mi/10.1 km; 6450 ft/1966 m). The panorama from this point is varied. Many peaks are visible to the south and west; Grand Valley lies to the north. Hikers should take the short walk from the pass to the top of the unnamed peak (6701 ft/2042 m) to the southwest. The view of Mount Olympus alone makes it worthwhile. Here, too, is one of the best places to see McCartney Peak (6784 ft/2068 m), which is only 1.5 mi/2.4 km distant, and the cirque at the head of the Lillian River. The stagnant Lillian Glacier, the river's source, is merely a remnant of the once extensive glacier that filled the valley.

Descending sharply from Grand Pass to Cameron Creek, the trail reenters the forest, where it crosses several little meadows covered with luxuriant growth, including wildflowers such as lupine, Columbia lily, bleeding heart, columbine, shooting star, and bluebells. On the shale slides the low-growing phlox is abundant. The trail down from the pass is steep, primitive, often wet, and inclined to be slippery, and it is no place for novice hikers. One should use caution in making the descent, in any event.

The trail ends at a junction with the Cameron Creek Trail (8.0 mi/12.9 km; 4200 ft/1280 m) below Cameron Basin.

46 BADGER VALLEY TRAIL

Length 4.5 mi/7.2 km
Access Grand Ridge Trail
USGS Maps Mount Angeles; Maiden Peak
Agency Olympic National Park

This route to Grand Lake via Badger Valley begins 0.2 mi/0.3 km east of Obstruction Point, on the **Grand Ridge Trail**, at 6050 ft/1844 m elevation. The path descends along Badger Creek to its confluence with Grand Creek, then follows the latter up Grand Valley. By combining this path with the **Grand Pass Trail**, the hiker can make an excellent loop trip.

The name Badger Valley has no relation to badgers, which do not live in the Olympics. A ranger who patrolled the area years ago had a horse he called Badger. Supposedly he named the valley after the animal.

The trail first switchbacks down slopes of barren shale. Near the point where the zigzags end, water can be obtained from a brook that flows throughout the summer and fall. The trail then descends gradually as it traverses meadowland broken by clusters of subalpine fir and Alaska cedar. Wildflowers are abundant, including anemones, thistles, and daisies. Directly ahead a barren mountain appears to block the lower valley. This is Emerald Peak, which rises about a mile northeast of Grand Lake.

After crossing several brooks, the trail goes through a fringe of trees and out into a big meadow where it intersects the **Elk Mountain Trail** (0.8 mi/1.3 km; 5300 ft/1615 m), which climbs to the Grand Ridge Trail. The route then follows a draw to Badger Creek and alternately traverses forest and open country before coming out into a huge meadow. Not far below, the trail skirts an area where an avalanche destroyed many trees. The big meadow below, the last one on the descent, has a scattering of silver fir, western white pine, and Alaska cedar.

The trail then switchbacks down through stands of western hemlock and Douglas-fir. The latter are surprisingly large for this high altitude. After descending to an emergency camp (2.8 mi/4.6 km; 4000 ft/1219 m), where fires are permitted, the trail crosses Badger Creek above its confluence with Grand Creek. The route then traverses avalanche paths and crosses Grand Creek on a logjam below a pool and double waterfall.

Here, at the base of Emerald Peak, the trail turns south into Grand Valley and climbs again, following the course of Grand Creek. The route breaks out into country where one has views of the mountainsides, then reenters the forest. The trail in this section is rocky and eroded, thus provides poor footing. An unusual but interesting phenomenon here is the large number of trees ornamented with burls.

The trail now climbs sharply as it goes by a 40-foot waterfall. The forest consists mostly of subalpine fir, with a bit of western white pine. The grade then moderates; the path crosses Grand Creek and meanders through stands of subalpine fir broken by marshy spots overgrown with willow, then comes out to Grand Lake (4.3 mi/ 6.9 km; 4740 ft/1445 m). Here it winds along the west side through forest and meadow made colorful by the blooms of wildflowers, including thistles and pearly everlasting. A side path leads to campsites on the lake's south shore.

The route ends at a junction with the Grand Pass Trail (4.5 mi/7.2 km; 4950 ft/ 1509 m) west of Grand Lake.

47 GRAND RIDGE TRAIL

Length 7.6 mi/12.2 km
Access Deer Park Road; Obstruction Point Road
USGS Maps Maiden Peak; Mount Angeles
Agency Olympic National Park

Varying in elevation from 5000 to 6500 ft/1524 to 1981 m, this trail follows Grand Ridge from Deer Park to Obstruction Point. Most of the time it is above timberline, where the succession of spectacular views is outstanding, but subalpine trees are present at low points on the route. The hiker should carry water because it is usually not available.

The trail is accessible by road at both ends—the Deer Park Road in the east, the Obstruction Point Road in the west. The Forest Service planned to connect the roads, and construction crews worked from both ends. However, the western crew stopped near Obstruction Point, and the one at Deer Park built less than a mile of road. Later the National Park Service considered reviving the project, but hikers, conservationists, and ecologists objected to converting the Grand Ridge Trail, the highest in the Olympic Mountains, into a road, and the plan was abandoned.

The trail begins near Deer Park Ranger Station (5230 ft/1594 m) on Blue Mountain, and at first follows the abandoned road which the Forest Service had planned to link up with the Obstruction Point Road. Because the trail descends through heavy stands of subalpine fir and lodgepole pine, the views are limited at first. Leaving the roadbed, the trail traverses a succession of meadows, then climbs steeply through subalpine forest toward Green Mountain. On this exposed ridge, the wind howls in the trees, but with each upward step the views improve—both to the north overlooking Morse Creek and to the south across the Graywolf River.

As the trail traverses around Green Mountain, it goes through stands of subalpine fir, mountain hemlock, and lodgepole pine—predominantly the latter. At a saddle (2.0 mi/3.2 km; 5500 ft/1676 m) west of the peak one can look across the Strait of Juan de Fuca to the mountains on Vancouver Island. Port Angeles is also visible—especially prominent are Ediz Hook and the smoke pouring from the Crown Zellerbach mill. Dungeness Spit stands out to the northeast, with the San Juan Islands and the Coast Mountains of British Columbia beyond.

West of the saddle the trail ascends through stands of subalpine fir, and the hiker can look back and see Blue Mountain and the Deer Park Road. The peak's lower slopes are forested with both old- and second-growth trees, fire having swept the mountainside many years ago. The burned areas are now covered with young trees; the patches of virgin timber stand out as darker green.

Beyond a swale known as Grassy Valley (2.5 mi/4.0 km; 5500 ft/1676 m), the trail climbs to broad, open meadows which are covered with grasses that wave in the wind. The path here is a deep trench in the tundralike meadows. The views are spectacular, especially to the east and south. They include not only the scenes observed from the saddle near Green Mountain, but also the Cascades, dominated by Mount Baker and Glacier Peak. Closer at hand are The Needles and Blue Mountain in the Olympics. Grand Ridge is clearly visible from this point all the way back to Deer Park. This stretch just traversed is lower than what lies ahead, and it is mostly covered with trees.

As it works around a rocky peak, the trail goes through a band of firs, then crosses an outcrop of shale and sandstone. The Cameron Glaciers are visible from this point, Elk Mountain is directly ahead, and the scene includes Grand Lake and Grand Valley. Crossing meadowland broken by patches of juniper, the trail meanders through sandstone strata inclined almost vertically, then traverses below the saddle next to Maiden Peak.

The short walk to Maiden Peak (6434 ft/1961 m) is well worth the time. The northeast slope drops sharply to a basin that harbors Maiden Lake. The distant views are similar to those observed from the big meadow above Grassy Valley, but they are more expansive and include the Strait of Juan de Fuca, Dungeness Flats, the San Juan Islands, and the Cascades. Near at hand stands Blue Mountain, with the Deer Park Road winding up its slopes. The Olympics to the south are in full view, and away to the northwest one can see Port Angeles and the Hurricane Ridge Road cutting across the face of Klahhane Ridge. However, the view to the west is blocked by the vast, arid bulk of Elk Mountain.

Beyond the saddle the trail crosses meadows below a ridge of upturned strata, then descends to Roaring Winds Camp (4.5 mi/7.2 km; 6000 ft/1829 m), located at timberline in the notch between Maiden Peak and Elk Mountain. (Permits are limited between May 1 and Sept. 30. Reservations are recommended.) The peaks obscure the view, but the campsite is well-named because cold winds rush through this gap, where ground-hugging subalpine firs are interspersed among rock outcrops. The hiker who wishes to camp here can either carry water or melt snow obtained from a snowfield several hundred feet down the north slope.

The trail then zigzags up to the broad plateau called Elk Mountain. Here for nearly 2 miles the path's elevation exceeds 6500 ft/1981 m, making it the highest trail in the Olympic Mountains. Lying above timberline, this country consists of tundralike meadows, where fields of smooth stones covered with lichen are interspersed among tufts of grass. Hawks soar overhead looking for prey, and twittering finches flit among the grasses while searching for insects.

The view from the broad, open slopes of Elk Mountain is identical with that from Maiden Peak, with one notable exception. Mount Olympus is now in full view, attended by lesser peaks, including Christie, Meany, Ferry, Stephen, and Carrie. Previously they were hidden from view by Elk Mountain itself.

Crossing shale slides, the trail intersects with the **Elk Mountain Trail** (5.6 mi/ 9.0 km; 6575 ft/2004 m), then skirts just below the summit. Again one should walk to the top (6764 ft/2062 m) in order to enjoy the view to the north.

After traversing the plateau, the trail descends to the low point between Elk Mountain and Obstruction Peak, where it contours the head of Badger Valley. Beyond the junction with the **Badger Valley Trail** (7.4 mi/11.9 km; 6050 ft/1844 m), the trail follows the abandoned roadbed to Obstruction Point (7.6 mi/12.2 km; 6100 ft/1859 m) on the south side of Obstruction Peak. Barren peaks and ridges, still flecked with snowfields in late summer, rise beyond the green depths of Badger Valley.

48 ELK MOUNTAIN TRAIL

Length 2.0 mi/3.2 km
Access Badger Valley Trail; Grand Ridge Trail
USGS Map Maiden Peak
Agency Olympic National Park

Formerly a way trail that received little or no maintenance, this pathway has apparently graduated to bona fide National Park trail status and now appears to be well maintained. This route connects the **Badger Valley Trail** with the **Grand Ridge Trail** and makes possible a triangle hike that is particularly interesting as an "owl walk" during a full moon. Beginning at Obstruction Point, the hiker can either take the Badger Valley Trail to the lower trailhead or the Grand Ridge Trail to the upper trailhead, then follow the trail up or down, as the case may be, returning via the other route. The path overlooks Badger Valley, one of the most beautiful vales in the Olympics. The route provides good views of the nearby peaks and ridges, including a cirque on Lillian Ridge that contains a small pond.

The lower trailhead (5300 ft/1615 m) is located on the Badger Valley Trail, 1.0 mi/1.6 km from Obstruction Point, in a grassy meadow undermined with marmot dens and broken by islands of subalpine fir and scrubby Alaska cedar. The trail climbs sharply, gaining 1275 ft/389 m in 1 mile. Among the low-growing plants found along the path are juniper, huckleberry, and mountain ash. The wildflowers include pearly everlasting, thistle, lupine, paintbrush, cow parsnip, harebell, and mountain aster.

After traversing slopes dotted with clumps of subalpine fir, the trail emerges into tundralike meadows. The Needles are visible on the horizon. At this point the switchbacks end, and the trail meanders a bit as the terrain steepens. The route is indistinct, the path disappearing in spots, but intermittent cairns mark the way. The slopes, covered with short grasses for the most part, are barren where snow lies late in the season.

Other peaks now come into view. One can see Mount Cameron with its glaciers, also Mount Deception; eventually Mount Olympus rises above the horizon. Angling to the east, the trail contours the slope through matted, low-growing juniper, and Grand Lake is now visible.

The trail ends where it intersects the Grand Ridge Trail (1.0 mi/1.6 km; 6575 ft/2004 m) near the top of Elk Mountain, 2.0 mi/3.2 km east of Obstruction Point.

49 THREE FORKS TRAIL

Length   4.5 mi/7.2 km
Access   Deer Park Road
USGS Maps   Maiden Peak; Tyler Peak
Agency   Olympic National Park

This is the original "upside down trail," the best known of several such routes in the Olympics. The term came into use to describe a trip where one can drive to high elevation, then hike down the trail rather than beginning at the lower trailhead and climbing up from below. The difference in elevation between the beginning and ending trailheads on this route is 3300 ft/1006 m, attained in a distance of 4.5 mi/7.2 km.

The trail starts near Deer Park Campground (5400 ft/1646 m) and descends the mountainside via nineteen switchbacks, ending in a junction with the **Cameron Creek Trail** at Three Forks. The name Three Forks refers to the fact that three streams—Cameron Creek, Grand Creek, and the upper Graywolf River—come together near this camp to form the lower Graywolf.

When walking down this trail, hikers are likely to be fresh and full of energy and move along rapidly. However, the continuous descent is hard on the knees, although easy on the lungs. The reverse is true when hikers return to Deer Park, which they have to do unless they exit from Three Forks via one of three escape routes. However, these escape routes are all longer by many miles than the Deer Park to Three Forks hike, and two of them take the hikers over Grand Pass and Graywolf Pass, both of which are higher than Deer Park. The most practical solution is to rest at Three Forks several hours, then climb back up to Deer Park.

At first the trail descends steeply through meadowland and groves of subalpine fir, where juniper bushes sprawl along the ground. The meadows are colorful during August with lupine, thistle, and bluebells. The views of the surrounding country are excellent. One looks directly up the valley of Grand Creek, and to the south The Needles are visible; also other peaks, including Mount Cameron and its glaciers. Elk Mountain and Maiden Peak rise to the west. The view to the east looks out over the lower Graywolf Valley.

Near the trail's beginning a way path leads left to the summit of Blue Mountain (6007 ft/1831 m), crossing the Deer Park Road as it does so. The trail then goes through a grove of subalpine firs to a junction (0.2 mi/0.3 km) with the **Deer Ridge Trail**. Beyond this point it switchbacks down the mountainside. Although the path is not overly steep, it is continuously downhill and thus hard on the knees. The Graywolf Valley is glimpsed now and then through the forest.

At the beginning the trees are mostly subalpine fir. After a bit, the grade eases and the trail enters unbroken forest, now a mix of several species—Douglas-fir, lodgepole pine, silver fir, and western white pine. The stands are dark, shaded, and cool, with only a thin undergrowth of salal and vanilla leaf. As the trail loses elevation, the views disappear, until only glimpses of the peaks are had through the forest canopy.

After following a spinelike ridge, the trail switchbacks down through stands of Douglas-fir and western hemlock. Beyond the fourteenth switchback, the trail approaches a narrow ravine (2.8 mi/4.5 km). A sign, obviously intended for the hiker coming up from Three Forks, states that it is the last water. Here a little side path leads down to the stream.

The trail parallels the draw, and the murmur of the brook breaks the silence. Veering to the west, away from the ravine, the trail descends at a gentler grade, then goes east again. One can hear the Graywolf River faintly—or perhaps it is the sound of Grand Creek and Cameron Creek combined with that of the river. Once again the trail approaches the draw (3.3 mi/5.3 km), where a couple of paths lead down the steep bank, apparently made by hikers to obtain water. One can no longer hear the river, but a bit later it is audible again, then the sound is lost completely. Apparently, the configuration of the topography affects the sound waves as they travel through the forest.

Eventually the trees become primarily Douglas-fir, and they are larger, their trunks and branches coated with lichen. Cool breezes sweep up the slope, and the whisper of the wind in the treetops accents the creaking caused by tree trunks now and then rubbing against each other. At one point several yew trees add a note of botanical interest.

Turning a spur, the trail makes five short switchbacks as it approaches Three Forks, and the roar of Grand Creek rises from the valley. The trail then comes out onto a tiny meadow on the stream's north bank, near its confluence with Cameron Creek. At this point the trail intersects the Cameron Creek Trail (4.5 mi/7.2 km; 2100 ft/640 m).

Three Forks Shelter stands at the north edge of the opening. Although in this deep forest setting the sun comes up late and goes down early, the place is popular with backpackers. Fishermen like to come here in October, after the frost has killed the insects and the fish are hungry. (The shelter is closed in November.) No sounds are present save those of nature—the rushing of Grand Creek, the wind in the trees.

50 DEER RIDGE TRAIL

Length 5.0 mi/8.1 km
Access Slab Camp Route; Deer Park Road
USGS Maps Maiden Peak; Tyler Peak
Agencies Olympic National Forest and Olympic National Park

This route ascends Deer Ridge, the eastern spur of Blue Mountain, and ends at Deer Park. The trail starts in the national forest on FS Road 2875 just beyond Slab Camp (2540 ft/774 m). Motorbikes are not permitted. At first the path parallels the road, but soon climbs above it, and one can see snowy peaks ahead. Left is the valley of Slab Camp Creek, leading to the Graywolf River. The virgin forest was destroyed by fire, and burned stumps are scattered through the stands of stunted Douglas-fir that have grown up since.

The trail has a moderate grade for about a mile, then steepens as it climbs Deer Ridge. The trees are also larger and taller. Although steadily uphill, the route is cool and shaded, the rock outcrops covered with mosses and lichens. The trail then rounds a spur and traverses to View Rock (1.5 mi/2.4 km; 3200 ft/975 m), which overlooks the Graywolf and the snow-covered peaks beyond. Directly below, a clearcut mars the vista down to and across the river. At this point one can hear, faintly, the distant murmur of the stream. Extensive clearcuts are visible in the northeastern foothills of the Olympics; beyond them, the Cascades rise above the clouds that often blanket Puget Sound.

As it makes a long traverse, the trail climbs almost imperceptibly. A seep pool and little stream (1.7 mi/2.7 km; 3300 ft/1006 m) provide the first water. The tiny spring is perpetual; one can obtain a cool drink here at any time.

Leaving the second-growth forest behind, the trail enters a stand of virgin Douglas-fir, but the trees are not large, and the trunks and limbs are covered with lichen. After passing a second spring (2.0 mi/3.2 km; 3600 ft/1097 m), the trail steepens considerably, and the trees are much larger. Here an abrupt transition occurs—the forest changes from timber type trees to bushy ones. This is a high-altitude stand—the trees are scattered, and the ground cover is sparse.

The trail crosses a spur and comes out onto a narrow, spinelike ridge covered with contorted firs and pines. The ridge provides a splendid view into the Olympics—a vista of the upper Graywolf and Cameron Creek watersheds, with mountains at the head of each. (The spectacular views, however, still lie ahead—in the high meadows within the national park.)

The path leaves the ridge and traverses the mountainside. The views become more frequent—one has vistas from almost every rock outcrop and opening in the forest. After rounding several spurs and crossing a grassy swale, the trail enters Olympic National Park (3.6 mi/5.8 km; 4750 ft/1448 m).

Within the park the trail goes below basalt rocks covered with stonecrop. The conifers are large for this altitude, and consist of subalpine fir, lodgepole pine, and Douglas-fir. This is the upper limit of the latter's range.

As the country becomes parklike, the bushy firs and pines contrast with the slender subalpine firs. The latter predominate on the cool and shaded north side of the ridge; the firs and pines on the warm and sunny south side.

Leaving the dense stands, the trail crosses meadows that are dotted with pines and firs, then circles the head of a gully. The views ahead are striking, and include the upper Graywolf, The Needles, Baldy, and neighboring summits. Although one is not apt to look back, the hiker who does so can see Glacier Peak topping the Cascades.

After weaving through basalt upthrusts, where juniper sprawls among the rocks, the trail enters a dense stand of lodgepole pine, then traverses scree slopes as it circles to cross two gullies. Both are dry in late summer and fall, but water is available here early in the season. The almost barren mountainsides support a thin growth of juniper.

The trail crosses a big meadow, a colorful flower garden in early summer, where the views are unobstructed, then intersects the **Three Forks Trail** (5.0 mi/8.1 km; 5360 ft/1634 m) beside a stand of subalpine fir. One can reach the Deer Park Road from this point by going right 0.2 mi/0.3 km on the Three Forks Trail.

51 SLAB CAMP TRAIL

Missing bridge due to be replaced in 2004
Length 3.1 mi/5.0 km
Access Slab Camp Route
USGS Map Tyler Peak
Agency Olympic National Forest

This is another "upside down trail," one that descends from the trailhead to a lower elevation. The trail is now closed because the log with handrail that spanned the Graywolf River and served as a bridge was swept away by floods and has not been replaced; accordingly, it is not a viable alternate way to reach the lower Graywolf Trail. The trail, which is continuously in the forest, follows Slab Camp Creek from Slab Camp to the Graywolf River. It is used principally as a shortcut to the middle Graywolf and, when a missing bridge is replaced, will offer this area's best access to the upper Graywolf region. A washed-out bridge has made the Lower Graywolf Trail impassable at the 4.2-mile mark, eliminating it as an access route for the Graywolf region's higher elevations. The upper Graywolf, meanwhile, can be reached more readily via the Three Forks Trail from Deer Park.

The trailhead is located on FS Road 2875, approximately four miles from its intersection with FS Road 2870. Three primitive campsites are located adjacent to the parking area. The trail begins in a dense stand of second-growth Douglas-fir, and the path descends to the Graywolf River in four steps—first, a gradual loss of elevation, followed by a steep drop; then a gentle grade for a longer distance, followed by another precipitous descent to Duncan Flat. Most of the way the route is over moraine left by the Cordilleran Ice Sheet during the Ice Age.

Near the trail's beginning, one can look southward, across the Graywolf Valley, and see Baldy (6797 ft/2072 m) in Olympic National Park, with its high meadows on the upper reaches of Slide Creek. The forest along the trail has a dense understory of rhododendron, and the floral display here in late June is remarkable. This slope was swept by fire years ago, which destroyed the original forest; a few old firs survived, and the big stumps of others are scattered among the small trees.

As it makes the final descent, the trail closely parallels Slab Camp Creek, then crosses the stream (together with Graywolf River the only source of water on this route) and comes out onto Duncan Flat (2.1 mi/3.4 km; 1500 ft/457 m), which supports a stand of old-growth cedar and fir. Because of the dampness here, the ground is covered with moss. At this point a side path leads left to two riverside camps.

The trail now parallels the river upstream to the site of a washed-out log bridge, which is scheduled for replacement in 2004. What if you arrive here before the new crossing is complete? Adventurous hikers can still make the crossing if they are good swimmers, but it is not recommended that they make such an attempt. It is a dangerous crossing, particularly at high water. Yet for those who make the ford, once on the far side it is possible to climb through fir and cedar to a junction with the Lower Graywolf Trail at Camp Tony (3.1 mi/5.0 km).

Slab Camp received its name many years ago after several boys hiked into the Olympics to camp. They neglected to take a tent but improvised a shelter from slabs of bark they stripped from the trunks of fallen trees. The boys have long since departed, but the name Slab Camp lingers on.

52 NED HILL TRAIL

Abandoned trail; no longer maintained
Length 1.2 mi/1.9 km
Access Slab Camp Route
USGS Map Tyler Peak
Agency Olympic National Forest

Although it has been abandoned by the Forest Service, the Ned Hill Trail is in good condition. The trail leads to the summit of Ned Hill, where a makeshift fire lookout used in the 1930s still stands. No water is available on the trail.

The unmarked path begins on the south side of FS Road 2878, 0.3 mi/0.5 km from its junction with FS Road 2875 at Slab Camp. At first the trail climbs through moderately large second-growth fir having a dense undergrowth of rhododendron, salal, and Oregon grape. Near the top the trees are much smaller, more scattered, and one has glimpses of the mountains, but they are only partial views—of Blue Mountain, Baldy, and Tyler and Maynard Peaks.

The summit (1.2 mi/1.9 km; 3450 ft/1052 m) is a disappointment—one has no view at all because the peak is overgrown with tall trees. The old lookout consists of a crude platform, perhaps 20 feet high, built on top of two standing tree trunks and two poles alongside. Several rungs of the access ladder are missing, as is part of the platform. The structure is unsafe, and one climbs it at considerable risk—which is pointless because it is not high enough to look out over the trees.

Ned Hill never had a live-in lookout; the fire guard at Slab Camp went up occasionally, during spells of hot, dry weather, to observe the country when the fire danger was high. This was fifty years ago, before the trees had grown high enough to obscure the view, and one could look out over the area devastated by the Maynard Burn, a forest fire that occurred in the early 1900s. Most of this area is now covered with dense stands of second-growth fir.

DUNGENESS-GRAYWOLF

The Dungeness watershed lies in the northeastern Olympics. The river has two major branches—the East Fork, commonly called the Dungeness, and the West Fork, known as the Graywolf (or, alternatively, the Greywolf, Gray Wolf, or Grey Wolf—the name is not spelled consistently). Jim Taplin's 1930 trail guide map shows the West Fork as Cameron River, with the upper Graywolf designated as Grey Wolf Creek. The Dungeness and Graywolf are each less than 25 miles in length, but they descend nearly 5000 ft/1524 m from the high snowfields to their confluence at Dungeness Forks; thus they are rapid streams.

The first man-made trail in the Olympics was constructed in this district in 1882 by soldiers stationed at Fort Townsend. They built a path "to and across both branches of the Dungeness River" before they abandoned the undertaking. Their destination was the high Olympics, which they called the Snowy Range.

Because this district is sheltered from the full impact of winter storms by the peaks to the south and west, it has the lightest precipitation in the Olympics and is actually semiarid in late summer. Consequently, glaciers are few in number and tiny in size. The snow disappears early from the high country, making this area popular with backpackers. The peaks and ridges outlining the Dungeness-Graywolf often rise above 7000 ft/2134 m; thus they are among the loftiest in the Olympics, and they challenge the rock climber.

Most of the Dungeness Valley (the watershed of the East Fork) lies in the Olympic National Forest. In fact, a loop of peaks that almost coincides with the boundary between the national forest and Olympic National Park forms a horseshoe around the upper valley. The culminating points are Mount Deception and The Needles to the west, Mount Constance to the south, and Buckhorn Mountain to the east. Fringe districts, such as Royal Basin and Home Lake, together with the upper Graywolf, are located within the national park.

The watershed of the West Fork, or Graywolf, includes not only the Graywolf Valley but also the valleys of the stream's two major tributaries, Cameron Creek and Grand Creek. This watershed is paralleled on the east by Graywolf Ridge, which is capped by Mount Graywolf and the series of towers called The Needles. The watershed is bordered on the west by the divide beyond which lies the Elwha. Graywolf Pass, at the head of Graywolf Valley, stands between Mount Deception and Mount Cameron.

ROADS

Because a large part of this region is in the national forest, many roads have been built to tap stands of commercial timber, but hikers need concern themselves only with the ones that provide access to trails. Much of the area at the higher elevations is still unspoiled, and it is traversed by a number of interesting paths.

Palo Alto Road. This is the main route of entry into the Dungeness country. The road leaves US 101, the Olympic Highway, 1.5 mi/2.4 km west of Sequim Bay State Park, or 2.8 mi/4.5 km east of downtown Sequim. The route goes by

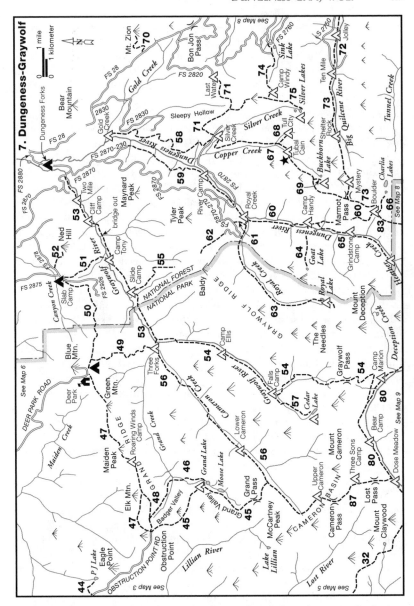

prosperous ranches and through stands of second-growth timber as it climbs into the foothills. The designation Palo Alto ends at a three-way junction (7.6 mi/12.2 km) with FS Road 2880 and FS Road 28 (the Bon Jon Pass Road).

Bon Jon Pass Road (FS Road 28). This road begins at a three-way intersection with FS Road 2880 and the Palo Alto Road, 7.6 mi/12.2 km from US I01. Traveling south-southwest on Palo Alto Road, FS Road 2880 bears right and the Bon Jon Pass Road (FS Road 28) angles left. FS Road 28 then leaves the Dungeness and cuts across the northeastern foothills, alternately going through virgin timber, logged-off country, and second growth.

At Bon Jon Pass (9.2 mi/14.8 km; 2900 ft/884 m), the road crosses over into the Quilcene watershed, then descends the Little Quilcene Valley to the national forest boundary (13.9 mi/22.4 km), ending at a junction with the Lords Lake Road (14.5 mi/23.3 km) near Lords Lake.

FS 2880. This road begins at a junction with the Bon Jon Pass Road and the Palo Alto Road, 7.6 mi/12.2 km from US 101. The narrow, one-lane road, with turnouts, descends steeply to the Dungeness River (1.0 mi/1.6 km) and the Dungeness Forks Campground, which is located in the triangle formed by the confluence of the Dungeness and Graywolf. The road ends at an intersection with FS Road 2870 (1.9 mi/3.1 km).

FS Road 2870. This road leads to several trailheads, including Lower Dungeness Trail, Gold Greek Trail, Upper Dungeness Trail and Lower Graywolf Trail. The road's upper portion was once known as FS Road 2860, but the Forest Service eliminated that number and closed the lower segment of what had been 2860, between FS Road 28 and the Lower Dungeness/Gold Creek trailheads. In the process, the Forest Service also decommissioned the East Crossing Campground located along that former stretch of road.

To reach FS 2870, drive west from Sequim on US 101 for 2.5 miles. Turn south on Taylor Cutoff Road, then follow Lost Mountain Road to the right. Proceed to the intersection with FS Road 2870 and turn left. Pass an intersection with FS Road 2875 (see below) and travel south-southeast of FS Road 2870. At 4.5 mi/7.2 km beyond the intersection with FS 2875, reach the relocated trailhead for the Lower Graywolf Trail, at one time an access route to the middle and upper Graywolf regions. The Lower Graywolf, though, has suffered an irreparable, impassable bridge washout 4.2 miles from its trailhead, leaving it 1.9 miles short of its junction with the Slab Creek Trail. Alternatives for reaching the upper Graywolf are now the Slab Creek Trail or the Three Forks Trail out of Deer Park.

In 1.5 mi/2.4 km from the Lower Graywolf trailhead, intersect with FS Road 2880, which goes left. FS 2870 heads south. In a few miles FS Road 2870-230 meets FS Road from the left. This spur road climbs until it ends at the trailhead for both the Lower Dungeness and the Gold Creek trails. Staying south on FS Road 2870, the road makes a long, gradual descent toward the Dungeness River. It later reaches a fork, where FS Road 2870-270 bears right and traverses the flanks of Tyler Peak. It is closed, however, 1.7 mi/2.7 km from its intersection with FS Road 2870 due to slides and erosion. This spur road continues as a footpath to the unmarked Upper Maynard Burn Way Trail (3.4 mi/5.5 km from the junction), then comes to a dead end (3.6 mi/5.8 km).

FS Road 2870 traverses logged-off country as it descends to the Dungeness River where, at 1.6 mi/2.6 km from its intersection with FS Road 2870-270, the Upper Dungeness Trail begins. The road crosses the river, heads northeast to Silver Creek, then climbs to the Tubal Cain Trail (3.6 mi/5.8 km beyond the river). Nearby, one can find the southern terminus of the Gold Creek Trail and the west end of the Little Quilcene Trail. Neither trailhead is signed. The road then continues to a dead end in a maze of clearcuts (15.8 mi/25.4 km).

FS Road 2875. This road leads to the Slab Creek Trail, previously noted as the only route that now permits access to the upper Graywolf area. Find it not long after turning off Lost Mountain Road to FS Road 2870. FS Road 2875 begins at its intersection with FS Road 2870, just inside the forest service boundary.

53 LOWER GRAYWOLF TRAIL

Length 4.2 mi/6.8 km to a washed-out bridge, where the trail ends; originally 10.6 mi/16.9 km. Bridge not scheduled for repair.
Access FS Road 2870
USGS Maps Tyler Peak; Mount Zion
Agencies Olympic National Forest and Olympic National Park

This trail penetrates a low-lying section of the Olympic National Forest that is still primitive—a once common feature that has become a rarity due to extensive logging and road building. However, the Graywolf River is now adequately protected. The upper Graywolf is in the national park; the lower Graywolf, within the recently established Buckhorn Wilderness Area in the national forest.

The Graywolf is a beautiful, clear stream that flows, in its lower reaches, through a scenic canyon cut in pillow basalt. The country traversed by the trail is relatively dry, covered principally with stands of fir, but water is available from numerous streams, as well as the river. Rhododendrons splash the somber forests with pink blooms in late spring; Indian paintbrush displays darker shades of red in open areas, and the showy bunchberry is conspicuous on the forest floor.

The trailhead is located roughly one mile west from its previous site, northwest of the bridge that crosses the Graywolf River (at the switchback in the road). The trail can also be reached by going south on the Taylor Cutoff Road (leaves US 101 just west of the Dungeness River crossing) to the Lost Mountain Road (2.6 mi/4.2 km), right on the latter to FS Road 2870 (5.1 mi/8.2 km), then left on FS Road 2870 to the trailhead (10.1 mi/16.2 km; 950 ft/290 m).

The trail begins in the virgin forest and climbs high above the rushing Graywolf, then traverses a steep sidehill and comes out into an old clearcut where several kinds of thistles grow luxuriantly among the huge stumps of the trees that were logged. The path crosses this clearcut, then meanders through the forest to a junction (2.0 mi/3.2 km) with a spur trail that comes down from the former trailhead on FS Road 2870–180. Two Mile Camp (1100 ft/335 m) is located just beyond the junction. Here, at least during the spring and early summer, when the stream is high, one can hear the "river voices"—only they sound more like a chorus singing than the chatter of people talking.

The path climbs up and down, ascending to an observation knoll (3.2 mi/5.2 km; 1500 ft/457 m) overlooking Graywolf Canyon, then switchbacks down to the river at Cliff Camp (0.8 mi/6.1 km; 1250 ft/381 m). The route follows the stream through its narrow gorge, where the Graywolf forms a succession of rapids and pools. Again the trail switchbacks and climbs high, only to descend to Sutherland Creek, once more coming back to river level just below where Divide Creek enters the Graywolf on the opposite side. An old sign, warped by the growth of the cedar to which it is nailed, indicates Divide Creek Camp (4.6 mi/7.4 km; 1360 ft/415 m), which is located by the river just below the confluence of the creek and the Graywolf.

The trail comes to a premature end at the site where a bridge previously spanned the river. No alternative route for crossing the river exists, and the forest service reports it has no plans to replace the bridge. For those who have viewed this route as their access corridor to the middle and upper Graywolf regions, your alternative is the Slab Camp Trail. A bridge has been missing at that trail's three-mile mark for several years, but a replacement bridge is slated to be installed in 2004. Check first with rangers on the status of that new crossing before setting out on the Slab Camp Trail. Making that ford during high-water season is viewed as dangerous, though achievable by people knowledgeable and experienced in crossing wilderness rivers.

The Lower Graywolf Trail intersects with the Slab Camp Trail at Camp Tony, 1.9 mi/3.1 km upriver from the bridge washout. Hikers can reach Camp Tony via the Slab Camp Trail, then travel southwest on the Graywolf Trail toward Three Forks camp.

The trail now climbs steadily, away from the river. The forest provides a good habitat for the blue grouse, which may be observed on occasion. The path switchbacks as it climbs more steeply, then the trail contours around rock ribs and buttresses high above the canyon, where various kinds of rocks are exposed—pillow basalt, red limestone, basaltic sandstone, and shale. The mountainsides drop away steeply, and at one point the hiker can see the river below. Logging scars are visible on Deer Ridge, directly across the canyon.

Beyond this point the trail descends and crosses a rock slide, where fire and avalanche have destroyed much of the virgin timber. The slopes ahead exhibit the light green that is characteristic of young trees, mottled by dark patches of old growth. This area was devastated by the Maynard Burn, a fire which occurred in the early 1900s. The burned slopes are now covered with thick stands of firs not much larger than broomsticks, and many snags rise above them.

The trail then descends toward Slide Camp. The ground is covered with moss, and the trees are so close together their limbs overlap; thus walking along the path reminds one of going through a tunnel. Slide Camp (8.0 mi/12.9 km; 2150 ft/655 m) is nondescript, little more than a couple of tent sites beside a brook that crosses the trail. The junction with the **Baldy Trail** is located just beyond the stream, which is a tributary of Slide Creek. The latter flows down the north side of Baldy.

After switchbacking down to Slide Creek, the trail enters Olympic National Park (8.8 mi/14.2 km; 2000 ft/610 m). The path is still high above the Graywolf, which can be heard but is lost to sight in its canyon. After making a long, gradual ascent, paralleling the river, the trail descends to a junction with the **Cameron Creek Trail** (10.5 mi/16.9 km; 2125 ft/648 m) near the Graywolf. As one approaches the stream, the din becomes pronounced. Here, where it is damper and the soil is better, the trees are much larger. They consist chiefly of Douglas-fir, western hemlock, and red cedar, plus the usual deciduous species. At this point the route becomes the **Upper Graywolf Trail.**

54 UPPER GRAYWOLF TRAIL

Length 12.9 mi/20.8 km
Access Lower Graywolf Trail; Cameron Creek Trail
USGS Maps Maiden Peak; Wellesley Peak; Tyler Peak
Agency Olympic National Park

The Upper Graywolf Trail begins at a junction (2125 ft/648 m) with the **Cameron Creek Trail** and the **Lower Graywolf Trail,** not far from Three Forks. The trail leads south, along the east bank of the river, climbing gradually through stands of fir, hemlock, and cedar. Because it is not a glacial stream, the Graywolf

River is clear, and its swift waters make a chain of cascades, rapids, and waterfalls, with deep, clear pools intervening. The river bed is filled with large boulders, and the stream is often spanned by fallen trees.

At Nameless Camp (1.0 mi/1.6 km) the trail crosses the river to the west bank and climbs high above the stream in order to get by a big slide. The trail then closely follows the river and ascends to a bench, where a few old firs, the survivors of an ancient forest, stand among the hemlocks. The undergrowth here is sparse, the ground covered by thick pads of emerald-green moss.

Beyond Camp Ellis (2.7 mi/4.3 km; 2900 ft/884 m), which is located among tall cedars and hemlocks, the trail wends its way through the forest, then traverses an area ravaged by avalanches. Here it climbs above a deep ravine carved by a creek that cascades down the cliffs in a double waterfall (one above the other). The growth of slide alder is thick, but one can look up and down the valley and also across to a silver forest—a grove of fire-killed trees—high on the far mountainside. The path then enters the track where an avalanche swept down to and across the river, demolishing trees on the opposite slope.

Leaving the devastated area, the trail again makes its way through stands of fir and cedar. Patches of snow, protected from the sun, remain until late summer in shaded places.

Falls Shelter (5.4 mi/8.7 km; 3900 ft/1189 m) is located near the river but distant enough that one can hear the "river voices." This is an illusion often experienced in the wilderness, especially by the solitary hiker—momentarily mistaking the chatter of a stream for the indistinct murmur of people. At this point one can find the **Cedar Lake Way Trail** in the fringe of trees near the shelter.

The heavy forest growth ends in this vicinity. The trail crosses Cedar Creek, then alternates from one side of the river to the other as it winds upward through stands of subalpine trees. The ground cover is luxuriant, well-watered by numerous little streams. Consequently, wildflowers are abundant: Columbia lily, Sitka valerian, thistles, arnica, lupine, and daisies. Buttercups and shooting stars bloom alongside the melting snowdrifts. Again one can hear the river voices as the trail goes back and forth through meadowland and groves of subalpine trees, where in early summer the path is likely to be hidden by snow.

After climbing through stands of Alaska cedar, the trail crosses the river again, but the stream is now little more than a creek. The path climbs steeply, with many switchbacks, up the west side of the valley, breaking out into open country cooled by the breezes that descend from Graywolf Pass. (A cross-country route to Cedar Lake, an alternative to the Cedar Lake Way Trail, leaves the trail here, at the head of a little gorge, and climbs west to the divide. The ascent over heather slopes and snowfields is steep but not difficult. The route goes by the upper of three lakes lying between the ridge and the river, then climbs to the low point in the ridge and descends meadowland to Cedar Lake.)

The trail now crosses the river again—the fifth and last time beyond Falls Shelter—and enters the meadows of Graywolf Basin, where tiny brooks tumble over rock ledges as they rush madly down the mountainsides. The views are both impressive and expansive. Northward one can look down the Graywolf Valley toward the Strait of Juan de Fuca, while directly east The Needles cap the ridge that extends north from Mount Deception. The southwestern skyline is a mass of rocky peaks splotched with snowfields. The meadows are made colorful by a sea of wildflowers: Sitka valerian, lupine, common bistort, daisies, gentians, elephant's head, paintbrush, and red mountain-heather. They do not all blossom at the same time, but over the course of several weeks. During late summer the plumed seed pods of the anemone wave in the wind.

As it crosses snowfields at the head of the Graywolf, the trail climbs to a little muddy tarn, then leaves the meadowland behind and ascends barren talus to Graywolf Pass (9.5 mi/15.3 km; 6150 ft/1875 m). This gap is flat enough for camping, but cold and windy, and snow must be melted for water. Nevertheless, it is a spectacular viewpoint. On warm, sunny days a stiff breeze from the south is invariably present. The view back to the north looks down the Graywolf—across the meadows to the timbered lower slopes. The upper Dosewallips Valley is to the west, bounded by several high peaks—Claywood, Fromme, Sentinel, and Wellesley. Mount Anderson rises beyond the latter. If one leaves the pass and scrambles a bit along the east ridge, Lost Peak and Mount Olympus can be seen. Between Olympus and Anderson, the snow-clad peaks surrounding Elwha Basin are visible in the distance. Much closer to hand, to the east, are Deception, Constance, Mystery, and Little Mystery, with Gunsight Pass between the last two. The vast sweep of the Dosewallips is to the south; The Brothers are on the horizon.

The trail then descends to the Dosewallips via a series of seemingly endless switchbacks. The trail is well laid out, however, and not really steep. At first it goes through open country, where it crosses meadows that nature has landscaped with groves and solitary specimens of subalpine fir. Here the view of Mount Deception and the two Mysteries, across the U-shaped valley of Deception Creek, is notable. One can hear the muffled sound of the Dosewallips and now and then the shrill whistle of a marmot. Surprisingly, little streams flow across the trail throughout the summer. This south-facing slope is well exposed to the sun; consequently, during the fall the huckleberry bushes turn flaming red and purple. So, too, the mountain ash.

Below the meadows the trail descends through forests of western white pine and Alaska cedar, and one can look down the Dosewallips from several points and see Piros Spire in the distance. About 2 miles below Graywolf Pass the trail enters the Douglas-fir forest, coming to a junction with the **Dosewallips Trail** (12.9 mi/20.8 km; 3600 ft/1097 m) between Camp Marion and Bear Camp.

55 BALDY TRAIL

Abandoned trail; no longer maintained
Length 3.5 mi/5.6 km
Access Lower Graywolf Trail
USGS Map Tyler Peak
Agency Olympic National Forest

Neither signed nor maintained, this steep, abandoned trail starts on the uphill side of the **Lower Graywolf Trail** just beyond the draw at Slide Camp, in the Olympic National Forest. The route climbs relentlessly up the mountainside, but the views make the trip worthwhile. The path itself is not long, but the trailhead (2150 ft/655 m) is located 5 miles from Slab Camp, the nearest point that can be reached by automobile.

Ascending through stands of stunted, second-growth Douglas-fir and a thick undergrowth of salal, the trail at first follows a ridge, but soon leaves it and traverses the sidehill. This area was devastated by the Maynard Burn in the early 1900s. Old stumps are abundant; logs lie strewn through the forest in apparent disorder. The trail then switchbacks up the slope, and the stands—which now include lodgepole pine—are more open, allowing one a glimpse or two up the creek. As the trail climbs higher, the hiker can see the meadows on Baldy, as well as a vista up and down the Graywolf. Elk Mountain, Maiden Peak, and Green Mountain are visible to the northwest, but Blue Mountain is hidden by Deer Ridge. Logging clearcuts stand out across the Graywolf River.

The trail crosses a little stream, the only source of water on this route. Western hemlock is abundant here; also, for the first time, mountain hemlock is present. At this point the trail turns northeast and climbs to the ridge between Slide Creek and Divide Creek. Directly ahead, to the east, the hiker looks across the canyon of the West Fork of Divide Creek, and the sound of the stream comes up from below. One has only to glance back, in the opposite direction, to see Grand Ridge beyond the Graywolf Canyon.

Heading directly south, the trail follows the ridge, which is thinly forested with stunted firs. The rocky mass of Tyler Peak rises to the southeast; the vista in the opposite direction overlooks the Graywolf River and Grand Creek, and the ridges lying on either side.

Beyond an old, abandoned campsite, the path becomes indistinct, and the hiker who is preoccupied with the scenery is apt to lose the trail and stumble around in the brush momentarily. The hiker must also watch his or her footing because of the tangled undergrowth and the fact that now the trail steepens and is choked with a dense growth of mountain azalea. The trees are chiefly subalpine fir, mountain hemlock, and lodgepole pine, and they are scattered on the slopes. Although one must struggle through the brush, the views improve with almost every upward step. Across Slide Creek the slope has been swept bare by avalanches—broken rocks and stumps are strewn down the mountainside. One can look back and see the Grand Ridge peaks; in late fall they are apt to be frosted with fresh snow.

Eventually the brush is left behind, the country becomes much more open, and the terrain flattens somewhat. The trail, such as it is, ends (3.0 mi/4.8 km; 5700 ft/1737 m) on the northern slope of Baldy, but it doesn't matter. One doesn't need a trail now because the route is apparent. The deep valley of Divide Creek is to the left, with a long, rocky ridge beyond; the canyon of Slide Creek lies to the right. The view to the northeast includes the Strait of Juan de Fuca, northern Puget Sound, and the San Juan Islands, with Mount Baker high on the horizon.

Here, close to timberline, the subalpine firs and lodgepole pines are dwarfed and few in number, and the smooth, rounded ridge leads past the beautiful meadows at the head of Slide Creek. Tufts of grass wave in the wind; sprawling junipers hug the ground, where layers of splintered, broken shale are turned on edge. Often a cold breeze sweeps across the slopes at this altitude.

The north summit of Baldy (3.5 mi/5.6 km; 6600 ft/2012 m) consists of large sandstone blocks. At this point peak baggers have built a big cairn of slabs. The wind often howls fiercely here, but the view is spectacular—northeast, the Strait of Juan de Fuca, the San Juan Islands, and Mount Baker; northwest, Blue Mountain, Klahhane Ridge, and Mount Angeles. Graywolf Peak (7218 ft/2200 m) rises to the southwest. Nearby is the summit of Baldy (6797 ft/2072 m), about a half mile distant and slightly higher than the north peak. On a good day one should, if time permits, make the trek across to the summit.

56 CAMERON CREEK TRAIL

Length 11.3 mi/18.2 km
Access Lower Graywolf Trail; Upper Graywolf Trail
USGS Maps Tyler Peak; Maiden Peak; Wellesley Peak
Agency Olympic National Park

This trail follows Cameron Creek to its headwaters in Cameron Basin, then climbs to Cameron Pass. Beyond this high divide, the route (now known as the **Lost Pass Trail**) continues to the Dosewallips River.

The trail starts near Three Forks in a three-way intersection (2125 ft/648 m) that marks the division between the **Lower Graywolf Trail** and the **Upper Graywolf Trail**. The path follows down the east bank of the Graywolf, past a camp, to a high log (with handrail) that spans the river just below the entry of Cameron Creek. Normally both streams are clear, but on warm afternoons during late summer and fall Cameron Creek sometimes becomes milky white with glacial silt, only to clear again during the night.

After crossing the Graywolf, the trail follows the north bank of Cameron Creek past the point where Grand Creek flows into the stream, then comes to a junction, in a tiny meadow, with the **Three Forks Trail** (0.3 mi/0.5 km; 2100 ft/640 m). Often it is cool here because cold air flows down the valley and settles at this point.

The trail crosses Grand Creek near Three Forks Camp, then follows beautiful Cameron Creek, at times along its banks, at others high above the stream. The route leads through stands of large Douglas-fir. The creek has many deep pools, which alternate with rapids; and trout up to a foot long test the angler's skill.

As it makes its way up the valley, the trail crosses Cameron Creek four times, beginning and ending on the north side of the stream. The trail then climbs away from the creek through stands of big Douglas-fir and enters the first of six meadows that extend from Cameron Creek up the mountainside forming the valley's northern slope. The meadows were created by avalanches, snow having swept down from the ridge above. On the divide between Cameron Creek and the Graywolf, to the south, Shelter Peak (6590 ft/2009 m) rises above the timbered slopes. Beyond the meadow, the trail winds through a forest of old firs.

At the edge of the second meadow, which extends on both sides of Cameron Creek, stand the ruins of the Lower Cameron Shelter (5.3 mi/8.5 km; 3800 ft/1158 m). The shelter was struck by a falling tree and rendered unusable. This area is of botanical interest because groves of ancient Engelmann spruce growing on the flats between the trail and Cameron Creek were discovered here by big tree hunters Robert Van Pelt and Arthur Jacobsen. The largest trees are more than 6 feet in diameter and about 175 feet tall.

The route now alternately traverses forest and meadowland, with beetling cliffs overlooking the trail. Marmots whistle protests in the open country; from the fifth meadow the Cameron Glaciers are visible to the south. The sixth and last meadow in the series is a large open expanse. Directly opposite, on the south side of Cameron Creek, the slope is strewn with avalanche debris. Beyond this meadow the trail ascends to a junction with the **Grand Pass Trail** (7.6 mi/11.2 km; 4200 ft/1280 m).

The trail now climbs steeply through thickets of slide alder, willow, Alaska cedar, and salmonberry. The trail has been cut through; otherwise the jungle would be impenetrable. Eventually the trail emerges into partially open country below McCartney Peak, where one can look down the V-shaped valley of Cameron Creek to Three Forks and observe the avalanche chutes alternating with lines of trees that extend up the steep mountainsides.

Upper Cameron Camp (10.0 mi/16.1 km; 5400 ft/1646 m) is located beside a little stream near the northern end of Cameron Basin, where meadow and subalpine forest are intermingled. This wild and lonely basin is a delightful place to explore, its remoteness from well-traveled paths adding to its charm. Occupying a glacial cirque about a mile long and somewhat more than a half mile wide, the basin is surrounded by snow-clad peaks and ridges, including McCartney Peak to the northwest, and Mount Cameron to the east. Although the floor is more or less level, the terrain is varied, the meadows broken by rocky, tree-covered knolls. Near the southern end, at the foot of the shale slopes that lead up to Cameron Pass, the basin is flat and marshy. This area is the home of countless insects and thus not a good place to camp. Little moss-lined brooks, edged by wildflowers, meander across the flats. The displays are gorgeous—avalanche lilies bloom first, followed by buttercups, bog orchids, anemones, elephant's head, lupine, bistort, asters, and arnica.

As it crosses the basin, the trail becomes indistinct, and the route—marked by cairns because the path is hard to follow—traverses meadowland. At the basin's head the trail improves and makes long switchbacks across shale slopes and snowfields, then short ones as it climbs a barren moraine to Cameron Pass (11.3 mi/18.2 km; 6450 ft/1966 m). This is the low point in the ridge.

The view from the pass is splendid but still better from the peak to the west, which is reached by a short walk. Here, near the center of the high-country Olympics, one can look down into Cameron Basin, and all about are snowy peaks, including Mount Olympus in the distance. Directly east is Mount Cameron, with its glaciers and snowfields; far to the southwest is Low Divide. (See **Lost Pass Trail** for description of the route from the pass to the Dosewallips River.)

57 CEDAR LAKE WAY TRAIL

Abandoned trail; no longer maintained
Length 3.0 mi/4.8 km
Access Upper Graywolf Trail
USGS Map Wellesley Peak
Agency Olympic National Park

This well-beaten way trail begins near Falls Shelter (3900 ft/1189 m), on the **Upper Graywolf Trail**, and climbs through the meadow behind the structure. Near the upper end, where Cedar Creek tumbles down a steep slope, Mount Deception (7788 ft/2374 m), the highest peak in the eastern Olympics, can be viewed above the snowfields at the head of the Graywolf River. The trail then enters the forest, where many trees are adorned with fancy burls.

The trail sidehills through the timber, then crosses a scree slope and climbs sharply, switchbacking a half-dozen times, before ascending an avalanche track overgrown with Alaska cedar and slide alder. Here the route parallels Cedar Creek, and one has good views of The Needles.

As it crosses a meadow where it winds through groves of subalpine forest, the trail traverses marshy spots. The cliffs above, to the right, are masked by thick growths of Alaska cedar. The trail can be lost easily at the far end of this meadow, where it turns left and crosses Cedar Creek below a waterfall. The cascade, narrow at the top, widens as it spreads out over ledges.

The trail climbs through the forest east of the creek and comes out into another marshy area—a mix of subalpine forest, meadow, little streams, and brush-covered terrain. However, the country gradually becomes more open and rocky, and the trees are now mostly subalpine fir. In late summer the grassy openings are covered with masses of lupine and gentian.

Breaking out into a big meadow surrounded by peaks and ridges, where streams cascade down the slopes, the trail ascends to Cedar Creek, then crosses the stream and climbs about a hundred yards to the outlet of Cedar Lake (3.0 mi/4.8 km; 5280 ft/1609 m).

This scenic, mile-high lake lies in a bowl, the lower part of an old glacial cirque. With an area of 21 acres, it is one of the largest subalpine lakes in the Olympics and is popular with fishermen because it contains rainbow trout. The outlet is at the northwestern end, where the lake is bordered by a fringe of subalpine firs, and here the wind often howls in the trees. A good campsite is located at this point. The lake's beautiful, clear green waters reflect the surrounding slopes. On the north side the lake is bordered by grassy meadows that sweep back to groves of tall subalpine firs. Apparently, the lake's depth does not fluctuate much but remains more or less constant, sustained by the melting snowfields. The peaks south of the lake comprise the eastern part of Cameron Ridge. Highest is The Pup (7073 ft/2156 m).

Although the way trail ends at Cedar Lake, hikers may return to the Upper Graywolf Trail by using Cedar Pass (6000 ft/1829 m) southeast of the lake. The route crosses heather meadows. The view from the ridge is splendid—one can see The Needles, Mount Deception, and Mount Mystery rising beyond the headwaters of the Graywolf. The Upper Graywolf Trail climbing to Graywolf Pass is also visible.

The route down to the Upper Graywolf Trail traverses slopes covered with heather and boulders and goes by three subalpine lakes. Blocks of ice often float in the upper or largest lake throughout the summer. The route reaches the Upper Graywolf Trail about a mile below Graywolf Pass.

58 GOLD CREEK TRAIL

Length 6.4 mi/10.3 km
Access FS Road 2870-230
USGS Map Mount Zion
Agency Olympic National Forest

This trail, the lower portion of the old Tubal Cain Trail, makes a good woodland walk. Reach the trailhead by driving south from Sequim on Palo Alto Road to its three-way intersection with FS Road 28 and FS Road 2880. Bear right on FS Road 2880 and drive 2.0 mi/3.2 km to the intersection with FS Road 2870. Turn left on FS Road 2870 and travel 2.0 mi/3.2 km to the intersection with FS

Road 2870-230 (or just 230). Turn left on 230. The trailhead awaits at the end of this spur road.

The trail begins in a deep forest setting (1250 ft/381 m) and climbs to a bench above the Dungeness River. Here it goes by a large monolith, then veers away from the river to cross Gold Creek.

Gold Creek Shelter (0.2 mi/0.3 km; 1220 ft/372 m) stands on the south side. Beyond it the trail switchbacks up the spur between the Dungeness and Gold Creek, climbing through fir and cedar forest, where winter wrens trill their happy song. The path then makes a long traverse to the south, climbing as it parallels the Dungeness, which can be heard rushing through its canyon. This area was swept in the past by fire, which destroyed much of the virgin timber. The trees are smaller than those near the creek and river, and they consist mostly of stunted second-growth fir with patches of old-growth.

Upon gaining a point where one can look across the Dungeness to Three O'Clock Ridge, the trail descends to Sleepy Hollow Creek, only to regain the lost elevation by switchbacking up the far side. Rhododendrons now appear as an understory, and they are abundant the rest of the way, the blossoms making showy displays in June. The river can be heard occasionally, and now and then snow-clad peaks are visible up the valley.

The trail goes through the lower part of a clearcut (2.4 mi/3.9 km) which apparently was logged from a road on the slope above. The area is thickly overgrown with rhododendron, manzanita, and little firs, and the views up, down, and across the Dungeness Valley are unbounded.

Going back into the forest, the route traverses high above the Dungeness, but the river is not visible. The trail ascends and descends, gaining and losing elevation, and the views are intermittent. At 5 mi/8.1 km, clearcuts and FS Road 2870 are visible below. Beyond them one can see the peaks that fringe Royal Basin.

The trail ends (6.4 mi/10.3 km; 3300 ft/1006 m) on FS Road 2870 opposite the entrance to the parking area for the Tubal Cain Trail. The upper trailhead is not marked; the path merely comes out to the road.

59 LOWER DUNGENESS TRAIL

Length 5.8 mi/9.3 km
Access FS Road 2870-230
USGS Maps Mount Zion; Tyler Peak
Agency Olympic National Forest

This trail and the Gold Creek Trail now share the same trailhead. See trail 58 for directions.

The trail is used primarily by hunters, fishermen, and mountain bikers—and by people just looking for a pleasant woodland walk. However, it might well be termed the trail of surprises. One expects it to be a river bottom path; instead, the first part traverses the side of a canyon, reaching points high above the Dungeness, where the views are splendid. The forest alternates between patches of old-growth Douglas-fir and stands of second growth. Apparently, fire swept through portions of this valley in the past—in places many old trees exhibit fire-blackened trunks, but in other localities they do not appear to have been burned.

After descending from the trailhead to cross a small stream, the trail makes a long upward traverse. The river is far below and inaccessible, but the sound it makes as it rushes through the narrow, rocky canyon carries up to the trail.

As it rounds a bend, the trail climbs to a point where one can look across the valley to slopes scarred by a clearcut and a road that slices across the face of the mountain. This is the logged area that the Gold Creek Trail traverses. The trail then ascends through stands of old fir to an open spot, where the hiker looks across and up the Dungeness Valley to a peak with a stumplike tower—the north end of the ridge lying between the Dungeness River and Copper Creek.

The trail descends steeply to Cougar Creek, then climbs again, with views now and then through the trees. The roar of the Dungeness is now pronounced. The old firs are scattered, and the country has a parklike appearance that reminds one of the east slope of the Cascades. The undergrowth consists primarily of maple and red currant. During the fall the maples turn golden; thus they contrast brightly with the dark green conifers.

Making a semicircle as it rounds Three O'Clock Ridge, the trail goes between a buttress and a little rocky point (3000 ft/914 m). Standing on the point, facing east, one can, by turning slightly, take in a spectacular 180-degree view—from down valley (due north) to the head of the Dungeness (due south). With the exception of the Gold Creek Trail clearcut, which is downstream and not conspicuous, the scene is a vista of unspoiled forest clothing the canyon walls. The peak with the stumplike tower stands at the head of the valley; the river is hundreds of feet below.

The trail then crosses a narrow slide where the path has been obliterated for perhaps 8 or 10 feet. One must use care in traversing this ticklish spot to avoid taking a nasty spill down the steep slope. Beyond the slide the trail ascends to a junction with a side path (2.5 mi/4.0 km) that climbs up to FS Road 2870 (3.7 mi/6.0 km, via the road, from the lower trailhead).

Zigzagging down the steep mountainside, the trail descends toward the river and crosses three streams. Bungalow Creek, the middle one, is the largest. Eventually, the path reaches river grade, coming out to River Camp, where an old shelter stands on the banks of the Dungeness (4.3 mi/6.9 km; 2100 ft/640 m). This shelter was restored in 1985 by volunteers and has been kept up well since.

Beyond this camp the trail crosses a washout, then traverses Douglas-fir forest as it parallels the river. The fairy slipper orchid is numerous here in the springtime. The trail crosses Mueller Creek, then comes out to FS Road 2870 near the bridge across the Dungeness River (5.8 mi/9.3 km; 2500 ft/762 m).

60 UPPER DUNGENESS TRAIL

Length 6.3 mi/10.1 km
Access FS Road 2870
USGS Maps Tyler Peak; Mount Deception
Agency Olympic National Forest

The trail begins in a setting of tall, old-growth Douglas-fir on the west side of the Dungeness where FS Road 2870 crosses the river (2500 ft/762 m). The

Dungeness River is beautiful, unsurpassed in clarity because it is not a glacial stream. The trail follows the river to Camp Handy, then climbs above the valley to Boulder Shelter, where it intersects the **Constance Pass Trail** and the **Upper Big Quilcene Trail**. Obtaining water along this route is never a problem because many little streams cross the path.

At first the trail has a more or less level grade as it follows the river through stands of Douglas-fir to a junction with the **Royal Basin Trail** (1.0 mi/1.6 km; 2800 ft/853 m). Excellent campsites are located here at the confluence of the Dungeness and Royal Creek. The two streams are about equal in size at this point. The trail enters the Buckhorn Wilderness upon crossing Royal Creek, then goes by another campsite located between the trail and the river.

Making its way through the firs, the trail remains on a level grade as it parallels the river. The stream is picturesque—the green water cascades around and over countless rocks, logs, and barriers in the river bed; large fern-covered boulders over-look deep, clear pools, where fishermen stand and cast their lines, hoping to reel in a big one. The trail goes by a salt lick (1.6 mi/2.6 km), where wild animals, especially deer, may be observed on occasion.

After traversing opposite a slide, the trail crosses the Dungeness (2.4 mi/3.9 km), then climbs through stands of large fir as it contours the hillside. One can look across the river to beautiful meadows. At Camp Handy (3.2 mi/5.2 km; 3100 ft/ 945 m), reached by a couple of side paths, the hiker emerges from the cool, shaded forest onto a little meadow flooded with bright, warm sunshine. A shelter stands by the forest's edge at the base of the steep hillside. A good campsite is located by the river near the willows, another in the timber south of the shelter.

Camp Handy lies in the center of the upper Dungeness Valley, which is in the Buckhorn Wilderness. The grassy meadow is fringed by impenetrable willow thickets to the north and south, and bordered by the river on the west, the evergreen forest on the east. Here one can look up and down the breeze-swept valley—to the

Camp Handy, Upper Dungeness

heavy stands of conifers beyond the willows, to the timbered ridges rising above them. The top of Tyler Peak is visible due north, downriver.

Beyond this camp the trail climbs in earnest and goes by the unmarked junction with the **Heather Creek Trail** (3.5 mi/5.6 km), which leads to the right. The forest is mostly fir, but the trees have not pruned themselves well at this altitude, and stubby dead branches extend outward from the trunks like spokes. Rhododendrons now appear as an understory, growing thickly in places.

As it climbs above the river, the trail ascends steadily but at an easy grade, traversing a steep mountainside, and one can hear the chatter of the stream far below. The forest gradually changes to a mixture of fir and hemlock, and the trees become much smaller. Many are bearded with growths of lichen. The rhododendrons also disappear. With increasing elevation, the ground cover becomes more varied: in addition to salal and vanilla leaf, one now sees mountain azalea, pipsissewa, lupine, and juniper.

During the long, gradual ascent, the trail crosses numerous streams; thus water is readily available. At Slide Creek (5.0 mi/8.1 km), the stream is bordered by slide alder, and just beyond this point lodgepole pine occurs, a reminder that one is on the dry side of the Olympics.

This section is broken by viewpoints, which provide vistas of the upper Dungeness and the snow-clad peaks beyond, including Mount Constance. A big meadow borders the river below, but the stream is hidden by the thick growth along its banks. The meadow lies at the foot of an avalanche track, where snow accumulates, thus preventing the growth of trees.

Because it now more or less contours the mountainside, the trail becomes less steep, then goes slightly downhill. At the same time, the forest changes to subalpine fir, with openings where one can see a barren peak with a rock slide on its western face. Here the trail comes out to a willow-fringed creek, which it crosses to a little meadow strewn with huge chunks of basalt and blocks of pillow lava. This is the lower end of a big basin, and before the trail was rerouted one could look up and see the trail to Marmot Pass crossing the rock slide on the barren peak. A campsite is located in the meadow; just beyond it, however, Boulder Shelter sits on a grassy knoll surrounded by subalpine forest. The trail forks near the shelter (6.3 mi/ 10.1 km; 4950 ft/1509 m). This point marks the end of the Upper Dungeness Trail. The right branch becomes the Constance Pass Trail, the left branch the Big Quilcene Trail.

61 LOWER MAYNARD BURN WAY TRAIL

Not maintained
Length 0.5 mi/0.8 km
Access Royal Basin Trail
USGS Map Mount Deception
Agency Olympic National Forest

The route up the south side of Baldy is known as Maynard Burn Way, not only to distinguish it from the Baldy Trail (which goes up the north side) but also because it leads into the southern edge of the area devastated by the Maynard Burn in the early 1900s. This forest fire destroyed the virgin timber on Maynard Peak, Baldy, Tyler Peak, and Ned Hill.

Originally the trail extended unbroken from Royal Creek to the 6000-ft/ 1829-m level on Baldy. However, the extension of FS Road 2860 into the Mueller Creek drainage destroyed all but a fragment of the lower part. This remnant, which ascends from the Royal Basin Trail to FS Road 2860–120, is now called Lower Maynard Burn Way. The longer stretch above the road is known as Upper Maynard Burn Way.

Lower Maynard Burn Way begins (2850 ft/869 m) about 200 yards up the **Royal Basin Trail,** after the latter makes two switchbacks. The unmarked trail goes uphill to the right. Although not maintained, it is in good condition, but climbs fairly steeply, traversing stands of Douglas-fir and western hemlock.

Near its start, the path crosses a muddy area, then climbs around a spur and comes out upon the ridge, which it follows, the slopes falling away at a moderate angle. The old firs here are craggy, lacking symmetry, with dead limbs that stick out from their trunks in all directions.

The trail emerges into a clearcut (0.5 mi/0.8 km; ca. 3300 ft/1006 m) at a big loop in FS Road 2870–270, 2.8 mi/4.5 km beyond the junction of FS Roads 2860 and 2870–270.

62 UPPER MAYNARD BURN WAY TRAIL

Not maintained
Length 3.5 mi/5.6 km
Access FS Road 2870-270
USGS Maps Mount Deception; Tyler Peak
Agency Olympic National Forest

This path is more interesting than the Lower Maynard Burn Way Trail because it leads to high, subalpine country. The trailhead (3600 ft/1097 m) can be reached by walking 1.7 mi/2.7 km beyond the end of FS Road 2870–270, a branch of FS Road 2870.

The unmarked route climbs a steep bank on the left, or uphill, side of the road. Nothing indicates the presence of a trail, but one can see a Cat track on the slope above. The path climbs up to and joins this track at a switchback, then follows it straight up the mountain at an uncomfortably steep angle. Apparently, the track was bulldozed by the Forest Service to serve as a fire-protection lane.

The trees, mostly Douglas-fir, are scattered in thin stands, and the ground supports a sparse growth of salal and lupine. The firs are typical of those found at the higher altitudes—the crowns are not symmetrical, and limbs are numerous. Many trees are covered with lichen.

The trail follows the narrow ridge, which drops away sharply on both sides. The route is steep and arduous, but cool breezes are usually present, making the hike pleasant. As the trail climbs higher, it follows the Cat track where it cuts a swath through a thick stand of lodgepole pine. The route gradually becomes less steep, and the track is overgrown with hundreds of little lodgepole pines, with silver firs and western white pines interspersed among them. Here the track is bordered on both sides by old-growth trees—an almost pure stand of lodgepole pine.

The end of the Cat track is marked by a turnaround or lookout point (1.3 mi/ 2.1 km; 4850 ft/1478 m), where the national park, national forest, and wilderness area all come together. Beyond this point the trail follows the boundary between the national park and the national forest for about a mile and assumes a much easier grade as it meanders through thick stands of subalpine fir.

Entering the Buckhorn Wilderness, the route breaks out into beautiful meadowland with excellent displays of wildflowers and hoop-skirted subalpine firs. Bluebells are found in large quantities. Here one can look across the valley of the creek that heads below the ridge between Baldy and Tyler Peak.

The trail ends in the meadows near a grove of lodgepole pines (ca. 6000 ft/ 1829 m) below the eastern false summit of Baldy (6500 ft/1981 m). But one does not need a trail to clamber up to this point, or to go on beyond to the true summit (3.5 mi/5.6 km; 6797 ft/2072 m). The country consists of tundralike meadows, where tufts of grass wave in the wind, and little birds twitter among the rocks. The views are magnificent and well worth the climb. (See **Baldy Trail** for description of the view.)

63 ROYAL BASIN TRAIL

Length 7.0 mi/11.3 km
Access Upper Dungeness Trail
USGS Maps Mount Deception; Tyler Peak
Agency Olympic National Park

This route follows Royal Creek to its headwaters in Royal Basin, one of the finest bits of high country in the Olympics. The stream was originally called Roy Creek, but somehow the name was changed. However, the present name is appropriate because Royal Basin would be a suitable place to entertain kings and queens. The basin, which cannot be observed in its entirety from one viewpoint, consists of several terraces or ice-carved basins, where meadows intermingle with groves of trees, forested knolls, and glacier-polished knobs.

The trail begins in the national forest at a junction with the **Upper Dungeness Trail** near the confluence of the Dungeness River and Royal Creek (2800 ft/853 m). About 200 yards up the trail an unmarked path leads uphill, to the right. This is the beginning of the **Lower Maynard Burn Way Trail**. The Royal Basin Trail continues straight ahead.

As it follows the course of Royal Creek, the trail climbs sharply, overlooking the sparkling stream, which is a succession of rapids, cascades, and waterfalls. Huge boulders scattered about the mountainside add an interesting note. The forest is mostly Douglas-fir and western hemlock, and as the trail climbs out of the bottoms the trees become smaller because the soil is thin and stony. An understory of rhododendron is present in places.

Upon entering the national park (0.4 mi/0.6 km), the trail veers away from Royal Creek, but water is available from numerous brooks along the way. Although

Arrowhead Meadow, Royal Basin Trail

the creek is now seldom in view, one can hear its thunderous booms. The path then crosses several avalanche tracks, which provide views of the peaks ahead, including The Needles. Two beautiful camps are located on the banks of Royal Creek in the intervening timbered areas.

Beyond these camps the cliffs of Graywolf Ridge overlook the valley, and the route becomes less steep as it traverses more or less open country. Royal Creek is now close at hand, and its thundering—intensified by Royal Creek Falls—reverberates through the valley. The falls are located where the rock formation changes from slate and sandstone to more resistant basalt. The mountainsides are rough, covered with rock slides and scattered stands of subalpine trees. Higher up, the meadows are smoother, and the trail goes by a couple of camps located in groves of silver fir. After traversing a marshy area, where water tends to stand, thus turning the path into a series of little pools, the route breaks out into the lower part of Royal Basin.

The trail meanders through a large meadow strewn with big boulders, then crosses willow-fringed Royal Creek and climbs through stands of silver fir to the north end of Royal Lake (6.0 mi/9.7 km; 5130 ft/1564 m), which occupies a glacier-scoured depression and drains to Royal Creek.

The pork chop–shaped lake, which contains Eastern brook trout, is surrounded by rocky, tree-covered knolls. The old campsite at the south end has been closed to restore the natural vegetation, but one can camp among the trees nearby. Look for designated sites. (Reservations needed May 1–September 30.) The lake is encircled by a well-beaten path, and the views are good—Graywolf Ridge rises to the north, Mount Deception and Mount Fricaba stand to the south. The terrain surrounding the lake is a blend of open country and stands of silver fir and subalpine fir.

Beyond the lake, the trail climbs over a rise, then descends to another meadow, where Royal Creek makes a double cascade as it tumbles down the mountain. Big Rock, also known as Shelter Rock, is located at the meadow's edge. This huge chunk of pillow lava overhangs on the west side. The campsite beneath it can accommodate a number of people, and during storms hikers sometimes take refuge here.

An excellent display of Jeffrey's shooting star is located just above Shelter Rock. The trail now climbs through forest to Arrowhead Meadow, so called because of its shape. Bordered by steep slopes, this meadow is flat, with a rounded, tree-covered knoll in the center. At the meadow's upper end, the trail climbs among sandstone boulders to still another level. This is the main basin, an area of expansive, rolling meadows, with steep headwalls at the upper end. The meadows are sprinkled with countless boulders composed of sandstone and pillow lava. The views in every direction are impressive—Mount Deception rises to the south, The Needles to the west, other rugged peaks to the east.

A campsite near the stagnant Deception Glacier, on the northeast face of Mount Deception, marks the end of the trail (7.0 mi/11.3 km; 5700 ft/1737 m). Near the camp a muddy lake, milky with glacial flour, gives birth to a silt-choked stream. This is the beginning of Royal Creek. No inlet is visible; apparently the water seeps through the moraine, where great chunks of pillow lava lie piled in jumbles. The adjacent meadows are colorful with lupine and gentian in late summer.

One can walk up the rounded hogback west of the lake to a big rock that makes an excellent post to observe the jagged pinnacles that rise above the scree. The upper valley of Royal Creek, below the lake, has a definite U shape, indicating the glacier once extended down the valley a considerable distance. Deer roam the meadows, and elk are sometimes observed. Marmots are everywhere, and mountain goats clamber on the nearby cliffs. The neophyte should not venture beyond this point, but the experienced mountaineer can climb up and over or around Mount Deception to Deception Basin, which lies between Mount Deception and Mount Mystery. However, the basin can be reached more easily via the **Dosewallips Trail.**

The pinnacles of The Needles, west of Royal Basin, are composed chiefly of upended beds of pillow lava and provide some of the best rock climbing in the Olympics. The rock breaks easily, however, and is generally inferior to the granite found in the Cascades.

64 GOAT LAKE WAY TRAIL

Not maintained
Length 1.8 mi/2.9 km
Access Upper Dungeness Trail
USGS Map Mount Deception
Agency Olympic National Forest

This path begins on the west bank of the Dungeness River, opposite Camp Handy (3100 ft/945 m) on the **Upper Dungeness Trail**, and can be reached by either wading the river or crossing on a logjam just south of the camp. Both ends of the trail are vague and indistinct, but most of the way the route is well defined. However, it is steep and arduous, gaining more than a half mile of elevation in less than 2 miles.

The trail begins as a poor path that follows down the river's west bank to the first creek that comes in from the west, then follows this tributary's north bank. (In the fall, this may be only a dry and rocky channel.) At the base of the slope, several paths converge to form the trail leading uphill. Here the route is confused by innumerable game trails, which tend to go everywhere except the direction the hiker wishes to go. Above this point, however, the route is well defined. The precipitous ascent is brutal, especially on a hot afternoon—a grueling grind that elicits grunts and groans from the backpacker.

The path skirts a slide bordering a deep gully, climbing steeply along the edge of the raw earth. Here one can look south and see craggy peaks with snowfields. The trees are also craggy—rough-barked, with many dead limbs projecting outward from the trunks. The undergrowth is largely salal, kinnikinnick, and rhododendron.

As the trail climbs higher, one can see a lofty meadow across the Dungeness, in the Marmot Pass area. The trail now follows a spinelike ridge of slate and shale, and one has to clamber along ledges, over rocks and tree roots, while clinging to bushes and little trees. The path is similar in this respect to the infamous Lake Constance Trail. Many trees have burls, some of them quite large. At one point the hiker can look back and down and see the shelter and meadow at Camp Handy.

After the path tops the gully and slide (0.7 mi/1.1 km; 4700 ft/1433 m), the grade eases somewhat, but it is still precipitous. Here, at the upper levels of the unbroken forest, the trees become scrubby, almost subalpine in character. The path then goes through dense thickets of slide alder, where the ground is marshy. A way has been cut through—otherwise the jungle would be impenetrable. Little openings appear, covered with lush grasses and plants; "Christmas" trees are scattered on the slopes, and a small stream courses down through the swale.

At the base of a steep hillside covered with sandstone boulders intermixed with scree (1.0 mi/1.6 km; 5250 ft/1600 m), the path climbs sharply again. The country is mostly open, with scattered subalpine firs and a few pines. Marmots are abundant. Here the ascent is particularly trying—often one takes a step upward in the loose scree, only to slide back two.

Eventually the hiker tops a rise and looks out upon the calm waters of Goat Lake (1.8 mi/2.9 km; 5930 ft/1807 m). The deep blue lake, covering an expanse of 8 acres, lies in a cirque at the base of a rugged, snow-flecked peak and is surrounded by stretches of meadow, groves of subalpine trees, and outcrops of sandstone covered with black lichen. A barren talus slope rises to the west.

65 HEATHER CREEK TRAIL

Way trail, not maintained
Length 4.0 mi/6.4 km
Access Upper Dungeness Trail
USGS Map Mount Deception
Agency Olympic National Forest

This route is not marked with a sign, and the Forest Service does not list it in its literature. Nevertheless, it is a fairly good trail, and with limited maintenance could be made into a first-class one. The path ends near the national park boundary on the upper reaches of Heather Creek.

The trail begins as a log-blocked side path (3175 ft/968 m) on the **Upper Dungeness Trail**, 0.3 mi/0.5 km beyond Camp Handy. The path leads downhill, to the right, descending toward the Dungeness River through scrubby forest having the characteristic understory of salal and rhododendron found in the northeastern Olympics. After crossing a small stream, the trail approaches the Dungeness at an old camp where a cabin stood close to the river. The structure was destroyed in 1981, and nothing remains but a pile of logs.

At this point the trail goes upstream through the conifer forest, paralleling the Dungeness but avoiding its willow-choked banks. The route alternately traverses stands of old fir and grassy glades. Two camps are located in this area—the first in a grove of firs, the second (Grindstone Camp) in a meadow opposite Milk Creek, which flows down the slope to the west to join Heather Creek, thus forming the Dungeness River. The path meanders as it detours around windfalls and washouts. The flat bottomland disappears, and the trail climbs a little ridge before descending to Heather Creek (2.0 mi/3.2 km; 3260 ft/994 m). The stream is not bridged; one must either wade or look around for a log spanning the creek.

The trail then follows a rounded ridge, and one can hear the booming of Heather Creek below. As the path climbs through the forest, where the ground is covered with boulders and moss, the hiker is surprised to come upon an old hunters' camp (2.9 mi/4.7 km; 3475 ft/1059 m) littered with heaps of debris. The piles include broken glass, whiskey and beer bottles, assorted jars, gasoline cans, and rusted tableware. Burned timbers denote the site where a cabin once stood.

At this point the trail jogs to the right and climbs steadily through scrubby little firs and hemlocks. At times one can look across the Dungeness Valley and see the rock tower that marks the end of the Charlia Lakes Way Trail. The trail then enters the first of two areas where avalanches have destroyed the timber. Here one can see rocky, forested peaks and ridges, with some meadowland at the higher elevations.

The character of the forest changes, with willow and slide alder mixed among the conifers. Many of the latter are covered with burls. The country becomes increasingly rough; big rocks lie scattered among the trees, and the slope drops steeply to a canyon on the left. The trail then enters a big basin overgrown with impenetrable thickets of slide alder and willow, where a good deal of debris has been left by avalanches. The basin is encircled by rocky mountains, with two peaks forming a wall at its head. The higher one is Little Mystery.

The trail descends along the basin's edge to Heather Creek. A cabin, identified by a sign as Heather Creek Camp, once stood on a knoll on the stream's far side, almost hidden by brush and stunted evergreens covered with burls.

This cabin was located in the vicinity of the national park boundary, which has not been marked in this area. The trail ends here (ca. 4.0 mi/6.4 km; ca. 4000 ft/1219 m).

66 CHARLIA LAKES WAY TRAIL

Not maintained
Length 1.0 mi/1.6 km
Access Upper Dungeness Trail
USGS Map Mount Deception
Agency Olympic National Forest

A way trail that leads to high places and wide views, this route begins about 250 yards south of Boulder Shelter at the end of the **Upper Dungeness Trail,** at 5000 ft/1524 m. The trail is not marked, but it is surprisingly good. However, it is no longer listed in Forest Service literature.

At first the path climbs through stands of subalpine fir where the undergrowth is largely azalea. The grade soon eases, however, and patches of meadow are mixed among the firs and rock outcrops. After crossing a little ridge, the route meanders through alpland where the views across the Dungeness River include The Needles, Mount Deception, Graywolf Ridge, Baldy, and Tyler Peak.

After going through a gap in the ridge to a campsite by a little pond, the trail works its way out onto a rocky ledge where one has an unobstructed view of Mount Constance and the upper Dungeness. The path follows the ridge, traversing meadowland, where clumps of lodgepole pines defy the elements. The vistas in every direction are splendid.

As the trail climbs a steep slope between rough peaks, the mountains to the southwest, beyond the headwaters of the Dungeness, come into view. The path switchbacks up the slope, climbing through broken rubble at the foot of a rock tower about 100 feet high, then ends on the ridge crest (1.0 mi/1.6 km; ca. 6500 ft/1981 m).

At this point one can look down the valley of Tunnel Creek and see a bit of Hood Canal, with Glacier Peak beyond it on the horizon. The smaller of the Charlia Lakes is visible from a spot a bit downslope, but in order to see the larger lake one has to scramble a hundred yards or so up the peak to the north. The hiker should watch for mountain goats because the country is ideal habitat for the animals.

Rocky peaks rise both north and south of the lakes, which drain eastward to Tunnel Creek, a tributary of the Big Quilcene River. The lakes are almost a thousand feet below the ridge, and in order to reach them the hiker must "heel down" the steep slope. The soft soil affords good footing on the descent, but the climb back up is strenuous. One lake is little more than a round pothole (5700 ft/1737 m), but the other is much larger, irregular in shape, and bordered by trees (5500 ft/1676 m). The lakes contain Eastern brook trout.

67 TUBAL CAIN TRAIL

Length 8.8 mi/14.2 km
Access FS Road 2870
USGS Maps Mount Zion; Mount Townsend; Mount Deception
Agency Olympic National Forest

Originally this trail extended from Dungeness Forks to Marmot Pass, but man's penchant for building roads has taken its toll. The lower portion below Gold Creek has been destroyed; the middle section, between Gold Creek and Silver Creek, has been isolated from the upper part by FS Road 2870, and is called the **Gold Creek Trail**. Only the upper section is known today as the Tubal Cain Trail.

The trailhead (3300 ft/1006 m) is located on FS Road 2870, 3.6 mi/5.8 km beyond the Dungeness River crossing. The path is smooth, with a gradual grade, and lends itself to rapid walking. After going by Silver Creek Shelter, it crosses the stream, takes a westerly course as it climbs around the spur between Silver Creek and Copper Creek, then heads due south, paralleling the latter. The gain in elevation is almost imperceptible. After the first mile, the forest changes to a mix of Douglas-fir and western hemlock. Now and then the hiker is rewarded with a glimpse of distant peaks up the valley.

About 1899, copper, manganese, and other minerals were discovered at the sites of Tubal Cain and Tull City, on the lower flanks of Iron Mountain. Men took mining claims and packed equipment and ore along this part of the 18-mile trail. However, during the winter of 1911 severe snowstorms swept the district, and spring floods and avalanches destroyed the mine shafts. Consequently, the miners left.

The lower slopes traversed by this trail were burned during the early 1900s, when the mining activities were under way, and the route now traverses scrubby stands of second-growth fir. The heavy undergrowth consists mostly of rhododendron, and the display of pink blossoms is spectacular in early summer.

Not far beyond County Line Creek, where one leaves Clallam County and enters Jefferson, the hiker can look across the valley and see a band of meadowland high up the slope, with thick timber not only below but also above. This is characteristic all along the ridge west of Copper Creek.

Near Tull Canyon Creek the rhododendron jungle disappears, and the trail swings to the southwest. The **Tull Canyon Trail** (3.2 mi/5.2 km; 4150 ft/1265 m) climbs the hillside to the left. The Tubal Cain Trail now enters dense stands of second-growth fir, where the ground is barren, but presently the path leaves the dark forest, crosses a tributary of Copper Creek, then parallels the latter to Tubal Cain Camp (3.6 mi/5.8 km; 4350 ft/1326 m), which is located on Copper Creek.

The camp is located in a grove of subalpine fir near the Tubal Cain Mine. One should not explore the mine tunnel because it is unsafe. The main shaft goes back 2800 feet, with 1500 feet of side tunnels. The old buildings have been gone for years, but debris lies scattered about. Backpackers have utilized the stoves, pipes, and barrels at campsites located among huge chunks of pillow lava in the dark, damp, and gloomy woods. The best camping place, however, is a little island in Copper Creek, where one can enjoy the sunshine.

The trail crosses the creek at this point. This is the last water on the route unless one makes a side trip to Buckhorn Lake. As the path climbs through beautiful meadows, one can see the Strait of Juan de Fuca to the north. Beyond an area where fire-killed snags have been knocked down by avalanches, the trail traverses open slopes providing wide vistas of the basin at the head of Copper Creek.

The **Buckhorn Lake Way Trail** (5.5 mi/8.9 km; ca. 5300 ft/1615 m) is not marked, and the hiker intending to visit the lake should watch for a path leading downhill to the left, because the lake is not visible from the trail.

As it switchbacks up the shale slopes, the path alternates between meadow and subalpine forest. At Buckhorn Pass (7.0 mi/11.3 km; 5900 ft/1798 m), on the divide between Copper Creek and the Dungeness, the trail turns south and follows the ridge. The valley at the head of Copper Creek lies to the left, below Iron Mountain and Buckhorn Mountain. One can also look back to the north and see Peak 6628. Beyond it lies the Strait of Juan de Fuca, with Mount Baker and Mount Shuksan gleaming on the horizon.

The trail now attains its highest elevation (6300 ft/1920 m), then traverses the shale slopes on the west side of Buckhorn Mountain. The landscape is dotted with stunted whitebark pines and subalpine firs, but they do not obscure the views, which now include the country to the south as well as the strait to the north, with the peaks in Canada beyond.

As the trail descends high meadowland where the subalpine lupine waves in the wind, the hiker is treated to a succession of splendid views—the upper Dungeness, Del Monte Ridge, Alphabet Ridge, and numerous rugged peaks. They include Constance, Mystery, Fricaba, Deception, The Needles, and Warrior. The wind sweeps across the ridge, and one cannot help but wonder what it is like here during a winter storm.

The trail then descends to Marmot Pass, the gap in the ridge at the head of the Big Quilcene, where it ends in a junction with the **Upper Big Quilcene Trail** (8.8 mi/14.2 km; 6000 ft/1829 m).

68 TULL CANYON TRAIL

Way trail, not maintained
Length 0.7 mi/1.1 km
Access Tubal Cain Trail
USGS Map Mount Townsend
Agency Olympic National Forest

Although short and steep, this trail contains a couple of surprises. The path begins on the **Tubal Cain Trail** at 3.2 mi/5.2 km just beyond a big rock (4150 ft/1265 m), and climbs steeply uphill. The first surprise is right at the start—the dark, forbidding entrance to a miners' tunnel at the base of a cliff. One can discern the floors and walls for some distance, then all definition disappears in the murky darkness.

The trail skirts beneath the moss-padded cliff, then traverses through stands of broomstick-size fir and hemlock, and makes its way among rough boulders of broken basalt. Upon coming to a vantage point that overlooks the ridge to the west, the trail goes through stands of larger trees, and the grade eases. The trail then forks.

The left branch leads out to a swampy area at the lower end of a beautiful valley—and the second surprise. Here, scattered among thick growths of willow, lie the remains of an Air Force B-17 that crashed on January 19, 1952, during a blinding snowstorm. Three men were killed; five survived. •

The right branch goes to a campsite, then to the remnants of an old cabin (0.7 mi/ 1.1 km; 5000 ft/1524 m). The roof is gone; only the walls are standing. This was the site of Tull City, another ill-fated mining venture contemporary with the Tubal Cain development. Beyond the cabin, a well-developed way trail extends up the valley about a half-mile to meadowland.

Large boulders are strewn about the marshy area. At this point one can look up Tull Canyon, which is overshadowed by a rocky peak on the right.

69 BUCKHORN LAKE
WAY TRAIL

Not maintained
Length 0.5 mi/0.8 km
Access Tubal Cain Trail
USGS Map Mount Townsend
Agency Olympic National Forest

The primitive trail that leads to Buckhorn Lake begins at a junction with the **Tubal Cain Trail,** 1.9 mi/3.1 km beyond Copper Creek, at ca. 5300 ft/1615 m. The intersection is not marked, and the hiker traveling north on the Tubal Cain Trail is apt to mistake the path for a switchback and wind up at Buckhorn Lake when the intended destination is Copper Creek.

The path descends through stands of subalpine fir, crosses a small stream, then climbs a bit, rather sharply, only to descend again to Buckhorn Camp. Two campsites are located here, adjacent to a little creek in the forest, where chipmunks scurry about, anticipating the opportunity to commit larceny. But the trail doesn't end here; it goes on, descending again, to Buckhorn Lake (0.5 mi/0.8 km; 5150 ft/1570 m).

The lake is not visible from either trail; it could well be called Hidden Lake. One wonders how it was discovered. Most likely a prospector spotted it from the top of Iron Mountain, then set out to find it. The lake lies in a beastly, miserable hole and has a rocky shore, but the path comes down to the muddy upper end near the inlet creek. The tarn, which is stocked with rainbow trout, is surrounded by dense stands of subalpine fir. One little tent site is located here, but it is not level. The best camp is up in the woods with the chipmunks.

QUILCENE

The Quilcene watershed, located in the midst of the district once called the Jupiter Hills, encompasses the areas drained by the Big Quilcene River and the Little Quilcene River in the northeastern Olympics. The streams, separated by the Quilcene Range, flow into the head of Quilcene Bay less than a mile from each other. The Quilcene country is separated from the

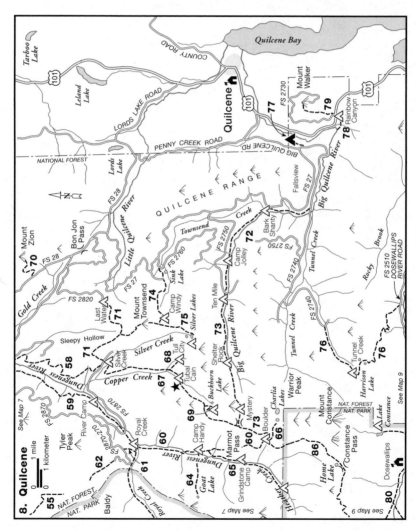

Dosewallips on the south by a long, narrow ridge extending from Mount Turner to Mount Constance; from the Dungeness on the west by the Constance Range; and from the district to the north and east by low divides.

Most of the land lying in the Quilcene watershed is rugged. The Big Quilcene heads at about 6000 ft/1829 m near Marmot Pass, the Little Quilcene at the same level on the north slope of Mount Townsend; but each stream is less than 20 miles in length. The Big Quilcene has two major tributaries—Townsend Creek and Tunnel Creek.

This area lies in the heart of the rain shadow, the driest district in the Olympic Mountains. Yet it is not truly arid; in fact, in the river bottoms the forests are luxuriant. With the concurrence of the Forest Service, the timber industry has severely exploited this district. Logging roads penetrate almost everywhere; clearcuts are legion. The only remaining areas that can be considered truly primitive are the upper valleys of the Big Quilcene and Tunnel Creek.

ROADS

Access to the trails in this area is provided by the Olympic Highway, US 101, which skirts the region on the east, and by several logging roads in the national forest.

Bon Jon Pass Road (FS Road 28). This road begins at Lords Lake, near the national forest boundary, and is reached by driving 2.0 mi/3.2 km north of Quilcene on US 101, then turning left onto County Road 30 (Lords Lake Road) and following it 3.4 mi/5.5 km to a junction, near Lords Lake, where FS Road 28 begins. The latter follows the Little Quilcene River in a northwesterly direction, climbing to Bon Jon Pass (5.3 mi/8.5 km), then traversing across the foothills to the Palo Alto Road on the Dungeness (15.7 mi/25.3 km). It leads to the Mount Zion Trail.

FS Roads 27, 2740, 2750, and 2760. These roads are all reached by driving 1.4 mi/2.3 km west of Quilcene on US 101, then turning right onto Penny Creek Road just north of the Big Quilcene River. At 1.4 mi/2.3 km the Big Quilcene River Road branches to the left and continues for 3.0 mi/4.8 km until it divides (4.4 mi/7.1 km from US 101). At this point the left branch becomes FS Road 2740; the right branch, FS Road 27.

FS Road 27. This road begins at the junction with FS Road 2740 and the Big Quilcene River Road. FS Road 2750 branches left at 6.1 mi/9.8 km; FS Road 2760 at 9.1 mi/14.7 km. After crossing Skaar Pass (11.1 mi/17.9 km), FS Road 27 continues to FS Road 28 (16.0 mi/25.8 km).

FS Road 2740. The road begins at the intersection with FS Road 27 and the Big Quilcene River Road and descends through virgin timber into Big Quilcene Canyon. After crossing the Big Quilcene River above the confluence of Tunnel Creek, the road follows the latter stream and provides access to the Tunnel Creek Trail (6.6 mi/10.6 km).

FS Road 2750. This road branches left from FS Road 27, 6.1 mi/9.8 km beyond the intersection of FS Road 27, FS Road 2740, and the Big Quilcene River Road. The road goes up the Big Quilcene Valley to Wet Weather Creek and Ten Mile Shelter (4.6 mi/7.4 km). The Upper Big Quilcene Trail begins on the uphill

side just beyond the shelter; the upper trailhead of the Lower Big Quilcene Trail can be found near Wet Weather Creek on the downhill side of the road.

FS Road 2760. This primitive road, noted for its rhododendron display in late June and July, branches left from FS Road 27 at 9.1 mi/14.7 km, and provides access to the popular Mount Townsend Trail, 0.9 mi/1.4 km from its junction with FS Road 27.

FS Road 2820. The road branches left from FS Road 28, 0.2 mi/0.3 km west of Bon Jon Pass, and leads to the Little Quilcene Trail.

FS Road 2730 (The Mount Walker Road). This road leaves US 101 5.0 mi/ 8.1 km southwest of Quilcene and climbs to the top of Mount Walker, ascending steadily as it almost encircles the peak. At 3.2 mi/5.2 km a viewpoint overlooks the country to the south and east, including Mount Rainier. The road forks at 4.1 mi/ 6.6 km. The right branch goes about 600 yards to the South Viewpoint (2730 ft/ 832 m); the left branch extends approximately 250 yards to the North Viewpoint (also 2730 ft/832 m). Each viewpoint has a loop at the end.

The South Viewpoint overlooks Dabob Bay and Dabob Peninsula, Hood Canal, Puget Sound, the Cascades, and the eastern foothills of the Olympics. The North Viewpoint has a sweeping view of the Olympics from Mount Jupiter to Mount Townsend, and it also overlooks the Quilcene Range to the north, and the neighboring lowlands. The lower slopes of the range have been badly scarred by patch logging.

70 MOUNT ZION TRAIL

Length 1.8 mi/2.9 km
Access FS Road 28
USGS Map Mount Zion
Agency Olympic National Forest

Mount Zion stands somewhat isolated, its slopes draining to four systems—on the west, via Gold Creek, to the Dungeness River; north, to a tributary of Jimmycomelately Creek; east, into Snow Creek, and on the south to Deadfall Creek, a tributary of the Little Quilcene. The peak does not, therefore, belong to any particular watershed; but because it is more closely linked with the Quilcene than the Dungeness, it has been included here.

The trailhead (2950 ft/899 m) is located on FS Road 28, 2.0 mi/3.2 km from Bon Jon Pass, where a parking lot and a permanent restroom have been constructed.

This trail is at its best in late June or early July, when the rhododendrons are in bloom. The floral display rivals that on Mount Townsend as one of the finest in the Olympics. The smooth, well-laid-out trail is a delight to walk.

The route climbs at a moderate grade, ascending slopes covered with second-growth fir and an understory of rhododendron. Lichen clings to the trunks of the trees and the branches of the rhododendrons; the ground is covered with salal and ferns. Columbia lilies bloom alongside the path in the summer; their seed stalks sway in the autumn winds.

The only source of water on this route is a trickle on the right side of the trail (0.6 mi/1.0 km)—enough to hold a cup under and obtain a drink.

The trail climbs to the northwest, then makes a big bend and reverses its direction 180 degrees. After traversing beneath outcrops of basalt, the path climbs a bit, via a half dozen switchbacks, then goes by more examples of volcanic rock.

Upon the summit (1.8 mi/2.9 km; 4274 ft/1303 m), the trail breaks out into the open, but little trees are scattered around. The actual top is a smooth, flat area where a lookout cabin once stood. Built in 1929, it was removed in 1975.

The views are excellent. High peaks are visible to the southwest, including snow-flecked Mount Deception and The Needles, but flat-topped Mount Townsend dominates the scene because it is closer. Lower peaks and ridges can be seen to the northwest. The Strait of Juan de Fuca lies to the north, partially obscured by the ridge in the foreground. Mount Baker rises to the northeast, beyond Puget Sound, which is often covered by clouds, but on a clear day one has a glorious view of the water and the Cascades.

71 LITTLE QUILCENE TRAIL

Length 4.2 mi/6.8 km
Access FS Road 2820; FS Road 2870
USGS Map Mount Zion
Agency Olympic National Forest

The trailhead (ca. 4200 ft/1280 m) is located at the 4.0 mi/6.4 km point on FS Road 2820, which is reached via the Bon Jon Pass Road. The trail begins in a big clearcut that has been slash-burned and is now covered with blackened stumps and fireweed. As the trail climbs above and parallels the road, it crosses a little stream—the only water on the route. This was the site of Last Water Camp before much of the trail was obliterated by logging.

Beyond the clearcut the trail goes through a fringe of second growth before it enters the virgin forest—at this point Douglas-fir and western hemlock, with the typical understory of rhododendron and azalea that is found in the eastern Olympics. The trail climbs sharply to a more or less level area covered with subalpine fir and lodgepole pine. An old sign riddled with bullet holes indicates that this is Little River Summit (0.9 mi/1.4 km; 4800 ft/1463 m), the divide between the Little Quilcene and the Dungeness Rivers.

Open spots permit one to look out over the patch logging in the foothills to the Strait of Juan de Fuca. When the weather is benign, this is a pleasant place, but during storms the wind shrieks in the subalpine firs, creating a wilderness symphony.

The trail crosses into the Sleepy Hollow watershed, where it traverses thick stands of subalpine fir. Here it climbs again, but not so steeply, going up and down like an elevator as it makes its way through lodgepole pine and subalpine fir to the intersection with the **Mount Townsend Trail** (2.0 mi/3.2 km; 5275 ft/1608 m), near the head of Sleepy Hollow and below the crest of Dirty Face Ridge.

How Dirty Face Ridge and Sleepy Hollow received their names is not known, but one is tempted to speculate that the former may have referred to the smoke-grimed faces of men fighting a forest fire—or perhaps they were miners from Tubal Cain returning to civilization.

Beyond this point the trail is not maintained, and it is sometimes called the Dirty Face Ridge Trail or the Sleepy Hollow Trail. The path climbs onto Dirty Face Ridge, where it winds among bushy pines and upthrusts of pillow lava. The forest is the same mixture of lodgepole pine and subalpine fir, with the former predominating. The views are excellent. Mount Townsend looms to the south, little more than a mile distant; Iron Mountain and Buckhorn Mountain are in full view. More distant are the peaks at the head of the Dungeness. The view to the northeast embraces Puget Sound and the Cascades, with Mount Baker the major peak. Below, to the north, are forested ridges, with a few clearcuts discernible in the distance.

The trail then traverses below the ridge, leaving the subalpine country, and the views disappear. But as the path circles around to the southwest, logging roads and clearcuts are visible along Silver Creek and the Dungeness.

The views again disappear as the trail begins a precipitous descent that is hard on the toes. Unbelievably, it gets steeper, until the rocky trail is little more than a gully. The route goes through stands of stunted trees and thick growths of rhododendron, where the display of blossoms in early summer is reason enough to hike over the trail. Although water is usually not available, the path crosses a seep (4.0 mi/6.4 km) where it can sometimes be obtained. The trail improves beyond this point—it is no longer rocky and loses much of its steepness as it comes out to FS Road 2870 (see Dungeness-Graywolf chapter) on the uphill side (4.2 mi/6.8 km; 3400 ft/1036 m). No sign is present to indicate that this is the trail's western terminus. The person driving on the road merely sees a path going up the mountainside. The parking area for the **Tubal Cain Trail** is down the road just a bit.

72 LOWER BIG QUILCENE TRAIL

Length 5.8 mi/9.3 km
Access FS Road 27; FS Road 2750
USGS Maps Mount Townsend; Mount Walker
Agency Olympic National Forest

The Big Quilcene Trail once extended unbroken almost the full length of the valley, and it was known as the Rainbow Trail. However, FS Road 2750 now extends far up the valley, and where it crosses the river it cuts the trail in two. The lower and upper segments are now known, respectively, as the Lower Big Quilcene Trail and the **Upper Big Quilcene Trail.**

The Lower Big Quilcene Trail begins at Big Quilcene Campground (1300 ft/396 m), a primitive camping area reached by driving 0.4 mi/0.6 km on FS Road 27, then going left 0.3 mi/0.5 km on FS Road 2700–080. The upper trailhead is located on FS Road 2750, 4.6 mi/7.4 km from its junction with FS Road 27.

The trail follows the Big Quilcene River, at first utilizing the grade of the abandoned Bark Shanty Road, so long unused it is now carpeted with grass. The path, bordered by second-growth fir, alder, and maple, soon enters the Port Townsend municipal watershed, where it comes to an overlook. The view south, across the canyon, includes beautifully forested slopes that have been marred by numerous clearcuts. The river itself is hidden by trees along its banks.

The route now contours high above the Big Quilcene, and one can glimpse the stream, clear and sparkling, in the depths of the canyon. Old firs stand between the trail and river, but the uphill slope has been logged and is now covered with second growth. At this point the trail enters virgin forest, largely Douglas-fir. A glance backward reveals fir-clad mountainsides scarred by clearcuts, but across the Big Quilcene the forest is untouched. The broad path, still following the old road, is now practically level as it contours the mountainside. Upon approaching the river, the trail crosses several streams.

One now makes the first of two crossings of the Big Quilcene. The stream, spanned by an old wooden bridge, flows over a bed of boulders, many covered with mosses and plants. On the west side, the trail traverses a stand of tall firs. Here an unmarked path leads, right, to Bark Shanty Camp (2.4 mi/3.9 km; 1440 ft/439 m), just below the confluence of Townsend Creek and the river. The campsite is a little spot surrounded by tall evergreens. The old road ended at this point.

The trail recrosses the river above the point where Townsend Creek flows into the Big Quilcene and then climbs a bit as the valley becomes more canyonlike. The path then enters stands of second growth on land that was logged some years ago, all the way to the river. Not even a fringe of trees was left standing. One can look upstream and see logging roads on the mountainside, clearcuts covered with young stands of fir, and dark expanses of old-growth forest above. The trail then goes through an area logged in 1983–84. The slopes on both sides of the river were shorn of trees to the stream's edge. Only the stumps remain of the large firs and cedars that bordered the trail, and the path threads its way through head-high second growth.

The trail then reenters the forest, here a mixed stand of fir and hemlock. The undergrowth consists of rhododendron, Oregon grape, and salal; the ground is often covered with moss. The trail crosses three creeks, where the hiker must hop across from boulder to boulder. At Jolley Creek, the last one, a side path leads downhill to Camp Jolley (5.0 mi/8.1 km; 2000 ft/610 m).

The trail climbs to a point where one can look down and see the river flowing in its narrow channel like a millrace. A logged patch is visible to the right, through the trees, and one can see FS Road 2750 on the slope above.

The roar of the river comes up from below as the trail rounds a spur, and the keen-eyed hiker can dimly perceive the cause through the trees—a falls 15 or 20 feet high. The path now enters what the Forest Service calls a partial cut—a selectively logged area. Many trees were left standing; consequently, the land has not been left desolate, as is often the case.

The trail comes out into a clearcut grown up with hemlock and fir and climbs to FS Road 2750 about a hundred yards east of Wet Weather Creek (5.8 mi/9.3 km; 2500 ft/762 m). This is the upper trailhead of the Lower Big Quilcene Trail. Ten Mile Shelter is just ahead, on the uphill side adjacent to Wet Weather Creek. The Upper Big Quilcene Trail begins just beyond the shelter.

73 UPPER BIG QUILCENE TRAIL

Length 6.7 mi/10.8 km
Access FS Road 2750
USGS Maps Mount Townsend; Mount Deception
Agency Olympic National Forest

This route traverses the Buckhorn Wilderness. The trailhead (2500 ft/762 m) is located on FS Road 2750 just beyond Ten Mile Shelter (4.6 mi/7.4 km), near where the road crosses the Big Quilcene River. The shelter stands on a bench above the road, next to Wet Weather Creek; but, as the name implies, it was 10 miles up the trail before the road was built.

The trail, which is well maintained by a number of volunteer groups, climbs gradually through stands of old-growth fir, cedar, and hemlock, primarily the latter. Rhododendrons are abundant and in early summer brighten the forest with masses of pink flowers. Many big, moss-covered boulders lie scattered about, and ferns grow among the rocks. The trail comes out onto the banks of the Big Quilcene, then switchbacks upward through silver fir and western hemlock, leaving the river far below rushing wildly through the forest.

The trail then returns to the river and a side trail leads, left, to Shelter Rock Camp (2.6 mi/4.2 km; 3650 ft/1113 m), located in a stand of tall hemlock beside the Big Quilcene, which at this point is scarcely 10 feet wide. Why the camp received its name is puzzling. The only large boulders nearby are two modest-sized ones.

Beyond this camp the trail once again climbs up and away from the river, but parallels a small stream, the last source of water until one approaches Camp Mystery. As it traverses a steep, sun-baked mountainside, the path crosses a large boulder field where, during the winter and spring months, avalanches sweep down from Iron Mountain and Buckhorn Mountain. The river's canyon is to the left, and one can look up toward Marmot Pass. The trail then crosses scree slopes of another avalanche zone. Buckhorn Mountain stands to the north, the slope above the trail culminating in pinnacles of basalt. Across the narrow valley rise steep ridges and Peak 6852, with Mount Constance beyond.

Camp Mystery (4.6 mi/7.4 km; 5400 ft/1646 m) is located in a stand of subalpine fir beside a stream. A cragged ridge rises to the north, and rugged peaks are visible to the south. This is a good place to make a base camp because running water is available, and the place is sheltered from the wind.

The trail now climbs steadily toward Marmot Pass, and the trees are much smaller, the stands thinner. The route goes through an area of large boulders interspersed with meadows and groves of subalpine fir, where a little stream tumbles down from the heights above. This is the last source of water. At this point considerable damage has been done to the trail by people who have cut across the switchbacks. The trail zigzags up the slope beneath outcrops of basalt, and one can look down the Big Quilcene Valley and see Puget Sound—and, beyond it, Glacier Peak topping the Cascades. The trail then breaks out into large meadows, through which it climbs to a junction with the **Tubal Cain Trail** at Marmot Pass (5.3 mi/8.5 km; 6000 ft/1829 m).

Upon reaching the pass, one is inclined to linger and savor the panorama that extends across the upper Dungeness. The view includes some of the highest peaks in the Olympics, including Fricaba, Deception, The Needles, and Graywolf Ridge. The pass is merely the low point in the Constance Range, the ridge that extends north from Mount Constance to the headwaters of Copper Creek. Here the wind seldom, if ever, stops blowing, howling fiercely as it whips across the notch, whistling in the subalpine firs that cling to the nearby ridge, while the grasses and wildflowers wave wildly. Occasionally, however, the wind is toned down to a subdued susurration, and when this occurs the pass is a pleasant place to be. One cannot help but wonder, however, what it must be like here during a winter storm.

Double-peaked Buckhorn Mountain (6988 ft/2130 m; 6956 ft/2120m), which rises about a mile northeast of the pass, offers still better views of the northeastern Olympics. The ascent of the mountain, which owes its name to a fancied resemblance of the peak to deer antlers, is nontechnical, via a prominent boot path visible from the pass. The much-used route is generally snow-free by mid-July. Hikers should stay on the boot-beaten path to avoid trampling the heather.

Beyond the pass the trail crosses a rock slide, then makes "the grand traverse"—alternately going through groves of subalpine fir and across meadowland brightened by bluebells, lupine, and yarrow in late summer, with splendid views of the Dungeness Valley and the rugged peaks. The trail then descends, crossing rock slides and meadows dotted with subalpine firs, and lodgepole and whitebark pines. This is one of the few places where whitebark pine grows in the Olympics, but about half the trees are dead. The trail then skirts a field of big, rough boulders at the foot of a talus slope, where water is available. This is the first stream since just beyond Camp Mystery.

The trail enters a dense stand of subalpine fir as it drops down to a junction with the **Constance Pass Trail** and the **Upper Dungeness Trail** near Boulder Shelter (6.7 mi/10.8 kin; 4950 ft/1509 m).

74 MOUNT TOWNSEND TRAIL

Length 6.3 mi/10.1 km
Access FS Road 2760; Little Quilcene Trail
USGS Maps Mount Townsend; Mount Zion
Agency Olympic National Forest

This path, one of the best maintained in the Olympics, begins on FS Road 2760 at approximately 3000 ft/914 m elevation and penetrates the perimeter of the Buckhorn Wilderness. The trail ascends through the various life zones and provides superlative vistas of the surrounding country. At first the trail meanders by Sink Lake, which is half swamp and half stagnant lake. In late summer it appears to be turning into a grassy meadow with a stream running through it.

After passing a well-maintained trailside shelter, often used by equestrians, the route climbs to the terminus of an abandoned road (1.0 mi/1.6 km; 3500 ft/1067m). This is the former trailhead—now usually referred to as the upper trailhead—and it is readily accessible via the abandoned road, but the road itself is not signed to indicate it provides access to the Mount Townsend Trail, and the hiker who follows the road signs will end up at the lower trailhead instead.

The trail ascends through stands of fir and hemlock having a dense understory of tall rhododendron. When the bushes are in bloom, during early summer, they convert the forest into a green-and-pink fairyland. Here the trail parallels Townsend Creek, which flows through a canyon to the left. Although the stream can be heard, it is not visible and the trail does not approach it here.

The smooth path climbs steadily at a moderate grade. Near a series of rock outcrops the forest changes to a mixture of subalpine fir, western white pine, and silver fir. Although Douglas-fir and western hemlock are still present, they are now conical in form, with branches extending to the ground. Numerous open spots occur, and here wildflowers such as the lupine and pearly everlasting grow abundantly. Kinnikinnick creates green mats among the rocks above and below the trail; its red berries are colorful in the fall.

The trail traverses beneath a pillow lava outcrop, and at this point the hiker can look down the valley and see a curious blend of virgin timber, second growth, clearcuts, and logging roads. The grade eases as the trail crosses Townsend Creek near its source (dry in late summer and fall). This is typical high country—meadows with scattered groves of subalpine trees; slopes covered with juniper, thimbleberry, and huckleberry brush that turns blazing red in the fall. A few lodgepole pines are present. Examples of pillow lava are visible everywhere.

As the trail climbs higher, the views widen to include Discovery Bay to the left of the Quilcene Range, Puget Sound to the right. A rocky ridge looms up to the south. Making a "viewpoint turn," the trail enters a stand of tall subalpine fir, where a side path leads to Camp Windy (3.6 mi/5.8 km; 5300 ft/1615 m), located in a tiny meadow. The nearby Windy Lakes are little more than potholes, but in late summer they provide the only water along this trail. If the water is used, it should be boiled or filtered.

Beyond Camp Windy the trail climbs through stands of subalpine fir to a junction with the **Silver Lakes Trail** (3.9 mi/6.3 km; 5650 ft/1722 m). The trail then ascends high, open meadows where juniper bushes hug the ground. The Quilcene Range and Mount Walker are visible to the southeast, and one can see Windy Lake (the larger one) directly below.

The crest of Mount Townsend is a long, narrow ridge with a gentle incline on the west, but a steep drop on the east; thus it resembles a tilted block. The mountain has two summits a half mile apart—the higher one to the south (6280 ft/1914 m), the lower to the north (6212 ft/1893 m). They are merely the highest points on the plateau. Upon attaining the summit ridge, the trail crosses to the west slope, skirting below the south summit as it traverses grassland to the saddle between the peaks. Here the trail divides (5.0 mi/8.0 km). The main trail goes left; the right branch is a spur that leads to the north summit. Once the site of a lookout cabin, this point is littered with bits of broken glass and pieces of cable.

Mount Townsend is fully exposed to the west wind, which at times howls mightily here, the grasses waving wild accompaniment. The view is one of the best in the Olympics. Numerous peaks are visible to the southwest—The Needles, Deception, Constance, Inner Constance, Mystery, Warrior, Iron Mountain, and The

Brothers. One has only to turn and look in the opposite direction, however, to see Puget Sound, the Strait of Juan de Fuca, and the Cascades, the latter capped by volcanic cones. On a day that is exceptionally clear, the keen-eyed person can discern the buildings in Seattle. But the distant views are not the only attraction. The lucky hiker may also see ravens wheeling and turning overhead. The birds love the wind and are often observed over the peak.

Descending from the summit ridge, the trail goes by knobby chunks of pillow lava in high meadowland that is essentially treeless. The peaks to the southwest remain in full view. As the trail descends, stunted pines and subalpine firs appear. The path then switchbacks; here the landscape is sprinkled with bushy lodgepole pines that stand as solitary specimens among upthrusts of basalt. The trail makes a descending traverse at the south end of Dirty Face Ridge, then rounds a point. Ahead one can see the long scar made by FS Road 2950 where it slashes across the slopes beyond the Dungeness, with one clearcut after another below the road, strung out like beads on a necklace.

The trail descends sharply as it crosses to the ridge's east side and switchbacks down into the timber. Here the subalpine firs and lodgepole pines are much taller and larger. Entering a dense stand, the trail comes to a junction with the **Little Quilcene Trail** (6.3 mi/10.1 km; 5275 ft/1608 m).

75 SILVER LAKES TRAIL

Length 2.5 mi/4.0 km
Access Mount Townsend Trail
USGS Map Mount Townsend
Agency Olympic National Forest

The trail begins 0.3 mi/0.5 km above Camp Windy on the **Mount Townsend Trail** at 5650 ft/1722 m and traverses beneath outcrops of rock. Windy Lake is visible below, but the view disappears as the path goes into a thick stand of subalpine fir. Then, climbing toward the ridge crest, the trail makes its way through an area of tortured basalt—blocks, towers, and incipient cliffs, with upthrusts sticking out of the ground.

At the exposed notch (5700 ft/1737 m), where the trail crosses the south ridge of Mount·Townsend, the wind often whips through the trees. On this side the slopes overlook Silver Creek Basin and the peaks at the head of the valley. Logging roads are discernible to the north, down the valleys of Silver Creek and the Dungeness River.

As it descends toward the basin's head, the trail makes long traverses between switchbacks. The country consists of open meadowland and groves of subalpine firs. Bluebells bloom alongside the path, where rocks stick up like toes among the flowers.

The trail dips down to where the trees thicken into an unbroken stand. Here it goes beneath a cliff, the low point in the route, then climbs again. After crossing a stream—the only place where water is available—the trail ascends through the subalpine firs. The country becomes meadowy again just before the trail terminates at the larger and better known of the two Silver Lakes (2.5 mi/4.0 km; 5425 ft/ 1654 m), the source of Silver Creek.

The lake, shaped like a teardrop, lies in an amphitheater or glacial cirque that is almost encircled by rough peaks. The east and west sides—which pinch together at the north, or outlet, where the creek begins—are bordered by stands of subalpine fir. At the broad south end, meadowland rises toward the ridge that leads to the peaks southwest of the lake. The huge boulders scattered along the lake's west side have fallen from the cliffs above and now rest at the foot of talus slopes. Diving Rock, at the lake's southeast corner, is often used by swimmers on warm summer days.

Although the trail ends here, a way path loops around the lakeshore, and another one climbs the hill north of the lake to a campsite, then descends to the second lake. About half the size of the upper lake, it lies directly north, about 500 yards distant, at 5290 ft/1612 m. Both lakes contain Eastern brook trout.

The Silver Lakes can be reached via an alternate route, an unmaintained way path that joins the main trail less than a mile from the lakes. Follow the instructions given for reaching the Upper Dungeness Trail via FS Road 2860, cross the Dungeness River, then drive 3.6 mi/5.8 km, still on FS Road 2860, to the Tubal Cain Trail; cross Silver Creek, and continue to an obscure, abandoned logging road which has space for parking two or three vehicles. No signs indicate the trail begins nearby until one hikes up 300 feet of unmaintained path to a large bulletin board and sign-out station. The trail at this point is surprisingly good and shows evidence of being used, but it is often overgrown. Beginning on the west side of Silver Creek, the trail soon crosses to the east side (no bridge). The path more or less follows the creek, and after climbing a bit of precipitous terrain, where hikers must use care, it ends in a junction (2.2 mi/3.5 km) with the main route. After merging with it, the way trail becomes an imperceptible component of the remaining 0.8 mi/1.3 km to the lakes.

76 TUNNEL CREEK TRAIL

Length 7.3 mi/11.8 km
Access FS Road 2740; Dosewallips River Road
USGS Maps Mount Townsend; Mount Jupiter
Agency Olympic National Forest

This route traverses the Buckhorn Wilderness, climbing to Fifty-Fifty Pass (5050 ft/1539 m) at the head of the South Fork of Tunnel Creek. The hike should start on the Tunnel Creek side; no sane person deliberately backpacks over this trail from the Dosewallips River.

The trail begins at 6.6 mi/10.6 km on FS Road 2740, where it crosses the South Fork of Tunnel Creek (2600 ft/792 m). At first the path parallels Tunnel Creek, ascending through hemlock forest as it traverses above the stream. Camp Monk (0.5 mi/0.8 km), an attractive site across the creek, has space for one tent. A sign indicates the camp was established in 1959. The path then veers away from the creek and climbs through an imposing stand of old-growth western hemlock and silver fir. Although the creek is no longer visible, it can be heard faintly. As it approaches the creek again, the trail becomes fairly level and parallels the stream.

At Tunnel Creek Shelter (2.7 mi/4.3 km; 3800 ft/1158 m) the good trail ends;

beyond this point the route is steep and rough. The trail crosses the creek, then switchbacks a dozen times as it climbs steeply to the Twin Lakes—first to Karnes Lake (4600 ft/1402 m), then to Harrison Lake 3.7 mi/6.0 km; 4750 ft/1448 m). The lakes are bordered by mountain hemlocks. The trees are large on this cool, northern slope, the preferred habitat of this species. Karnes Lake contains rainbow trout. A poor campsite is located at the south side of Harrison Lake.

Above Twin Lakes the trail becomes steeper and rockier as it climbs the shaded north slope, then goes up a long draw leading to meadowland and stands of subalpine fir. Near the divide one is treated to the most spectacular view of Mount Constance to be had in the Olympics—an unobstructed look at the vertical east face, only 2 miles distant but a half mile higher. The barren cliffs are flecked with patches of snow.

At Fifty-Fifty Pass (4.1 mi/6.6 km; 5050 ft/1539 m), the hiker can see The Brothers, but the view of Mount Constance is now obscured by the trees. Mount Rainier stands high on the distant skyline. Often the peaks rise above a layer of clouds covering the Dosewallips Valley, the lowlands, and Puget Sound.

Beyond the divide the trail descends at a steep grade to the Dosewallips River, losing almost a mile of elevation in just over 3 miles. At first the path traverses meadows and groves of subalpine firs, where it goes by an unusual topographic feature—a deep-dish swale that should be a lake but isn't. The grassy swale probably resulted from ground creep. With high banks all around, it has no place for an outlet, but it is dry. Apparently the soil here is too porous for the basin to hold water.

Beargrass is abundant in the meadows; huckleberry and azalea bushes grow thickly clustered among the scattered, hoop-skirted firs. The route crosses open, rocky slopes having good views down the Dosewallips. On a clear day one can distinguish the Cascades, Hood Canal, and Puget Sound. Mount Jupiter and The Brothers rise directly across the valley. The trail meanders through upthrusted basalt, then enters the shaded coolness of the unbroken forest, here a mixture of old growth and second growth. Apparently fires swept up the mountainside, destroying much of the virgin timber, but patches escaped—stands of tall, slim Douglas-firs, with lichen clinging to the trunks and foliage.

The path now becomes so steep that the hiker is likely to have blistered toes before reaching the road. As the trail descends, it goes into the upper level of the rhododendron belt, where this plant forms a dense understory. One can hear the Dosewallips rushing in its channel far below. The trail descends to Gamm Creek (6.2 mi/10.0 km; 2750 ft/838 m), the only water source between Harrison Lake and the Dosewallips. The creek makes a triple falls above the trail as it cascades down a mossy cliff.

The trail descends a bit before traversing to the east, then switchbacks to avoid the canyon of another creek. Without further ado, it plunges straight down the mountainside, although making a switchback now and then. The steady descent is hard on legs and knees. Upon reaching the road and level ground, the hiker is inclined to stagger like a sailor for a few minutes.

The south trailhead (7.3 mi/11.8 km; 500 ft/152 m) is located on the Dosewallips River Road, 9.0 mi/14.5 km from US 101 (see Dosewallips chapter).

77 FALLSVIEW LOOP NATURE TRAIL

Length 0.1 mi/0.16 km
Access US 101
USGS Map Mount Walker
Agency Olympic National Forest

Fallsview Campground, in the Olympic National Forest, is located 3.5 mi/ 5.6 km southwest of Quilcene on US 101. The nature trail begins at the far end of the campground and makes a little loop (0.1 mi/0.16 km), coming back to its point of origin. The path goes to a couple of overlooks. The slope below them is almost vertical, therefore the Forest Service has installed a cyclone fence to prevent accidents. Several picnic tables are located among the trees beyond the overlooks. During early summer, when the rhododendrons are blooming, the forest is especially attractive.

At the viewpoints one can see a waterfall which plunges down a cliff that is almost obscured by the forest. The Big Quilcene River is below; the falls are on a tributary stream that flows down the southern end of the Quilcene Range. The best view is obtained from the second overlook. Here one can see the falls from top to bottom, ribboning down perhaps 150 ft/46 m into a pool in the river.

Another path, labeled Trail to River, begins near the loop trail and switchbacks down to the Big Quilcene. Wooden handrails provide security, because many people who are not hikers walk up and down this path, which comes out onto a big rock at the river's edge (0.2 mi/0.3 km). At this point the Big Quilcene dashes against the rock, then makes a sweeping turn to the left. The scene is striking, and one is reminded of the whirlpool at Goblin Gates on the Elwha.

For a longer hike in this area, ask the staff at the Quilcene ranger station how to find the Notch Pass Trail, a historic Indian route reopened in 1999. It climbs 500 ft/169 m in 2.0 mi/3.1 km to Notch Pass, then descends another 2.5 mi/4.0 km to a junction with the Lower Big Quilcene Trail. The hard-to-spot trailhead is on FS Road 010 (usually unmarked), in the vicinity of paved FS Road 27.

78 RAINBOW CANYON NATURE TRAIL

Length 0.5 mi/0.8 km
Access US 101
USGS Map Mount Walker
Agency Olympic National Forest

The Rainbow Picnic Area (727 ft/222 m) is located on US 101 in the Olympic National Forest near Walker Pass, 4.9 mi/7.9 km southwest of Quilcene. Overnight camping is not permitted; this is a day-use area maintained by the Quilcene Lions.

The delightful Rainbow Canyon Nature Trail leads to Rainbow Canyon on the Big Quilcene River. The walk is particularly pleasant in mid-October, when the fall color is at its peak. The trail begins in the picnic area and descends the mountainside via a half dozen switchbacks through stands of tall Douglas-fir and an understory of salal, vine maple, and sword fern. The trail first comes to a point overlooking the river, then to the brink of a side canyon. Here, on Elbo Creek, a tributary stream, a waterfall plunges down into a round pool. The canyon walls are lined with ferns.

The trail then descends to the river, coming out among alders and boulders at the water's edge (0.5 mi/0.8 km; 600 ft/183 m). This is Rainbow Canyon. Apparently the name stemmed from the graceful curve that the river makes at this point as it flows past a cliff garlanded with ferns and vine maple and topped by evergreen forest.

Originally this trail was the beginning of the Big Quilcene Trail, which was known fifty years ago as the Rainbow Trail and extended almost 20 miles to Boulder Shelter on the upper Dungeness.

79 MOUNT WALKER TRAIL

Length 2.0 mi/3.2 km
Access FS Road 2730
USGS Map Mount Walker
Agency Olympic National Forest

One can either drive up Mount Walker on FS Road 2730 or walk the trail to the top. Or, simpler yet, leave a car at the lower trailhead, drive in another vehicle to the summit, then hike down the trail. Nonhikers who drive up the road amble 50 yards to the knoll to see the view; people who hike the trail walk a delightful 2 miles.

The lower trailhead (750 ft/229 m) is located 0.3 mi/0.5 km from US 101 on the Mount Walker Road (FS Road 2730). Motorbikes are not allowed, and water is not available along the trail. The upper trailhead is located at the North Viewpoint.

The trail has one disadvantage—the hiker can hear traffic noise, particularly the sound of trucks, on the highway below. The trail is a broad, smooth path that starts in a stand of tall Douglas-fir, the undergrowth consisting of salal, Oregon grape, red huckleberry, vine maple, and rhododendron. Although the latter are beautiful, better displays can be found elsewhere in the Olympics; for example, on the trails to Mount Townsend, Tubal Cain, and Mount Zion.

As it climbs steadily, the path alternates between switchbacks and traverses, part of the time following a ridge. The trail heads toward the north summit, with the south summit to the right, beyond a deep ravine. The trees get smaller as the trail climbs higher, and near the top the path crosses a sunny slope where little firs and pines are scattered at random, as if a giant hand had tossed the seed carelessly.

The trail comes out onto a windswept knoll. This is the North Viewpoint (2.0 mi/ 3.2 km; 2730 ft/832 m), which overlooks the mountains to the west, the Quilcene Range to the north, and the lowlands east of the range. A wooden bench has been provided, where one can sit and contemplate the view.

Now lined by rocks, the trail leads from the knoll to the road and the parking area nearby. During winter months when the road is snow-covered, the road is gated.

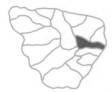

DOSEWALLIPS

The Dosewallips watershed, centrally located in the eastern Olympics, is long and narrow except in its upper part. The latter, lying within the national park, broadens to form a triangular-shaped area. This triangle results from a dendritic or treelike stream pattern—the North Fork and the West Fork of the Dosewallips River, together with Silt Creek, combine to form the trunk,

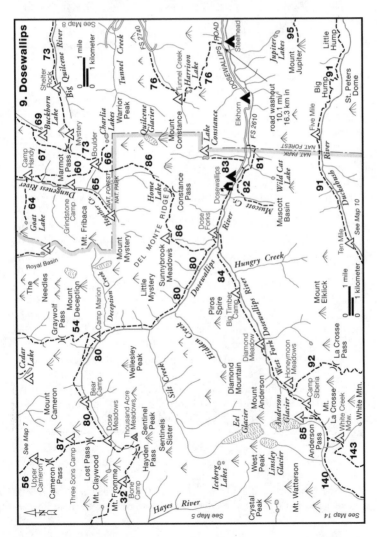

which then flows eastward to Hood Canal. Of the three branches, only Silt Creek—which probably should be considered the main stream—is glacial in origin, having its source in the Eel Glacier on Mount Anderson. This is the largest glacier in the eastern Olympics.

Numerous tributaries contribute to the river's volume. After heavy rains the Dosewallips is prone to serious flooding and at times has destroyed bridges and portions of the road or trail along its banks. During the summer, after the snowpack is gone and the temperature is high enough for the ice to melt, the river becomes cloudy with glacial flour transported by Silt Creek. The Dosewallips is then particularly dangerous and can be difficult to wade across because one cannot see the bottom and thus avoid stepping into deep holes. In early fall, before the rains commence, when the temperature is cold enough to retard melting, the river is crystal clear and often low enough to be easily waded.

The valley is enclosed by lofty peaks and ridges, including some of the highest in the Olympics. Mount Anderson, the hydrographic apex of the Olympic Peninsula, stands between the upper reaches of the West Fork and Silt Creek. A high ridge extends northward from the mountain to Hayden Pass, beyond Silt Creek, where the headwaters of the North Fork are encircled by the Five Peaks—Claywood, Fromme, Lost, Sentinel, and Wellesley. A large expanse of subalpine country is located here, including the splendid Thousand Acre Meadows.

Cameron Ridge divides the Dosewallips from Cameron Creek and the Graywolf River on the north. The mountainsides drop steeply from the ridge to the Dosewallips. The eastern end of the ridge is connected to the loop of high peaks that surrounds the upper Dungeness River. The most prominent summits in this chain are Constance, Deception, Mystery, and Little Mystery. The high country lying between Mount Mystery and Mount Constance is commonly called Del Monte Ridge.

Below the national park boundary, the valley is bounded on the north by the high ridge between the Dosewallips and Quilcene watersheds. On the south the valley is bordered throughout its length by a ridge of lesser elevation, beyond which lies the Duckabush. This ridge is capped by several rugged peaks—Elklick, LaCrosse, White Mountain, and Jupiter.

ROADS

The Olympic Highway, US 101, which follows Hood Canal in this area, provides approaches to the Dosewallips River Road from the north and south.

Dosewallips River Road (FS Road 2610). No road in or near Olympic National Park has generated more controversy in recent years than this popular but storm-damaged access route to some of the park's prime east-side scenery.

Following strong storms in late 2001, a 300-foot section of the road finally washed away just west of milepost 10. This left a nearly five-mile gap between the washout and road's end, the location of a heavily-used drive-in campground (Dosewallips) and a couple of always-busy trailheads. Another campground accustomed to capacity crowds, Elkhorn, was also blockaded by the washout.

Some voices clamored to have the road, which begins just north of the tourist-friendly hamlet of Brinnon on US 101, rebuilt in order to restore a beloved access point that attracts active and sedate visitors alike. Others, such as those who did not mind walking or biking the 10-mile round trip to reach road's end, insisted the closure reestablished a natural serenity in the area and campaigned to leave the washout alone.

In March 2004, the Forest Service announced a $556,000 project intended to rebuild the road, building a ¾-mile section of road that would impact a four-acre parcel of land, nudging the road deeper into a hillside at the spot of the washout. Two environmental groups, citing disruptions to a salmon-spawning habitat and impact on old-growth forest in the area, appealed the decision. Further challenges are anticipated, and no one is predicting when (or if) the project will begin.

Drive-up access to all of the trails described in this section is blocked by the washout. Plan on hiking (or mountain biking) up to an extra 4.8 mi/7.7 km to reach the starting points outlined in trips 80 through 87.

Leaving Brinnon, your last supply stop, the road follows the river and travels through private land, then state land, then national forest, and finally the national park.

The valley is bordered by high ridges on both sides, and as the road follows the river it passes by stump ranches on the bottomland. At Rocky Brook a footpath formerly led to nearby Rocky Brook Falls, but since development of a hydropower plant here the picturesque falls have been closed to the public.

The country becomes more rugged after the road enters the Olympic National Forest (5.5 mi/8.9 km). Leaving the cutover lands and second growth behind, the road winds through virgin forest as it traverses primitive country still in its natural state. The asphalt ends at 7.0 mi/11.3 km, and the road is graveled the rest of the way. Elkhorn Campground (10.6 mi/ 17.1 km; 700 ft/213 m), now inaccessible by vehicle, sits one-half mile west of the road closure and is located in a stand of tall Douglas-fir on the banks of the Dosewallips. The road now becomes steep and narrow, climbs high above the river and goes by what was known years ago as the Lower Jumpoff, then enters Olympic National Park (12.9 mi/20.8 km).

Within the park the road crosses Constance Creek, then skirts the base of a cliff of pillow basalt. The road now climbs sharply as it edges by Dosewallips Falls— a series of cataracts where the river, confined to a narrow channel, cascades over big boulders. At the head of the falls (the Upper Jumpoff of the old days), a place has been provided to load and unload horses.

The road descends through the forest to Dosewallips Campground in Muscott Flat (14.7 mi/23.7 km; 1600 ft/488 m), where campsites and picnic tables are located among large cedars. The road ends just beyond the campground at the Dosewallips Ranger Station (14.9 mi/24.0 km).

80 DOSEWALLIPS TRAIL

Length 15.4 mi/24.8 km
Access Dosewallips River Road (FS Road 2610)
USGS Maps The Brothers; Mount Deception; Wellesley Peak
Agency Olympic National Park

The Dosewallips Trail begins at Muscott Flat (1600 ft/488 m), where the road ends, and follows the river to its source, then climbs sharply to Hayden Pass, on the Elwha-Dosewallips Divide. Throughout its length, the trail crosses creeks (a dozen are named) and chattering brooks; thus, obtaining water is never a problem. The cold, clear streams tempt the backpacker, especially on a hot day, to pause often for a drink. During spells of warm weather, when the snow melts rapidly, they become brawling torrents.

Near the trailhead, an alternate route, known as the Terrace Trail, branches to the left. This parallel side path, less than a mile long, traverses a bench above the river, then ascends to join the main trail, which climbs up and down between Muscott Flat and Dose Forks. Both paths meander through fir, hemlock, and cedar, with undergrowth of salal, rhododendron, and vine maple. During early summer the rhododendron blossoms add vivid splashes of pink to the somber forest.

The trail divides at Dose Forks (1.4 mi/2.3 km; 1800 ft/549 m). The left branch is the **West Fork Dosewallips Trail**. The main trail goes right, climbing by Soda Springs, where animals are attracted to the mineralized water that seeps from the rocks. The path now contours high above the Dosewallips, which flows through a deep canyon for several miles. Again the trail forks (2.5 mi/4.0 km; 2182 ft/665 m), with the **Constance Pass Trail** branching to the right. The main trail goes left, still traversing high above the river, and crosses Upper Twin Creek just below lovely Calypso Falls. Diamond Mountain can be glimpsed occasionally, and from a spot opposite Hidden Creek one has a distant view of Hatana Falls.

After negotiating a recent blowdown for about a half-mile, the path crosses Deception Creek (7.8 mi/12.6 km; 3156 ft/962 m), the largest tributary coming in from the east. Good campsites are located on the stream's far side and at Camp Marion, a half-mile beyond. The trail then climbs over a steep spur and enters a valley of great beauty, where it meanders alternately through open country and stands of subalpine trees. Wildflowers bloom profusely. Columbia lily, broadleaf arnica, beargrass, cow parsnip, and columbine are abundant, but many other species are also present. The vegetation often grows waist high, and on warm summer days the fragrance of the plants is pronounced.

Beyond the junction with the **Upper Graywolf Trail** (9.2 mi/14.8 km; 3600 ft/1097 m), patches of subalpine forest, mostly silver fir, alternate with meadows. This is primarily open country, and sweeping vistas are present at almost every turn of the trail. Massive peaks loom darkly above flower-filled meadows: Wellesley Peak to the south; Cameron Ridge to the north; Lost Peak, Mount Claywood, and Mount Fromme up valley in the west; Mystery and Little Mystery down valley to the east.

At Bear Camp (11.0 mi/17.7 km; 3850 ft/1173 m), a shelter stands near the trail. Two waterfalls in the river at this point constitute a barrier to trout moving upstream; thus fishing in the Dosewallips ends here.

The path then goes through dense stands of subalpine forest to the junction with the **Lost Pass Trail** in Dose Meadows (12.8 mi/20.6 km; 4450 ft/1356 m). This lush meadowland, covered with grasses and wildflowers, sweeps upward to the high peaks and ridges. The naked cliffs of Mount Fromme, crowned with snow cornices until late summer, enclose the meadows on the west; Lost Peak pokes above the mountainsides to the northeast. The river, now little more than a creek, plunges through a gorge lined with evergreens. Columbine and shooting star brighten the stream's banks.

Wildlife is abundant. One is sure to see and hear marmots as they sun themselves by their burrow entrances. Deer are remarkably tame, and elk may be observed, though rarely. Bears sometimes prowl around the campsites at night, looking for edible items. More often heard, however, are the "river voices," accompanied at times by the scudding sound of boulders moving on the river bottom.

The term "river voices" was coined by Frank O. Shaw when he and Richard Baldwin camped here in 1932. The men mistook the gurgling sounds made by the Dosewallips for the indistinct murmur of voices in the distance. They looked up, expecting to see a troop of Scouts coming up the trail, only to realize they had been deceived by the river.

The trail now trends toward Mount Fromme, then abruptly turns south. Again entering subalpine forest, the path crosses a footbridge spanning the river, then switchbacks and climbs to Camp Number Three (14.5 mi/23.3 km; 5300 ft/1615 m),

Dose Meadows and Mount Fromme

which was established by The Mountaineers in 1920. The camp is hidden on a terrace above the trail, just north of a little brook, but it is seldom used because most hikers are unaware of its existence.

One can leave the trail at this camp and travel cross-country, going directly up heather slopes to the northeast, to reach an outstanding example of subalpine meadowland. The so-called Thousand Acre Meadows—actually they are about half the size the name implies—occupy a glacial cirque shaped like a mitten, complete with thumb. The meadows are believed to have been named by Captain Lloyd B. Hunt, skipper of the *Burro,* a Puget Sound freighter. The attractions here are varied: gorgeous displays of wildflowers brighten the slopes in summer; later, dwarf huckleberries ripen to delicious sweetness. Two brooks, sustained by melting snow, flow across the open country, then down through the forest to the Dosewallips.

Beyond Camp Number Three the trail half-circles the subalpine basin north of Sentinel Peak. This basin, the source of the Dosewallips, is noted in midsummer for fields of avalanche lilies blooming alongside melting snowbanks. Near the streams, pioneer violets, glacier lilies, and buttercups mingle together to form bright splashes of yellow. During late summer, lupine laces the meadows with patches of intense blue.

The trail crosses the river again—now so small one can jump across—and switchbacks up to Hayden Pass. The steep slope is often covered with snow, and until midsummer the hiker may be confronted by a cornice on the summit ridge. This sometimes makes the ascent difficult.

Hayden Pass (15.4 mi/24.8 km; 5847 ft/1782 m), the low point between Sentinel Peak and Mount Fromme, is merely a spine of rotting shale that supports a few wildflowers and stunted trees. The eastern flanks of the peaks, facing the Dosewallips, exhibit pronounced concavity, the result of glacial sculpting. The western slope, leading down to the Elwha River, is much less abrupt. The name Hayden Pass honors General John L. Hayden (1866–1936), who commanded Puget Sound's harbor defenses early in the twentieth century.

Lieutenant Joseph P. O'Neil and Private John Johnson traveled through the Hayden Pass area when scouting toward Mount Anderson in 1885, but the first party to cross the pass from the Dosewallips to the Elwha was probably a group of five prospectors who started on Hood Canal in the summer of 1890. O'Neil named Mount Claywood (6836 ft/2084 m) for Major Henry Clay Wood, Assistant Adjutant General, who published the orders that directed him to reconnoiter the Olympics in 1885. The Mountaineers named Mount Fromme (6655 ft/2028 m) in 1920 to honor Rudo L. Fromme, then Supervisor of the Olympic National Forest, who accompanied the outing and obtained the assistance of the Forest Service in building a trail. (The party thought the lower peak, closer to the pass, was Mount Claywood, therefore mistakenly named the higher one Mount Fromme, but the names are reversed on today's maps.)

The view from Hayden Pass is outstanding. High peaks outline the Dosewallips Valley to the north and east. Beyond the Bailey Range, on the western horizon, Mount Olympus thrusts skyward, but closer at hand, to the south, double-peaked Mount Anderson rises above flower-strewn meadows. Cross-country hikers can approach the mountain by traversing south, along the flanks of Sentinel Peak, then following along the Dosewallips side of the divide. The route becomes progressively more difficult but eventually emerges onto the meadows along Silt Creek, below the Eel Glacier.

Beyond Hayden Pass, the path is known as the **Hayden Pass Trail** and continues to the Elwha River.

81 OLD DOSEWALLIPS TRAIL

Abandoned fragment, no longer maintained
Length 1.5 mi/2.4 km
Access Dosewallips River Road (FS Road 2610)
USGS Map The Brothers
Agencies Olympic National Forest and Olympic National Park

Fifty years ago the Dosewallips River Road ended at Elkhorn Camp (now Elkhorn Campground), and the Dosewallips Trail began at that point. At the Lower Jumpoff, about midway between Bull Elk Canyon and the present national park boundary, the trail crossed the river, then followed up the south side, intersected the Muscott Basin Trail, and recrossed the river at the head of Dosewallips Falls. This crossing was known as the Upper Jumpoff, and the Jumpoff Ranger Station was located here.

The ranger station and the bridges at the crossings have been gone for years. Today, of course, the road follows the river to Muscott Flat, and the Dosewallips Trail begins there, that part of the old trail on the river's north side between Elkhorn and Muscott Flat having been destroyed by the road construction. However, one can still find the abandoned trail on the south side between the two crossings.

This section begins in the national forest but soon crosses into the national park. Near the Lower Jumpoff, in the national forest, it is so overgrown as to be virtually nonexistent, but in the national park it is in reasonably fair condition. Because the only feasible approach today is via the Upper Jumpoff, the trail description begins there and goes downstream. The Upper Jumpoff (1500 ft/457 m) is located at the packer's station just above Dosewallips Falls. At this point the river can be safely forded in late summer and early fall.

On the south side one can find the old trail among the firs and cedars at the base of the mountainside. The trail climbs away from the river, going by a boulder about 12 feet high. The logs that lie across the path have been cut out, and near the boulder the trail is covered with old, moss-covered puncheon.

The trail climbs to a junction (1700 ft/518 m), beside a mossy rock, with another trail, where a board is nailed to a tree. The legend has faded away, but it apparently indicated that the **Muscott Basin Trail** led to the right. The old river trail goes left, or downstream, toward the Lower Jumpoff.

This area was swept by fire in the past, and the slopes are now covered with thick stands of young trees. Rising among them are a few old firs with blackened trunks. The trail climbs above the river, then goes by a couple of knolls that are covered with moss and kinnikinnick. Here one can look down the Dosewallips Canyon.

As it winds through the forest (a mix of trees of all sizes), the trail crosses a glade covered with ferns, vanilla leaf, and bigleaf maple, and works its way through mossy boulders to Tumbling Creek, which flows over a bed of solid rock. The route now becomes brushy. The next stream, Brokenfinger Creek, may have been appropriately named; more than likely someone broke his finger while crossing the slippery rocks and logs.

The trail has countless logs lying across it, but the thick growth of little trees is more frustrating. Only an inch or two in diameter, they grow in the trail itself, with brushy limbs that make it difficult to force one's way through.

Beyond Brokenfinger Creek, the trail goes into the national forest (1.2 mi/ 1.9 km), but the boundary line is not marked. The path descends to the river, where it disappears entirely. Formerly, it led to the Lower Jumpoff, then climbed the opposite bank to where the road now traverses (1.5 mi/2.4 km; 1200 ft/365 m).

82 MUSCOTT BASIN TRAIL

Abandoned fragment, no longer maintained
Length 2.0 mi/3.2 km
Access Old Dosewallips Trail
USGS Map The Brothers
Agency Olympic National Park

The path begins south of the Dosewallips River at a junction (1700 ft/ 518 m) with the **Old Dosewallips Trail** near the Upper Jumpoff, the point where the Old Dosewallips Trail crossed back to the river's north side. One must ford the stream to reach the trail, and caution should be exercised. When the river is low and clear, the bottom is visible, and it is easy to wade; but when it is higher and discolored by glacial silt, it is treacherous because one could unknowingly step into a deep hole and be swept downstream.

A moss-cushioned boulder beside the trail marks the point where it departs from the Old Dosewallips Trail. As it traverses the mountainside high above the stream, the route parallels the river for about a mile, and one must constantly climb over logs that have fallen across the path. The ground is padded by hummocks of moss several inches thick, and the footpath has been abandoned so long that it, too, is covered with thick growths of moss in many places.

After crossing a rock slide composed of big, moss-covered boulders, the trail climbs a bit, then traverses through a stony area. The forest is a mixture of Douglas-fir and western hemlock; the heavy undergrowth is chiefly salal and rhododendron.

The trail goes by several huge boulders composed of pillow lava. They are from 30 to 40 feet high, with moss and ferns clinging to their sides. Beyond them the trail makes an ascending traverse on the steep slope, climbing through stands of fir and hemlock where many large boulders, cloaked with moss, lie scattered about.

The route then intersects (ca. 1.0 mi/1.6 km; 2100 ft/640 m) a primitive way trail that climbs up from the Dosewallips. One can cross the river at the Dosewallips Campground and climb this path to the Muscott Basin Trail. Although shorter, it is a poorer approach. Beyond this junction the trail turns south, paralleling Muscott Creek, and crosses a steep gully that runs straight up and down the mountain, then comes out to a more or less open area, where the creek is visible below. The trail descends to the stream and crosses to the other side (2.0 mi/3.2 km; 2900 ft/884 m).

The undergrowth along the creek is luxuriant, mostly willow and salmonberry. At this point one can look up the valley and see the ridge at the head of Muscott Basin.

The trail now ends at the creek crossing, although bits and pieces of the old path—mostly obscured by slide alder, willow, and vine maple—can be found for another mile or so. The path then disappears in a thick tangle of brush. One is easily discouraged here. Ahead are seemingly endless, impenetrable thickets. However, the hiker who perseveres will come out into the more or less open country of Muscott Basin, which is a good place to camp.

This is the usual approach to Wild Cat Lake, which is located in the next basin to the east, near the head of Tumbling Creek. The lake, which contains Eastern brook trout, can be reached by climbing over the ridge between the two basins.

83 LAKE CONSTANCE TRAIL

Length 2.0 mi/3.2 km
Access Dosewallips River Road (FS Road 2610)
USGS Map The Brothers
Agency Olympic National Park

The Lake Constance Trail is a boot-built track which was created by the trampling of human feet over many years. Although it scarcely rises to the dignity of a decent footpath, it receives heavy use because it is not dangerous if one exercises caution. However, the trail's steepness—it ascends 3250 feet in 2 miles—makes it a strenuous route for the backpacker.

The path begins on the Dosewallips Road (roughly 4.0 mi/6.4 km beyond the 2001 road washout) at Constance Creek (0.3 mi/0.5 km beyond the park boundary; 1400 ft/427 m) and climbs steeply northward. As it follows the creek's course, the route goes straight up the forested mountainside, and one must hold onto the little trees while ascending the difficult places.

About midway the terrain levels out briefly. At this point Half Acre Rock (1.0 mi/1.6 km; 3200 ft/975 m) either fell from a high cliff or was left by the glacier that came down from above. The huge block of basalt lies east of the trail, and its exploration makes an interesting side trip. The most unusual feature here is The Guillotine, a rock formation large enough to behead Paul Bunyan.

The route now becomes more difficult, and one has to clamber over fallen trees and fight through thick brush; in the steepest places the hiker must cling to the limbs or exposed roots of small trees when ascending or descending. At one point the only possible way necessitates walking in the edge of the creek bed. During the last half mile, the trail climbs steeply over rock ledges and ascends a low precipice over which the creek plunges, leaping free of the rock. The trail climbs sharply almost to the brink of the lake, then the grade eases.

The path ends at Lake Constance (2.0 mi/3.2 km; 4650 ft/1417 m), which lies cupped in a rocky bowl, or glacial cirque, at the base of Mount Constance. The lake is bordered by subalpine forest which is overshadowed by walls of pillow basalt, rocks that erupted on the floor of an ancient sea, the lava beds now standing almost vertical. The 11-acre lake, which once was stocked with Eastern brook trout, varies in color from intense blue to emerald green, depending upon the light, and

Lake Constance

mirrors the surrounding cliffs and crags. The lake was formed by glacial action and rock slides. An enormous talus cone lies at the base of a cliff to the northeast.

Mountain goats are abundant here. Wool clings to the brush, and the curious animals often approach campsites, especially at night. Marmots and birds are also present. Unfortunately, because of overuse, camping is now by reservation only, and the lake water is polluted. Camping quotas are in effect May 1–September 30. Contact the Wilderness Information Center for details.

84 WEST FORK DOSEWALLIPS TRAIL

Length 9.1 mi/14.7 km
Access Dosewallips Trail
USGS Maps The Brothers; Mount Steel
Agency Olympic National Park

This route, also known as the Anderson Pass Trail, provides the shortest, quickest approach by trail to Mount Anderson, the dominant peak of the eastern Olympics. The trail begins on the **Dosewallips Trail** at Dose Forks (1800 ft/549 m), in a setting of tall firs, about a half mile below the confluence of the two branches of the Dosewallips River, and follows the West Fork to Anderson Pass.

Good campsites are located at Dose Forks along the north bank of the river, upstream from the bridge. The trail crosses the Dosewallips, where sunlight streaks down, glinting the waters, then meanders through forests of Douglas-fir having an understory of rhododendron, huckleberry, and salal. During early summer the pink rhododendron blossoms accent the dark green of the conifers; bunchberry and queencup beadlily carpet the forest floor.

The trail crosses the West Fork (0.9 mi/1.4 km; 1800 ft/549 m) just above Dose Forks, the point where the North Fork and the West Fork come together. Both streams flow through steep-walled canyons—the West Fork through a slot carved in thick sandstone beds turned on edge. The high footbridge overlooks the confluence of the two streams, where the clear waters of the West Fork mingle with the milky ones of the North Fork, the latter carrying a heavy load of glacial silt from the Eel Glacier on Mount Anderson.

On the north side the trail climbs through stands of fir and hemlock, but the soil is thin and stony, and the trees are not large. After an extended climb, the trail reaches a high point (2429 ft/740 m), where one can look across the West Fork. The route then descends sharply to Big Timber Camp (2.7 mi/4.3 km; 2300 ft/701 m), located by the river in a stand of Douglas-fir. Vine maple forms an understory beneath the old firs, which are not as large as the name would imply. Beyond this camp the rhododendrons disappear, and the up-and-down trail meanders through a dark forest, where pads of moss cover the ground, bunchberry and queencup beadlily blossom in June, and vine maple and devil's club grow in the damper places.

Excellent campsites are located at Diamond Meadow (5.3 mi/8.5 km; 2692 ft/821 m), a pleasant place among the tall trees, where the hiker can listen to the birds singing and the river rushing by. The small glade—kept free of timber by avalanche snow that melts late in the season—is overgrown with cow parsnip, vanilla leaf, and huckleberry.

About a half mile beyond the meadow, the trail crosses the West Fork via the Lower Log Bridge, then steepens as it climbs up the now canyonlike valley, ascending what geologist Rowland W. Tabor calls a riser in a ladder created by an alpine glacier during the Ice Age. The river becomes a series of cascades thundering down a narrow defile, swirling among sandstone boulders left by the glacier. At the Upper Log Bridge the trail recrosses to the north side and comes out into Honeymoon Meadows (7.5 mi/12.1 km; 3527 ft/1075 m), where the terrain flattens to form the step of the ladder.

The origin of the name Honeymoon Meadows is disputed. One account alleges the Edward Diamonds, who were married on Christmas Day in 1885, honeymooned here; another, that the A. E. Smiths did so in 1925. The second version is more plausible because no trail existed in 1885 and the country would have been snowbound in December. The open meadows here are covered with lush grasses and clumps of false hellebore. At their western edge, the **LaCrosse Pass Trail** (7.6 mi/ 12.2 km; 3627 ft/1105 m) branches to the left.

Beyond this junction, the trail ascends sharply through subalpine forest to Anderson Pass Shelter (8.3 mi/13.4 km; 4100 ft/1250 m), known to hikers as Camp Siberia or Little Siberia because cold winds sweep down from the Anderson Glacier. However, it is a luxury hotel compared to the climbers' high camp at Flypaper Pass, 2400 feet higher up the mountain. The nearby marshy spots are colorful in early summer with the blooms of shooting stars, marsh marigolds, and avalanche lilies. Winter wrens flit through the bushes, frequently pausing to trill their simple song.

West of the shelter, beyond a small stream, piles of big boulders extend up the mountainside, but the trail avoids them by turning north and climbing through the forest. An alpine pool at Anderson Pass (9.1 mi/14.7 km; 4464 ft/ 1361 m) mirrors the surrounding peaks, where one can look down the Dosewallips and see Mount Constance and Warrior Peak on the horizon. Here the trail merges with the **Enchanted Valley Trail**, the route coming up from the East Fork Quinault River, and the **Anderson Glacier Trail**, which climbs part way up the mountain.

85 ANDERSON GLACIER TRAIL

Length 0.7 mi/1.1 km
Access West Fork Dosewallips Trail
USGS Map Mount Steel
Agency Olympic National Park

This spur trail climbs from Anderson Pass (4464 ft/1361 m) on the **West Fork Dosewallips Trail** to the moraine alongside Anderson Glacier on the south side of Mount Anderson. The path ascends through stands of mountain hemlock, then switchbacks up steep slopes covered with heather, huckleberry, and fields of avalanche lilies. The trail ends at the moraine (0.7 mi/1.1 km; 5200 ft/1585 m), but one can wander at will along the rock wall and enjoy the views—north to Mount Anderson, which is often flecked with fresh snow after summer storms; south across the upper Quinault to White Mountain. A good campsite is located by a little tarn near the lateral moraine, which consists of huge, angular boulders and rocks of all sizes piled up in a long row. The glacier's terminus is littered with debris, and large chunks of ice float in the lake impounded between the ice and the moraine. The glacier has receded a great deal during the last sixty years, leaving a field of rubble—sharp, angular rocks strewn across the barren glacial bed. The silt-laden lake has also become much larger.

The glaciers on Mount Anderson are, despite their recession, the larger in the eastern Olympics, and the mountain looks truly alpine from this

Anderson Pass

sharp peaks overshadowing the ice. The ascent should be attempted only by experienced climbers.

86 CONSTANCE PASS TRAIL

Length 8.5 mi/12.7 km
Access Dosewallips Trail
USGS Maps The Brothers; Mount Deception
Agency Olympic National Park

This route begins at a junction with the **Dosewallips Trail** (2.5 mi/4.0 km from the road's end; 2182 ft/665 m) and climbs to Sunnybrook Meadows, then over Del Monte Ridge and Constance Pass, beyond which it contours above the headwaters of the Dungeness River. Although continuously uphill to the ridge crest, the trail is one of the smoothest in the Olympics, neither rocky, muddy, nor eroded by streams. Sunnybrook Meadows and Del Monte Ridge were named in 1926 by the Boy Scouts at Camp Parsons, near Hood Canal. They named the ridge after Billy Del Monte, their West Indian cook.

The trail makes the steep ascent above the Dosewallips River via long, sweeping switchbacks. The slopes are thinly clad with Douglas-fir and a bit of western white pine, and the forest floor is open in many places, but usually thickly overgrown with salal. As the trail climbs higher, views appear; one looks up the West Fork Dosewallips, which is bordered by snow-clad peaks—Elklick, LaCrosse, and Diamond. Wellesley Peak looms to the northwest. The sound of the Dosewallips comes up faintly from below.

Ascending the spur between Sunny Brook and Lower Twin Creek, the route alternately looks over the Dosewallips or across the slopes below Del Monte Ridge to Inner Constance (7339 ft/2237 m). The forest is denser here, the trees bearded with lichen, the rhododendrons abundant. A perennial seep spring near the trail (2.0 mi/3.2 km; 3600 ft/1097 m) is the only place where water can be obtained between the river and Sunnybrook Meadows.

The forest changes to subalpine growth, then the trail breaks out into Sunnybrook Meadows, an expanse of meadowland on the south slope of Del Monte Ridge. The meadows are luxuriant with lupine, beargrass, cow parsnip, and huckleberry and broken intermittently by groves of subalpine and silver fir. The trail crosses several streams which, collectively, form the headwaters of Sunny Brook. Across the Dosewallips Valley rise The Brothers and the ridges west of the peak. Sunnybrook Camp (2.5 mi/4.0 km; 5000 ft/1524 m) is located beyond the last creek, in a copse of silver fir and Alaska cedar.

The trail now climbs through meadows, where the hiker sees an expanding panorama of the Olympics, although the view to the northeast is blocked by Del Monte Ridge. Another campsite (3.5 mi/5.6 km; 5650 ft/1722 m) on a grassy knoll beyond a tarn overlooks the mountains to the west. A brook flows nearby. Higher up, the path switchbacks across meadowland and patches of finely broken shale. Low-growing juniper sprawls among rocks darkened by lichen.

The crest of Del Monte Ridge (4.0 mi/6.4 km; 6500 ft/1981 m), where the trail crosses, is a wide expanse of gravel and thin soil covered with tufts of grass and piles of broken rock. Marmots live among the boulders and rend the air with shrill whistles when hikers approach. A number of peaks are visible from the ridge, including Deception, Mystery, Little Mystery, and Inner Constance. The valley of the West Fork Dosewallips trends to the southwest.

The cross-country route to the Mount Mystery area begins at this point. One leaves the trail here and follows the ridge to Gunsight Pass (6350 ft/1936 m), so named because a sharp needle rises in the center of the notch between Mount Mystery and Little Mystery. The peaks are composed of basalt and thus contrast with the sandstones and shales of the ridge. Of special interest is Deception Basin, an alpine area bounded by Deception, Mystery, and Fricaba. A glacier and snowfield lie adjacent to each other on the north slope of Mount Mystery, the meltwater from them merging to form Deception Creek. One side of the stream is milky with glacial silt; the other side is clear.

Beyond the crest of Del Monte Ridge, the trail descends as it follows the narrow ridge. Barren talus slopes and perpetual snowfields—the source of the Dungeness River—lie on the northern slope, and directly ahead are the cliffs of Inner Constance and Mount Constance. The Brothers rise to the south. After rounding a spur, the trail overlooks a basin to the north where Home Lake occupies a hollow in the mountainside.

Constance Pass (5.0 mi/8.0 km; 5850 ft/1783 m) marks the eastern terminus of Del Monte Ridge, where it abuts the cliffs of Inner Constance. The contact line between the volcanic and sedimentary rocks is plainly evident.

The route now angles to the left, and the trail descends the north slope, crossing shale slides and meadowland. Home Lake (5.4 mi/8.7 km; 5350 ft/1631 m) has no visible outlet, but a stream flows into it on the upper side. The lake's level

Home Lake, Constance Pass Trail

fluctuates, leaving a ring around its margin in late summer. The setting is nonetheless scenic: the tarn's clear, greenish water reflects the rocky hillside to the west, and the neighboring slopes are covered with rough boulders and a few subalpine firs.

Below Home Lake the trail descends through subalpine forest, where huge chunks of basalt lie scattered among the trees. Lupine is abundant; in late summer the clusters of blue flowers contrast with the dark rock. The trail goes by a large snowfield, crosses a rock slide below the cliffs of Mount Constance, climbs slightly, then contours northward at the 5000 ft/1524 m level through open country and subalpine forests. On the right Warrior Peak overlooks the trail; left is a view across the upper Dungeness Valley and back to Constance Pass.

The trail crosses into the national forest (7.6 mi/12.2 km; 5000 ft/1524 m) and ends at Boulder Shelter (8.5 mi/12.7 km; 4900 ft/1494 m) in a three-way junction with the **Upper Dungeness Trail** and the **Upper Big Quilcene Trail**.

87 LOST PASS TRAIL

Length 2.8 mi/4.5 km
Access Dosewallips Trail
USGS Map Wellesley Peak
Agency Olympic National Park

This route leaves the **Dosewallips Trail** at Dose Meadows (4450 ft/ 1356 m) and climbs steeply up the north side of the valley. Now and then the trail switchbacks beneath outcrops of sandstone, where penstemons add a bit of color.

At Lost Pass (0.8 mi/1.3 km; 5500 ft/1676 m), the low point between Lost Peak and Mount Claywood, a wide expanse of country is in view: Lost Peak, Mount Claywood, Wellesley Peak, and Sentinel Peak are close at hand; Stephen Peak is visible in the distance.

The trail then skirts the headwaters of Lost River. Here are mountain meadows as beautiful as any in the Olympics, where wildflowers blossom with lavish abandon, growing in such profusion the hiker cannot avoid trampling them. During midsummer millions of avalanche lilies wave white petals with every passing breeze or rub shoulders with magenta paintbrush and common bistort. Other varieties are also present—fescue sandwort, subalpine spiraea, thistle, and arnica. Marsh marigolds, anemones, buttercups, and elephant's head brighten the moister spots. During late summer the meadows are colorful with lupine, buckwheat, arnica, paintbrush, and the aster fleabane, or mountain daisy.

Three Sons Camp (1.7 mi/2.7 km; 5400 ft/1646 m) is located between two brooks on a level area protected from the wind by subalpine trees. A rock slide comes down from Lost Peak almost to the camp. Beyond this campsite the trail climbs through meadowland covered with a riot of wildflowers—primarily asters, buckwheat, and lupine—and by dwarf huckleberry. When the fruit ripens in late summer, bears are attracted to the area.

As the trail gains altitude, Mount Olympus lifts its snowy crown above the meadows to the west, and Mount Anderson pierces the sky due south, beyond Hayden Pass. Near Cameron Pass the peaks of the Bailey Range come into view, as do the mountains near Low Divide.

The route becomes the **Cameron Creek Trail** at Cameron Pass (2.8 mi/4.5 km; 6450 ft/1966 m), where the hiker can look out over Cameron Basin toward the distant Strait of Juan de Fuca. The unnamed peak (6733 ft/2052 m) west of the pass can be reached by an easy walk. Here one has an unobstructed view of the Olympics in all directions. Mount Cameron stands directly east, with its steep glaciers on the north slope, and one can look down into Cameron Basin.

DUCKABUSH

Heading in the southeastern Olympics, the narrow Duckabush Valley forms a long arc from O'Neil Pass to Hood Canal. The forest growth on the valley's lower slopes is luxuriant, the dense stands of conifers masking the rough terrain, although cliffs at times break the green cloak, and avalanche paths scar many mountainsides. Because the mountains are lower here than they are to the north, the alpland is not extensive, but none of the meadows elsewhere is more beautiful than LaCrosse Basin at the head of the Duckabush River or Elk Basin on the First Divide.

The Duckabush is paralleled by steep ridges and snow-capped peaks. The ridge to the north, lying between the Duckabush and Dosewallips, reaches its maximum elevation in several peaks—Jupiter, Elklick, LaCrosse, and White Mountain; the one to the south, isolating the Duckabush from the Hamma Hamma and Skokomish Rivers, culminates in The Brothers, Lena, Hopper, Steel, and Duckabush. O'Neil Pass, at the head of the Duckabush, provides access to the Quinault.

Many short, swift tributaries flow into the Duckabush, adding to its volume. The largest ones are One Too Many Creek and Crazy Creek. The latter tumbles down from Elk Basin and the snowfields on Mount Stone. The river has its source in the stagnant Twin Glaciers on the north face of Mount Duckabush. Next to The Brothers, this is the most prominent peak in this area, and it has had five names— Susan, Skookum, Arline, Steel, and Duckabush. The first three have gone the way of the great auk, but the name Mount Steel was later given to a nearby peak. The name honors Will G. Steel, who helped Lieutenant Joseph P. O'Neil organize the 1890 U.S. Army–Oregon Alpine Club joint expedition.

The Duckabush is a swift river, and its waters are clear despite the fact that the Twin Glaciers help sustain the stream. The stream is characterized by numerous cascades and rapids, where the current swirls over and among large boulders. The blue green water, shaded by the overhanging maples and alders, flashes white whenever it breaks over moss-covered rocks and reflects innumerable glints from vagrant shafts of sunlight.

The wilderness of the upper Duckabush is adequately protected because it lies within Olympic National Park, and since 1984 the 6-mile segment between Little Hump and the park boundary has been part of The Brothers Wilderness and thus equally well protected. However, the last few miles between Little Hump and Hood Canal flow through lands subject to commercial activity. The Duckabush in its entirety should be declared a "wild river" in order to keep it free from development.

The upper Duckabush was first explored in the summer of 1890 by the O'Neil expedition and by a party led by Judge James Wickersham of Tacoma.

ROADS

Duckabush River Road (FS Road 2510). This road leaves US 101, the Olympic Highway, 3.5 mi/5.6 km south of Brinnon on the Hood Canal and goes by

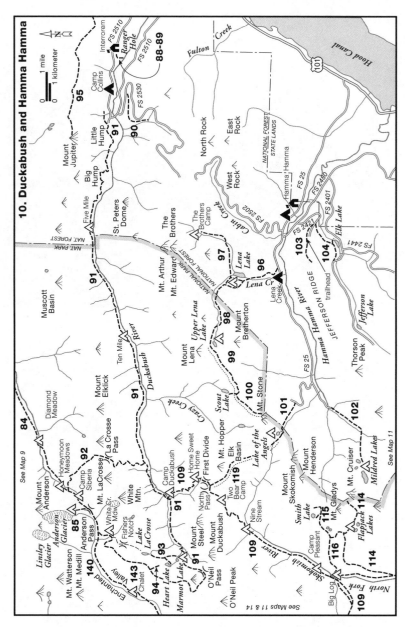

10. Duckabush and Hamma Hamma

woodland homes and through stands of large second-growth Douglas-fir. The road enters the Olympic National Forest at the old Interrorem Guard Station (3.6 mi/ 5.8 km). The rustic cabin, built in 1906, was the first government building constructed on the Olympic Forest Reserve (before it was renamed Olympic National Forest). The road then penetrates wild, rugged country. Camp Collins (5.0 mi/

Looking down the Duckabush

8.1 km) is an automobile campground on the north bank of the Duckabush. At 6.0 mi/9.7 km, FS Road 2510–060 branches to the right and provides access to the Duckabush Trail.

The river road continues up the valley a short distance, then crosses the Duckabush to the south side and heads back toward Hood Canal. At 6.4 mi/10.3 km the road forks. FS Road 2510 continues as the left branch; the right branch becomes FS Road 2530. The Murhut Falls Trail begins on FS Road 2530 one mile beyond the junction of that road with FS Road 2510.

FS Road 2510–060. This stub road, on the eastern slopes of Little Hump, at the foot of Mount Jupiter, is slightly more than one-tenth of a mile in length and begins 6.0 mi/9.7 km from US 101 on FS Road 2510. The road leads to the registration station for the Duckabush Trail, adjacent to a commodious parking area that will accommodate at least twenty vehicles. Hikers should not leave valuables in cars parked here because serious vandalism has occurred at this trailhead.

Mount Jupiter Road (Cormorant Way). Access to the Mount Jupiter Trail is provided by the Mount Jupiter Road, which is signed Cormorant Way at its junction with US 101 just south of Black Point. The junction, 0.9 mi/1.4 km north of the Duckabush River Road (FS Road 2510) and 3.0 mi/4.8 km south of the Dosewallips River Road (FS Road 2610), can be spotted easily because a small bulldozer sits perched atop a huge stump some 12 to 15 feet high on the east side of US 101. Note: Mount Jupiter Road has seasonal closures.

To reach the trailhead, drive west on Cormorant Way 5.9 mi/9.5km. The road meanders through clearcuts and stands of second-growth fir where logging is actively occurring. One should be alert for logging trucks and also watch for guidance signs at intersections with other roads. Parking at the trailhead (ca. 2100 ft/640 m) is limited, and drivers should use spots that will not interfere with the movements of the logging trucks.

88 RANGER HOLE TRAIL

Length 0.8 mi/1.3 km
Access Duckabush River Road (FS Road 2510)
USGS Map Brinnon
Agency Olympic National Forest

The trail begins at the old Interrorem Guard Station (175 ft/53 m), on the Duckabush River Road, just beyond the national forest boundary. The square log cabin, with its pyramidal, shake-covered roof, dates from 1906; Emery Finch, son of Hoodsport pioneers, served as the first ranger. The fishing hole below the station was called Ranger Hole because the ranger lived at the guard station.

The well-maintained trail begins near the cabin and traverses an area, logged years ago, that now supports what are probably the largest specimens of second-growth Douglas-fir to be found in the Olympics. The trees are up to 150 feet tall, and many are more than 2 feet in diameter.

Near the trail's beginning, the **Interrorem Nature Trail** circles to the left, but the Ranger Hole Trail heads directly toward the Duckabush River. At first the path is fairly level, and the forest has an understory of bigleaf and vine maple. The rotting stumps of the giant firs that were logged here give silent testimony to the forest's former grandeur.

The trail then descends and one can hear the river, but the sound is distant and muted. For a long, straight stretch the broad, smooth path forms an aisle through the trees, where the ground cover is mostly deer fern and sword fern. Winter wrens trill their song constantly from the heights of the bigleaf maples. The birds appear to be happy here in this pleasant environment, and the hiker often sees them flitting about beneath the arches of vine maple.

After descending at a moderate grade, the trail drops steeply, and the river becomes much louder. Masses of sword ferns border the path, which comes down to the river bottom and turns right, or upstream, to a campsite, then leads out to a promontory that overlooks Ranger Hole (0.8 mi/1.3 km; 125 ft/38 m).

Here, where countless fishermen have cast their lines, the Duckabush forms a deep pool of clear, green-tinted water. Above the pool the river swirls with white rapids as it rushes through a narrow chute between rock walls, then drops down a slot into the deep recess that forms Ranger Hole. The water, full of air bubbles, then wells up from below.

Ranger Hole is one of the most picturesque fishing spots in the Olympics, where the steelhead lie in wait—or did. According to anglers who know the area, the hole has been fished out, and one cannot catch anything, at least during the summer, when the river is high.

Below Ranger Hole the Duckabush flows broadly onward to Hood Canal.

89 INTERROREM NATURE TRAIL

Length 0.5 mi/0.8 km
Access Duckabush River Road (FS Road 2510)
USGS Map Brinnon
Agency Olympic National Forest

This nature trail forms a half-mile loop east of the **Ranger Hole Trail,** beginning and ending about 100 yards beyond Interrorem Guard Station (175 ft/ 53 m).

The path might well be called the Trail of the Giant Stumps. The ferns, the second-growth forest (Douglas-firs up to 30 inches in diameter) and the vine maple are beautiful, but the enormous stumps of the cedars and firs—7 to 9 feet in diameter—are more impressive. One is saddened to think that the trees were cut down merely to be sawed into boards.

As the trail circles around, it goes through a bower of vine maple, then comes out behind the guard station and rejoins the Ranger Hole Trail.

90 MURHUT FALLS TRAIL

Length 1.5 mi/2.4 km
Access Duckabush River Road (FS Road 2510)
USGS Maps Brinnon; Mount Jupiter
Agency Olympic National Forest

The beginning of the Murhut Falls Trail is not signed, but it is located on FS Road 2530, one mile beyond that road's junction with FS Road 2510. This trail is relatively unknown and is probably used mostly by people who reside in the vicinity.

The first mile isn't the usual mountain path but simply the track of an abandoned logging road. Although it appears to be well used, and looks as if it has been around a while, it is in relatively good condition. The trail climbs gradually at a fairly steep grade to the shoulder (1.0 mi/1.6 km; 1200 ft/366 m) of a mountain spur. The old logging road ends at this point, but a man-made trail goes on, crossing over the ridge, then descending to a point near Murhut Creek (1.5 mi/ 2.4 km; ca. 1400 ft/427 m), which follows down a steep-walled miniature canyon. The path then follows up the narrow valley of the stream to what is supposedly a vantage point from where the falls can be seen, but it is impossible to obtain a good view here because one stands in a narrow canyon at a lower elevation than the falls; consequently, the terrain above them is largely hidden. Because the stream emerges from a narrow gorge, the view of the falls is somewhat restricted by the topography.

Murhut Falls is a double cascade—both vertically and horizontally. The double upper falls drop about 70 feet into a basin, and then the water spills over the lip and plunges another 30 feet or so, both the upper and lower falls being divided into two streams each, with the result that the view, although restricted, is quite scenic.

91 DUCKABUSH TRAIL

Length 22.2 mi/35.7 km
Access FS Road 2510–060
USGS Maps The Brothers; Mount Jupiter; Mount Steel
Agencies Olympic National Forest and Olympic National Park

A disconcerting up-and-down route, the trail up the Duckabush River leads to beautiful subalpine meadows at the head of the valley, then climbs to O'Neil Pass on the Grand Divide. The trail begins in the national forest (440 ft/ 134 m) at the end of FS Road 2510–060, a spur slightly more than one-tenth of a mile long that branches from FS Road 2510 exactly 6 miles from US 101 near Hood Canal.

The trail at first follows an abandoned roadbed, then enters The Brothers Wilderness as it climbs over Little Hump (1.2 mi/1.9 km; 900 ft/284 m). The trail then descends to the river. This country was logged in the early 1900s, and thick stands of second-growth fir now obscure the grade of an old logging railroad.

The trail turns north, to avoid the river's gorge, and abruptly ascends Big Hump, a rocky buttress on the flanks of Mount Jupiter. As it climbs alongside moss-covered pillow basalt that was smoothed by glacial ice, the trail makes numerous short, steep switchbacks, ascending 1000 ft/305 m in about a mile. St. Peters Dome (4490 ft/1369 m) is visible across the river from a lookout point on the trail.

Rowland W. Tabor, a geologist with the U.S. Geological Survey, has pointed out that the Little Hump and Big Hump are risers of glacial steps in the canyon,

Marmot Lake

where the Duckabush Glacier cut deeply during the Ice Age. After the glacier retreated, the valley may have contained a lake dammed by the Big Hump until the river cut through the barrier.

Beyond Big Hump (3.5 mi/5.6 km; 1700 ft/518 m), which thus far has kept civilization from invading the upper Duckabush, the trail enters the gloom of undisturbed virgin forest. The branches of the tall, slim firs and hemlocks are covered with lichen. The route then descends to the river at Five Mile Camp (5.3 mi/8.5 km; 1200 ft/366 m).

The trail enters the national park (6.7 mi/10.8 km; 1300 ft/396 m) in a deep forest setting and climbs gradually, making descents from time to time. Ten Mile Camp (10.0 mi/16.1 km; 1500 ft/457 m), in a setting of large firs and cedars, is located close to the river. The turbulent stream, its bed filled with large boulders, booms continuously, and the sound is calculated to quickly lull the tired backpacker to sleep.

The isolation and solitude make the upper Duckabush one of the most attractive areas in the Olympics, the type of country that lures the dedicated backpacker. Above Ten Mile Camp the trail winds through dense stands of fir and hemlock, but intermittent breaks in the forest provide sweeping vistas of fir-clad mountainsides. Beyond the junction with the **LaCrosse Pass Trail** (15.8 mi/25.4 km; 2677 ft/816 m), the trail meanders through the forest, which now includes silver fir and grand fir in addition to the usual Douglas-fir and western hemlock. The trail then swings back to the river and crosses to Camp Duckabush, also known as Upper Duckabush Camp (17.5 mi/28.2 km; 2700 ft/823 m). Good campsites are located here beneath towering Douglas-firs.

A huge log that spanned the river at this point served as a hikers' bridge for many years, but recent floods have swept it away. Because no bridge has been built, crossing the river can be tricky early in the season. One can cross from the north bank to an island in the river, then cross from the island to Camp Duckabush on the south bank. Carry a long pole when wading to help you maintain your balance.

Near Camp Duckabush the trail intersects the **North Fork Skokomish Trail** (17.6 mi/28.3 km), then follows the route of the O'Neil expedition, which explored this country in the summer of 1890. The trail crosses Home Sweet Home Creek and traverses the slopes south of the river, crossing several streams—including Wild Bear Creek—where cataracts leap down cliffs. The route then alternates through patches of subalpine forest and open glades with rank growths of salmonberry, devil's club, and slide alder.

The trail now climbs steeply above the river, which cascades through a deep, narrow canyon, then descends to the stream and crosses to the north bank. The crossing can be difficult, particularly in early summer, when the river is high. At this time, too, the path may be hidden in places by patches of snow, sprinkled with forest litter, that contrast with the gloom of the shaded defiles.

The route leads sharply upward to Marmot Lake (21.1 mi/34.0 km; 4350 ft/ 1326 m), a gemlike tarn with a tree-studded isle near its center. The lake occupies an ice-carved basin and is edged by rolling meadows and groves of mountain hemlock and Alaska cedar, with cliffs to the northwest. Nearby is a junction with the **LaCrosse Basin Trail.** The lake was named on August 12, 1890, by two of Lieutenant O'Neil's scouts.

South of the lake the bluff overlooking the Duckabush provides a good view. Across the valley, Mount Steel and Mount Duckabush, clad with snow and ice, soar into the sky, and one can look down the Duckabush Valley and see Mount Jupiter, 15 miles distant.

Beyond Marmot Lake the trail climbs steadily toward O'Neil Pass, traversing subalpine meadows where, on warm summer afternoons, marmots sun on rocks near their burrow entrances and greet intruders with shrill whistles. This is the animal's danger signal, yet the creatures do not appear to be alarmed by the hiker's presence, and one can often approach them to within a few feet.

O'Neil Pass (22.2 mi/35.7 km; 4950 ft/1509 m) lies between Mount Duckabush and Overlook Peak. Lieutenant O'Neil's pack train crossed this pass on September 20, 1890, during his exploration of the southern Olympics. Beyond this point the route becomes the **O'Neil Pass Trail,** which contours around the mountain to a junction with the **Enchanted Valley Trail.**

92 LACROSSE PASS TRAIL

Length 6.5 mi/10.5 km
Access Duckabush Trail; West Fork Dosewallips Trail
USGS Map Mount Steel
Agency Olympic National Park

An across-the-ridge route between the Duckabush and Dosewallips Rivers, the LaCrosse Pass Trail begins (2677 ft/816 m) on the **Duckabush Trail** 1.7 mi/2.7 km east of Camp Duckabush, climbs steeply to LaCrosse Pass, then descends to the West Fork Dosewallips. As it climbs out of the Duckabush Valley, the trail ascends almost 3000 feet via many short, steep switchbacks. Most of the distance it goes through deep forest. One should carry water.

Near LaCrosse Pass, the views southward from the high meadows become spectacular. The pointed subalpine firs are silhouetted against cloud banks, and two peaks dominate the skyline to the southwest. The rocky, six-sided peak is Mount Steel, the lower of the two. This mountain, streaked with snowfields, reminds one of a turreted and buttressed castle. Beyond it Mount Duckabush outlines its jagged ridge crest and snow dome against the blue sky.

The view north from LaCrosse Pass (3.0 mi/4.8 km; 5566 ft/1697 m), which lies between Mount LaCrosse and Mount Elklick, is equally striking. The glacier-scarred bulk of Mount Anderson rises in lonely splendor above the neighboring peaks, and part of the Anderson Glacier is visible. This ice field is usually covered with snow until late summer, making it appear to be a large snowfield.

North of LaCrosse Pass the trail goes through luxuriant meadows bordered by clumps of subalpine fir. Buttercups, avalanche lilies, and other wildflowers create showy, colorful displays in midsummer; but the eye is mesmerized by Mount Anderson, which dominates the northern skyline until lost to sight when the trail enters the forest. The route then descends at a moderate grade to the **West Fork Dosewallips Trail** near the upper end of Honeymoon Meadows (6.5 mi/10.5 km; 3627 ft/1105 m). A good camping area is located here, isolated from the usually crowded one in Honeymoon Meadows.

93 LACROSSE BASIN TRAIL

Length 1.5 mi/2.4 km
Access Duckabush Trail
USGS Map Mount Steel
Agency Olympic National Park

LaCrosse Basin is a band of high country—the O'Neil expedition called it a level plateau—that extends about 3 miles in a north-south direction from Fisher's Notch to O'Neil Pass. This upland varies in width but is generally about a half mile across except in the north, where it broadens. Marmot Lake and Heart Lake are located at midpoint; Lake LaCrosse near the upper end. The lakes occupy glacier-carved depressions or little cirques. Broken by rocky knolls and groves of mountain hemlock, the basin is mostly open meadowland, where meandering brooks glint in the sunlight. During the winter the snow accumulates to great depths, and patches linger until late summer. Consequently, the lakes may remain frozen well into July, or sometimes early August. When bare spots appear on the mountainsides, the meadows turn into brilliant wildflower gardens, where elk, deer, and bear may be observed on occasion.

The trail through the basin traverses subalpine country equal to any found in the Olympics. The path begins at a junction with the **Duckabush Trail** near Marmot Lake (4350 ft/1326 m) and climbs steeply through subalpine forest to a viewpoint that overlooks the Duckabush Valley. Far to the east, Mount Jupiter appears to rise directly from the valley's center. The trail levels out, then forks (0.5 mi/0.8 km; 4900 ft/1494 m). The left branch meanders several hundred yards to Heart Lake (4850 ft/1478 m); the right branch traverses northward, with a few ups and downs, over meadowland, ending at Lake LaCrosse (1.5 mi/2.4 km; 4750 ft/1448 m). Beyond the ridge bordering LaCrosse Basin on the northeast, Buck Lake (5050 ft/ 1539 m) lies in the bottom of a small cirque. No trail goes to this deep blue tarn, and the steepness of the slope leading down to it discourages many from attempting the descent. The lake was originally called Indigo Lake by the O'Neil expedition.

Heart Lake is fairly large—16 acres in extent—and lies cupped in a deep hollow bordered on the north and west by steep slopes that extend up to a peak which overlooks the lake. A small peninsula juts into the water from the east. From the outlet, one can look down upon Marmot Lake and across to Mount Duckabush, which slashes the southern skyline. However, the best view of Heart Lake itself can be obtained from the ridge to the north, and it is especially scenic when the beargrass is in bloom and chunks of snow and ice float in the lake.

Lake LaCrosse, about half the size of Heart Lake, is shaped somewhat like a pear. The greenish waters are surrounded by lush meadows and by heather slopes that lead up to cliffs and rock slides. Below the lake's outlet the creek plunges over a ledge to form the lovely Cascades of the Holy Cross.

During the summer of 1890, LaCrosse Basin was explored for the first time— by the Banner Party, led by Judge James Wickersham, and by the Olympic Exploring Expedition, under the leadership of Lieutenant Joseph P. O'Neil. The latter was a joint endeavor of the U.S. Army and the Oregon Alpine Club.

On August 12, during a scouting trip, two of O'Neil's men (H. Fisher and N.

LaCrosse Basin and Lake LaCrosse

E. Linsley) named three lakes in the basin. The first one they came upon had a small isle in its center, and they named it Marmot Lake. They called the largest one Heart Lake because it was shaped like a heart, and they gave the name Lake of the Holy Cross to the third one because a moss-draped snag with two extended limbs resembled a cross overlooking the lake. About ten days earlier the Banner party had called it Lake Darrell.

In his official report on the expedition, Lieutenant O'Neil states that two lakes at the head of the Duckabush were named Francis and John. An expedition photograph clearly identifies Lake Francis as Lake of the Holy Cross; therefore Lake John must have been either Heart Lake or Marmot Lake.

The Lake of the Holy Cross later became known as Maltese Cross Lake, and eventually the name was shortened, probably through local usage, to simply Lake LaCrosse. Years later, in the early 1950s, the name Heart Lake was changed to Hart Lake by the U.S. Board on Geographic Names because a man named Hart alleged the lake had been named for his uncle, a prospector who had roamed the high Olympics in the pioneer days. The members of the Board were not aware at that time that clear, cogent, and convincing evidence to the contrary reposed in the vaults of The Mazamas, successor to the Oregon Alpine Club.

94 HEART LAKE WAY TRAIL

Not maintained
Length 0.5 mi/0.8 km
Access LaCrosse Basin Trail; O'Neil Pass Trail
USGS Map Mount Steel
Agency Olympic National Park

When traveling between LaCrosse Basin and Enchanted Valley, experienced backpackers often use this shortcut to avoid the long trek via O'Neil Pass.

The views are good, and the route is shortened almost 4 miles. However, this trail is rough and steep, and except for stunted subalpine trees, handholds are virtually nonexistent. This route is used mostly on descents; few care to struggle up the steep mountainside, preferring instead to take the delightful walk that overlooks Upper O'Neil Creek Basin and traverses the slopes above Enchanted Valley.

The way trail begins on the ridge (5170 ft/1576 m) just north of Heart Lake (reached via **LaCrosse Basin Trail**), next to a cluster of trees that resembles, from a distance, a large bush. The path descends steeply, with dwarfed evergreens providing much-needed handholds, to the **O'Neil Pass Trail** (0.5 mi/0.8 km; 4300 ft/1311 m), striking that route at a point about 3 miles south of White Creek Meadow. Years ago the way trail extended directly down to the floor of Enchanted Valley, following the route pioneered by Lieutenant O'Neil and his mules in 1890, but the path below the O'Neil Pass Trail has virtually disappeared and is no longer used.

95 MOUNT JUPITER TRAIL

Length 7.1 mi/11.4 km
Access Mount Jupiter Road
USGS Maps Mount Jupiter; Brinnon
Agency Olympic National Forest

The United States Exploring Expedition, commanded by Lieutenant Charles Wilkes, visited Puget Sound in 1841. This expedition gave the name Jupiter Hills to the northeastern Olympics. The term is no longer used, but it survives in Mount Jupiter, a peak on the southern fringe of the district.

Because the Mount Jupiter Trail is approached from Hood Canal and follows the Duckabush-Dosewallips Divide, it could be said to belong to both watersheds—or perhaps to neither. As a matter of convenience, it has been listed under the Duckabush in this book. No water is found along this route, and one should carry plenty because the hike is strenuous, much of it without the benefit of shade. Motorbikes are permitted on the trail; they have done considerable damage to the switchbacks.

The trailhead (2100 ft/640 m) is located 5.9 mi/9.5 km from US 101 on the Mount Jupiter Road (Cormorant Way). In mid-June one is surrounded by an apparently endless sea of colorful rhododendron blossoms.

The trail begins below the ridge on the slope facing the Duckabush River and starts to ascend at once, switchbacking through intermingled second-growth fir and rhododendron. Other plants include salal, bracken fern, Oregon grape, huckleberry, currant, beargrass, trillium, and the giant fawn-lily, which resembles an avalanche lily but has variegated leaves.

At first the views are little more than glimpses through the trees of peaks and waterways—the latter often covered by clouds. After about a mile, however, the trail enters the national forest and Mount Jupiter itself comes into view, although it looks remote. In fact, the hiker is likely to doubt that one can walk to the summit and back in one day.

Cascades of the Holy Cross

Still traversing below the ridge crest on the Duckabush side, the trail goes by a little campsite (1.8 mi/2.9 km), which has room for one tent. However, anyone intending to stay here would have to carry water up from below. Apparently, fire swept these slopes at one time, and many blackened snags remain. The trail then comes out upon the top of the ridge, where the hiker has the first view of the Dosewallips side.

The path now follows the ridge, not only climbing up and down but also shifting back and forth, first on one side, then the other—from the sunny south side above the Duckabush to the cold north slope overlooking the Dosewallips. On the south side one can gaze at The Brothers and hear the murmur of the Duckabush; on the north side, Mount Constance can be glimpsed occasionally, and the sound of the Dosewallips rises faintly from below. At times the route keeps to the spine itself, where one can look both ways through the trees. The alternating ascents and descents are disconcerting, however, because one realizes that during the return journey the descents will be ascents.

The trail passes another camp (2.7 mi/4.3 km) which has a well-built fireplace, with logs and benches, and space for several tents. But, again, water is not available.

At the trail's halfway point (3.6 mi/5.8 km; ca. 3300 ft/1006 m), a promontory to the left overlooks the Duckabush Valley. The rocky point provides a spectacular view of the country, including the delta of the Duckabush. One is most impressed, however, by the rock walls that extend down from each peak of The Brothers to enclose a snow-filled cirque on the east face of the mountain. Although the dramatic view is only a prelude—an hors d'oeuvre, so to speak—to what can be seen from the top of Mount Jupiter, this is a good place for hikers who do not wish to overextend themselves to turn back.

As the trail climbs higher, through outcrops of basalt, the views improve because the trees are smaller, the stands thinner. The ridge is now a rocky spine, and two peaks appear to block the way, but this is merely an illusion. The trail goes around them, climbing a ridge through a thick growth of rhododendron, mountain hemlock, and subalpine fir. The hiker is rewarded by a sweeping view down the Duckabush Valley, with Hood Canal and Mount Rainier beyond. The U-shaped valley reveals its glacial origin; ahead are rugged ridges composed of volcanic basalt. Although the trail gets rougher and rockier, the views are an unending delight. So, too, the flowers—phlox on the rocks, pioneer violets peeping from the crevices. However, the hiker walking the trail for the first time questions whether it will ever end.

The route now enters The Brothers Wilderness (5.0 mi/8.0 km; 4050 ft/1234 m), which was established in 1984 to protect the prominent, twin-peaked mountain known as The Brothers, as well as the primitive 6-mile segment of the Duckabush River between Little Hump and the national park boundary.

The trail goes beneath upthrusts of pillow lava, and the rhododendrons disappear, replaced by huckleberry, beargrass, and saskatoon, or western serviceberry. Many bleached snags—the trunks of old, fire-killed trees—stand on the hillside among the upthrusted rock. Upon turning a corner, where the path has been blasted from solid rock, the hiker is confronted by rough hummocks of basalt that support a few mountain hemlocks. Now hacked in living rock, the trail begins a series of abrupt switchbacks—thirty-three in all—as it makes the final steep ascent to the top of Mount Jupiter. During early summer the slopes here are likely to be covered with snow.

The summit (7.1 mi/11.4 km; 5701 ft/1738 m) consists of big blocks of broken sandstone, edged by scrubby little trees at the west end. The old fire lookout cabin that once stood here was destroyed about 1969, leaving the area littered with bits of broken glass, telephone wire, rusty nails and screws, and old insulators.

On a warm, sunny day, the hiker will wish to spend at least an hour on the summit. The breezes are cool and pleasant, the views glorious. This is one of the superlative panoramas in the Pacific Northwest, and the hiker sees—at least when the skies are clear—an array of beautiful scenes: close at hand, the foothills and snow-clad peaks of the Olympics, dominated by Mount Constance and The Brothers; beyond them, Hood Canal and Puget Sound with its islands. Haze softens the country to the south and east, but at times the keen-eyed person can discern the skyscrapers in downtown Seattle or ferry boats crossing Puget Sound. The Cascades loom beyond, topped by the volcanic cones of Mount Rainier and Mount Baker. Far to the north, the Coast Mountains of British Columbia are visible.

The calm, peaceful silence is accented by little sounds—the muted murmur of the Duckabush coming up from below, the rustling of the breezes in the tiny hemlocks, perhaps the humming of an insect now and then.

HAMMA HAMMA

One of the smaller rivers in the Olympics, the Hamma Hamma is less than 20 miles long and does not penetrate deeply into the mountains. The headwaters lie on the national park boundary in the Sawtooth Range, and except for the last few miles the river flows through the Olympic National Forest. Hamma Hamma is an Indian name meaning "big stink"—a reference to the unpleasant odor left by decaying salmon that died after spawning.

The North Fork Skokomish River forms a crescent around the headwaters of the Hamma Hamma, and the peaks on the divide between the streams—they include Washington, Pershing, Cruiser, Skokomish, and Stone—are as rugged as the higher peaks deeper in the Olympics. However, they are too low to support glaciers other than tiny, more or less stagnant patches of ice, although permanent snowfields are extensive. The ridges between the Hamma Hamma and the Duckabush district, to the north, are dominated by The Brothers, one of the most conspicuous peaks visible from Puget Sound. Lena Creek, the river's major tributary, has its source in the national park, but most of the other streams lie entirely in the national forest.

The lower slopes of the Hamma Hamma watershed were extensively logged in the early 1900s, and most of the virgin forest that survived the timber-cutting operations was destroyed by fire. Consequently, many weather-beaten snags rise above the heavy stands of second-growth fir that now mask the rough terrain. Thus this valley lacks the primitive aspect that characterizes much of the Olympics.

ROADS

Hamma Hamma River Road (FS Road 25). This road, formerly designated as 2490, leaves US 101 on Hood Canal, 2.3 mi/3.7 km north of Eldon, and ends in rugged, mountainous country on the upper Hamma Hamma. After the first mile, the route becomes a one-lane, blacktopped road with turnouts for passing. The views include the Hamma Hamma Valley to the left, and rugged, snow-flecked peaks ahead.

As it climbs above Hood Canal into the foothills, the road traverses north of the river and enters the Olympic National Forest (4.9 mi/7.9 km), where a side road (5.7 mi/9.2 km) leads to the popular Hamma Hamma cabin, which is available for overnight rental. (Contact Forest Service ranger stations in Hoodsport or Quilcene for details.) Beyond the Hamma Hamma Campground (6.0 mi/9.7 km), the road intersects FS Road 2502, the Cabin Creek Road (6.3 mi/10.1 km), then FS Road 2480 (6.4 mi/10.3 km), which crosses the river and provides access to the country to the south. FS Road 25 continues up the valley past the Lena Lake Trail and Lena Creek Campground (7.7 mi/12.4 km; 650 ft/198m), which is a good place to stay overnight. The two-lane pavement ends at the campground. The campground is primitive, with an old-fashioned water pump and outhouses; thus hikers feel more like they are camping out here than they do when they stay in the developed national park campgrounds.

Beyond Lena Creek the country becomes increasingly wild and rugged, and at

Boulder Creek (11.7 mi/18.8 km) a marker stands beside the road: "Near here is the grave of Carl Putvin, pioneer, trapper, and explorer. Born September 4, 1892, died January 10, 1913." At 12.0 mi/19.3 km the Boulder Creek Road (FS Road 2466) branches to the right. FS Road 25 then crosses Whitehorse Creek.

The valley narrows and the road crosses the Hamma Hamma River—here in a deep, narrow gorge—over a steel and concrete bridge that leads nowhere. The road ends abruptly on the opposite side at a turnaround and parking area (13.1 mi/21.1 km), where the Mildred Lakes Way Trail begins.

FS Road 2480. This road branches left from FS Road 25, the Hamma Hamma River Road, 6.3 mi/10.1 km from US 101 and crosses the river. At 0.3 mi/0.5 km FS Road 2421 branches to the right. This spur goes 1.5 mi/2.4 km, ending in a turnaround where two trails begin—the Elk Lake Trail and the Jefferson Ridge Trail. Beyond the junction with FS Road 2421, the road continues to a junction with FS Road 24 at Jorsted Creek.

Boulder Creek Road (FS Road 2466). This road, which is not maintained for public travel, branches right from the Hamma Hamma River Road 12.0 mi/19.3 km from Hood Canal. The road climbs steadily, paralleling Boulder Creek, and it is closed by a slide (0.8 mi/1.3 km), where limited parking is available.

Jefferson Creek Road (FS Road 2401). This road leads from FS Road 2480 to Elk Lake, then follows Jefferson Creek past Jefferson Lake, ending near the northeastern base of Mount Washington. The western end of the Elk Lake Trail is located on this road.

Note: All roads and trails described in this chapter are shown on the map in the Duckabush chapter.

96 LENA LAKE TRAIL

Length 3.2 mi/5.2 km
Access Hamma Hamma River Road (FS Road 25)
USGS Maps The Brothers; Mount Washington
Agency Olympic National Forest

This popular trail begins 7.6 mi/12.2 km from Hood Canal on FS Road 25, at 700 ft/213 m elevation. The path is virtually a boulevard—broad and smooth, with an easy grade. The original trail was much steeper, but about twenty years ago the Forest Service realigned it, thus making it considerably longer. Most of the year the trail is free of snow.

At first the trail climbs slopes covered with second-growth fir (the original stands having been logged). The path then enters virgin forest, where the understory consists of vine maple, bigleaf maple, huckleberry, and salal. Many hikers cut the long, sweeping switchbacks, where the trail closely parallels itself on the turns, but this should be avoided because it results in unsightly erosion.

After climbing some distance, the trail approaches Lena Creek. The stream rushes noisily in its canyon but is hidden by the forest. The trees are larger here, reflecting more favorable soil and moisture conditions. The trail traverses above the creek, then crosses the stream bed on a sturdy bridge (1.8 mi/2.9 km). The creek usually flows underground at this point; thus the bridge spans a dry channel consisting of big, moss-covered boulders, but one can hear the stream gushing forth from the rocks not far below the bridge.

The sound of Lena Creek fades as the trail climbs to a knoll, where one can look down the valley. The trail then traverses beneath cliffs of overhanging basalt and crosses a tributary of Lena Creek. An unmarked path leads to the right, just beyond the bridge. This is a remnant of the old trail, which approached the lake at the southwest corner. The new trail traverses above the lake, which is hidden by the timber.

Beyond the junction with the **Upper Lena Lake Trail** (2.8 mi/4.5 km; 2100 ft/ 640 m), the route descends to Lena Lake (3.0 mi/4.8 km; 1800 ft/549 m). The lake was created by rock slides that dammed Lena Creek, not by glacial action. The lake's level fluctuates, sometimes by 20 feet or more, reaching its low point in late summer or early fall. Apparently this results because the debris dam is composed of loosely consolidated material. (This probably explains why the outlet creek usually flows underground for some distance and why the trail crosses a dry channel.) When the water is low, stumps and snags protrude from the lake; when the water is high, bushes and small trees along the shore are submerged.

Having an area of 55 acres, Lena Lake is larger than the subalpine lakes, but smaller than several lowland lakes, in the Olympics. The lake, which contains rainbow and Eastern brook trout, is roughly quadrangular in shape, with the outlet at the south end. Lena Creek flows into the northwest corner; East Fork Lena Creek into the northeast corner. The lake is surrounded by forest-clad mountainsides

Lena Creek in the springtime

which are broken by outcrops of rock. Many camps along the shore, which have received heavy use over the years, are now closed because the Forest Service is attempting to restore the vegetation. The agency has built a splendid new camping area on the north side of the lake in a stand of huge, ancient firs to alleviate the burden on the lakeshore campsites.

The trail along the lake's western shore—which is part of the original trail—is little more than a mass of roots and rocks, crossed by numerous little streams. The forest consists of fir and hemlock.

The trail divides near a mass of pillow lava known as Chapel Rock. The left branch, the high water trail, goes over the rock; the right one, the low water trail, traverses beneath the rock and cannot be used when the lake is high. Chapel Rock is a warm, pleasant place, a tranquil spot that overlooks the lake.

One can see scars on the mountainsides, where the slides occurred that formed the lake. Except for an airplane now and then, or perhaps a distant logging truck, one hears nothing but nature's sounds. During the fall, when Lena Creek is low, the stream murmurs gently as it flows into the lake, but on hot days in early summer, when the snow melts rapidly in the high country, the booming sounds like distant cannonading.

Beyond Chapel Rock the high and low routes come back together, and the trail goes by Camp Cleland, situated among tall firs and hemlocks. Here one is likely to be besieged by camp robbers, those delightful feathered beggars known by a variety of names.

The trail ends at an intersection near the northwest corner of the lake (3.5 mi/ 5.6 km; 1900 ft/579 m). **The Brothers Trail** goes right; the path to the left, an abandoned remnant (0.3 mi/0.5 km in length) of the old trail to Upper Lena Lake, joins the new section of that trail northwest of Lena Lake.

97 THE BROTHERS TRAIL

Way trail, limited maintenance
Length 3.0 mi/4.8 km
Access Lena Lake Trail; Upper Lena Lake Trail
USGS Maps The Brothers; Mount Jupiter
Agency Olympic National Forest

This way path was created by people—primarily climbers headed for The Brothers—tramping up East Fork Lena Creek. The route, which is now maintained, begins at the northwestern corner of Lena Lake (1900 ft/579 m), where it intersects the **Lena Lake Trail** and the old route to Upper Lena Lake. At the very beginning, the trail crosses Lena Creek, which is spanned by several logs, and the hiker can take a choice of crossings. The trail then skirts the north shore, where it goes by a new camping area located in a stand of giant firs. Excellent campsites are located here, but one must obtain water from the lake.

Leaving the lake, the way trail—now a mass of rocks and roots—enters The Brothers Wilderness and begins to climb as it follows East Fork Lena Creek through the Valley of Silent Men. The name stems from the days when Olympic College conducted climbing classes in the mountains, beginning in the late 1940s. When scaling The Brothers, the participants camped the night before at Lena Lake, then arose at an early hour to make the ascent. As the climbers plodded up this valley in the semidarkness, conversation languished, and it was christened the Valley of Silent Men. Although it is quiet and peaceful, one can hear the murmur of Lena Creek in the distance, and now and then the raucous cry of a raven.

The trail descends to the East Fork, which at this point flows underground except when the snow is melting in the high country, or after heavy rains. Big, moss-covered boulders are everywhere, and old, rotting logs lie across the path. Huckleberry grows rank, mixed with devil's club and vanilla leaf.

As it follows the creek bed, the trail climbs sharply, and presently one can hear running water ahead. The route now goes up the narrow valley through thickets of vine maple, salmonberry, huckleberry, devil's club, and alder. The flat along the creek disappears, and the trail climbs out of the creek bed. The valley is little more than a V-shaped cleft shaded by the dark, gloomy hemlock forest. The creek is now a flowing stream—noisy, rollicking, full of cascades—and the trail crosses to the east side to a camp (1.5 mi/2.4 km; 2300 ft/701 m). The path is rocky, and the hiker has to use care when walking among the boulders. The trail then goes back to the west side, to another camp (1.9 mi/3.1 km; 2450 ft/747 m), only to return once more to the east side. The creek is larger here; apparently some of the water is lost downstream due to subterranean drainage. Many huge boulders have fallen from the cliffs above; all are thickly padded with moss, indicating that the slides occurred years ago.

The trail now climbs steeply through stands of hemlock and silver fir to a large basin at the southeastern base of The Brothers. After going by a brackish, mossy pond, the route crosses the creek to The Brothers Camp (3.0 mi/4.8 km; 3000 ft/ 914 m). This is the end of the maintained trail. The fairly large camping area (it can accommodate about a dozen tents) occupies the triangle where two branches of the creek come together. This site is often used by climbers as an overnight camp prior to making an ascent of The Brothers.

The neophyte should not venture farther because the route is poorly marked. In fact, beyond this point the trail is strictly a way path used by climbers.

98 UPPER LENA LAKE TRAIL

Limited maintenance
Length 4.0 mi/6.4 km
Access Lena Lake Trail; The Brothers Trail
USGS Maps The Brothers; Mount Washington
Agencies Olympic National Forest and Olympic National Park

This trail formerly began at the northwest corner of Lena Lake, where it intersected with the Lena Lake Trail and The Brothers Trail. Now, however, it starts farther south, at a junction (2100 ft/640 m) with the **Lena Lake Trail** west of the lake. The new section connects with the old trail northwest of the lake. The distance to Upper Lena Lake from Lena Lake is only 4 miles, but the last half is so rough and steep the backpacker is inclined to believe it is much farther.

Initially, the trail goes through stands of Douglas-fir, red cedar, hemlock, and

Upper Lena Lake

silver fir as it traverses above Lena Lake, which is not visible, then veers to the northwest. Here it parallels Lena Creek, which is also hidden. The stream roars loudly when the water is high but murmurs faintly when it is low. The new section ends where it merges (0.4 mi/0.6 km) with the old trail coming up from the northwest corner of the lake. (The abandoned section provides an alternate approach via Lena Lake. See Lena Lake Trail description.)

As it switchbacks up the mountain, the trail gets rougher and is often crisscrossed with tree roots. The big Douglas-firs disappear, and the forest is now composed mostly of hemlock and silver fir.

Upon entering Olympic National Park (1.2 mi/1.9 km; 2550 ft/777 m), the trail climbs a bit, then descends to Lena Creek but does not cross the stream. The growth of devil's club is luxuriant, and on the creek's far side an avalanche fan is covered with vine maple and bigleaf maple. This slope turns brilliant red and yellow in October.

Leaving Lena Creek, the trail crosses a large tributary that comes in from the south. A campsite is located on the opposite side. The trail then steepens as it climbs through a wet area, where many little streams cross the path, but the worst places are covered with puncheon. Water is abundant, and on a hot day the hiker needs it. As the trail ascends rocky gullies, it virtually becomes a staircase of roots and rocks, washed by small brooks. The path is bordered by luxuriant undergrowth; if the jungle of salmonberry, devil's club, slide alder, currant, elderberry, and Alaska cedar were not cut back by the trail crew, it would be impenetrable. The way is not only steep but also much like walking in a creek bed. The trail then climbs out onto a promontory, where one can sit in the sunshine and enjoy the view down the valley. The trail, chipped out of living rock, then works its way up among knobs and knolls composed of basalt.

Disconcertingly, the route goes up another rocky gully bordered by devil's club and salmonberry, while to the right Lena Creek cascades down a rocky defile. The trail then crosses the creek, which here flows over a bed of solid rock. A sign indicates that fires are not permitted beyond this point.

The trail switchbacks into and out of the forest as it climbs above the canyon. The trees are mostly Alaska cedar, mountain hemlock, and silver fir. Huge boulders lie scattered about, in fields of wildflowers—mostly lupine, arnica, bluebells, daisies, valerian, cow parsnip, and thistle. The trail parallels Lena Creek, which is not always visible but its rushing sound can be heard continuously.

Climbing ever more steeply, the trail traverses a sidehill covered with boulders, and one can see a wall of trees ahead—behind which lies Upper Lena Lake. The trail then attains a point where the lake is visible. At this point it forks, but both branches lead down to the water. The right one follows the shore to the northwest corner, where it becomes **Scout Lake Way Trail;** the left branch traverses south along the ridge (from where Mount Rainier can be seen, resplendent in the afternoon sunlight), then descends to the lake's outlet, where it crosses Lena Creek (4.0 mi/6.4 km; 4550 ft/1387 m).

Upper Lena Lake lies between Mount Lena (5995 ft/1827 m) and Mount Bretherton (5960 ft/1817 m). The 26-acre lake occupies a depression carved in the slate and sandstone by an Ice Age glacier and is surrounded by meadows, scree slopes, and subalpine forest. The lake is reported to have rainbow trout, but the fishing season is limited by the fact that the lake sometimes remains frozen well into June. A seasonal ranger station, staffed only in the summer months, is located here. Mount Bretherton was named for Bernard J. Bretherton, the naturalist with the 1890 O'Neil expedition. Why this peak was chosen to bear his name is puzzling because this mass of basalt lies in the watershed of the Hamma Hamma, one of the streams the expedition did not explore.

The area around the lake has been virtually loved to death—paths go everywhere through the heather because people tend to take a direct route to any destination. Consequently, the National Park Service is attempting to obliterate many paths by covering them with burlap and posting signs indicating they are not to be used. In addition, the trampled sites at the lake's northeastern corner have been closed to camping in order that the vegetation may reestablish itself; but good camps that can be used are located along the northern shore, and just south of the outlet creek on the east side.

This basin is a peaceful, tranquil place. When the sun disappears behind the western ridge, the trees on the skyline appear to be on fire, the foliage illuminated like the filament of a light globe. During the evening the lake's reflections are silvery at first, but as night comes on, the surface darkens, with luminescent sparkles breaking the surface, particularly when the rainbow trout leap high.

99 SCOUT LAKE WAY TRAIL

Not maintained
Length 3.0 mi/4.8 km
Access Upper Lena Lake Trail; Lena Lake Trail
USGS Maps The Brothers; Mount Washington; Mount Skokomish
Agency Olympic National Park

The trail that leads from Upper Lena Lake to Scout Lake is another way path created by human feet, but parts of it are as good as a constructed trail. For all practical purposes, it may be considered an extension of the **Upper Lena Lake Trail.**

The trail begins near the lake's west shore (4550 ft/1387 m), where it crosses a creek, then climbs through grassy areas, patches of heather, and thickets of stunted mountain hemlock, Alaska cedar, and subalpine fir. During the fall, mountain ash and dwarf huckleberry make splotches of blazing red on the mountainsides. The delectable huckleberries are abundant in late summer, often causing hikers to dawdle along the trail. The scenery is splendid—Mount Bretherton rises ahead, to the left, but the summit is hidden from view by lower buttresses.

Beyond a narrow, grass-choked lake, the trail crosses meadowland that sweeps high onto the slopes above. A stream here provides the last water for several miles as the trail ascends to and follows the ridge lying between Upper Lena Lake and Scout Lake, alternating between subalpine fir forest and meadow country, where dwarf huckleberry is abundant. Ahead one can see a cluster of peaks—Washington, Ellinor, and Pershing—cradling snowfields on their northern slopes; to the left, between the ridge and Mount Bretherton, is the deep valley of Boulder Creek. The trail then comes to a point where one can look down into the Duckabush Valley and see the ridges beyond, with Mount Anderson on the horizon. The path becomes less distinct now, but cairns indicate the way, and the terrain is not difficult.

The trail crosses to the Duckabush side of the ridge at Scout Lake Pass (1.7 mi/2.7 km; 5150 ft/1570 m), which is marked by a large cairn. Here one has an excellent view of Mount Anderson. At this point the trail leaves the ridge and descends through heather meadows and sandstone outcrops to Deerheart Lake (2.2 mi/3.5 km; 4970 ft/1515 m). The little tarn is enclosed by rocky slopes, with Mount Stone rising beyond. This is the first place where water is available on this side of the ridge, and a one-tent campsite is located at the lake's south end.

Below Deerheart Lake the trail parallels the outlet stream, crossing it three times, then goes by a turnip-shaped lakelet (2.4 mi/3.9 km). At this point one should leave the trail and travel cross-country, going left through easy terrain to meadows, thus avoiding the steep descent to Scout Lake via the trail. The route is longer but much safer. The hiker should go south as far as the big meadow, where the **Stone Ponds Way Trail** can be followed north to its intersection with Scout Lake Way Trail.

Experienced and adventurous hikers can continue on the trail, which beyond the lakelet becomes progressively steeper, with several ticklish places to scramble down. The route goes through rock slides and thickets of azalea and Alaska cedar, coming out beside a knoll where one has a good view of Scout Lake. The intense blue, almost indigo, expanse is impressive. Then, just below this point, the hiker has to clamber down a spot that is difficult to negotiate with a heavy pack. At the brink of an almost vertical face that falls away 40 feet or so, it is necessary to hold onto a root and swing out over space like a circus aerialist while searching for friendly footing. One must then move crablike to a mass of tree roots, from where it is possible to work downward to less precipitous terrain.

Below this point the terrain loses much of its steepness, and the trail turns north and joins the Stone Ponds Way Trail (2.6 mi/4.2 km; 4500 ft/1372 m). The two trails coincide from here to Scout Lake; the route goes north, down a steep, rocky ravine, through scrubby subalpine trees, to a flat at the head of Scout Lake (3.0 mi/4.8 km; 4250 ft/1295 m).

Scout Lake is about the same size as Upper Lena Lake, but it is long and narrow, with the outlet at the north end. The lake is bordered by steep slopes—heavily forested on the east side, less densely so on the west, where the cliffs are broken by slides and talus slopes. The view across the water of the forested ridges is peaceful and tranquil. The lake contains rainbow trout.

Camping is prohibited at the lake, which has no beach of significance. The rockbound shore is inaccessible on the west because a cliff comes down into the water, creating a barrier, but one can clamber over the big sandstone boulders on the east side. The stream that flows into Scout Lake at the upper end and out the lower is designated as One Too Many Creek on recent maps, but this is not in accord with older maps, which denote it as a branch of Crazy Creek.

100 STONE PONDS WAY TRAIL

Length 2.8 mi/4.5 km
Access Scout Lake Way Trail
USGS Map Mount Skokomish
Agency Olympic National Park

This route coincides with **Scout Lake Way Trail** from Scout Lake as far south as the point (0.4 mi/0.6 km; 4500 ft/1372 m) where the Scout Lake Way Trail reaches the base of its steep descent from Deerheart Lake. The Stone Ponds Way Trail then continues south toward Mount Stone, climbing through meadows dotted with tree-covered knolls, outcrops of rock, and little ponds. One can see St. Peters Gate straight ahead.

The trail comes out into a big meadow and vanishes, but it can be found again on the far side, where it leads up to Stone Ponds Pass (1.0 mi/1.6 km; 4900 ft/ 1494 m), then descends to Stone Ponds, two small lakes (1.2 mi/1.9 km; ca. 4600 ft/ 1402 m) at the head of a branch of Boulder Creek. The trail ends at this point.

The Stone Ponds, aquamarine in color, are bordered by meadows, subalpine forest, scree, and large boulders. The scene is tranquil, quiet except for the sound made by a waterfall in the creek above. The sheer, smooth cliffs of Mount Stone tower above the lakes.

The route to St. Peters Gate (2.0 mi/3.2 km; 5900 ft/1798 m) climbs over heather, scree, and snow. The "gate" is a U-shaped notch in the southeast ridge of

Mount Stone. This ridge forms the divide between Boulder Creek and Whitehorse Creek, tributaries of the Hamma Hamma River.

Beyond St. Peters Gate the route descends to Lake of the Angels (2.8 mi/4.5 km; 4900 ft/1494 m), the source of Whitehorse Creek, located just below the saddle between Mount Stone and Mount Skokomish. The **Putvin Trail** can then be followed from the lake to the Boulder Creek Road.

101 PUTVIN TRAIL

Way trail, limited maintenance
Length 4.0 mi/ 6.4 km
Access Hamma Hamma River Road (FS Road 25)
USGS Map Mount Skokomish
Agencies Olympic National Forest and Olympic National Park

This trail was named for Carl Putvin, an early-day explorer in the Olympic Mountains. The trailhead (1580 ft/482 m) is located on FS Road 25 at the Putvin Historical Marker. It can also be accessed from the Boulder Creek Road (FS Road 2466).

The path at first climbs over rocky terrain lying between Boulder Creek and an abandoned Forest Service road. It traverses slopes covered by second-growth fir, where the ground cover consists largely of salal, beargrass, kinnikinnick, and vine maple. The trail then crosses the old road and enters the Mount Skokomish Wilderness. The noisy chatter of Whitehorse Creek can be heard just ahead, but the stream itself is hidden by vine maple thickets. Upon approaching the creek, the trail veers right and switchbacks up the steep mountainside, climbing through the forest until it breaks out into more or less open country, where it levels out. The trees here are mostly subalpine fir and Alaska cedar. One can look across the Hamma Hamma Valley and see Mount Pershing and Jefferson Ridge. At this point (2.0 mi/ 3.2 km; 3360 ft/1024 m), a side path branching left descends to a camp on Whitehorse Creek, then to another site in the woods beyond.

The route now crosses a fairly level basin. The creek bottom is overgrown with impenetrable thickets of slide alder, vine maple, and willow, but the trail traverses the hillside through thimbleberry, thistle, huckleberry, cow parsnip, and bracken fern. Various kinds of wildflowers bloom here; the most prominent is pearly everlasting.

The trail crosses rock slides, then becomes progressively steeper and more exposed as it ascends the headwall. Here the hiker has to cling to rocks, roots, and bushes, and one place, about 10 feet high, requires a bit of climbing agility, especially when the rocks are wet and slippery. However, the terrain becomes easier above this point, where a reward awaits—at least in late summer. Great quantities of huckleberries can then be gathered—both the large, blue-black kind and the low-growing purple ones, with their exquisite flavor.

The trail follows the headwall's rim, then descends to a small stream where a side path (3.0 mi/4.8 km) leads to a campsite in a grove of trees. All through this section one can hear the roar made by Whitehorse Creek as it plunges over the headwall, and occasionally one can see the waterfall.

The Pond of the False Prophet, so called because it is sometimes mistaken for Lake of the Angels by weary hikers plodding up the trail, marks not only the entry into Olympic National Park but also the beginning of subalpine meadowland. However, the route is choked with brush in many places. The round lakelet is bordered by lush grasses and timbered knolls, and rough boulders that have fallen from the cliffs above lie scattered over the meadows. Mount Skokomish rises to the southwest; Mount Stone to the north.

The trail crosses Whitehorse Creek and again climbs steeply, zigzagging up open slopes, where wildflowers bloom profusely among the rocks. Here one finds a variety of species: false hellebore, paintbrush, buckwheat, anemone, alumroot, and buttercups. Also present are bluebells, arnica, asters, and thistles. One can look down on the little pond, up to St. Peters Gate on Mount Stone. Mount Rainier and the Cascades also come into view. Now and then the silence is broken—either by the shrill whistles of marmots or the croaking of ravens circling overhead.

The trail then levels out, going alongside Whitehorse Creek, which flows down a little V-shaped gorge to the right. Lake of the Angels lies directly ahead, in a beautiful meadow called the Valley of Heaven (4.0 mi/6.4 km; 4900 ft/1494 m), where patches of snow linger until late summer.

The lake, which lies in a glacial cirque, is shaped like a teardrop, with the outlet to the northeast, at the pointed end. The cirque occupies a niche below the ridge that links Mount Stone and Mount Skokomish. On the west and south, the sandstone cliffs of Mount Skokomish rise directly from the lake's shores; on the north the mountainsides lead up to the cliffs of Mount Stone. Only on the east, where it faces the cirque's open end, is the lake bordered by level meadows. One can camp on this flat but the wind, chilled by the snowfields on Mount Skokomish, sometimes sweeps fiercely across the lake, and it is better to pitch the tent in a sheltered spot.

The trail ends at the lake, but a rudimentary path, broken in places, climbs heather slopes to the ridge (5250 ft/1600 m) between Mount Stone and Mount Skokomish. The gap is marked by one of nature's cairns—a huge boulder capped by another weighing several hundred pounds. A campsite is located nearby, but water is not available. The view to the west includes several peaks—Duckabush and Steel, with Olympus between and beyond them; Chimney Peak and Hopper. One can also look back to the east and see the Cascades (dominated by Mount Rainier), Puget Sound, Hood Canal, and the foothills of the Olympics. St. Peters Gate is visible on the skyline, and Lake of the Angels is directly below. The lake is especially beautiful in mid-October, after it has frozen over and the first snowfall has whitened the peaks. The surface then resembles a beaded silver screen.

Beyond this gap the cross-country route becomes the **Mount Hopper Trail**.

102 MILDRED LAKES WAY TRAIL

Limited maintenance
Length 5.5 mi/8.9 km
Access Hamma Hamma River Road (FS Road 25)
USGS Map Mount Skokomish
Agency Olympic National Forest

One of the primitive "roots and rocks way trails" found throughout the Olympics, this path leads to several subalpine lakes at the eastern base of the

Sawtooth Range in the Mount Skokomish Wilderness. The trailhead (1678 ft/ 511 m) is located at the end of FS Road 25.

Near its beginning the trail crosses little streams, but beyond them water is not available for some time. At first the trail is fairly level and goes through stands of second-growth fir, the virgin timber having been cut, then burned. The huge fir and cedar stumps are silent reminders of the forest's former glory. Looking back, one can see the Boulder Creek Road and the logging scars on the ridge south of Mount Bretherton.

As it traverses the mountainside, the trail gradually steepens. Upon reaching the end of the logged area, it enters virgin forest—at this point mostly western hemlock and silver fir, with only an occasional large Douglas-fir, the forest having been logged to the "fir line."

Up to this point the hiker will wonder why this route has such a bad reputation and will probably be inclined to dismiss it as hyperbole. However, the path now deteriorates, and it alternately consists of rough stones or masses of tree roots that are slippery when wet. The trail steepens as it climbs over a ridge of upthrusted sandstone and loose boulders. Here one can look both right and left, through stands of little trees, to rocky peaks. The sharp Sawtooth Range looms ahead; the sound of a rushing stream can be heard to the right. The route then descends to a large creek, a major tributary of the Hamma Hamma River. The stream is bridged by a log, but one is better advised to make a quick dash through the shallow riffles. Two campsites are located here (2.4 mi/3.9 km; 3000 ft/914 m).

The trail climbs steadily, crosses another stream, then comes to a deep, steep-sided ravine where in times past a large log spanned the abyss. At its most harrowing point, the log put hikers 25 feet above the rocky ravine. The log has since been removed, requiring hikers to now descend into the ravine, then clamber up the other side.

The trail now goes straight up the mountain, climbing a rock staircase. Many hikers give up at this point, but the grade eases once this obstacle is overcome. The path emerges at a campsite located among outcrops of sandstone in the heather-covered meadows on a little ridge. The peaks of the Sawtooth Range are visible, apparently near, yet far away.

Descending steeply through subalpine forest, the trail crosses a wet area, where dark ponds lie among sandstone ribs that protrude from the heather. At the second pool a little mountain hemlock, its trunk twisted like a pretzel, awaits the photographer at the water's edge. The forest here is beautiful, growing among big boulders composed of basalt.

Bordered by mountain hemlocks, the Mildred Lakes lie in basins scooped in the sandstone by a glacier that came down from the nearby Sawtooth Range. Huge blocks of basalt, carried down by the ice from the peaks above, lie scattered about. The first lake now comes into view (4.9 mi/7.9 km; 3850 ft/1173 m). A rock sticks out of the water near the far end, and many large chunks of basalt edge the shores, where the trail goes by several campsites littered with debris. The trail then traverses a mixture of forest and meadow dotted with many little ponds to another lake (5.5 mi/8.9 km; 3900 ft/1189 m). This one is the largest subalpine lake in the Olympics. The deep lake, which covers an expanse of almost 40 acres, is shaped like a whale, with the head pointed southwest, the tail northeast. The rocky shores—in places they are smooth sandstone faces—drop steeply to the water.

The trail ends here. The rugged peaks of the Sawtooth Range, now only a mile distant, overlook the lake on the north and west. Mount Lincoln stands to the left, Mount Cruiser and Alpha to the right.

This lake is about six times as large as the first one, and the setting is calm, peaceful, serene. Unfortunately, the campsites are littered with cans, broken bottles, jars, and plastic food containers. Above the rim of forest, the cliffs support a jungle of Alaska cedar, and bits of meadowland appear here and there; mostly, however, the sheer cliffs alternate with scree slopes that extend up to the walls of the Sawtooth Range.

The third lake in the trio lies somewhat to the north, away from the trail.

103 JEFFERSON RIDGE TRAIL

Limited maintenance
Length 2.8 mi/4.5 km
Access FS Road 2421
USGS Map Mount Washington
Agency Olympic National Forest

The trailhead (1100 ft/335 m) is located at the end of FS Road 2421, which can be reached by FS Roads 2480 and 25.

At first the trail climbs at a moderate grade through an area that has been logged and is now covered with stands of second-growth fir and a heavy undergrowth of salal, rhododendron, and vine maple. As the path switchbacks up the mountainside, it crosses an old Cat track, which goes straight up the hill. The trail more or less parallels this skid road, which it recrosses; then, beyond the sixteenth switchback, the trail quits fooling around and follows the track directly up. This makes the route steeper and more arduous. Eventually, however, the trail leaves the sun-drenched slope and enters the cool and shaded virgin forest. The path now veers away from the Cat track and again has a pleasant grade.

Upon attaining the crest of Jefferson Ridge, the trail follows the divide, zigzagging as it ascends through the forest, which now contains a good deal of western hemlock. Once again the trail and Cat track coincide, and the route steepens as it follows the skid road.

The hiker then receives a surprise—the trail skirts the edge of a big clearcut on the south side of the ridge. Here it goes out into the warm sunshine, where tiny evergreens are beginning to establish a foothold among the rhododendrons and fireweed. At this point one can see Hood Canal, but most of the hiker's attention is devoted to clambering up the steep slope, where the trail was obliterated by logging. The path, consisting of loose stones and gravel, goes straight up the mountainside.

Snow cornice on ridge

Beyond the logged area the trail goes back into the forest and either follows the ridge crest or traverses to one side. The path now goes by the only hazard on the route—a deep cave or hole right beside the trail, where one can look straight down.

Presently, the trail leaves the cool shade of the woods, comes out onto the ridge top, and ends just ahead, where the fire lookout cabin formerly stood (2.8 mi/ 4.5 km; 3832 ft/1168 m). One of the last lookouts constructed in the Olympics, the building was erected in 1961 at a cost of $60,000, then destroyed six years later, when lookouts were abandoned in favor of airplanes and helicopters. Nothing remains but a pile of debris—concrete blocks and footings, burned timbers, cable, melted glass, bolts, and sheet iron.

When the cabin was built, the trees were cut down, thus creating an impressive 360-degree vista. However, young ones are now growing up and beginning to obscure the scene. Due north stand The Brothers, only 5 miles distant. The view clockwise from that mountain includes the ridges and foothills, then bits and pieces of Hood Canal and the low hills beyond, with the Cascades, topped by Mount Rainier, on the horizon; the ridges from Hood Canal to Mount Washington, which are covered with a multitude of recent clearcuts; then the peaks of the Olympics— Washington and Pershing; the Sawtooth Range, capped by Cruiser; Skokomish; Stone, with its snowfield; Bretherton and Lena, and back to The Brothers. Far to the north, in the gap between Lena and The Brothers, one can see a rounded peak with a snowfield (Mount Deception) and a steep pyramid (Mount Mystery).

On a warm summer day, the lookout is a pleasant place to linger. Cool breezes sweep across the ridge, and one can hear the signals made by loggers working in the foothills, occasionally the purr of a plane flying over the mountains, or perhaps the clatter of a helicopter. Yet, oddly enough, one has the sensation that this is a place of solitude.

104 ELK LAKE TRAIL

Length 2.3 mi/3.7 km
Access FS Roads 2480; FS Road 2401
USGS Map Mount Washington
Agency Olympic National Forest

A fragment of a once major trail, this path extends from FS Road 2421 to FS Road 2401. The trailheads are accessible by driving FS Road 25 to FS Road 2480. The eastern trailhead can be reached by following FS Road 2480 to FS Road 2421, then going up the latter to its terminus. The southern trailhead is approached by continuing on FS Road 2480 to its junction with FS Road 2401, then taking the latter to the parking area at Big Elk Lake. One can continue on FS Road 2401 to the western trailhead.

The path is not marked at the eastern trailhead (1100 ft/335 m), but it is obvious. The trail goes through stands of fir, hemlock, and large madrona. The sound of Jefferson Creek rises from the canyon to the left. The route is characterized by slight ups and downs as it traverses the mountainside, alternately going through virgin forest and clearcuts overgrown with little conifers, maple, alder, tangled blackberry vines, and thickets of salal and Oregon grape. One looks from the openings across Jefferson Creek to FS Road 2441, which is bordered by logged areas and patches of virgin timber. The older clearcuts are grown up with young firs; the more recent ones are still barren.

The trail then forks (1.2 mi/1.9 km; 1100 ft/335 m). The left branch leads to the southern trailhead on FS Road 2401; the right branch continues up Jefferson Creek, going near Big Elk Lake (1050 ft/320 m). The flat land adjacent to the lake is marshy, and the outlet is plugged by logs and debris.

Big Elk Lake (also known as Lower Elk Lake) varies from 6 to 10 acres in size and was formed by a landslide that created a natural dam across Jefferson Creek. The lake is edged by meadows and thick growths of willow, with stands of tall conifers farther back. Two campsites are located here—one near the outlet, the other on the lake shore. However, the once-beautiful scene has been spoiled by logging. Looking up the valley, one sees the end of the ridge that rises between Washington Creek and Jefferson Creek. The north side is still clothed with virgin forest, but the south side has been completely stripped. Had esthetics been considered, this mountain would not have been logged—or at least not in such a ruthless manner.

Beyond Big Elk Lake the trail goes through virgin forest having a dense undergrowth consisting mostly of little hemlocks. Below, on the left, Jefferson Creek gurgles and ripples, reflecting glints of sunlight. Presently, the trail emerges onto FS Road 2401 (2.0 mi/3.2 kin; 1200 ft/366 m).

The branch path descends steeply to the lake, then follows the shore to the outlet, where it crosses a boulder-filled overflow channel that is dry during the summer. The path then intersects with the main trail (0.3 mi/0.5 km; 1100 ft/335 m).

Little Elk Lake (also known as Upper Elk Lake) is about one-third to one-half the size of Big Elk Lake and is located approximately a quarter mile south of its neighbor. Both lakes are stocked with Eastern brook trout.

PART II

WINDWARD OLYMPICS

The western and southern slopes of the Olympic Mountains constitute the windward side because the prevailing winds at this latitude in the northern hemisphere come from the west and southwest. Accordingly, the windward side stands as a barrier which receives the full effect of the storms that sweep inland from the North Pacific. Most of the storms occur during the winter and spring, and when they travel inland the marine air masses become unstable, because they are warmer than the land over which they move. The result is raininess, overcast skies, and high humidity. As a consequence, the western and southern slopes of the Olympics are deluged by the heaviest precipitation in the conterminous United States—estimated to vary from 140 to 200 inches annually, with still greater amounts occurring in the wettest years. However, on the fringes of the windward belt, where this district blends into the leeward zone, the precipitation is, of course, lighter, although it probably exceeds 100 inches.

At the lower elevations most of the moisture falls in the form of rain, and this has led to the development of the famous rain forests in the lowland valleys; but at the higher altitudes, the bulk of the precipitation occurs as snow, which piles up to great depths. On the loftier peaks, such as Mount Olympus, more snow falls than can melt during the succeeding summer, and this has resulted in the formation of glaciers at an exceptionally low elevation for this latitude.

The trails in the Windward Olympics are located farther from the centers of population; therefore they are not so readily accessible nor so well known as the ones in the Leeward Olympics—at least to most residents of western Washington. They also suffer from the stormier, poorer weather, which makes them less attractive—from that standpoint—than the trails in the Leeward Olympics. The bulk of the trails are in the national park. The few that are located in the national forest are chiefly fragments of a once extensive network that has been greatly diminished by the heavy emphasis on logging during the past quarter century.

Hall of Mosses, Hoh Trail (Photo by Frank O. Shaw)

Because the southern and western slopes of the Olympics are less precipitous than the northern and eastern sides, the Windward Olympics comprise approximately 60 percent of the area covered by the mountains. However, they have fewer trails and less trail mileage. With the exception of Mount Olympus, the Windward Olympics are also lower than the Leeward; thus the bulk of the high country is to be found in the latter section.

North Fork Skokomish River emerging from box canyon

NORTH FORK
SKOKOMISH

The Skokomish River flows through the southeastern Olympics to Hood Canal. The river's two branches—the North Fork and the South Fork—come together about 7 miles from the Big Bend of the canal. The North Fork Skokomish has its source in a glacier and snowfields on Mount Skokomish, on the national park boundary, and makes a big loop through the southeastern Olympics, leaving the park a mile below Staircase, where it flows into Lake Cushman. This branch of the river is bounded on the east by rugged peaks composed of basalt—Stone, Skokomish, Henderson, Copper, and the Sawtooth Range, which extends from Mount Lincoln to Mount Cruiser. The valley is bordered on the north and west by other peaks, largely sandstone, that are equally precipitous—Hopper, Steel, Duckabush, and the ridge extending from Mount Duckabush to Mount Olson.

During the Ice Age, an alpine glacier moved down the valley of the North Fork Skokomish, deepening it, and the Cordilleran Ice Sheet pushed westward against and into the Olympics, depositing material that dammed the river. This combined action created Lake Cushman, which was discovered and named in 1852. The original lake covered about a square mile, but it was enlarged approximately 600 percent in the mid-1920s, when the City of Tacoma built a power dam on the North Fork about 5 miles below the lake. The reservoir inundated the lake as well as several miles of the river. The lake contains king salmon, and several kinds of trout—rainbow, Eastern brook, silver, and Dolly Varden.

Within the national park, above Lake Cushman, the North Fork often forms dark pools, then plunges through rock-walled channels, with a show of white water, as it tumbles over boulders. Then, again, the river may flow at a smooth and tranquil pace. The stream has numerous tributaries—short ones flowing from the east, longer ones coming from the west. The latter are paralleled by ridges that lie at right angles to the river. Six Stream is the largest tributary. Several creeks—Four Stream to Nine Stream, inclusive—were named for camps of the 1890 O'Neil expedition.

The upper valley, within the national park, is a splendid example of primeval landscape. The ever-changing vistas are accompanied by the music of the Skokomish as it dashes over rocks, its cascades scintillating in the sunlight. The forest here contains some of the finest Douglas-fir and western red cedar in the national park. Trees more than 250 feet tall, with diameters of 6 to 8 feet, are common. Because the valley has a southerly orientation, the rainfall is heavy, resulting in a luxuriance of plant growth that rivals the rain forests of the western Olympics.

Most of the trails in this watershed are located in the national park, but several short ones are found in the national forest.

The North Fork Skokomish was explored in 1890 by the O'Neil expedition and by a party led by Judge James Wickersham. Since that time, however, the lower part of the valley has been savagely exploited, and the approach now gives little hint of the beauty to be found within the national park.

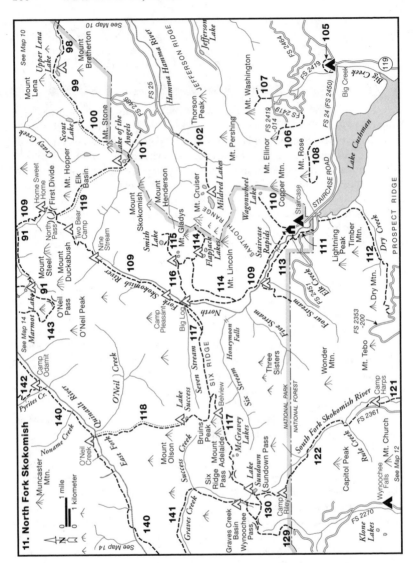

ROADS

Jorsted Creek Road (FS Road 24). This road, formerly designated as 2450, begins on US 101, 2.3 mi/3.7 km south of Eldon. The route first goes through private and state land. The Lilliwaup Camp and Picnic Area (6.9 mi/11.1 km) is maintained by the Department of Natural Resources. At 7.2 mi/11.6 km, FS Road 2419, the Big Creek Road, branches to the right. After entering the Olympic National Forest, FS Road 24 intersects the Hoodsport Road (8.8 mi/14.2 km). Big Creek Campground is located just beyond the junction. The road crosses Big Creek, then traverses above Lake Cushman.

Cushman Falls (11.1 mi/17.9 km) plunge down the cliffs on the right. They were named for Alfred Cushman, who visited the lake out of curiosity in the 1890s, having seen the name Lake Cushman on a map. He remained and took a homestead near the falls. Lightning Peak, originally called Storm King, is visible straight ahead. The peak was denuded by a forest fire in the early 1900s, and the blaze made enough light that one could read a newspaper at midnight 4 miles away at Cushman House, William T. Putnam's resort on the lake.

Beyond the Mount Rose Trail (11.5 mi/18.5 km), the road winds along the shores of Lake Cushman to a junction with FS Road 2451, the Lightning Peak Road (14.0 mi/22.5 km), at the head of the lake. When the reservoir's level is low, hundreds of giant stumps are visible, the ghosts of a once great forest. The Bear Gulch Picnic Area is located just beyond this junction. At this point the road goes into the virgin forest and enters Olympic National Park (14.2 mi/22.9 km). Here a surprise greets the visitor: the graveled road changes to blacktop.

Within the park the scarred lands are left behind, and the road penetrates a region little changed by the hand of man. Bordered by towering firs, the road follows the North Fork, ending at the Staircase Ranger Station (15.2 mi/24.5 km; 800 ft/ 244 m) and an automobile campground. At this point trails radiate into the surrounding country.

Lake Cushman Road (State Route 119). This road begins at Hoodsport on Hood Canal and climbs over low hills, then through the Cushman Recreation Area, where summer homes have been built in the forest. The sinuous road climbs through second-growth forest to a viewpoint (6.0 mi/9.7 km) that looks across the lake to Mount Washington and Mount Ellinor. Camp Cushman (7.0 mi/11.3 km) has facilities for overnight camping. The road ends where it intersects FS Road 24 (9.0 mi/14.5 km). (The route to the national park now turns left and follows FS Road 24.)

Big Creek Road (FS Road 2419). This road begins 7.2 mi/11.6 km from Hood Canal on FS Road 24. The road climbs half way up Mount Ellinor and Mount Washington and provides access to the trails on these peaks.

Lightning Peak Road (FS Road 2451). This logging road branches left from FS Road 24 at the head of Lake Cushman, crosses a causeway to the west side of the Skokomish, then climbs to the upper watersheds of Elk Creek and Four Stream. The Dry Creek Trail can be reached by this road.

105 BIG CREEK NATURE TRAIL

Length 1.3 mi/2.1 km
Access FS Road 24
USGS Map Hoodsport
Agency Olympic National Forest

The Big Creek Campground, constructed by the Forest Service in 1981–82, is located on FS Road 24, the Jorsted Creek Road, just beyond the junction with the Hoodsport Road. The Big Creek Nature Trail makes a 1.3 mi/2.1 km loop that encircles the campground (ca. 900 ft/274 m). Although one can walk the path in either direction, it is described here as if one were traveling counterclockwise.

Going into the woods to the right of the campground entrance road, the trail follows an almost level grade as it winds through scrubby stands of second-growth fir. The underbrush consists of salal, bracken fern, vine maple, huckleberry, and beargrass. (The Skokomish Valley is one of the few places where beargrass grows naturally at low elevation.)

After coming out to an old road, which it follows briefly, the trail descends slightly, and one can hear Big Creek ahead. The path parallels the stream, which is about 15 to 20 feet wide, then crosses it on a little wooden bridge. The trees are larger here, and western red cedar is also present. The vegetation along the creek is luxuriant—the maples are garlanded with mosses; sword ferns carpet the damp ground.

The trail traverses a steep sidehill above the creek, then recrosses the stream over another bridge and strikes the entrance road opposite the point where it started (1.3 mi/2.1 km).

106 MOUNT ELLINOR TRAIL

Length 2.8 mi/4.5 km
Access FS Road 2419
USGS Map Mount Skokomish
Agency Olympic National Forest

The ascent of Mount Ellinor is much shorter now than it was in 1898, when Henry Gannett, geographer of the U.S. Geological Survey, accompanied Arthur Dodwell and Theodore F. Rixon to the summit. The men wanted to get a look at the new Olympic Forest Reserve—3483 square miles of untouched wilderness that Dodwell and Rixon had been employed to survey. At that time one had to climb without benefit of roads or trails. Eventually, however, the trail was established, but as late as the 1950s people began the climb at a low elevation near Lake Cushman. Today, however, the Big Creek FS Road (2419) goes halfway to the summit, making the ascent considerably less strenuous—and much less interesting. One should carry water because the trail follows a dry ridge.

The path has two trailheads. The lower one (ca. 2800 ft/853 m) begins on FS Road 2419, the Big Creek Road, 4.6 mi/7.4 km beyond its intersection with FS Road 24; the upper trailhead (ca. 3600 ft/1097 m) can be reached by driving another 1.6 mi/2.6 km on the Big Creek Road, then going 1.0 mi/1.6 km on FS Road 2419–014. Many hikers interested solely in reaching the summit approach via the upper trailhead because it shortens the route 1.5 mi/2.4 km, but in doing so they miss the delightful walk along the forested ridge.

Upon leaving the lower trailhead, the trail climbs the narrow ridge through mature stands of western hemlock and Douglas-fir. The undergrowth is sparse, and saprophytes are frequently observed. The trail ascends at a moderate grade to a junction (1.7 mi/2.7 km; 3900 ft/1189 m) with the path that comes from the upper trailhead, only 0.2 mi/0.3 km distant.

The trail steepens and gets rougher as it climbs to Chute Flats (2.4 mi/3.9 km; 4500 ft/1372 m). Although water is not available here, a crude campsite is located among the trees. The flats are noted for beargrass, Indian paintbrush, lupine, columbine, false hellebore, arnica, heather, and phlox.

Because Mount Ellinor is a comparatively easy ascent, hundreds of people scramble to the top every year. The climb has been made still easier in recent years by the Olympians of Grays Harbor. Assisted by other volunteer trail builders, they extended the trail from Chute Flats to the summit. Beyond the flats the path goes through subalpine country, paralleling the climbers' chute route as it does so. Hikers ascend this path, which follows the west ridge of the mountain to the rocky summit, but many climbers stick to tradition and go up The Chute, which is easy to ascend in the spring and early summer when it is filled with snow. At this time one can, during the descent, glissade from the top of The Chute to the bottom, rapidly losing more than a thousand feet of elevation. Later, after the snow has melted, going up and down The Chute is time-consuming and requires caution because loose stones clatter down from above. Climbers can avoid this hazard by using the path built by the Olympians.

The views from the summit (2.8 mi/4.5 km; 5944 ft/1812 m) are splendid, particularly early in the season when the Olympics are snow-covered, although clouds often obscure the surrounding scene. Many peaks are visible in the distance; close at hand are Mount Washington and Mount Pershing. Away from the Olympics the vista includes Hood Canal, Puget Sound, and the Cascade Range.

107 JEFFERSON PASS TRAIL

Way trail, limited maintenance
Length 1.6 mi/2.6 km
Access FS Road 2419
USGS Map Mount Washington
Agency Olympic National Forest

The trail begins at the upper edge of a clearcut (3000 ft/914 m) on FS Road 2419, the Big Creek Road, 6.7 mi/10.8 km from its junction with FS Road 24. The broad, smooth path climbs at a gentle grade through mature fir and hemlock forest. The elevation is comparatively high, yet the firs are 3 feet or more in diameter, which explains why logging operations have gone so far up the mountainside.

This route leads to a Class IV climbing route, requiring ropes and belays to climb Mount Washington. Most climbers use Route 1A to reach the summit of Mount Washington. Refer to *Climber's Guide to the Olympic Mountains* (The Mountaineers). After making several long traverses, the trail crosses a level saddle. The Douglas-firs have disappeared, and the forest is now exclusively western hemlock and Pacific silver fir. A pile of logs that block the way (1.1 mi/1.8 km; 3850 ft/ 1173 m) marks the end of the maintained trail, but the path continues about a half mile down into the Jefferson Creek drainage. Although the abandoned section is in fair condition, the fallen logs have not been cut out. The path descends from the saddle, then traverses, with views out across the valley of Jefferson Creek. After crossing a stream, the trail goes into a jungle of slide alder, Alaska cedar, and devil's club, where it disappears (ca. 1.6 mi/2.6 km; 3300 ft/1006 m).

At the log pile in the saddle, a climbers' scramble route leads, left, up the mountainside. This steep, rough path is less than a half mile long and is better suited to mountain goats than hikers, although it was created by climbers' boots. One clambers over a succession of roots, moss-covered boulders, and logs, the path going directly up a spur. After a steep climb, the trail comes out onto a precipitous, rocky ridge, where it ends. The view is good—Mount Washington is straight ahead, and one can see Lake Cushman, the peaks west of it, the Big Bend of Hood Canal, Mount Rainier, and part of Puget Sound.

108 MOUNT ROSE TRAIL

Length 4.8 mi/7.7 km
Access FS Road 24
USGS Map Mount Skokomish
Agency Olympic National Forest

Mount Rose was named for Albert A. Rose, one of the first settlers on Lake Cushman. He arrived in the mid-1880s and used a log raft to ferry supplies across the lake to his claim.

The steep trail that leads almost directly to the summit of Mount Rose climbs more than 3500 ft/1067 m in a little under 3 miles. The trailhead (767 ft/234 m) is located on FS Road 24, the Jorsted Creek Road, near the north shore of Lake Cushman, 2.8 mi/4.5 km west of the intersection of FS Road 24 with State Route 119.

Because the trail ends in a loop, like a cowboy's lariat, one has four options on how to hike the trail. The shortest, at 5.6 mi/9.0 km, is to go up and down the so-called summit route; the longest, at 8.2 mi/13.2 km, is to go up and down the ridge route. In between, both at 6.4 mi/10.3 km, are two more options: up the summit route and down the ridge route or up the ridge route and down the summit route.

Upon leaving Lake Cushman, the trail quickly gains elevation, climbing steadily as it switchbacks and twists its way through second-growth fir, where salal almost hides the big stumps left by the loggers. Most of the virgin timber was either cut or burned, but patches remain. As the trail alternately goes through stands of second and old growth, the contrast between the two is marked. The young trees are small; the old ones are tall, straight as arrows, 4 to 5 feet in diameter, with lichen clinging to the trunks.

The route at this point enters the Mount Skokomish Wilderness (1.1 mi/1.8 km; 2000 ft/610 m), which was established in 1984 to protect the rugged, primitive country adjacent to the southeast corner of Olympic National Park. The wilderness area's boundary, at least in the vicinity of Mount Rose, follows the 2000-ft contour line, which means that everything on the mountain above that elevation is protected.

At the seventh switchback, the trail steepens as it goes by outcrops of moss-covered rock, where manzanita and madrona are present. This is a good place to bask in the sunshine on a warm day. The view of Lake Cushman is good, the shadows of the trees extending down from the lake's edge like black beards.

The ridge now drops steeply on both sides, and the trail climbs sharply. Thick pads of mosses compete with a ground cover of kinnikinnick and beargrass. Before the trail was rebuilt recently, it was rough in many places, and one often walked on a bed of roots and rocks. Occasionally, when the wind is blowing in the right direction, one can hear a stream flowing in the depths of the forest below.

The trail now forks (1.8 mi/2.9 km; 2600 ft/610 m). The left branch, known as the summit route, heads more or less directly toward the peak of Mount Rose. The right branch of the ridge loop makes the beginning of the alternate ridge route. Orange diamonds mark the route to the top.

Both routes lead to the top of Mount Rose (4301 ft/1311 m). Via the summit route, the total distance is 2.9 mi/4.7 km, and by the ridge loop route the total distance is 3.6 mi/5.8 km.

Above the fork, the main trail or summit route goes through heavy forest and rock gullies, then sparse forest for some distance. There are a number of switchbacks, and the final pitch is quite steep. This route is harder to follow than the ridge loop way, especially in early season when snow covers the ground.

The ridge loop route leads through fir and hemlock forest as it makes a long upward traverse and crosses two small streams. Beyond the brooks it switchbacks upward to the saddle between Mount Rose and Mount Ellinor. The path climbs steeply as it veers away from the saddle. Near the ridge crest it goes by four large silver firs that stand in a row, growing so closely to each other that their trunks have welded together, thus creating a wall.

The trail strikes the ridge, turns left, and follows the narrow, rocky spine through stands of hemlock, Alaska cedar, Douglas-fir, and silver fir. Mount Ellinor is glimpsed through the trees. The trail now becomes indistinct but descends slightly as it heads to the base of a little basalt peak which rises perhaps 30 feet above the general level. This is the top of Mount Rose (4.8 mi/7.7 km; 4301 ft/1311 m). The climb up the north side is a simple scramble, but the space on top is limited and will accommodate not more than two or three people. Hikers not subject to vertigo can look almost straight down to Lake Cushman and see Lightning Peak rising beyond. Visible in the distance are a number of peaks, among them Mount Rainier to the southeast and Mount Steel to the northwest, at the headwaters of the North Fork Skokomish.

109 NORTH FORK SKOKOMISH TRAIL

Length 15.6 mi/25.1 km
Access FS Road 24
USGS Maps Mount Olson; Mount Skokomish; Mount Steel
Agency Olympic National Park

The major trail that parallels the North Fork Skokomish leaves the valley at Nine Stream and climbs over the First Divide to the Duckabush River, where it merges with the **Duckabush Trail.** Except for the first few miles, where the trail follows the east side of the river, the route coincides with that taken by the O'Neil expedition in 1890.

The trail begins at the Staircase Ranger Station, where FS Road 24, the Jorsted Creek Road, now ends (800 ft/244 m). The road formerly extended another 4 miles, but this section was closed in 1973 because it was difficult to maintain. The old roadbed is now considered part of the trail.

Beyond the ranger station the trail climbs to a point that overlooks the river. The valley is bordered by steep mountains clad with virgin forest, and the river meanders on the bottomlands. During early morning and late afternoon, the trees cast dark shadows across the sun-splashed Skokomish. The trail then descends to Slate Creek (0.5 mi/0.8 km), which is spanned by a foot log. Slides in the early 1990s destroyed the bridge that was located at this point.

The old road now goes through majestic stands of virgin forest—chiefly Douglas-fir, red cedar, and hemlock, intermingled with grand fir and deciduous species such as cottonwood, bigleaf maple, alder, and vine maple. Many of the Douglas-firs and cedars are 6 to 8 feet in diameter, more than 250 feet tall, and over five hundred years old. The undergrowth is luxuriant—much like the west side rain forests—consisting of sword ferns, salmonberry, devil's club, and other moisture-loving plants. During April and May, trilliums are conspicuous, and the fairy slipper orchid lurks in the greenery on the forest floor.

At 1.0 mi/1.6 km a side path branches left and leads to the Rapids Bridge, which arches over the river between two large rocks. The bridge formerly made possible a 2-mile loop trip which began and ended at the ranger station. However, the bridge cannot presently (1999) be used to cross the river because it was severely damaged by storms during the winter of 1998–99, and whether or not it will be rebuilt is not known at this time.

As it parallels the river, the old roadbed footpath climbs into the district blackened in 1985 by the Beaver Fire, a conflagration which destroyed 1400 acres of virgin timber, mostly on this side of the river. Many of the trees were more than four hundred years old. The junction with the Mount Lincoln Way Trail (2.4 mi/3.9 km) was destroyed, located as it was in the midst of the devastated area. The National Park Service does not plan to rebuild the Mount Lincoln Trail.

The trail goes through the fire-blackened forest as far as the **Flapjack Lakes Trail** (3.7 mi/6.0 km; 1475 ft/450 m). The old roadway ends just beyond this junction. The path then contours the mountainside, traversing stands of fir, cedar, and hemlock untouched by fire. This section is bordered by huckleberry bushes, and in midsummer, when the berries ripen, hikers make slow progress because they often stop to sample the fruit. The river, lost to sight below, makes its presence known by a constant roar, and one can also hear the rush of the larger tributaries.

The trail crosses Madeline Creek, where clumps of deer ferns make a fine display, then Donahue Creek, the next major stream. Near this creek a large fir that fell across the trail during the 1970s was 540 years old, indicating the tree was growing when Columbus set sail across the Atlantic. This fir was typical of many that stand in this area.

At the next intersection (5.5 mi/9.0 km; 1500 ft/457 m), the **Black and White Lakes Way Trail** climbs steeply to the right, and a well-beaten path to the left descends to Big Log Camp, a popular site on the banks of the river. Beyond this junction, the trail traverses a flat covered by large cedars and firs, then crosses the North Fork Skokomish. Here the river, narrowly confined between rock walls, is deep, swift, and clear. On the west bank, the **Six Ridge Trail** branches to the left (5.9 mi/ 9.5 km; 1475 ft/450 m).

The trail now coincides with the route of the O'Neil expedition as it follows

North Fork Skokomish River

the west side of the river. The forest alternates with glades overgrown with thickets of salmonberry and devil's club, and occasionally the path traverses bottomland, where maples are festooned with ferns and mosses. The flats are miniature examples of the rain forests found in the western Olympic valleys.

Aptly named Camp Pleasant (6.7 mi/10.8 km; 1600 ft/488 m) is located among the maples on a sunny, breeze-swept spot by the river. Beyond this camp the trail is shaded by giant firs, but near Eight Stream one can look up the river and see Mount Steel. Between Eight Stream and Nine Stream, the trail alternates between forest dominated by ancient firs and small glades grown up with willow, slide alder, salmonberry, and ferns.

The trail then crosses Nine Stream, a major tributary that flows down from the snowfields on Mount Duckabush. On warm summer afternoons it becomes a brawling torrent. Camp Nine Stream (9.6 mi/15.5 km; 2000 ft/610 m) is located on the north side, where the O'Neil expedition had one of its major camps.

At this point the trail begins to climb, switchbacking through stands of fir toward the First Divide, the watershed between the Skokomish and Duckabush Rivers. After about a mile, the large forest growth is left behind, replaced by higher altitude species, including silver fir.

Two Bear Camp (11.6 mi/18.7 km; 3800 ft/1158 m) was named in 1924 by George Conaway, foreman of the crew that built the trail. Every morning when they were working on this section, the men saw two bears in the meadow above, so Conaway suggested they call it Two Bear Camp. Since that time the meadow has grown up with slide alder and salmonberry. The camp is located beside a small stream, not far above Canaday Cataract, which was named for Lewis Canaday, who led a party of backpackers across the Olympics about 1950.

Beyond Two Bear Camp, the trail breaks out into an open area covered with a rank growth of slide alder, willow, and salmonberry, then climbs through meadows filled with colorful masses of wildflowers—lupine, columbine, valerian, bluebells, Columbia lily, thistle, bistort, arnica, and marsh marigold, to name a few. The largest meadow, located just above a little canyon, was the site of the O'Neil party's Camp Number Ten.

Camp Lookabout (12.4 mi/20.0 km; 4300 ft/1311 m), just below the First Divide, was popular with visitors in the 1890s and early 1900s. At this point the old O'Neil Trail leads left, or northwest, to North Pass, where the expedition crossed the divide. Hikers sometimes mistake this abandoned path for a continuation of the North Fork Skokomish Trail, but the latter turns right at this point and contours beneath the ridge to a junction with the **Mount Hopper Way Trail** (12.7 mi/20.4 km; 4540 ft/1384 m). Numerous wildflowers, including the rare white bog orchid, bloom with lavish abandon here, and the trail, now in open meadow where avalanche lilies nod in the vagrant breezes, goes by a small tarn, then tops the First Divide (12.9 mi/20.8 km; 4688 ft/1429 m). One can look down from this point to Home Sweet Home Creek and across the upper Duckabush to White Mountain and Mount LaCrosse, which are scarred by avalanche chutes. On warm, clear days this is a pleasant place, but during storms the wind surges mightily here, and one must seek shelter from the driven rain.

The trail switchbacks down the north slope, then crosses Home Sweet Home Creek at the edge of a lovely subalpine meadow. On the far side a branch path leads across the flat, grassy expanse to Home Sweet Home Shelter (13.5 mi/21.7 km; 4198 ft/1280 m). The basin, recessed on the northwest side of Mount Hopper, is often covered with snow until late July, but after the snow disappears it is blanketed with avalanche and glacier lilies. Later in the season, lupine and buckwheat make equally showy displays. Mount Steel and Mount Hopper overlook the basin, and when the weather is stormy the clouds roll over North Pass from the Skokomish side. They dance across the meadow, swirling in surrealistic patterns, swooping here and there, coming down and touching the ground at times, then leaping high, like youthful gods gamboling in sheer delight.

Beyond Home Sweet Home, the trail descends through stands of large Alaska cedar, western hemlock, and silver fir. The route traverses above the creek, which is hidden by the dense forest, then crosses a slide. Below this point the route enters the Douglas-fir forest and descends to a junction with the **Duckabush Trail** near Camp Duckabush (15.6 mi/25.1 km; 2695 ft/821 m).

110 WAGONWHEEL LAKE TRAIL

Length 2.9 mi/4.7 km
Access FS Road 24
USGS Map Mount Skokomish
Agency Olympic National Park

This steep trail climbs 3250 ft/991 m in just under 3 miles, ending at Wagonwheel Lake on the northwestern slope of Copper Mountain. Because water is not available on this route until one reaches trail's end at the lake, hikers should carry a good supply.

The trail begins at the parking area behind the Staircase Ranger Station (900 ft/274 m) at the end of FS Road 24, the Jorsted Creek Road, and at first climbs through a stand of large second-growth Douglas-fir, where remnants of virgin forest are present in the form of fire-blackened snags. The understory consists of maple, both bigleaf and vine, and the ground is covered with salal and sword ferns.

After going by a prospector's hole, which goes straight down about 12 feet, the trail begins to switchback, and the trees are smaller. Ascending steadily, the route climbs to the crest of the spur between Slate Creek and Lincoln Creek, where Mount Lincoln is visible through the trees. Western white pine seedlings and rhododendrons are intermingled with the salal and ferns, and poison oak is also present here. This is one of the few places this plant is found in the Olympics.

More switchbacks lie ahead. As it follows the ridge, the trail goes into the big timber—stands of old-growth western hemlock untouched by fire. The trunks are covered with lichen, and thick undergrowth carpets the ground.

After making the last switchback, the trail goes straight up the narrow ridge, thus steepening considerably. The trail then leaves the ridge, and the grade eases, the route contouring the north slope through stands of hemlock, silver fir, and Alaska cedar. Beneath the cliffs to the right, the path crosses an avalanche slope overgrown with a thick tangle of slide alder that impedes one's progress. Although the hiker can make better time across this place during the spring months, when the slope is covered with deep snow, one must keep an eye out for avalanches.

The trail then goes back into the big timber and crosses a little creek which issues from Wagonwheel Lake (2.9 mi/4.7 km; 4150 ft/1265 m). The lake is bordered by a dense stand of conifers.

Why this lake was given this name is a mystery. The tarn is oval, not round like a wheel, and lies cupped in an egg-shaped basin on the north side of Copper Mountain.

111   SHADY LANE

Length 1.0 mi/1.6 km
Access FS Road 2451
USGS Map Mount Skokomish
Agency Olympic National Park

This path is the national park section of the old Dry Creek Trail, which was severed from the national forest part by construction of FS Road 2451. The trail follows the west side of the North Fork Skokomish to the head of Lake Cushman.

Beginning across the river from the Staircase Ranger Station (785 ft/239 m), at the end of FS Road 24, the trail goes south toward Fisher's Bluff and crosses Elk Creek. A dark hole then looms up in the cliff just ahead—a tunnel that prospectors abandoned after they had penetrated 15 or 20 feet into the mountain in a vain search for manganese and copper. During the summer the tunnel is dry and one can walk in and look out; but in the winter the floor is often covered with water.

As it skirts the base of Fisher's Bluff, the path follows a ledge that overlooks a deep pool in the river. This shelf was blasted in the cliff about 1910 by miners who volunteered to do the work if the Forest Service provided the powder. The name Fisher's Bluff honors Private Harry Fisher, a member of the 1890 O'Neil expedition. The bluff was the first obstacle the party faced in building a mule trail up the Skokomish. Trout were abundant in the river during the pioneer days, and O'Neil's troopers caught a great number while fishing from the rocks at this point.

Beyond the bluff the path goes through groves of giant fir, cedar, and hemlock on the level bottomlands. This area is one of the finest examples of virgin forest on the eastern side of the national park. Many trees are 6 to 8 feet in diameter, with heights in excess of 250 feet, and one fir near the park boundary is 11 feet in diameter. The luxuriant understory beneath the conifers consists of bigleaf and vine maple, with black cottonwood close to the river.

During the late 1950s the National Park Service permitted the Forest Service to build FS Road 2451 across this corner of the park in order to tap stands of timber on the upper reaches of Elk Creek and Four Stream, an area that would (and logically should) have been included in the park had the boundaries been drawn on topographic lines. Without regard to the effect it would have upon the beautiful groves along Shady Lane, the road builders blasted tons of rock from the mountainside in order that the road could climb above Fisher's Bluff. The rocks tumbled down the slope, destroying the trees and leaving ugly scars that spoiled the beauty of the forest backdrop. Worse still was the loss of solitude. On weekdays, logging trucks roar up and down the road, kicking up dust and breaking the silence that the hiker should experience when walking among the big trees. One can look away from the destruction but cannot ignore the noise. Before this road was built, the only sounds to be heard were the sighing of the wind in the trees and the distant murmur of the river.

Beyond the national park boundary (0.9 mi/1.4 km; 768 ft/234 m), the route goes through second-growth forest to a road where summer homes have been built. This road leads into FS Road 2451 (1.0 mi/1.6 km), which approaches via the causeway at the head of Lake Cushman. The path continues on the other side of FS Road 2451 as the **Dry Creek Trail.**

One of the delights of Shady Lane is to leave the trail opposite the rock slides caused by the road construction and wander to the river, then go south and circle back west to the trail again. This walk takes one through groves of huge cedars and firs and along glades near the river where deer are likely to be observed. One of the firs has an osprey's nest in its top, and the birds can be observed from a vantage point among the trees.

112   DRY CREEK TRAIL

Length 7.3 mi/11.8 km
Access FS Road 2451
USGS Maps Lightning Peak; Mount Tebo
Agency Olympic National Forest

The Dry Creek Trail originally began at Staircase Ranger Station, but the part in Olympic National Park—detached from the remainder by FS Road 2451— is known today as **Shady Lane**. The trail now begins on the south side of FS Road 2451, just beyond the causeway at the head of Lake Cushman.

The route starts as a Cat track in the midst of summer home development that is still under way. The forest is second-growth fir, but huge stumps are scattered through the woods—all that remains of the big firs and cedars that once stood here. The trees were cut when the City of Tacoma built a dam on the North Fork Skokomish in the 1920s, thus enlarging Lake Cushman. Primitive roads branch out in various directions from the bulldozer track, and the trailhead (750 ft/229 m) is just beyond them.

As it follows the lake, the trail alternates between skirting the driftwood-clogged shore and traversing the hillside above. Then, beyond a viewpoint where the hiker can look across to Mount Rose, the path starts to climb, and in places it is covered with old puncheon. A spur trail (0.9 mi/1.5 km) goes downhill to the left to Dry Creek (0.6 mi/1.0 km from the junction).

The ascent is seemingly interminable as the trail follows the grade of an old logging road. The forest here is composed mostly of alder and maple. After descending to a campsite (3.0 mi/4.8 km; 1543 ft/470 m), the trail crosses Dry Creek— except it is not dry but a shallow stream about 15 feet wide. However, with care one can cross on a wobbly log and slippery rocks. The trail now climbs again, but it is in poor condition and so little used that it is carpeted with thick moss. The path then enters the virgin forest (3.5 mi/5.6 km), consisting of stands of silver fir, western red cedar, and western hemlock, with a little Douglas-fir. Deer ferns grow thickly beneath the trees.

As it switchbacks, the trail climbs steadily, and at one point the hiker has a good view across Dry Creek Valley to Lightning Peak. The trail then attains the crest of Prospect Ridge (5.5 mi/8.9 km; ca. 3000 ft/914 m). Here one can look both to the north and south, and signs of logging operations are visible ahead as the trail follows the narrow ridge westward through gloomy forests of silver fir and Alaska cedar. Presently, one sees clearcuts in every direction—the hills appear to have been shaved by Paul Bunyan's razor.

The trail switchbacks as it follows the ridge until it reaches the pass (6.7 mi/10.8 km; 3650 ft/1113 m) between Dry Mountain and the west end of Prospect Ridge. After topping this gap, the trail—which is now much better—descends into the basin at the head of LeBar Creek, ending where it comes out to FS Road 2353–200 (7.3 mi/11.8 km; ca. 3200 ft/975 m). (See the description of FS Road 23 in the South Flank chapter.)

The trail formerly extended down to and across LeBar Creek, and connected with the South Fork Skokomish Trail at Camp Comfort, but that portion has been obliterated by logging. After crossing the causeway over the North Fork Skokomish River, the trailhead is 0.25 mi/0.4 km ahead on the left. The steep trail climbs through old-growth forest 2.2 mi/3.5 km to the ridge, where it makes a brief loop. Total distance: 4.5 mi/7.2 km.

113   STAIRCASE RAPIDS TRAIL

Length 3.5 mi/5.6 km
Access FS Road 24
USGS Map Mount Skokomish
Agency Olympic National Park

This delightful trail, popular with hikers, both novice and veteran, leads to beautiful scenes as it follows the North Fork Skokomish River to Four Stream along the route taken by the O'Neil expedition in 1890. The trail then climbs above Four Stream and ends abruptly. The route is entirely in the deep forest, which consists of fir, hemlock, and western red cedar. The huge trees rise above a lush undergrowth that is almost as luxuriant as that in the rain forests.

The trail begins at the end of FS Road 24 across the river from Staircase Ranger Station at the edge of the clearing that was formerly occupied by the Staircase Resort (800 ft/244 m). Near the trail's beginning, a side path leads, left, to the remains of a giant western red cedar that fell in January 1999, apparently from old age. About 14 feet in diameter, it was one of the largest trees in the valley and estimated to be eight hundred years old. The tree had been admired for years by hundreds, perhaps thousands, of visitors and had often been photographed. The trail then comes out onto the banks of the Skokomish. The crystal clear stream, every rock on the bottom visible, flows rapidly here, the rushing water muffling the twittering of the birds that dwell in the forest.

Another side path descends to picturesque Red Reef Pool, where the river has cut a narrow channel through a dike composed of red limestone. The stream surges wildly through the break into a deep basin or pool, where the upwelling water, releasing air gathered during its mad rush, bubbles like champagne. The trail then climbs a bit, and another path leads, right, to Dolly Varden Pool, which is bordered by rock ledges. Although not as scenic as Red Reef Pool, it is nonetheless impressive because the river boils and foams as it plunges over huge boulders.

Above the pools the trail winds through conifer forests beside the river, which cascades down a narrow defile. The path then edges Staircase Rapids (0.8 mi/1.3 km), where the stream flows over a series of low terraces. Tall trees shade the banks, and cool breezes are usually present.

The name Staircase derives from The Devil's Staircase, as O'Neil's route over Fisher's Bluff became known in the 1890s, after a visitor called it that upon returning from a trip up the river. The path at that time was largely a staircase of roots to which one had to cling when climbing up and down the bluff. Eventually the place became known simply as Staircase, and the name was later given to the rapids.

Beyond Staircase Rapids the trail veers away from the Skokomish and climbs Dead Horse Hill, the moraine deposited by the alpine glacier that came down the valley during the Ice Age. Near the top a path leads, right, to the closed Rapids Bridge. Here, one could formerly make a connection with the North Fork Skokomish Trail, to create a 2-mile hike from and to the ranger station. However, the bridge was so badly damaged by storms during the winter of 1998–99 that it was rendered unusable. Past the bridge the trail descends to Beaver Flats, a swampy area covered with cedar, fir, and moss-padded maple, alder, and cottonwood. This place is attractive any time, but especially during the spring, when the new growth appears, and in October, when the maple leaves turn golden. Unfortunately, the area was damaged in August 1985, by the Beaver Fire, ignited during hot, dry weather by hikers who built an illegal campfire. The dead, blackened trees contrast starkly with the surrounding verdant growth.

Leaving the burned district, the trail goes by Copper View Camp (1.7 mi/2.7 km), located where the river makes a big curve. This camp provides a good view downstream of Copper Mountain. Four Stream (2.0 mi/3.2 km) commemorates the O'Neil expedition's fourth mule trail camp, which was located nearby. The trail crosses the creek, climbs a bit, and then forks. The left branch (little used because it doesn't really lead anywhere) switchbacks upward through stands of hemlock, fir, and cedar, turns south and parallels Four Stream, then crosses into the national forest, where it comes to a dead end (3.5 mi/5.6 km; 1800 ft/549 m). The right branch, which is merely a stub, leads down to a riverside camp located in a grove of giant firs.

Beyond the camp one can travel cross-country up the river and find traces now and then of O'Neil's mule trail leading to the South Branch, or Jumbo's Leap (Five Stream), and the West Branch (Six Stream). The name Jumbo's Leap was given by O'Neil's troopers to the South Branch when an old hound named Jumbo made a desperate leap into the canyon. After the Cushman Dam was built, enlarging Lake Cushman, the trail up the river was relocated on the east side as far as Big Log Camp, where it crossed and rejoined O'Neil's trail. The old section between Four Stream and Big Log Camp was then abandoned—and such historic scenes as Jumbo's Leap and Honeymoon Falls, once familiar to many, became virtually unknown.

However, these places may become well known again in the near future. In

1982 the Bremerton, Washington, Order of the Arrow Chapter of the Chief Seattle Council, Boy Scouts of America, with the approval of the National Park Service, marked the route of the O'Neil Trail from Four Stream to Seven Stream. The organization registered the entire route of the O'Neil expedition's mule trail as a historic hiking trail with National Headquarters, Boy Scouts of America. Previously, the Order of the Arrow Chapter had marked and registered the route of the Press Expedition (via the Elwha, Goldie, and Quinault Rivers) as a historic hiking trail.

114 FLAPJACK LAKES TRAIL

Length 5.6 mi/9.0 km
Access North Fork Skokomish Trail
USGS Map Mount Skokomish
Agency Olympic National Park

This route, which leads to Flapjack Lakes and the mile-high Gladys Divide, at the head of the Hamma Hamma River, is popular not only with hikers and anglers but also with alpinists headed for high adventure in the nearby Sawtooth Range, which provides some of the best rock climbing in the Olympic Mountains. Because the area is heavily used, the number of persons permitted to camp overnight at the lakes has been limited since the early 1970s.

The trailhead is located near the end of the old, abandoned road that is now considered an extension of the **North Fork Skokomish Trail**. This point is 3.7 mi/6.0 km beyond the Staircase Ranger Station, at an altitude of 1475 ft/450 m.

The trail climbs an easy grade through stands of western hemlock and Douglas-fir, and at the first switchback goes by a small campsite where water is available in a nearby stream. After zigzagging upward, the trail turns north and makes a long, ascending traverse. Occasionally, one can see the mountains beyond the North Fork Skokomish River. Huckleberries are abundant along this part of the trail, and when the berries are ripe hikers often stop to feast.

As the trail approaches Madeline Creek, one can hear the stream cascading down the slope. The trail descends to the creek and crosses via a bridge of boulders to a campsite on the far side (2.0 mi/3.2 km; 2100 ft/640 m). Beyond this camp the route parallels Donahue Creek, and the trail climbs again as it switchbacks up the mountainside. Because the grade is steep, this stream consists of a series of waterfalls and cascades. A couple of poor campsites are located here (3.5 mi/5.6 km), then the trail crosses the stream. The creek was named for a prospector who planted trout in the Flapjack Lakes in the early 1900s. He was assisted by a man named Bonell.

At this point the route intersects the **Smith Lake Trail** (3.6 mi/5.8 km; 3500 ft/1067 m), which leads left to Black and White Lakes and Smith Lake. The Flapjack Lakes Trail continues to the right, climbing directly to the two lakes (4.1 mi/6.6 km; 3900 ft/1189 m). A seasonal ranger station is located at this point.

The Flapjack Lakes are the source of Donahue Creek. The eastern or larger lake is more or less round, which no doubt gave rise to the name inasmuch as the western lake is irregular in outline, shallow, and apparently evolving into a marsh. The lakes, which contain Eastern brook and rainbow trout, are surrounded by the forest and have several campsites. The ones with the best views are located between the lakes. Because the area has been overused, the water is polluted and unsafe to drink without treatment. Overnight camping is now by reservation only.

The campsites at the lakes are often used as an operations base by climbers headed for the Sawtooth Range. The rugged peaks, composed of blocks and pinnacles of pillow lava and breccia, loom above the lakes. The crags of Mount Lincoln stand at the southern end. Also visible are The Fin and Picture Pinnacle. The lava beds here are tilted on edge, and the sharp peaks were created by erosion along parallel cracks.

East of Flapjack Lakes the trail ascends through meadowland to Gladys Divide (5.6 mi/9.0 km; 5000 ft/1524 m), the saddle between Mount Gladys and Mount Cruiser. The divide overlooks the headwaters of the Hamma Hamma, but the view directly east is blocked by Mount Cruiser (6104 ft/1861 m). An easy walk leads to the rounded top of Mount Gladys (5600 ft/1707 m), where the view is better. Mount Anderson rises above the ridge to the north, and Mount Olympus is visible far to the northwest.

Mount Cruiser was named for the Bremerton Ski Cruisers. The peak, which is visible from Puget Sound, was first climbed in 1937, and its vertical basalt cliffs challenge the mountaineer. The highest peak in the Sawtooth Range, it stands near the national park boundary and is considered one of the more difficult rock climbs in the Olympics.

The Murdock Lakes, the source of the Hamma Hamma River, lie on the north slope of Mount Gladys. They were named for L. F. Murdock, a photographer who roamed the southeastern Olympics in the late 1890s and early 1900s.

115   SMITH LAKE TRAIL

Way trail, not maintained
Length 2.1 mi/3.4 km
Access Flapjack Lakes Trail
USGS Map Mount Skokomish
Agency Olympic National Park

Most of this route—which first leads to Black and White Lakes, then to Smith Lake—traverses high, subalpine country. The trail branches left from the **Flapjack Lakes Trail** at the Donahue Creek crossing (3500 ft/1067 m).

After climbing through stands of western hemlock, the trail traverses north along the sidehill, and the forest changes to mountain hemlock, Alaska cedar, and silver fir, with an understory of vine maple. The leaves of the latter turn gold and scarlet in October, thus making a colorful autumn display.

As the trail climbs higher, one can look out across the Skokomish Valley to a number of sharp peaks. They include Mount Church, Wonder Mountain, and the Three Sisters, with Mount Lincoln far to the left.

Upon leaving the sidehill, the trail crosses over into the deep woods, then goes into an old burn. Here a thick growth of mountain ash and vine maple contrasts with the weathered trunks of old snags. Fireweed and pearly everlasting are abundant, and huckleberries grow everywhere in great profusion. Signs of civilization

are present at the site of the Black and White Mine (1.2 mi/1.8 km): the foundation of a cabin, and a piece of machinery the miners used. The claim dates back to
1907, and during World War I, copper and manganese ore was packed out by mule
train. The trail then intersects with the **Black and White Lakes Way Trail** (1.3 mi/
2.1 km; 4200 ft/1280 m).

At least four versions explain the origin of the name Black and White: that it
stemmed from the mottled manganese ore; that it originated with the prospectors,
who celebrated their discovery with a bottle of Black and White brand Scotch
whisky; that it was elk hunters rather than miners who named the place for the
whisky; and that the miners' last names were Black and White because prospectors
usually named their claims after themselves.

The three Black and White Lakes, named after the mine, are not visible from
the trail, but lie a short distance ahead, to the right. Two are little more than potholes, but the largest one attains respectable size. This lake is long and narrow and
has fairly steep shores, too abrupt for campsites except near the south end. The old
burn surrounding the lakes is huckleberry country, one of the best places in the
Olympics to pick the delectable fruits because the berries ripen to perfection in
the warm sunlight in late September. Both the large black variety and the dwarf,
low-growing kind are present. During the fall the entire slope turns flaming red
and purple, when cool breezes vie gently—in a mild tug-of-war—with the waning
warmth of Indian summer.

Meandering through the burn, the trail climbs over the ridge north of the
lakes. Here one has a view up the Skokomish to Mount Duckabush and Mount
Steel and can look back and see the largest of the Black and White Lakes. The path
then traverses the north side of Mount Gladys through heather, huckleberry, mountain ash, and the bleached snags left by a fire that swept through here years ago.
Patches of old-growth trees relieve the stark severity of the ghost forest.

After leaving the burn, the trail goes through a mixture of forest and meadowland. Not far beyond a small pond, a branch trail (1.6 mi/2.6 km) descends, left, to
Smith Lake. The right branch, which was once the main trail, can be followed about
a mile farther, alternately traversing meadowland and groves of mountain hemlock.
The trees are festooned with lichen, and the wind murmurs as it travels from grove
to grove. The ground supports a luxuriant growth of azalea, heather, and huckleberry, and in late summer the meadows are resplendent with fields of blue lupine.
At one time the trail contoured beneath Mount Henderson, then descended to the
North Fork Skokomish opposite Eight Stream, where Chris Hamer, a retired log-
ger turned prospector, once had a cabin. He was found dead, lying in front of his
home, in the fall of 1918. Hammer Creek (spelling changed) was named for him.

The left branch of the trail, the main route today, descends sharply to Smith
Lake, most of the way going through forest. The last part is virtually a staircase of
roots and rocks, and one must use care when clambering down. The trail ends at
the lake (2.1 mi/3.4 km; 3970 ft/1210 m), the source of Hammer Creek.

Smith Lake lies in a forest-rimmed bowl, and its log-choked waters reflect various hues of green. The logs were probably carried down the crescent-shaped avalanche track on the slope to the east. Two campsites are located by the lake—one
near its outlet, the other on the north side. The lake is fairly large and is stocked
with rainbow and cutthroat trout. The slopes to the north and east are topped by a

silver forest of fire-killed trees. The mountainside to the northwest drops steeply toward the Skokomish; to the south the forested slopes that the trail descends rise above the lake.

116   BLACK AND WHITE LAKES WAY TRAIL

Not maintained
Length 2.0 mi/3.2 km
Access North Fork Skokomish Trail
USGS Map Mount Skokomish
Agency Olympic National Park

This trail has little to recommend it other than that it serves as a connecting link, thus making a loop trip possible. Backpacking up this route is not advised. The hiker's itinerary should therefore be planned so that one goes down the trail. Because water is not available on this path, a full water bottle should be carried.

The path begins at 1500 ft/457 m elevation on the **North Fork Skokomish Trail** opposite Big Log Camp. This is in the big timber, where the undergrowth is lush in the shaded, moist environment. Donahue Creek, out of reach in a canyon to the right, parallels the trail, which ascends the western spur of Mount Gladys. After about a half mile the large timber is left behind and most of the trees resemble broomsticks, although an old fir scarred by fire can be spotted now and then. The trail is extremely steep, and when one negotiates this route—whether going up or down—the shade is welcome on warm summer days. The Douglas-firs gradually disappear, and at the upper levels the trees are primarily western hemlock.

Emerging from the forest (1.6 mi/2.6 km), the trail climbs a spur, then crosses two humps that were ravaged by a forest fire years ago. Many dead trees still stand, their trunks bleached by weathering and blackened by the fire. The burned district contrasts sharply with nearby areas still clothed with green forest. Huckleberry bushes grow thickly, and the berries ripen to perfection because they receive lots of sunshine.

The trail crosses a meadow in the fire-killed silver forest to a junction with the **Smith Lake Trail** near Black and White Lakes (2.0 mi/3.2 km; 4200 ft/1280 m). To complete the loop take the Smith Lake Trail to the **Flapjack Lakes Trail**, which in turn connects to the North Fork Skokomish Trail.

117   SIX RIDGE TRAIL

Limited maintenance
Length 9.6 mi/15.5 km
Access North Fork Skokomish Trail; Graves Creek Trail
USGS Map Mount Olson
Agency Olympic National Park

One of the most strenuous routes in the Olympics, this trail climbs from the North Fork Skokomish to the east end of Six Ridge, which it then follows to

Six Ridge Pass. The many ups and downs test the mettle of the veteran hiker, and one can readily understand why the O'Neil expedition abandoned its attempt to build a pack-mule trail along this ridge.

The trail begins where the **North Fork Skokomish Trail** crosses the river (1475 ft/ 450 m) above Big Log Camp. At first the path, shaded by maples and alders, closely parallels the river, then it crosses Seven Stream where the creek emerges from a narrow canyon. Hikers should fill their water bottles here because water is not available during the next 5 miles. At this point the trail leaves the river bottom and switchbacks up a truncated spur to Six Ridge, which the O'Neil party called Deer Mountain. The forest is old growth, but the trees are not large. Huckleberries are abundant, and this is an excellent place to gather the fruit in a good year. The berries are usually ripe by early August.

Although the trail ascends steadily, via short switchbacks, the grade is not steep. As altitude is gained, one can glimpse the Skokomish Valley through the trees. Higher up, the slope eases and the switchbacks end, but the trail steepens as it climbs directly along the top of Six Ridge, which is flanked on the south and north sides, respectively, by Six Stream and Seven Stream. This serrated ridge is characterized by knobs that alternate with vales and depressions, thus causing the trail to go up and down. The configuration was caused by slumping and downward creeping of the steep valley sides. North and south, across the deep parallel valleys, one can see similar ridges. The distant mountainsides to the south, in the national forest, are scarred by logging operations. Cool breezes murmur in the mountain hemlocks, which are heavily bearded with lichen, and in late afternoon the ridge casts purple shadows in the forested valleys.

The ups and downs on the ridge seem interminable when one is backpacking, but eventually the trail breaks out into more or less open country on the ridge's south slope. This district was swept by fire in the past, and the blackened trunks of old snags rise above the brush. They create an eerie, almost surrealistic scene when the ridge is shrouded in fog. The trail then switchbacks up through the brush and fire-killed trees. Splashes of color are added by the mountain ash berries and the lupine blossoms.

After coming out upon the ridge top, the trail goes by a campsite near a tiny tarn, where water can be obtained (4.9 mi/7.9 km; 4400 ft/1341 m). The path follows the ridge through meadowland and rough outcrops of rock, where a few snowfields persist until late summer in shaded places. One looks north to Seven Ridge, south to Five Ridge. The latter is capped by the Three Sisters. Lake Cushman lies to the southeast. Directly ahead are Bruins Peak and Mount Adelaide.

Beyond a junction with the **Mount Olson Trail** (5.4 mi/8.7 km; 4400 ft/ 1341 m), the route descends into subalpine country on the south side of Six Ridge, where meadows alternate with groves of mountain hemlock. Here the trail crosses two swampy meadows and several brooks—the first running water beyond Seven Stream.

Camp Belview (6.4 mi/10.3 km; 4100 ft/1250 m) is located by a little stream near the edge of the second meadow. The open country is bordered by the steep slopes of Bruins Peak (5605 ft/1708 m), and snow avalanches down onto the meadow during the winter. The Sawtooth Range marks the eastern horizon, over which the sun rises to brighten Camp Belview in the morning.

The trail is less distinct beyond this point, but it contours a steep mountainside, alternately going through subalpine forest and marshy meadows, where the path often disappears. Little brooks are now abundant, in marked contrast to their absence between Seven Stream and Camp Belview.

Eventually, the route emerges onto a broad expanse of drier meadowland. The trail continues to alternate between subalpine forest and open country flecked with outcrops of rock. The route climbs over a spur, then descends to the larger of the two McGravey Lakes (8.5 mi/13.7 km; 4000 ft/1219 m).

The lake lies in a bowl beside a domelike outcrop of smooth rock and is surrounded by meadows dotted with mountain hemlocks. Beargrass waves in the breezes, murmuring brooks flow into the murky green lake, and bees hum busily in the heather fields. Nearby is the slightly smaller second lake, reflecting mountain hemlocks in its quiet waters.

The McGravey Lakes were named for John McReavy, a prominent pioneer, after he trekked through this area with several companions in the 1890s. McReavy was often called McGravey, and it is not clear whether the tarns were first called McReavy or McGravey. He lived at Union City, on Hood Canal.

Beyond the lakes the trail is poor, with several missing links where the route crosses meadows. The trail then enters a large meadow and climbs straight up, but the path is indistinct in places and one can be misled by elk trails. The grass is often higher than the cairns that mark the route, but hikers should watch for them because the path can be lost easily near Six Ridge Pass (9.6 mi/15.5 km; 4560 ft/1390 m). The pass marks the narrow ridge crest, and Mount Olympus and other peaks are visible to the northwest. Beyond this point the route becomes the **Graves Creek Trail**.

118   MOUNT OLSON TRAIL

Abandoned trail, no longer maintained
Length 8.5 mi/13.7 km
Access Six Ridge Trail
USGS Map Mount Olson
Agency Olympic National Park

This trail provides access to splendid high country that is remote from the well-traveled paths and thus not overrun with visitors. This solitude is due in part to the fact that one has to make a strenuous trek just to reach the trail. The part from Six Ridge to Lake Success is in fair condition, but the section between the lake and the East Fork Quinault River has been abandoned and is impossible to follow in places.

The trail begins on Six Ridge at the point (4400 ft/1341 m) where the **Six Ridge Trail** leaves the ridge, starting its descent to Camp Belview. As the Mount Olson Trail follows the ridge, it goes through meadowland having an abundance of beargrass and heather. The trees are mostly scattered mountain hemlocks. The views are excellent and include the Three Sisters to the south. The ridge narrows gradually to a spine a few feet wide, where the slopes fall away sharply on both sides, and one can look directly down on Six Stream on the south or Seven Stream on the north. The terrain is unusual, characterized by upright formations of rock and deep slump holes that are filled with heather or snow.

Beyond this spinelike ridge the trail crosses the upper edge of a large meadow, where the path is not well defined, then switchbacks steeply as it climbs to a promontory (4900 ft/1494 m) just below Bruins Peak. Across the headwaters of Success Creek, Mount Olympus marks the horizon, rising above the gap between two nearer peaks. The trail skirts below Bruins Peak on the north side, then crosses shale slopes, rock slides, and snowfields as it traverses westward beneath rock buttresses. The route now turns north, climbing to a notch in the divide between Success Creek and Seven Stream. The view down the valley of Seven Stream includes the Sawtooth Range, Mount Skokomish, and Mount Stone. At this point one can be misled by a blazed and flagged game trail that goes down into the headwaters of Seven Stream. The correct route stays high, however, more or less following the ridge.

As the trail contours north, Lake Success is visible below, near the lower edge of the basin on the western side of the divide. The trail then descends to the lake (3.0 mi/4.8 km; 4200 ft/1280 m). The little tarn is roughly rectangular in shape, with rockbound shores, and a campsite is located on the west side. The lake is surrounded by beautiful subalpine country, where mountain hemlocks stand as isolated specimens and in little clusters. The rolling heather meadows become masses of pink blossoms in late July, mixed with the white heads of beargrass, which is abundant but often cropped close by the elk. Wildlife tracks are everywhere—and the animals themselves can be observed on occasion. The view from the low ridge south of the lake is splendid—one looks down Success Creek toward the Quinault. The roughness of the canyon's steep walls is masked by heavy timber; thus they appear to be smooth.

Beyond Lake Success the route, marked by blazes, goes northwest, skirts the head of a branch of O'Neil Creek (where the hiker should avoid following a game trail down), then climbs over a saddle (4.5 mi/7.2 km; 4800 ft/1463 m) on the east shoulder of Mount Olson, just below the peak. Here one has an excellent view of the peaks flanking the headwaters of the East Fork Quinault, including Mount Anderson, Chimney Peak, and Mount Duckabush. The peaks rise above intervening forested ridges.

The trail descends a rock slide to a snowfield, then traverses a large meadow northeast of Mount Olson. The peak's north ridge, with a stand of fire-killed trees, is to the left. The trail angles to the left and descends the north ridge through heavy timber, where it becomes virtually impossible to follow. In fact, the cross-country hiker will make better time now by ignoring the trail and going due north by compass, picking out the best route while traveling. The slope is brushy, and it is steep in places.

Near the bottomlands the ridge pinches out between O'Neil Creek and the next stream west. At this point one is likely to strike the old trail again on a bench. The path goes through a forest where huge red cedars are scattered among the hemlocks. The trees are tall and straight, and were they more numerous one would be reminded of the redwoods. This stand is impressive enough to warrant the clearing and reopening of the trail by the National Park Service.

At the foot of the slope the trail comes out to the East Fork Quinault near the place where O'Neil Creek flows into the river opposite O'Neil Creek Camp (8.5 mi/ 13.7 km; 1150 ft/351 m). At this point it is necessary to wade the river, unless one can find a log spanning the stream. Normally it can be forded safely after mid-July, when it is only knee deep. The Enchanted Valley Trail can be reached on the north side of the river, just beyond O'Neil Creek Camp.

119   MOUNT HOPPER WAY TRAIL

Way trail, limited maintenance
Length 6.0 mi/9.7 km
Access North Fork Skokomish Trail
USGS Maps Mount Skokomish; Mount Steel
Agency Olympic National Park

Mount Hopper was named for Roland and Stanley Hopper, two brothers who settled on Lake Cushman in the 1890s. The peak stands near the head of the North Fork Skokomish River, and the trail leading to it begins at a junction (4540 ft/ 1384 m) with the **North Fork Skokomish Trail,** just below the First Divide. The trail, which receives only limited maintenance, is characterized by numerous ups and downs as it traverses around the western and southern sides of the peak.

At first the trail descends a bit through stands of mountain hemlock, then levels and climbs slightly. Windfalls are numerous, and they have not been cut out; thus one has to clamber under and over logs. The undergrowth consists largely of huckleberry. Most of the way, the trail alternately traverses forest and patches of meadowland. The latter become predominant toward the end, and the hemlock changes to subalpine fir. During the summer the meadows are wildflower gardens, where beargrass and lupine are abundant. The vistas from the open areas look across to the peaks beyond the North Fork Skokomish. Mount Skokomish (6434 ft/ 1961 m) stands in full view. The tiny Skokomish Glacier, the source of the North Fork, occupies a depression on its northern slope. Mount Henderson is visible to the right.

Beyond a grassy, boulder-strewn meadow, the trail climbs sharply, ending at Fisher's Pass (2.0 mi/3.2 km; 5040 ft/1536 m), which overlooks Elk Basin, the subalpine country at the head of Crazy Creek. One can walk from here to the summit of Mount Hopper in about an hour by following the south ridge. The view of mountains in every direction makes it well worth the effort—not to mention the delicious Olympic onion, found in abundance on the higher slopes.

Lieutenant O'Neil's scouts named Elk Basin in 1890, when they surprised a large herd of elk here and killed about a dozen animals. Lying at the southeast base of Mount Hopper, this cirque is bounded on all sides except the northeast by rugged cliffs. The place is quiet and peaceful, isolated from the well-traveled paths. Aside from the wind in the trees, or perhaps the bugle of an elk, one hears few sounds other than the gurgle of the little streams and the rush of the bigger ones down below. The basin has three levels, and a game trail along the north side provides the best means of going from one level to another. A good camp is located on the upper level beneath mountain hemlocks on a knoll beside a little stream.

Mount Skokomish, Mount Hopper Trail

The trail becomes an indistinct way path beyond Fisher's Pass and traverses meadowland and subalpine forest as it follows the ridge between Mount Hopper and Mount Stone to the Great Stone Arrow (5.0 mi/8.0 km; 5350 ft/1631 m). This pass is located at the western base of Mount Stone, between the headwaters of the North Fork Skokomish and the branch of Crazy Creek that heads in the Hagen Lakes. The lakes lie on the north side of Mount Stone, and one can see the largest one from the pass.

Beyond the Great Stone Arrow, so-called because rocks have been placed in the heather to form a directional sign, the route crosses talus slopes on the western side of Mount Stone, then climbs to another pass (6.0 mi/9.7 km; 5250 ft/1600 m) that overlooks Lake of the Angels on the Hamma Hamma side of the divide. A rough way path, broken in places, then descends the heather-covered slopes to the lake.

Campsite in Elk Basin

SOUTH
FLANK

What could be termed the South Flank of the Olympics, the area between Lake Cushman and Lake Quinault, lies almost entirely within the Olympic National Forest. This district consists of the watersheds of the South Fork Skokomish, Satsop, Wynoochee, and Humptulips Rivers. Only small areas at the head of the South Fork Skokomish (near Sundown Pass) and the Wynoochee (near Wynoochee Pass) are located within the national park. The South Flank was explored by the O'Neil expedition in the summer of 1890.

This once-lovely, heavily forested country has not been treated kindly by the timber industry and the Forest Service. Although formerly traversed by many miles of trail, the entire area has been dedicated almost exclusively to timber production during the last forty years. As such, it has been subjected to intensive logging, and the trails have fared worse here than elsewhere in the Olympics.

On the Wynoochee and Humptulips, roads have been built to the national park boundary and logging has occurred adjacent to park lands. Also on the Wynoochee, the U.S. Corps of Engineers built a flood-control dam that inundated several miles of the valley.

Most of the trails in the South Flank have been obliterated by logging roads, which have proliferated until they go everywhere. The virgin timber—practically all of it slated to be cut—has disappeared at an alarming rate. Few trails are left; the ones that still exist are but fragments of what was once an extensive network—and they remain because the timber companies haven't gotten around to logging the forest in those areas.

One is appalled, when driving through the South Flank, at the devastation that man can inflict upon the land. The roads traverse essentially three kinds of country—untouched virgin forest; old cutover land now restocked with second-growth forest in various stages; and recent clearcuts, which are raw and barren. The Forest Service argues, of course, that the trees will come back—and this is true, as evidenced on the old clearcuts. But one will never again have the opportunity to see an unblemished landscape because new clearcuts pop up as fast as the land restocks itself. Perhaps it would have been better had the agency cut it all in one fell swoop, then let the land lie undisturbed for fifty or sixty years, thus preventing the forest from looking like a moth-eaten coat.

In 1946 the eastern part of the South Flank was locked into an agreement between the Forest Service and the Simpson Timber Company (now terminated, according to the Forest Service). This contract gave Simpson exclusive rights to national forest timber in exchange for letting the agency manage Simpson's private timberlands. Although the Forest Service reserved the right to set aside tracts where, in its opinion, the esthetic or recreational values were paramount, or where, as a result of logging, severe erosion was likely to occur, and to prohibit or limit timber cutting on those lands, apparently little has been done in that regard. In fact, the agreement virtually converted a large section of the Olympic National Forest—public land that belongs to everybody—into

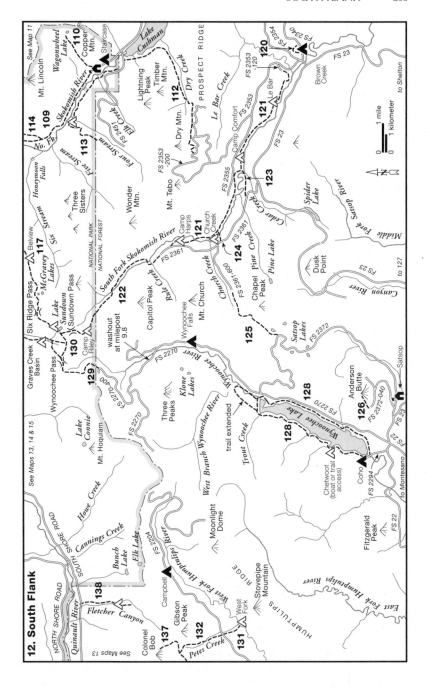

12. South Flank

Simpson's private preserve, with the result that wilderness recreation was largely excluded. The hiker or backpacker who goes into this area felt like an intruder. As often as not one drove miles up a Forest Service road only to find it blocked, several miles from the trailhead, by a logging operation, without any warning signs having been posted to that effect.

Although the South Flank is cut up, sliced, and gouged by many logging roads, hikers need concern themselves only with the ones that provide access to the few trails remaining in this district.

ROADS

South Fork Skokomish Road. This road provides the main approach to the trails on the South Fork Skokomish. The road starts 0.6 mi/1.0 km south of the Skokomish River crossing on US 101 and goes up the valley of the South Fork past prosperous country homes, where garden patches flourish. The land is devoted primarily to dairy farms and cattle raising. The road forks at Mohrweis (5.5 mi/8.9 km). The right branch becomes FS Road 23.

FS Road 23. Beginning at Mohrweis, this road first climbs a bit, then levels as it goes up the valley of the South Fork Skokomish. Frequently bordered by maples that turn golden in the autumn, creating a picturesque scene, the road twists and turns as it makes its way through the rugged southeastern corner of the Olympic National Forest. At 9.1 mi/14.7 km, FS Road 2353 branches to the right from FS Road 23 and crosses the South Fork Skokomish to a four-way intersection, where FS Roads 2361 and 2340 lead to the Lower South Fork Skokomish Trail and Brown Creek Nature Trail, respectively. FS Road 23 forks again at 13.2 mi/21.3 km. At this point it turns left and climbs to Spider Lake; the right hand branch is FS Road 2361.

Spider Lake (9.3 mi/15.0 km) is deep, with an irregular shape. Apparently it was created by a slide because many dead snags stick up out of the water. They are all that is left of the forest that once flourished on what is now the lake bottom.

Beyond the lake, FS Road 23 winds through a confusing array of logging roads, many of them not signed, to the trailhead of the Spoon Creek Falls Trail (31.0 mi/49.9 km). The road then crosses the West Fork Satsop River, here flowing in a narrow, vertical-walled gorge about 150 feet deep. At 31.9 mi/51.4 km, a shortcut road branching to the right leads to FS Road 2372 and the Satsop Ranger Station. FS Road 23 forks at 32.8 mi/52.8 km. FS Road 2372 bears right, FS Road 23 goes left, and at 33.7 mi/54.3 km, FS Road 23 unites with FS Road 2270 at a point about 100 yards north of a 90-degree turn in FS Road 22. This changes FS Road 22's direction from north–south to east–west, the north-south leg going to Montesano, the east-west branch to Wynoochee Lake and beyond.

Alternatively, the Spoon Creek Falls Trail can be reached from Montesano via FS Road 22, following it to its junction with FS Road 2270 (33.2 mi/53.4 km). From the junction drive 100 yards north to the terminus of FS Road 23 and follow that road to the trailhead (35.9 mi/57.8 km).

FS Road 2361. This road follows the South Fork Skokomish. At 3.5 mi/5.6 km, FS Road 2361–600 branches left, leading to the Church Creek Trail. FS Road 2361 ends at 5.5 mi/8.9 km, where the Upper South Fork Skokomish Trail begins.

Wynoochee Valley-Donkey Creek Road (FS Road 22). This road begins on

US 12 just west of Montesano. The first 17 miles are paved, where the road goes through farm land, stump ranches, and stands of second-growth timber in the lower Wynoochee Valley. Upon entering the national forest, the road traverses a mixture of cutover land and virgin forest. At a major intersection (33.2 mi/53.5 km), FS Road 22 goes left, FS Road 2270 straight ahead, and FS Road 2372 to the right. At 33.5 mi/53.9 km, on FS Road 22, FS Road 2294 branches right and leads to the Wynoochee Dam and Coho Campground (0.8 mi/1.3 km and 1.3 mi/2.1 km, respectively, from the junction). FS Road 22 crosses the foothills to a junction with the West Fork Humptulips Road, FS Road 2204 (46.6 mi/75.0 km), then comes out to US 101 (54.7 mi/88.1 km), 3 miles north of Humptulips.

FS Road 2270. This road begins where it intersects FS Roads 22 and 2372, parallels Wynoochee Lake to a junction (4.5 mi/7.2 km) with the other end of FS Road 2372, then follows the river. Wynoochee Falls Campground (7.9 mi/12.7 km) is primitive, and the space is limited, but it is the best place to camp in this area. The road is washed out at milepost 9.8, blocking vehicle traffic. Should the road be reopened in the future, it penetrates deeper into the mountains, where extensive logging operations are under way. The Wynoochee Trail can be reached by leaving FS Road 2270 at its junction (11.7 mi/18.8 km) with FS Road 2270–400, then following the latter 1.7 mi/2.7 km to the trailhead.

FS Road 2372. This road begins at a junction with FS Road 22 adjacent to the latter's intersection with FS Road 2270. The road then forks (0.9 mi/1.4 km). The right branch is FS Road 23; the left branch is FS Road 2372, which follows the Satsop River to its headwaters. After going by the western trailhead of the Church Creek Trail (7.3 mi/11.8 km), which leads to Upper Satsop Lake, the road winds high above Wynoochee Lake, then descends to FS Road 2270 near the head of the lake (12.3 mi/19.8 km).

FS Road 2372–040. This road ascends Anderson Butte almost to the summit and provides access to the last remnant of the old Anderson Butte Trail. Because it has many vistas overlooking clearcuts, this road is popular with deer and elk hunters. The road begins at a junction with FS Road 2372 at a point 1.3 mi/2.1 km east of the intersection of FS Road 2372 and FS Road 2270 north of Grisdale. The road forks at 2.5 mi/4.0 km. One should follow the left branch as far as it is drivable (3.0 mi/4.8 km from FS Road 2372; 2800 ft/853 m). (See description of Anderson Butte Trail for further instructions.)

West Fork Humptulips Road (FS Road 2204). This road begins at a junction with FS Road 22 near the Humptulips Ranger Station, on the southern boundary of the national forest, and follows the West Fork Humptulips to its headwaters. The views along the way include Stovepipe Mountain and Moonlight Dome—romantic names for the peaks east of the upper West Fork.

Opposite Stovepipe Mountain, a small parking area (10.5 mi/16.9 km) marks the point where the road bisects the Petes Creek Trail, dividing it into upper and lower sections. The beautiful Campbell Tree Grove (13.5 mi/21.7 km) is located at the foot of Moonlight Dome. Formerly known as the Big Tree Grove, this is a small area of large Douglas-fir in a district composed primarily of smaller species. This grove has been preserved, but logging has occurred close to it, as well as above and beyond it on the south slope of the ridge that forms the boundary between the national forest and the national park. The grove is similar to the Big Tree Grove near Willaby Creek on Lake Quinault.

The Forest Service built a road through the grove, thus allowing one to drive among the big trees, but it would have been better to have built a parking area nearby, with a nature trail through the grove, where people could walk and really see and appreciate the trees. However, the campground—which is not extensive, but consists of a few tent sites and picnic tables—is not in the big trees section but close by.

120 BROWN CREEK NATURE TRAIL

Length 0.8 mi/1.3 km
Access FS Road 23
USGS Map Lightning Peak
Agency Olympic National Forest

This nature trail, located adjacent to Brown Creek Campground on the South Fork Skokomish, begins and ends on FS Road 2340, but the trail itself is not marked. The path lies north of the road, and it makes a circle around a beaver swamp and a pond filled with water lilies. The elevation is about 600 ft/183 m above sea level, and the trail has several entrances or exits.

Beginning at the campground sign and going clockwise, the trail climbs a bit through second-growth Douglas-fir to a high point that overlooks the pond and swamp, which has a beaver hutch in the center. The trail then goes through an extremely dense stand of second-growth fir and comes out to a service road. After following the road about 50 yards, the path returns to the forest, where it descends to the flats near the campground. Here it goes through vine maple thickets, and it is bordered by large alders and bigleaf maples. The trail completes the circle at the campground sign (0.8 mi/1.3 km).

This is a delightful walk. On the flats the path meanders through what is almost a rain forest, where birds twitter constantly.

121   LOWER SOUTH FORK SKOKOMISH TRAIL

Length 8.9 mi/14.3 km
Access FS Road 2361; FS Road 2353–120
USGS Maps Mount Tebo; Lightning Peak
Agency Olympic National Forest

Fifty years ago the South Fork Skokomish Trail extended almost the full length of the river, beginning near Mohrweis, outside the national forest. Since then, however, logging operations have destroyed the lower third of the trail, and the midsection (the present Lower South Fork Skokomish Trail) has been detached from the upper third by FS Road 2361. This midsection is now paralleled by logging roads on both sides of the river; thus the hiker is never far from the sound of vehicular traffic.

As late as 1950, this part of the national forest was a vast expanse of untouched virgin forest—a primeval wilderness of giant trees. Today, however, clearcuts are visible everywhere, and the old growth is disappearing rapidly. Fortunately, the Forest Service has preserved a narrow strip of old-growth timber along the South Fork Skokomish River; unfortunately, the City of Tacoma, which dammed the North Fork in the 1920s, is studying the feasibility of building a power dam here. The structure would create a 1600-acre reservoir with a maximum depth of 250 feet. Consequently, the magnificent forest bordering the river is threatened with destruction—in this instance not from logging but from hydroelectric development.

The trailhead can be reached by driving the South Fork Skokomish Road to Mohrweis, then following FS Road 23 to its junction with FS Road 2353. At this point turn right onto FS Road 2353, cross the South Fork Skokomish to a four-way intersection, then go left 1.0 mi/1.6 km on FS Road 2353 to FS Road 2353–120; finally, go left on the latter 0.4 mi/0.6 km to the trailhead (900 ft/274 m).

The trail begins in an area that has been logged and is now covered with second-growth fir, which gives not the slightest hint of the grandeur that lies ahead. However, the path soon enters the virgin forest, where huge Douglas-firs rise high above vine maple, sword ferns, and vanilla leaf. The path descends steeply to LeBar Creek, then meanders across the bottomlands along the South Fork Skokomish—through a wonderland of giant firs, moss-draped bigleaf maples, alders, black cottonwoods, and thickets of vine maple and salmonberry. All the trees are large. The firs—monarchs five hundred to seven hundred years old—range up to 9 feet in diameter and many of them are more than 250 feet tall.

The trail alternately goes through groves of fir and hemlock and glades that consist mostly of deciduous growth. The river is perfectly clear, which is surprising, considering the amount of logging that has taken place in the vicinity. Were it not for the views of denuded mountains, hikers might think they were in the Olympic rain forest, particularly when fog lies low above the sandbars. This country is especially beautiful in the fall, when the maple leaves turn color. During late October they shower down like flakes of gold with every passing breeze, carpeting the ground.

The trail enters a clearing where a few trees were cut years ago, as evidenced by rotted stumps with springboard notches. Apparently this was the site of the old LeBar Guard Station (2.0 mi/3.2 km). Beyond this clearing the path goes back into the big timber. Although many large firs are present, the forest gradually becomes less impressive, and the trail descends to a flat where a stream is spanned by a plank bridge with an A-frame superstructure made of poles. During the next mile the trail crosses half a dozen creeks, each having its own distinctive bridge. One has arched handrails; another curves like a crescent as it crosses two parallel streams.

Beyond this series of bridged streams, the trail skirts the lower edge of a big clearcut where logging debris was pushed down to the trail. The path then goes back into the deep forest, and hunters' paths come down from the road above, intersecting the trail at various points. The path also divides several times, with trails going forth in various directions, then coming back together, like a braided river channel. Consequently, it does not matter which one the hiker takes, except at one place the main trail goes right, uphill, and the left branch leads to Camp Comfort (4.3 mi/6.9 km; 630 ft/192 m) on the banks of the South Fork.

The trail then climbs high above the river where the stream makes a big curve, traversing on the crest of the bluff what the Forest Service calls a partial cut—a selectively logged area where many trees were left standing. The trail is more or less level, but at times it climbs up and down, either traversing at river level or considerably above. At 6.7 mi/10.8 km the path is opposite Church Creek Shelter, which is on the west side of the river. The shelter may sometimes be reached by wading, but this is not feasible most of the year.

Eventually, the trail comes down to the river again (7.3 mi/11.8 km), crosses on a logjam to the west side, then climbs to a high bench above, where it forks (8.5 mi/13.7 km). The right branch goes downhill to Camp Harps Shelter, which stands on the banks of the Skokomish. The left branch leads to an old road, which it follows to FS Road 2361 (8.9 mi/14.3 km).

122 UPPER SOUTH FORK SKOKOMISH TRAIL

Length 7.7 mi/12.4 km
Access FS Road 2361
USGS Maps Mount Hoquiam; Mount Olson; Mount Tebo
Agencies Olympic National Forest and Olympic National Park

This is the upper part of the old South Fork Skokomish Trail, which at one time extended about 25 miles along the river. The trailhead (1300 ft/396 m) is located at the end of FS Road 2361 in the deep forest.

Upon rounding a bend, the trail overlooks the box canyon of the Skokomish, where the river rushes through a basalt gorge. The trail parallels the stream briefly, then descends to Rule Creek and the Lower Skokomish Crossing (1.2 mi/1.9 km). One must boulder-hop across the creek, but the river is spanned by a log with a handrail. The forest in this area contains a number of huge Douglas-firs.

After crossing the river to the east side, the trail climbs above the stream, which is now to the left. Large, moss-covered boulders are scattered through the forest—here consisting mostly of silver fir and western hemlock with, at times, considerable Douglas-fir.

Tumble Creek (1.9 mi/3.0 km) is aptly named because it cascades down the steep mountainside in its rush to join the river. The trail then descends through a rocky area overgrown with maple and alder to the Upper Skokomish Crossing (2.2 mi/ 3.5 km), where camps are found on both sides of the river among the giant firs. At this point the trail crosses, via a foot log, back to the west side of the Skokomish. (One should not be confused by the USGS Mount Steel quadrangle, which erroneously shows the Upper Skokomish Crossing to be about a mile beyond Tumble Creek.)

The trail then crosses an avalanche track grown up with alder, maple, and little evergreens. The river flows beneath the surface here, and the trail, which is now fairly level, parallels the dry stream channel for some distance. Not far beyond the avalanche track, the river once again flows above ground.

At this point the trail ascends through stands of western hemlock and silver fir to Startup Creek (4.0 mi/6.4 km; 1800 ft/549 m). Like Tumble Creek, this stream has an appropriate name because the trail now climbs steeply above the deep Skokomish Valley as it ascends a glacier-cut step, and one can hear the stream rushing through its canyon.

The trail is fairly well maintained almost to the national park boundary (5.1 mi/ 8.2 km; 2700 ft/823 m), then becomes little better than a way path—largely a mass of roots from which soil has eroded away. Within the park, the route climbs steadily to Camp Riley (5.4 mi/8.7 km; 3000 ft/914 m), located in a cluster of trees near a little stream and a grassy marsh surrounded by stands of Alaska cedar, mountain hemlock, and silver fir. The trail now crosses several brooks as it alternates between forest and marshy meadows. The hiker must boulder-hop across a large stream, one of two that form the headwaters of the South Fork Skokomish. The trail then skirts another forest-rimmed meadow grown up with tall grasses. The path keeps to the right, switchbacking up the slope through stands of large silver fir and mountain hemlock to the edge of another meadow. Again the trail keeps to the right, and as it gains elevation, one can look down the valley and see forested ridges, and a national forest clearcut in the distance.

Coming out into heather meadows dotted with mountain hemlocks, the trail tops a rise and goes by a little pond, then a larger one. The meadowland ends abruptly, hemmed in by a wall of mountain hemlocks on the ridge ahead, where the trail climbs to Sundown Pass (7.2 mi/11.6 km; 4103 ft/1251 m). The view through the trees on the northern slope consists of a succession of forested ridges, with the tip of Mount Olympus rising above them.

Beyond Sundown Pass the trail descends through stands of mountain hemlock, then meadowland, where the terrain flattens, ending at an intersection, where forest and meadow merge, with the **Graves Creek Trail** (7.7 mi/12.4 km; 3820 ft/ 1164 m). At this point one can go either left or right—left to Graves Creek and the East Fork Quinault; right, to Sundown Lake and Six Ridge Pass.

123   CEDAR CREEK TRAIL

Abandoned fragment, not maintained
Length 0.3 mi/0.5 km
Access FS Road 2361
USGS Map Mount Tebo
Agency Olympic National Forest

This abandoned fragment, which is no longer maintained, is all that remains of the old trail, destroyed by logging, that extended from the South Fork Skokomish River up Cedar Creek to Spider Lake, then to the head of the Middle Fork Satsop River and across the divide to Canyon River. The trail has been reduced from 15 miles to a half-mile stub that serves only to provide access to the **Lower South Fork Skokomish Trail** above Camp Comfort.

The trailhead (1000 ft/305 m) is located on FS Road 2361, 1.1 mi/1.8 km beyond its intersection with FS Road 23. The trail begins in a stand of old hemlock, but the forest floor is brushy with a dense growth of little evergreens, maple, salal, deer fern, and other plants.

Overlooking the river briefly, the trail descends to the edge of a clearcut, where the thick branches of second-growth firs almost obscure the path. The trail then parallels the river. As it follows the boundary of the clearcut, it is bordered by big timber on the left, by second-growth fir on the right. The trail then turns toward the river, coming out to a gravel bar (0.5 mi/0.8 km; 750 ft/229 m).

One can safely wade the river in late summer and early fall, when the stream is low, to reach the Lower South Fork Skokomish Trail. At other times of the year it is dangerous to attempt the crossing.

124 CHURCH CREEK SHELTER TRAIL

Length 0.3 mi/0.5 km
Access FS Road 2361
USGS Map Mount Tebo
Agency Olympic National Forest

The Church Creek Trail originally extended from the South Fork Skokomish to the divide at the head of Church Creek, then to Upper Satsop Lake. However, the construction of FS Road 2361 bisected the trail, and the extension of FS Road 2361–600 up Church Creek destroyed part of the trail. Consequently, what is left consists of two fragments—an eastern stub (Church Creek Shelter Trail) and a western section (Church Creek Trail).

A sign on FS Road 2361 beyond its junction with FS Road 2361–600 indicates that Church Creek Shelter is a half mile distant, to the east.

The trail descends steeply through virgin forest to the river bottom, where it crosses a slough. Church Creek Shelter (0.5 mi/0.8 km; 900 ft/274 m) stands on a little bench above the river in a grove of tall firs. (The USFS map and the USGS Mount Tebo quadrangle show the shelter on the east side of the Skokomish, which is incorrect.)

The trail ends here, and in order to reach the **Lower South Fork Skokomish Trail** it is necessary to cross the river, which is usually too deep and swift to ford. Consequently, one must search about for a log spanning the stream.

125 CHURCH CREEK TRAIL

Length 3.5 mi/5.6 km
Access FS Road 2361; FS Road 2372
USGS Map Mount Tebo
Agency Olympic National Forest

The western section of the old Church Creek Trail begins on FS Road 2361–600, 2.0 mi/3.2 km from FS Road 2361. FS Road 2361–600 traverses beautifully forested country that has been stripped by Simpson Timber Company with the blessings of the Forest Service.

The trailhead (ca. 1500 ft/457 m) is located at a bend in the road, and at first the trail goes through a stand of large silver fir and red cedar, with a scattering of big Douglas-firs. However, the latter are soon replaced by western hemlock. Here the song of the winter wren is likely to be heard. The view looks out to clearcuts on the other side of the valley. The undergrowth is luxuriant—largely huckleberry, with trailing club moss here and there. Deer ferns are numerous, as are flowering plants, including trilliums, avalanche lilies, and beargrass.

As it climbs toward the divide, via twenty-four switchbacks, the trail—mostly a bed of tree roots—crosses several brooks and occasionally goes by waterfalls that cascade down the slopes. The streams are lined by marsh marigolds and pioneer violets, and during the spring the hiker should look for the fairy slipper orchid. With increasing elevation, the forest becomes chiefly western hemlock, but also present are the tall, straight trunks of the Alaska cedar; then silver fir becomes predominant, replacing the hemlock.

The trail climbs steeply through a stand of large silver fir and comes out on a destroyed bulldozer path that forces the hiker to travel north a quarter mile to pick up the trail again. A giant western hemlock, with two buttressed, pistol-butted limbs on one side, marks the approximate crest of the divide (2.0 mi/3.2 km; 3150 ft/960 m).

The trail then descends steeply, to the right of a gorge, through the silver firs. As the route loses elevation, western hemlock again becomes intermingled with the fir. The trail makes four sweeping switchbacks, then comes out to Upper Satsop Lake (3.2 mi/5.2 km; 2195 ft/669 m), the northernmost and largest of the five Satsop Lakes, which are scattered over the comparatively level terrain. This tarn was originally named Lake Margaret in 1890 by Frederic J. Church, a member of the O'Neil expedition.

The lake has no outlet and is irregular in shape because the water level varies. During late summer and fall the inlet stream flows underground. Close to the lake's edge are mounds of sand or gravel, possibly old moraine, which are covered with grass; behind them, the virgin forest—hemlock, silver fir, and Alaska cedar—encircles the lake, and the trees are reflected in its placid waters. Rank growths of willow and salmonberry cover the open area in places. The lake contains Eastern brook trout as well as a large population of newts, or water dogs.

Beyond the lake the trail meanders to FS Road 2372 (3.5 mi/5.6 km; 2300 ft/ 701 m).

126 ANDERSON BUTTE TRAIL

Fragment of abandoned trail, not maintained
Length 0.3 mi/0.5 km
Access FS Road 2372–040
USGS Map Wynoochee Lake
Agency Olympic National Forest

Once beautifully timbered with virgin forest, Anderson Butte is a precipitous mountain that rises almost a vertical half mile above the bottomlands that border the two rivers—the Wynoochee and West Fork Satsop—between which the peak lies, near the southern boundary of the Olympic National Forest. During the last thirty years, most of the old-growth timber on the mountain has been logged, and several roads now carve their way up the peak's steep sides.

The Anderson Butte Trail formerly climbed, via Anderson Creek, from the Wynoochee Valley bottomlands to a fire lookout cabin that was built on the summit in the 1930s. However, the structure was removed several years ago, and almost all of the path has been obliterated by logging. The extant remnant (ca. 0.3 mi/0.5 km in length) is in fair condition and leads through old-growth hemlock forest near the summit, then up the final rock peak. This extrusion of basalt rises above the forest and provides a good view of the surrounding country.

The trail can be reached by driving up FS Road 2372–040 as far as it is drivable (ca. 3.0 mi/4.8 km; 2800 ft/853 m). One can either ascend directly from this point or walk the road another half mile, losing a bit of elevation, then climb several hundred feet through stumps and logging debris in a big clearcut. The trail will be found in the virgin forest at the upper edge of the clearcut (ca. 3000 ft/914 m).

The path first climbs, making several switchbacks, then traverses along the base of the rock cap, approaching it from the east. The last hundred feet or so negotiate an exposed ledge on the rock face. Years ago the Forest Service installed a cable here as a safeguard, but all that remains today are the iron posts. However, one does not really need the security of a handrail; the ledge is a simple walk, not dangerous if the hiker is careful.

The view from the summit (3358 ft/1024 m) includes much of the southern Olympics. This vista was magnificent in the old days—an expanse of rolling foothills and ridges clothed with untouched virgin forest. However, during the last three decades the country has been badly scarred by logging. Today many slopes are covered with second growth, and the remaining stands of old growth are moth-eaten with numerous clearcuts.

127   SPOON CREEK FALLS TRAIL

Length 0.2 mi/0.3 km
Access FS Road 22; FS Road 23
USGS Maps Grisdale; Wynoochee Lake
Agency Olympic National Forest

This trail can be reached from Montesano via FS Road 22 and from Hood Canal via FS Road 23 (for specifics, see the Roads section). The well-built path descends steadily and steeply to Spoon Creek, going through a mixed forest of large and small conifers with some deciduous growth, primarily vine maple. The ground cover is mostly salal. The trail ends at the creek bank (0.2 mi/0.3 km), but to see the falls one must walk 200 yards or so up the creek bed, which consists primarily of curiously spotted rocks. This is possible only during the dry season, not after heavy rains or during the time of maximum snowmelt in the high country.

Spoon Creek Falls are in the creek itself, not in a tributary stream. The water leaps over a precipice, then descends almost vertically, beginning (at least during the dry season) as two separate but parallel streams that fall about 15 feet or so, then blend together as the water spreads out to make a total fall of perhaps a hundred feet into a dish-shaped bowl that somewhat resembles a Chinese soup spoon or ladle, which probably explains the name. The water ribbons down the rock into a little, quiet pool, then slides over the edge to continue its journey down the now virtually level creek bed. At 0.15 mi/0.24 km beyond the falls, the creek adds its waters to the West Fork Satsop River.

128 WYNOOCHEE LAKE SHORE TRAIL

Length 16.0 mi/25.7 km
Access FS Road 2294
USGS Map Wynoochee Lake
Agency Olympic National Forest

The Wynoochee Dam (764 ft/233 m) was built (1967–72) by the U.S. Corps of Engineers to control floods on the lower Wynoochee River. The dam created a reservoir 4 miles long, generally about a half mile in width, and as a consequence destroyed the habitat of many kinds of wildlife, including elk, deer, bear, and grouse. The Forest Service built a trail around the new lake.

The path is described here going clockwise. Horses and motor-bikes are not allowed. The trail alternately goes through stands of second-growth forest and patches of virgin timber. Big stumps in the second growth—which often consists of thickets composed of firs little larger than broomsticks—hint at the former majesty of the forest. If the present stands are left undisturbed, perhaps five hundred years from now the big trees will be present again. The trail also climbs up and down in order to cross spurs and ravines; consequently, the route gains and loses quite a bit of elevation. Most of the time the path is 100 to 200 feet above the lake. At various points one can look across the water to beautiful mountains that have been badly scarred by logging. Winter wrens sing happily in the forest, but they have to compete with the racket made by motorboats. Trilliums bloom on the forest floor.

The trail begins at the north end of Coho Campground (880 ft/268 m), which is reached via FS Road 2294 and FS Road 22. It traverses high above the lake, then crosses an old road; just beyond it, the trail forks (0.5 mi/0.8 km). The right branch leads down to Chetwoot Campground, where a few sites are located on the lakeshore. This is a walk-in, boat-in camp. The left branch traverses northward, then switchbacks down to Scatter Creek, which flows into an arm of the lake. After crossing the stream, the trail climbs the other side, and eventually comes out to a road, which it follows a short distance.

Beyond this point the trail descends to Beaver Flat, a swampy area overgrown with alders and maples. Looking up the valley, one can see Mount Church and Capitol Peak, which are snow-clad in the springtime.

The trail turns northwest, away from the lake, in order to skirt a high sand bank, where a slide has done considerable damage. This sand bank is badly eroded, arid, and clifflike, and should be avoided by hikers because it is a hazard. The path then angles back to the northeast and descends to Trout Creek. The stream is not bridged, but one can cross on a logjam.

Wynoochee Lake Shore Trail (Photo by Frank O. Shaw)

When the trail comes out to the head of the lake, the hiker may be disconcerted to find that it is necessary to ford the Wynoochee River (6.0 mi/9.7 km) because the stream is not bridged at this point. Beyond the ford, the trail goes into the woods and leads to a field that serves as a primitive automobile camp which has no facilities (motorists can reach it via FS Road 2372 from FS Road 2270.) The path climbs above this camp through stands of old-growth fir and hemlock. The forest on this side of the lake is more impressive because the stands of virgin timber are more extensive. But, as on the west side, the trail climbs up and down—sometimes near the lakeshore, more often high above.

After crossing a rock slide, then a road, the trail meanders through second-growth forest. The lake is no longer visible except for an occasional glimpse. The path crosses Sixteen Creek, then descends through the broomsticks to a parking area at the Wynoochee Dam (16.0 m/25.7 km).

129 WYNOOCHEE TRAIL

Abandoned trail, limited maintenance
Length 3.7 mi/6.0 km
Access FS Road 2270
USGS Map Mount Hoquiam
Agencies Olympic National Forest and Olympic National Park

Today the Wynoochee Trail is just a fragment of what it was forty years ago. At that time it extended almost the full length of the river where the stream flowed through federal land—more than 15 miles in the national forest, a couple more in the national park. The latter part of the trail still exists, but in the national forest the trail has been obliterated by logging, road building, and the impoundment of water behind Wynoochee Dam. The area is botanically interesting because big trees occur at comparatively high altitude; included among them are some of the largest western hemlocks found in the national park.

The trailhead (2500 ft/762 m) is not marked, but the path begins where FS Road 2270–400 makes a U-turn (1.7 mi/2.7 km beyond its junction with FS Road 2270) below a clearcut that is now mostly covered with blackened stumps.

The trail goes through old-growth forest, which contrasts sharply with the roads and logged areas that the hiker leaves behind when setting foot upon this route. After crossing into the national park (0.2 mi/0.3 km; 2700 ft/823 m), the trail—often little more than roots and rocks—climbs steadily at a moderate grade. The terrain drops steeply to the Wynoochee River, here in a deep canyon. The trees are large western hemlock and silver fir; the dense undergrowth is chiefly huckleberry. The blossoms of bunchberry dogwood form beautiful carpets beneath the trees in early summer.

Between the park boundary and Wynoochee Pass the trail crosses a halfdozen creeks and several brooks. Because the slope is steep, the streams are characterized by cascades and waterfalls. The trail crosses the Wynoochee (here a small stream) just below the confluence of a creek (1.6 mi/2.6 km), each stream having a waterfall. The one in the river is a double cascade.

The trail steepens as it approaches Wynoochee Pass, and the trees change to mountain hemlock and Alaska cedar. The path climbs a high-angled slope, crosses an avalanche track overgrown with scrubby Alaska cedar, then switches back to the north. Here, from a couple of windows in the hemlock forest, one can view the Wynoochee Bowl at the river's headwaters. Near the pass a cluster of huge, multitrunked Alaska cedars—old derelicts more dead than alive—stands on the steep sidehill above the trail.

At Wynoochee Pass (2.2 mi/3.5 km; 3600 ft/1097 m) tall mountain hemlocks mark the low point in the north–south ridge that rises between the Wynoochee River and Graves Creek. The terrain just beyond the pass is more or less level, a mixture of subalpine forest, outcrops of sandstone, and heather meadows, where beargrass and huckleberry are abundant and the white lupine may be found. The meadowland is not extensive. The trail goes by two ponds, then descends the eastern slope through stately forests of silver fir and western hemlock having the usual undergrowth of huckleberry. Here a faint path (2.5 mi/4.0 km; 3400 ft/1036 m), marked by pink ribbon, leads right, downhill, but is easily overlooked. This is the **Sundown Lake Way Trail.**

Although the slope on this side of the divide is not as steep, the trail descends sharply via switchbacks and a traverse to a rocky creek bed, which is usually dry in late summer or early fall. This is the headwaters of Graves Creek, and just beyond the boulder-filled channel, the route intersects the **Graves Creek Trail** (3.7 mi/6.0 km; 2700 ft/823 m).

130 SUNDOWN LAKE WAY TRAIL

Not maintained
Length 1.0 mi/1.6 km
Access Wynoochee Trail
USGS Map Mount Hoquiam
Agency Olympic National Park

This path, a shortcut created by hikers headed for Sundown Lake via the **Wynoochee Trail,** saves about a mile of travel. However, its real raison d'etre is that it makes it unnecessary, in order to reach the lake, to descend 700 feet to Graves Creek Basin, then regain the lost elevation by ascending the Graves Creek Trail. Nevertheless, the route is not only rough but also has quite a bit of up and down. Consequently, backpacking to the lake via the regular trails is actually easier.

The path begins 0.3 mi/0.5 km beyond Wynoochee Pass, on the east side of the divide, at 3400 ft/1036 m. The route first leads downhill, to the right, descending a gully to a meadow, then traverses to a second meadow and climbs a bit. The trail makes a more or less level traverse through the forest and thick brush, crosses a rocky gulch, and climbs—steeply at times—over slippery roots and rocks. The way is fairly obvious where it goes through the woods, but one has to search for the path where it crosses meadows and ravines.

Eventually, the trail comes out into subalpine country, where one can look down the valley of Graves Creek and see a pyramidal peak in the distance. The trail then descends through a stand of large mountain hemlock to the **Graves Creek Trail** (1.0 mi/1.6 km; 3400 ft/1036 m).

131 LOWER PETES CREEK TRAIL

Length 1.0 mi/1.6 km
Access FS Road 22 (Donkey Creek Road), FS Road 2204
USGS Map Colonel Bob
Agency Olympic National Forest

The West Fork Humptulips Road (FS Road 2204) bisects the old Petes Creek Trail; thus we now have a lower and an upper section. The lower part goes from the road down to the West Fork Humptulips River Trail. FS Road 2204 is washed out at milepost 3.5. Until it is repaired, use FS Road 2220 as a detour to return to FS 2204.

The trail begins on the downhill side of the road, 10.5 mi/16.9 km beyond the Humptulips Ranger Station, at 1000 ft/305 m elevation. At first, the trail overlooks Petes Creek as it traverses a bench forested with hemlock and red cedar. The smooth, mossy path is almost level, and upon veering away from the creek it penetrates dense thickets and stands of little trees.

At the edge of the flat the trail switchbacks down to the West Fork Humptulips (0.9 mi/1.4 km; 700 ft/213 m). The West Fork Humptulips River Trail continues downstream 7.0 mi/11.3 km to the trailhead located at the West Fork Humptulips Gorge Bridge or upstream 3.9 mi/6.3 km to Campbell Grove Campground.

A sign at the trail junction indicates that the West Fork Humptulips River Shelter is located on the other side, opposite the confluence of the river and Petes Creek. Hikers should use care when crossing the river. The water can be waded in late summer or early autumn, but at other times the crossing may be dangerous.

The stream's banks are fringed by alders, with conifers further back. Beyond rises Stovepipe Mountain, clothed with evergreen forest.

132 UPPER PETES CREEK TRAIL

Length 2.4 mi/3.9 km
Access FS Road 22 (Donkey Creek Road), FS Road 2204
USGS Map Colonel Bob
Agency Olympic National Forest

The trailhead is located on FS Road 2204, 18.9 mi/30.4 km northeast of US 101, at 1000 ft/305 m elevation. Because the road bisects the old trail, the upper section starts on the uphill side and climbs to Quinault Ridge. Although the grade is moderate at first, it becomes steeper as the path switchbacks up the mountain. This route penetrates the southern part of the Colonel Bob Wilderness.

The trail begins in western hemlock forest, with some red cedar and silver fir present, and meanders through the woods, crossing five rocky stream beds, which are dry in late summer and fall. The fourth one is Petes Creek (1.0 mi/1.6 km; 1600 ft/488 m). Evidently the streams flow underground where the trail crosses, because one can hear a waterfall on the slope above, to the right.

Beyond the crossings the trail steepens, becomes rocky, and begins to switchback, crossing several little streams and an avalanche slope overgrown with vine maple, alder, and salmonberry. As it climbs steadily, the path parallels Petes Creek, which at this point is a fairly large, flowing stream. A small camp (2.0 mi/3.2 km; 2480 ft/756 m) has space for one tent, with water available at a little brook just beyond.

The trail now breaks out into an area covered with salmonberry and slide alder, then crosses a rock slide. Hikers should be alert for rolling rocks, which tumble down the steep, barren slope—the slide on Gibson Peak—that rises above the trail. Many whitened snags (the aftermath of a fire in 1963) are visible near the top, mingled with the living trees. As the trail zigzags up this open slope, one can look down the Humptulips Valley and see a succession of forested ridges.

The trail switchbacks over a rock slide, then returns to the alder and cedar thickets. Gibson Peak dominates the view to the right, with a large talus cone below steep cliffs broken by a gully. The trail ends where it intersects the **Colonel Bob Trail** (2.4 mi/3.9 km; 3360 ft/1024 m) on the south side of Quinault Ridge.

EAST FORK QUINAULT

Like many rivers on the Olympic Peninsula, the Quinault has two branches in the mountains, and it drains a large part of the southwestern Olympics. The North Fork, flowing down from Low Divide, and the East Fork, which heads near Anderson Pass, come together in the foothills. The river then flows through a broad, level valley to Lake Quinault. Glacial action created this lake during the Ice Age, when an alpine glacier deposited rock debris across the valley, thus damming the river. The lake lies on the edge of the mountains, midway between the river's source and the Pacific Ocean. Below the lake the Quinault River meanders across the Quinault Indian Reservation.

The East Fork Quinault, sustained by glaciers on Mount Anderson, sweeps in an almost straight line down a long, narrow valley bordered by timbered mountains. The deep upper part, walled in by precipitous slopes, is known as the Enchanted Valley. On the northwest, it is flanked by the Burke Range, so named in 1890 by the Press Expedition for Judge Thomas Burke of Seattle. The most important peaks in this range, which soar to almost 7000 ft/2134 m, are Crystal, Chimney, and Watterson. Muncaster Mountain, rising between the East Fork and Rustler Creek, marks the range's western end. The major peaks southeast of the East Fork—LaCrosse, White, Duckabush, and Steel—exceed 6000 ft/1829 m in elevation.

Below Enchanted Valley the East Fork is bordered by high, forested ridges. The river is paralleled on the north by a ridge that extends from Muncaster Mountain to the forks of the river. South of the East Fork, the major tributaries—such as Graves Creek and O'Neil Creek—break the continuity of the ridges, beyond which lie the headwaters of the rivers that flow from the southern flanks of the Olympics.

Lake Quinault lies less than 200 feet above sea level, surrounded by low, forest-clad mountains which culminate in Colonel Bob (4492 ft/1369 m). The slopes north of the lake are in the national park, but the more impressive peaks and ridges to the south are in the national forest. The river flows into the lake's northeastern end, where it has built a delta, then exits on the southwest side. Approximately 4 miles long by 2 miles wide, the lake covers 3729 acres and lies within the Quinault Indian Reservation.

The Quinault Valley is rain forest country, with an average annual precipitation of 140 inches on the lowlands and much more on the high peaks at the head of the valley. Because the temperatures are mild and the rainfall abundant, the trees on the river bottoms grow to enormous size, and the undergrowth is dense and luxuriant.

The East Fork Quinault was explored by Charles A. Gilman and Samuel C. Gilman in 1889 and by the O'Neil expedition in 1890.

ROADS

South Shore Road. The trails south of Lake Quinault and all those in the East Fork's watershed are reached via the South Shore Road, which extends from the

248

Olympic Highway, US 101, near the outlet of Lake Quinault, to Graves Creek on the East Fork. The road has two branches coming in from US 101 that form a Y at the west end. The north leg leaves the highway 0.1 mi/0.2 km south of the Quinault River crossing, 20.3 mi/32.7 km east of the Clearwater Road junction. The south leg leaves the highway 12.7 mi/20.4 km north of the Donkey Creek Road (FS Road 22) junction. (The distances to points on the South Shore Road are given here as if one were coming via the south leg; if approaching by way of the north leg, add 0.3 mi/0.5 km to the stated distance to any point.)

Along Lake Quinault the road goes by homes built among the spruce and fir trees and provides access to the Quinault Loop Trail and Willaby Creek Campground (1.5 mi/2.4 km). The road then enters Quinault (2.0 mi/3.2 km), where various facilities are located—including a lodge, general store, and ranger station.

Beyond Falls Creek Campground (2.4 mi/3.9 km), the road goes past farms and woodland homes—many well kept and prosperous looking, others not. The road continues through cutover land to Cottonwood Camp (11.3 mi/18.2 km), a primitive campground, then enters Olympic National Park (11.8 mi/19.0 km) at Bunch Creek, where the road closely parallels the river. Here one can look up the U-shaped valley and see snow-crowned peaks in the distance.

Within the park the stump ranches and fields are left behind as the road traverses beautiful rain forest. At Cannings Creek a bridge across the Quinault (12.8 mi/20.6 km) provides access to the North Shore Road. Beyond this point the route penetrates splendid stands of large Douglas-fir and spruce, as well as groves of gnarled bigleaf maples, garlanded with heavy growths of selaginella and mosses.

During the summer months, backpacking permits and trail information can be obtained at Graves Creek Ranger Station (18.5 mi/29.8 km). Graves Creek Campground (18.8 mi/30.3 km), located in a stand of fir and maples, is comparatively quiet, due to its isolated location; thus little traffic noise is heard. Nearby is the site of Graves Creek Inn, built in the 1920s and operated by the Olson family for many years. The road terminates at Graves Creek (19.1 mi/30.8 km), where the Enchanted Valley Trail begins.

Lake Quinault

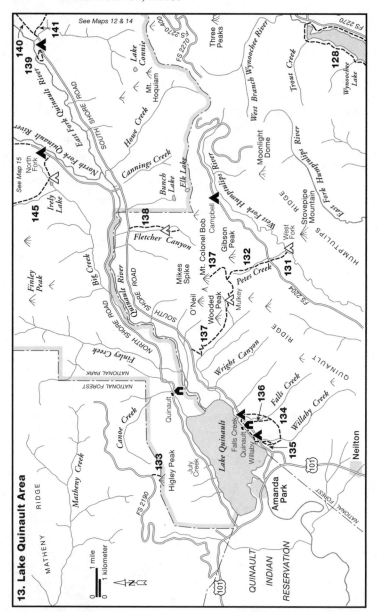

The South Shore Road is subject to frequent closures, especially during the rainy winter and spring months. Before hiking extensively in this area, one should consult the National Park Service as to the conditions prevailing at the time.

FS Road 2190. This logging road leaves the Olympic Highway 2.1 mi/3.4 km west of the North Shore Road intersection and climbs through timbered country and clearcuts. One has a good view of Mount Olympus and Mount Tom from this road, but the scene is impaired by clearcuts on the intervening ridges.

The road climbs almost to the top of Higley Peak, then continues into the Canoe Creek drainage. The signed Higley Peak Trail is located at 9.6 mi/15.5 km.

133   HIGLEY PEAK TRAIL

Length 0.5 mi/0.8 km
Access FS Road 2190
USGS Map Matheny Ridge
Agency Olympic National Forest

The old Higley Peak Trail began near the national park boundary on the Haas Road, northwest of Amanda Park. The trail climbed the spur between Prairie Creek and Higley Creek to Higley Ridge, then followed the ridge to Higley Peak (3.0 mi/4.8 km), also on the national park boundary, north of the lake. However, since the construction of FS Road 2190, this old trail has virtually vanished. Mention is made of it here because of its historic importance.

The present trail (in the national forest) begins 9.6 mi/15.5 km from US 101 on FS Road 2190, at 2800 ft/853 m, where two small parking spots are located. The trail climbs through silver fir forest to the summit of Higley Peak (0.5 mi/0.8 km; 3025 ft/922 m).

This peak overlooks everything named Quinault—the lake, the valley, the ridge beyond—as well as Mount Colonel Bob and the forested ridges that lead to the snowy peaks of the Olympics. However, the view to the north is obscured by trees. The old lookout cabin was constructed in 1932 by the Forest Service and used during World War II as one of the government's stations in the Aircraft Warning System. It was rebuilt on a wooden tower in 1964, then removed by helicopter in 1973. The building and tower are currently being used at Snohomish County Airport. A microwave reflector and tower that later occupied the space were removed in 2002.

Higley Peak was named for a pioneer family that settled on Lake Quinault. Alfred V. Higley, a Civil War veteran, and his son, Orte, arrived in October 1890, after following Lieutenant Joseph P. O'Neil's pack train across the Olympics from Hood Canal via O'Neil Pass.

134   QUINAULT LOOP TRAIL

Length 4.0 mi/6.4 km
Access South Shore Road
USGS Map Lake Quinault East
Agency Olympic National Forest

One of three trails south of Lake Quinault, this route makes an irregular closed loop that has no beginning or ending point, and it lies less than 500 feet above sea level. The trail is described counterclockwise, beginning at the parking area on the South Shore Road 200 feet northeast of the Pacific Ranger District, Quinault office.

The trail follows Falls Creek, which until 2002 had its banks lined with protective gabions (wire baskets filled with stones). The gabions (and a dam) have since been replaced with erosion-control structures made of rock and logs. A bridge over the creek leads to the campground and picnic area east of the creek; walk-in camp-sites on the west side are just ahead.

Coming out to the lake, the trail edges the shore, going by houses, garages, and boat landings, and one can hear the traffic on the nearby road. The path then crosses in front of Quinault Lodge. During hot, dry weather sprinklers on the roof of this imposing establishment keep it wet as a safeguard against fire.

The jungle along the lakeshore consists of a rank growth of blackberry, salmon-berry, skunk cabbage, thimbleberry, and hydrangea that has gone wild. The view is good across the lake to beautifully forested Higley Peak and the ridges to the north, but the mountainside to the northeast is scarred by a real estate development on private land within the national park boundaries. At one point the hiker can look up the Quinault Valley and see Mount Colonel Bob.

At Willaby Creek Campground (0.9 mi/1.4 km), the trail turns away from the lake, then crosses Willaby Creek and goes beneath the highway bridge that spans Willaby Gorge. The trail now enters the primeval forest, where the coolness is in-viting on a hot day. This section along the gorge, with its luxuriant display of rain forest vegetation and big trees, is the most beautiful and imposing part of the route. The broad, smooth path, bordered by protective guardrails, climbs as it parallels the steep-sided canyon, which is lined with ferns (particularly sword and maiden-hair), devil's club, huckleberry, and salmonberry. The trees are impressive: giant firs, spruces, and cedars lift lofty crowns high above the jungle that borders the clear, rock-bottomed stream. The forest floor is covered with oxalis and several kinds of ferns—deer, sword, and maidenhair. Signs posted along the trail give information about the rain forest.

The path climbs to a junction with the **Quinault Rain Forest Nature Trail** (1.2 mi/1.9 km). The trail then leaves the big firs as it descends through stands of western hemlock (apparently growing on an old burn), crosses Willaby Creek, and returns to the virgin forest. Here it enters a swamp where western red cedars are abundant, including numerous dead snags. The trail now consists of puncheon, much of it an elevated boardwalk that curves around the trees and piles of logs.

Leaving the bog, the trail follows Falls Creek to a junction with the **Lodge Trail** (2.9 mi/4.7 km), crosses the creek, and goes through stands of western hemlock. After crossing Cascade Creek—a series of cascades and pools—the trail descends to the South Shore Road and the parking area at Falls Creek (4.0 mi/6.4 km).

135 QUINAULT RAIN FOREST NATURE TRAIL

Length 0.6 mi/1.0 km
Access South Shore Road
USGS Map Lake Quinault East
Agency Olympic National Forest

This trail begins at the parking area on the South Shore Road west of Willaby Creek, 1.5 mi/2.4 km from US 101. The trail ascends through the Big Tree

Grove, one of the most impressive bits of old-growth Douglas-fir remaining in the Pacific Northwest. Although larger firs are found in the Olympics, this is an even-aged stand approximately five hundred years old. The stately trees are almost perfect in form, and they are all about the same size—6 to 10 feet in diameter and about 275 feet tall. The straight columns rise free of limbs for a hundred feet or more, and little pads of moss cling to the ribbed bark. Other species present include western hemlock, red cedar, and Sitka spruce. Oxalis and ferns carpet the ground.

Benches have been placed along the trail at various points, where one can relax and look—and absorb the mystery of the rain forest. Although the trail is short, one should not hurry through but take time to savor the magnificence. This is easy to do because the forest is quick to assert its primeval mood upon the visitor. One is both glad and sad—glad that this splendid remnant has been preserved; sad to realize that millions of acres of forest like this have been destroyed by fires and logging since the white man came to the Pacific Northwest. The Forest Service estimates that the timber growing here upon a single acre (approximately the size of a football field) would provide enough lumber to build forty average-size houses. However, the recreational and esthetic value of the trees is considered to be far greater than their value as lumber; consequently, they have been preserved for the enjoyment of present and future generations.

Because Douglas-fir requires mineral soil and sunlight to grow, it does not perpetuate itself in the shade. Therefore, an opening must have been made here about the time that Columbus set sail for the New World. The open area may have resulted from violent winds or perhaps from a fire such as occurs in the rain forest every hundred years or so during spells of unusually hot, dry weather.

Near the grove's eastern edge, adjacent to Willaby Creek, the trail ends in a junction with the **Quinault Loop Trail** (0.6 mi/1.0 km). Hikers can return to the parking lot by retracing their footsteps or by following the loop trail along Willaby Gorge to the road just east of the parking area.

136 LODGE TRAIL

Length 0.6 mi/1.0 km
Access South Shore Road
USGS Map Lake Quinault East
Agency Olympic National Forest

Used chiefly by tourists staying at Quinault Lodge, this trail extends southward and intersects with the **Quinault Loop Trail**, thus making possible a couple of loop hikes.

The graveled trail begins directly across the road from the lodge (220 ft/67 m) and climbs through a dense stand of small hemlock, where the undergrowth consists chiefly of red huckleberry and vine maple. The trail soon levels and changes to a dirt path about a yard wide—much broader than the typical backcountry trail. The trees are now larger; the route is bordered by excellent examples of Sitka spruce and western red cedar, with a few large Douglas-firs present. The forest floor is covered with many moss-covered logs and stumps and by a rich undergrowth of oxalis, ferns, and huckleberry.

The path traverses above Falls Creek, then ends in a junction with the Quinault Loop Trail (0.6 mi/1.0 km). The hiker who wishes to return to the lodge from this point has a choice of three routes: going back over the route just walked or traveling east or west on the Quinault Loop Trail. The distance via the Lodge Trail is less than going in either direction on the loop trail.

137   COLONEL BOB TRAIL

Length 7.2 mi/11.6 km
Access South Shore Road
USGS Maps Lake Quinault East; Colonel Bob
Agency Olympic National Forest

Colonel Bob is the highest of four peaks clustered together about 5 miles east of Lake Quinault and south of the Quinault River. The name McCallas Peak—for John McCalla, one of the first settlers on the lake—was given in 1890 to one or perhaps all four peaks (considered as one), consisting of Mount O'Neil, Colonel Bob, Gibson Peak, and Wooded Peak. Colonel Bob was named later for the noted nineteenth-century agnostic Robert Ingersoll; Mount O'Neil, so named in 1932 for Lieutenant Joseph P. O'Neil, leader of the O'Neil Expeditions, was formerly called Baldy.

This collection of peaks forms part of the south slope of the Quinault Valley, between the lake and the national park. The beautifully timbered mountains rise 4000 ft/1219 m above the bottomlands along the river. This area is now protected because it is within the Colonel Bob Wilderness, which was established in 1984.

The trailhead (230 ft/70 m), located on the South Shore Road, 6.0 mi/9.7 km from US 101. The terrain is steep, and the trail begins to climb at once through conifer forests, where the undergrowth is mostly sword and maidenhair ferns. Mixed with the slender hemlocks are huge firs and cedars. Higher up the slope, some of the large trees have been scarred by fire. The big trees are survivors of a former stand; the younger hemlocks have grown up since the fire.

The trail climbs steadily, paralleling Ziegler Creek, which can be heard below, to the right. As the path switchbacks up the mountain, the Douglas-fir gradually disappears, replaced by silver fir. Big rocks covered with mosses and ferns lie scattered through the forest.

Mulkey Shelter (4.0 mi/6.4 km; 2160 ft/658 m) is located in a marshy, jungled area infested with mosquitoes; therefore, one would be better advised to camp farther on at Moonshine Flats. The shelter was constructed by the Forest Service in 1930 to replace a cabin built about 1910 by Mart H. and Purl Mulkey. The brothers had a trapline that extended from the Colonel Bob area to Bunch Lake, where they had another cabin.

Making about a dozen switchbacks, the trail climbs sharply to Quinault Ridge (3200 ft/975 m). Here the terrain falls away sharply on both sides, and the forest is mostly western hemlock and silver fir. Now comes a disconcerting feature—the trail zigzags down, losing considerable elevation, before traversing beneath a rock cliff, where it crosses avalanche tracks.

Beyond the junction with the **Upper Petes Creek Trail** (5.5 mi/8.9 km; 3300 ft/ 1006 m), the route is devious, and unless one knows the way it is difficult to follow when covered with snow. The trail emerges from the deep forest and enters more or less open country. A cliff rises to the left, and ahead one can see a huge talus cone or slide on Gibson Peak. The trail is now rocky, not smooth like it was in the forest, and it crosses a little basin, where big boulders lie strewn helter-skelter. The tall grasses wave in the wind, accompanied by its murmur in the trees on the ridge. Wildflowers bloom profusely, mingled with smooth-slabbed rock outcrops. Here one will note daisies, lupine, thistles, Columbia lilies, arnica, and pearly everlasting.

Beyond this point the trail might well be called Salmonberry Lane. During the next half mile or so the path is bordered by a rank growth of the bushes. When the sweet, delicious berries ripen—usually around mid-August at this altitude—they are abundant, and the hiker is apt to linger and feast on the fruit.

Leaving the switchbacks and salmonberries, the footpath climbs to a gap (3700 ft/ 1128 m) that looks out over Fletcher Canyon to the peaks beyond the Quinault. The trail now veers to the left and descends to Moonshine Flats (6.3 mi/10.1 km; 3500 ft/ 1067 m). This subalpine basin lies between Colonel Bob and Gibson Peak, at the head of the canyon. Large boulders are scattered about, intermingled with beargrass, heather, and huckleberry. Several campsites are located beside Fletcher Creek, which

Forks of the Quinault

flows over a bed of living rock. The vegetation is typical of the Subalpine Zone; the trees are chiefly mountain hemlock and Alaska cedar.

Beyond the camp, the trail climbs steeply as it traverses beneath dark basalt cliffs and switchbacks up to the ridge, where the wind often howls in the hemlocks. Here one can look both north and south. The trail angles back east, beneath Colonel Bob, to a saddle above a rocky basin, beyond which rises a three-humped mountain. The last 100 feet lead up a rock face, via steps hacked in the rock, to the summit of Colonel Bob (7.2 mi/11.6 km; 4492 ft/1369 m).

The Forest Service built a fire lookout cabin on the top of this peak in 1932, but it was removed in 1967. Here one has an outstanding, unobstructed vista of the Quinault country—the lake, river, valley, timbered foothills, Pacific Ocean and snowy peaks to the north and east. Mount Olympus is visible on the skyline. The view to the south encompasses ridge after ridge, heavily forested but scarred by numerous clearcuts.

The summit is a pleasant place to spend some time on a warm, sunny day. The squawking of ravens in the forest below is the only sound heard above the whisper of the wind, and one feels far removed from the frenetic rush of civilization.

The impressive spire (ca. 4175 ft/1273 m) rising midway along the ridge between Colonel Bob and Baldy, or Mount O'Neil, is known as Mikes Spike. George A. Bauer and the late Mike Lonac spotted the pinnacle in 1974, and Lonac later made the first ascent. Climbers can reach it by leaving the trail near the base of the final peak and traveling cross-country about 200 yards.

138   FLETCHER CANYON TRAIL

Length 2.3 mi/3.7 km
Access South Shore Road
USGS Map Bunch Lake
Agency Olympic National Forest

This interesting but little-known trail begins on the South Shore Road 11.3 mi/18.2 km from US 101, at 400 ft/122 m above sea level. Near its beginning the trail goes by a big rock covered with mosses and ferns, then crosses a little stream, where a tiny pool collects drinking water. Ahead and to the right one can see an area where the wind has knocked down many trees. Because sunlight easily penetrates the thin forest canopy, red huckleberries grow profusely in the devastated area.

The trail avoids the windfall by switchbacking up to the left. Here it enters the dark realm of fir—dense stands of tall, slim evergreens. The forest floor is covered with ferns and mosses, and large boulders are scattered about. Although the grade eases where the trail crosses a rock slide, the ascent is unrelenting. The path is both smooth and rough, but generally the former, and as the trail traverses the mountainside the forest gradually changes to western hemlock and silver fir.

At 1.0 mi/1.6 km, the route climbs steeply through huge, moss-covered boulders. After going by a wall clad with mosses and ferns, the trail slides to the right—to use Forest Service slang—and descends to Fletcher Creek. The stream is bordered by currant and salmonberry bushes, and one can see a waterfall ahead.

A large foot log spans the creek, and the trail crosses to a campsite in Fletcher Bowl, a comparatively level area (1.9 mi/3.1 km; 1450 ft/442 m). Beyond the camp, the trail meanders through a heavy growth of salmonberry, where one cannot see the footpath, merely a "way" through the jungle; then, leaving the flat, the path leads uphill through hemlock forest. The trail is poor, dim in places, often scarcely discernible, but the way is marked with colored ribbons.

After topping a rise, the trail traverses above the canyon, then descends to the bottom, where it ends among the boulders in the rocky creek bed (2.3 mi/3.7 km; 1500 ft/457 m). During late summer the creek flows underground at this point. Slide alder and

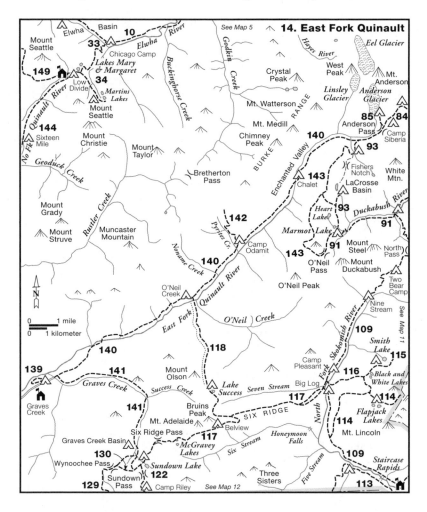

vine maple are abundant; avalanche debris is scattered everywhere.

One can, if he is foolish enough, travel cross-country from here to the Colonel Bob Trail, striking that route just below Moonshine Flats (4.5 mi/7.2 km), but it is rough going and not recommended. The hiker headed for Moonshine Flats would be better advised to take the Colonel Bob Trail.

139 GRAVES CREEK CAMPGROUND NATURE TRAIL

Length 1.0 mi/1.6 km
Access South Shore Road
USGS Map Mount Hoquiam
Agency Olympic National Park

Used mostly by casual walkers, this trail makes a circle adjacent to Graves Creek Campground. One should hike the trail counterclockwise, thus saving the best part for last. The trail is so described here.

The trail begins and ends near the river, at the campground's west end (570 ft/ 174 m). After traversing a lovely stand of bigleaf maple garlanded with mosses and ferns, the path descends to a flat by the river and crosses an old gravel bar. This former channel of the river is still largely devoid of vegetation. The trail then comes out onto a grassy bench above the Quinault. Although many large, old firs stand on the far side of the river, the forest along the trail is large second-growth fir and spruce on land that, in geological terms, was recently riverbed.

After a bit, the trail veers away from the river and crosses flats covered with typical rain forest, including a fairyland of impressive bigleaf maples. The trail then meanders through firs up to 4 feet in diameter, returning to the starting point (1.0 mi/1.6 km).

140 ENCHANTED VALLEY TRAIL

Length 18.9 mi/30.4 km
Access South Shore Road; West Fork Dosewallips Trail
USGS Maps Mount Hoquiam; Mount Olson; Chimney Peak; Mount Steel
Agency Olympic National Park

This major route, one of the most popular trails in the Olympics, apparently attracts every serious hiker at one time or another. People hear about it from other hikers, or they read something somewhere, so they have to go see for themselves. Few come back disappointed.

The trail begins where the South Shore Road ends at Graves Creek (600 ft/ 183 m). The road formerly extended 2.4 mi/3.9 km farther up the valley, but the section beyond Graves Creek is now part of the trail. The route ends at Anderson Pass, on the southern flanks of Mount Anderson.

Looking down the Enchanted Valley (Photo by Frank O. Shaw)

Beyond the old bridge over Graves Creek—now used only by foot traffic—the trail climbs to a junction with the **Graves Creek Trail** (0.1 mi/0.2 km). As it follows the old roadbed, the route goes through a magnificent forest of giant firs and cedars. Many trees are 6 to 8 feet in diameter and more than 250 feet tall. The undergrowth consists largely of huckleberry, vine maple, and devil's club. On the forest floor, queencup beadlilies and bunchberry dogwood add festive touches of color, scattered as they are among the sword and deer ferns.

A picnic table (2.4 mi/3.9 km; 1178 ft/359 m) marks the end of the abandoned road and the point where the forest changes to western hemlock and silver fir. The path descends steeply to the East Fork Quinault, and one can hear the river in the distance.

At the Pony Bridge (3.0 mi/4.8 km; 903 ft/275 m) the river plunges through a narrow gorge walled by layers of slate and sandstone inclined almost vertically, the rock sheathed with maidenhair ferns. A camp is located just beyond the bridge—the first of more than half a dozen riverside camps found along the trail in the next 2 miles.

The trail parallels the East Fork and is characterized by numerous ups and downs as it traverses moraine, terraces, and deposits of river gravel, descending to the stream's banks at the various camps. The forest now includes Sitka spruce, with a few big firs scattered among the alders and maples on the bottomlands. The broad-leaved trees are festooned with mosses, lichens, and liverworts. As it follows the meandering river, the trail winds through shadowy forest aisles.

The valley is pleasant, cooled by gentle breezes that come down from the snowfields at the river's head. Most of the time the Quinault rushes by noisily, but where it is deep and quiet the sound is soothing and peaceful. Except for the show of white water when it is broken by rapids, the river is pale green, especially in the morning; but it becomes turbulent on warm afternoons when the snow melts rapidly.

O'Neil Creek Camp (7.0 mi/11.3 km; 1179 ft/359 m), reached by a spur path, lies between the trail and river, opposite the point where O'Neil Creek flows into the East Fork. At this camp one can ford the Quinault to reach the abandoned **Mount Olson Trail** on the opposite side.

Beyond O'Neil Creek, the trail crosses numerous streams, several of them bordered by alluvial fans. A good campsite is located at Noname Creek (8.5 mi/13.7 km) and another at Pyrites Creek (10.0 mi/16.1 km; 1450 ft/442 m), where the old **Pyrites Creek Trail** begins. This site was named Camp Odamit by the party Lieutenant Joseph O'Neil sent to Mount Olympus in 1890. As it meanders up the valley, the trail crosses a number of small tributaries, but only one, Lamata Creek, has been named.

The path enters Enchanted Valley at the point where the river is spanned by a footbridge (12.6 mi/20.3 km; 1920 ft/585 m). Fred W. Cleator, a Forest Service employee, named Enchanted Valley in the late 1920s, when it was part of the Mount Olympus National Monument.

As the name implies, the valley is a lovely place, its charm enhanced by its isolation from highways and vehicular traffic. Perhaps it could best be described as somewhat resembling a miniature Yosemite. A glacier which filled the valley during the Ice Age deposited a moraine at the lower end. When the glacier retreated, the moraine dammed the river, thus creating a lake. However, both the glacier and the lake have been gone for thousands of years. On the valley floor the Quinault splits into a multitude of braided channels. The flats along the river, covered with lush grasses and alder groves, are bordered on the northwest by a cliff, 4000 ft/1219 m high, the sidewall of the Burke Range, which isolates the valley from the streams that flow to the Elwha River. The ridge from O'Neil Pass to Anderson Pass forms the less abrupt southeastern side, which is heavily forested. The valley floor is more or less open and free of evergreen forest—possibly due to heavy accumulation of snow during the winter.

When the snowdrifts on the Burke Range melt in early summer, hundreds of cascades plunge down the cliffs. They are responsible for another name, Valley of a Thousand Waterfalls. By late summer, when the snow is gone, most of them have disappeared, but a number remain. During the winter and spring, avalanches sweep down these cliffs, and the snow piles up, creating snow cones at the bottom. Accordingly, tiny ice fields cling to the mountainside near its base.

Enchanted Valley Chalet (13.3 mi/21.4 km; 2000 ft/610 m), a three-story log structure built in 1930, now serves as a ranger station only and is not available for visitor use except during an emergency. (The National Park Service does not consider poor weather to be an emergency.) The chalet stands near the western end of a flat, grassy meadow. The view from here includes the Linsley Glacier on Mount Anderson, as well as the valley's northwestern wall, with its waterfalls and pockets of ice. Fingers and islands of Alaska cedar break up the continuity of the barren cliffs, which are composed of slate and sandstone mixed with greenstone (a metamorphosed basalt).

At the head of Enchanted Valley, about 2 miles beyond the Chalet, the trail begins its ascent to Anderson Pass. The largest known western hemlock stands near the trail, its status proclaimed by a sign. The tree is almost 9 feet in diameter, and other hemlocks in the vicinity are nearly as large. The river, now constricted between steep, timbered slopes, cascades noisily over boulders and rocks. At this point Anderson Creek tumbles down from Linsley Glacier on Mount Anderson, adding its volume to the river.

As it climbs out of the valley, the trail makes an ascending traverse high above the roaring Quinault, going through stands of silver fir. The trail crosses White Creek just below a waterfall. This brawling stream flows down the north slope of White Mountain. Beyond the junction with the **O'Neil Pass Trail** (16.9 mi/ 27.2 km; 3200 ft/975 m), the trail switchbacks as it climbs steadily toward Anderson Pass. On warm days torrents of water plunge down the slopes of Mount Anderson, and on rare occasions the stillness may be broken by the crash of ice falling from Linsley Glacier. When the weather is hot, one should make the climb to the pass during the morning because the afternoon sun bears down upon this mountainside.

The view from Anderson Pass (18.9 mi/30.4 km; 4464 ft/1361 m) looks east across the valley of the West Fork of the Dosewallips, west down the Quinault. At the pass the route becomes the **West Fork Dosewallips Trail**, and the **Anderson Glacier Trail** ascends the lower slopes of Mount Anderson.

141   GRAVES CREEK TRAIL

Length 8.6 mi/13.8 km
Access Enchanted Valley Trail; Six Ridge Trail
USGS Map Mount Hoquiam
Agency Olympic National Park

The Graves Creek Trail branches right from the **Enchanted Valley Trail** just beyond Graves Creek bridge, follows the stream to its headwaters, then traverses the Graves Creek–Six Stream Divide to Six Ridge Pass. Of botanical interest on this route is the fact that large trees persist to comparatively high altitude. Several vantage points along the trail afford splendid views of the Graves Creek gorge and early-season waterfalls on the opposite mountainside.

The trailhead (646 ft/197 km) is located in a setting of western red cedar. The path first climbs above Graves Creek—which can be heard but is not visible— onto a bench covered with stands of hemlock, cedar, and fir. Little streams are numerous, and the ground is blanketed with luxuriant undergrowth, such as oxalis, vanilla leaf, queencup beadlily, and ferns (sword, deer, and maidenhair). This is also elk country, and the animals' tracks are everywhere. On occasion the lucky hiker may see a herd.

The trail gains elevation gradually, and the sound of the creek disappears. Then, after a bit, the trail descends, and Graves Creek, still hidden, can be heard again. In fact, this stream is just the reverse of what children are supposed to be like—it can be heard continuously but is almost never visible.

As it follows the creek's course, the trail traverses high above the deep, curving canyon. The forest here is in a state of transition. Large firs are not numerous, and several big ones have fallen in recent years. When a trail crew cut out sections of two trees that were lying across the trail, the men recorded the number of growth rings. One tree was 563 years old; the other, 643 years.

Traversing high above Graves Creek, the trail rises and falls as it crosses several streams. Now, for the first time, one can glimpse the creek occasionally, the white water rushing furiously through a box canyon walled in by timbered mountainsides. The creek has a steep gradient, with many falls and cascades, hence the booming and thundering. The sound is intensified after heavy rains or when the snow melt in the high country is at its peak.

The trail climbs steadily, crossing avalanche tracks overgrown with maple, salmonberry, and slide alder, then descends to Graves Creek just below its confluence with Success Creek (3.5 mi/5.6 km; 1880 ft/573 m). The stream is not bridged, and the crossing is difficult in late spring and early summer when the water is deep and swift; but one can cross easily in late summer and fall.

Beyond the ford the trail switchbacks up through hemlock and silver fir, makes a long traverse to a large creek, then descends to a camp on Graves Creek (5.3 mi/ 8.5 km; 2520 ft/768 m). The camp is located at the lower end of Graves Creek Basin, which consists of a series of openings in the forest where the stream is no longer in a canyon.

At this point the trail again crosses the creek, which must be waded if one cannot find a suitable log to serve as a footbridge. However, the stream is much smaller here. After crossing two avalanche tracks, the trail intersects the **Wynoochee Trail** (6.0 mi/9.7 km; 2700 ft/823 m) in a stand of western hemlock and silver fir, then switchbacks up the mountain, following the course of a stream.

Temporarily marked by ribbon tied to bushes beside a large cut log (6.6 mi/10.6 km; 3400 ft/1036 m), a faint track leads uphill on the right side of the trail. This is the eastern terminus of **Sundown Lake Way Trail**.

As it climbs higher, the trail breaks out into little bits of meadow on the steep sidehill, then bigger, more extensive openings. The trees are now mostly hemlock (both western and mountain) and subalpine fir. Here several rock-bottomed streams flow down the mountainside, where big boulders, covered with lichen and moss, lie scattered about. The view to the north down Graves Creek includes snow-clad peaks beyond the forested ridge in the foreground.

The junction with the **Upper South Fork Skokomish Trail** (7.2 mi/11.6 km; 3820 ft/1164 m) is located in a big meadow. This is lovely subalpine country—beautiful meadows framed by mountain hemlocks, with masses of showy white beargrass plumes and an abundance of dwarf huckleberries. The latter tempt one to linger even when time is pressing.

Beyond the meadow's far edge, the trail contours a steep slope through stands of large, pistol-butted mountain hemlocks. When the trees were young, the snow pushed against the trunks, causing them to lean; then they grew upright again, creating the pistol butt effect at the base of the trees.

A shelter once stood near the outlet of Sundown Lake (7.5 mi/12.1 km; 3900 ft/1189 m). No more. This oval-shaped tarn lies at the bottom of a steep-sided glacial cirque. The lake is bordered by narrow fringes of meadowland and brush, with forest above, and is oriented so that the outlet—and the only view from the cirque—is toward the setting sun in summer; hence the name. The lake is popular with fishermen because it is stocked with rainbow trout. A large meadow, where a few patches of snow linger throughout the summer, extends from the head of the lake to the ridge crest.

Beyond Sundown Lake the trail climbs through stands of big mountain hemlock as it traverses the cool, shaded north slope beneath low cliffs, then crosses broad meadows made attractive by groves of subalpine trees, rough sandstone boulders, and wildflowers, including the white lupine. The common blue lupine, beargrass, and false hellebore are abundant. Huckleberries also grow profusely here. The sweeping view is dominated by Mount Olympus on the horizon. The trail then climbs sharply, switchbacking up steep, forested slopes that alternate with meadowland as the route climbs to Six Ridge Pass (8.6 mi/13.8 km; 4650 ft/1417 m), where the path becomes the **Six Ridge Trail**. At this gap in the narrow divide, the gentle summer breezes murmur faintly in the hemlocks. During other seasons, however, the trees struggle for existence, pitting themselves against the fierce winds and the cold.

The view from the pass is splendid. Mount Rainier stands to the southeast, appearing ethereal and unreal. The Sawtooth Range, less than 10 miles distant, is dominated by Mount Lincoln and Mount Cruiser. One looks down the valley of Six Stream, which is bordered on the north by Six Ridge and on the south by the

Three Sisters. One of the McGravey Lakes glimmers in the forest below. Beyond the heavily-timbered ridges rise snow-clad peaks—among them Mount Henderson, Mount Duckabush, and Mount Olson.

142 PYRITES CREEK TRAIL

Abandoned trail, no longer maintained
Length 3.0 mi/4.8 km
Access Enchanted Valley Trail
USGS Map Chimney Peak
Agency Olympic National Park

An old trail that is virtually nonexistent today, this route should be reopened by the National Park Service to give backpackers access to the Burke Range, particularly the beautiful high country of Muncaster Basin. The trail is on the route taken by the party Lieutenant Joseph P. O'Neil sent to Mount Olympus in 1890.

The trail began—one hesitates to say begins—at Camp Odamit (1450 ft/442 m) on the East Fork Quinault River and followed Pyrites Creek about two-thirds of the way to the ridge between the East Fork Quinault and Godkin Creek. Although a few fragments can still be found, it is easier to forget the trail and just go straight up the mountain, traveling parallel to the creek, but following the bits and pieces of the path when they are encountered. The trail kept close to the creek the first half of the ascent, then angled away from the stream, ending not far above The Crow's Foot, where three branches of Pyrites Creek come together (3.0 mi/4.8 km; 3800 ft/1158 m).

143 O'NEIL PASS TRAIL

Length 7.4 mi/11.9 km
Access Enchanted Valley Trail; Duckabush Trail
USGS Maps Mount Hoquiam; Mount Olson; Chimney Peak; Mount Steel
Agency Olympic National Park

This trail begins at a junction (3200 ft/975 m) with the **Enchanted Valley Trail** near White Creek, 2.0 mi/3.2 km below Anderson Pass. The trail goes southwest to O'Neil Pass, at the head of the Duckabush River. This gap was used in 1890 by the O'Neil Expedition's mule train when it crossed the Grand Divide.

At first the trail climbs through the forest to an attractive camp at the lower end of beautiful White Creek Meadow (0.6 mi/1.0 km; 3750 ft/1143 m), which is characterized during the summer by vivid displays of wildflowers, particularly lupine. Here the hiker has a good view of Mount Anderson and Linsley Glacier. This is just below Bull Elk Basin, where the expedition killed an elk. The trail meanders over the meadow east of White Creek, then crosses the stream. (The experienced mountaineer can leave the trail here and travel cross-country to Lake LaCrosse.)

The trail then goes back into the forest and traverses below the ridge that borders LaCrosse Basin on the west. Because the slope is steep, this is an avalanche area, and after winters of heavy snowfall the route may be blocked by deep drifts until late summer. Most of the distance, however, the trail goes through scenic stands of conifers that alternate with snowslide tracks. This traverse overlooks Enchanted Valley, and when the skies are clear Lake Quinault and the Pacific Ocean glimmer in the distance. Mount Anderson and Linsley Glacier still dominate the northern skyline, but now one can look directly across Enchanted Valley to the Burke Range, topped by Chimney Peak (6911 ft/2106 m). The cliffs that form the northwest wall of the valley, crowned by snow cornices and streaked by cascades and water-falls, stand in full view, rising almost directly from the braided channel of the Quinault.

Beyond a junction with the **Heart Lake Way Trail** (3.8 mi/6.1 km; 4300 ft/ 1311 m), the trail comes out to a big basin (5.7 mi/9.2 km; 4700 ft/1433 m) on the northwest slope of Overlook Peak. This basin is often covered with snow. The path then rounds the peak's western spur, where it goes through dense growths of young conifers (mostly mountain hemlock), among which stand many large, dead snags. The thick undergrowth consists of heather, mountain ash, and huckleberry. The presence of the latter probably explains why O'Neil's men saw several bears on this mountain.

The trail almost encircles Overlook Peak as it contours above Upper O'Neil Creek Basin. Below the trail an old path—probably a remnant of O'Neil's mule trail—leads down into this beautiful area, where a small stream flows through the meadow. The expedition had its Camp Number Fifteen here. One should watch for elk; their tracks are almost always visible in the mud and snow. This basin is often covered with snowdrifts until midsummer, but when they disappear the wildflowers bloom profusely. Large marmots, mottled black and brown, whistle warnings when hikers approach. The narrow ridge to the south is covered with mountain hemlocks, and an elk path leads across it to O'Neil Creek Basin.

O'Neil Pass (7.4 mi/11.9 km; 4950 ft/1509 m) is merely a tree-covered notch in the ridge between Mount Duckabush (6233 ft/1900 m) and Overlook Peak (5700 ft/1737 m). The view is good when the peaks are not hidden by clouds: to the north are Mount Anderson, Linsley Glacier, and White Mountain; the bulk of Mount Duckabush is close at hand to the south. The eastern scene includes the upper Duckabush Valley and Mount Elklick; the western one, the Quinault Valley and O'Neil Peak. Beyond the pass the trail becomes the **Duckabush Trail.**

The hiker with a flexible schedule can make the trek over to O'Neil Creek Basin, one of the loveliest places in the Olympics, which may be reached by follow-ing the elk trail from Upper O'Neil Creek Basin. Lake Ben and two smaller, un-named tarns are located in the center, surrounded by subalpine meadows where the hiker can roam at will. Good examples of quartz can be observed in the rock slides, and the outcrops reveal evidence of glacial polish. The view down O'Neil Creek is striking, and several until recently unclimbed peaks rise directly south of the basin. The view from the divide east of the lakes makes the steep scramble up worthwhile because snow-clad peaks are visible in all directions, and one can look directly down to the North Fork Skokomish. Camp Nine Stream, little more than a mile distant, lies 3000 feet below the observer.

NORTH FORK QUINAULT

The North Fork Quinault River has its headwaters on Mount Seattle near Low Divide, and together with its numerous tributaries drains an area of rough, broken country. The lower slopes are clad with dense stands of virgin forest; at the higher altitudes many picturesque lakes and tarns dot the landscape. Near the river's source, several high, glaciated peaks stand between the Quinault and Elwha Rivers.

The North Fork is bounded on the east by Mount Christie—the dominant peak in the area—and the ridges at the head of Rustler Creek (also called Rusher Creek), which is the North Fork's largest tributary. The western part of the Burke Range rises between the North Fork and East Fork Quinault. On the west, the Quinault watershed is bounded by the mile-high Queets-Quinault Divide, which extends from Mount Noyes to Finley Peak.

As it makes its way out of the mountains, the North Fork Quinault twists and turns constantly like a dancer engaged in a wild fandango. The upper part of the river has a steep gradient, which James H. Christie, the leader of the Press Expedition, described as one continuous long waterfall. But the lower part, broad and deep, flows more quietly. Big Creek, a major tributary, flows underground the last few miles, disappearing in gravels and moraine southwest of Irely Lake.

Queets-Quinault Divide near the Skyline Trail

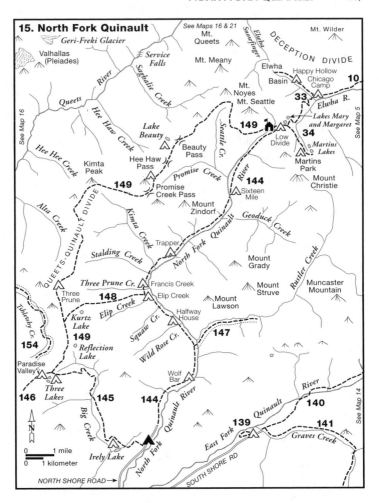

The Press Expedition was the first party to travel down the North Fork Quinault. The men climbed over Low Divide from the Elwha in the spring of 1890.

ROADS

North Shore Road. This road provides access to all trails in the district. Road closures are frequent, particularly during the winter and spring months. Therefore, before beginning a trip in this area one should check with the National Park Service as to current conditions. The road, which is paved for the first 11 miles, then gravel for the last 6, leaves US 101 near the national park boundary and follows the north shore of Lake Quinault through stands of old-growth forest and cutover land to July Creek Campground (3.5 mi/5.6 km; 219 ft/67 m). Beyond the lake, the road penetrates rougher country as it proceeds up the Quinault Valley past the Quinault Ranger Station (5.5 mi/8.9 km).

About 4 miles beyond Big Creek, the road goes through a meadow where one can look across the river to Colonel Bob and Mount O'Neil. Access to the East Fork Quinault is provided at a junction (13.9 mi/22.4 km) where a branch road leads, right, to a bridge that spans the Quinault just below the confluence of its two branches, and then connects with the South Shore Road. Beyond this junction, the North Shore Road parallels the North Fork, traversing splendid stands of large, old-growth Douglas-fir, where many trees are 275 feet tall, reaching 6 feet or more in diameter. Large cedars are also present, but they are not numerous.

The parking area at the Big Creek Trail (16.6 mi/26.7 km) will accommodate several cars. The road then goes by the North Fork Campground (16.9 mi/27.2 km), which has only a few sites. The facilities are primitive, and one must obtain water from the nearby river. The road ends at the North Fork Ranger Station (17.1 mi/27.5 km; 520 ft/158 m), where the North Fork Quinault Trail begins.

144 NORTH FORK QUINAULT TRAIL

Length 16.4 mi/26.4 km
Access North Shore Road
USGS Maps Bunch Lake; Mount Hoquiam; Mount Christie; Kimta Peak
Agency Olympic National Park

An up-and-down route, this arterial trail begins at the North Fork Ranger Station (520 ft/158 m) and follows the North Fork Quinault to Low Divide, the pass between the Quinault and Elwha Rivers. Most of the way the route goes through stands of virgin timber. Above Rustler Creek, the tortuous, twisting river flows almost continuously through a series of narrow canyons.

Hikers should take note that in some respects the North Fork Quinault Trail is more or less unique. In following this stream to Low Divide, one necessarily crosses several swift, rollicking tributaries, as well as the river itself about halfway up the valley at Sixteen Mile Camp. This area is subject to heavy winter rains; as a consequence, the bridges that span the tributaries are occasionally destroyed by floods. The bridges do not always get rebuilt immediately, confronting those hiking up or down the valley with several difficult, dangerous crossings. Before starting out, one is well-advised to contact the National Park Service and inquire as to the current status of the various creeks—whether they are bridged or unbridged.

The trail at first utilizes an abandoned, almost obliterated road bordered by splendid stands of fir, cedar, hemlock, and spruce. This rain forest has an understory of moss-draped bigleaf and vine maple, and a luxuriant growth of ground plants. The old roadbed ends at Wolf Bar (2.5 mi/4.0 km; 630 ft/192 m), a camp located on the river bank among deciduous trees and a vigorous stand of young fir.

Beyond this camp the trail leaves the level bottomlands and traverses terraces above the North Fork, opposite the confluence of Rustler Creek (4.0 mi/ 6.4 km; 700 ft/213 m), which flows into the North Fork from the east. The forest is now mostly western hemlock, and the trail traverses broken country, climbing over spurs that come down to the river at right angles between side streams. Frequently, especially after heavy rains or rapid snow melt in the high country, the smaller mountainside streams flow down portions of the trail, eroding it into a rocky channel that is sometimes a foot or more deep.

Halfway House (5.2 mi/8.4 km; 800 ft/244 m), now a trailside camp, was formerly the site of a lodge operated by the Olympic Chalet Company in the 1920s and 1930s. The building was located midway between Voorhies' packing station (near Fletcher Creek, where the South Shore Road then ended) and Low Divide. At that time the North Fork Trail was approached via the South Shore Road, and the traveler first had to cross the river in a canoe to Bunch's Ranch. Halfway House was later used as a trail shelter, but no sign of the building is present today.

Beyond this camp the trail follows a big curve of the Quinault for several miles. Here the river flows through a narrow canyon, and the path ascends and descends in order to cross a half-dozen tributary creeks which flow in steep, narrow gorges lined with devil's club and salmonberry. The first two creeks are Squaw and Elip. A good camp is located on the north bank of the latter (6.4 mi/10.3 km; 900 ft/ 274 m). The trail then climbs sharply, shaded by towering firs, to a junction with the **Elip Creek Trail** (6.5 mi/10.5 km; 1060 ft/323 m). Then follow in rapid succession the next four streams—Three Prune, Francis, Stalding, and Kimta. Three Prune Creek received its name in 1913 during the summer outing of The Mountaineers. The hikers arrived on schedule but the pack train did not, with the result that each person received three prunes for dinner. A campsite is located at Francis Creek (7.0 mi/11.3 km; 1100 ft/335 m) on the site of a former shelter. Kimta Creek, one of the larger streams, was the point where an 1890 scouting party led by Lieutenant Joseph O'Neil left the Quinault and climbed to the Queets-Quinault Divide.

Beyond Kimta Creek the trail goes by the site where Jasper Bunch, a Quinault pioneer, had a cabin that he used as a wilderness retreat. He lived on a ranch near the forks of the Quinault, and Bunch Lake and Bunch Canyon commemorate his name. The trail now heads to the northeast, following a big curve of the river. Trapper Shelter (8.5 mi/13.7 km; 1200 ft/366 m) is located in a stand of dense forest. The trail then crosses Rock Slide Creek, which flows down the southern side of Mount Zindorf. Beyond this point the canyon becomes increasingly precipitous, and a large landslide can be viewed on the slopes of Mount Lawson. This peak was named Mount Grady by the Press Expedition, but some time later the name Mount Lawson (which the expedition gave to a different peak) was shifted to this mountain.

The trail comes out to the banks of the Quinault, then reenters the forest at Twelve Mile Shelter (11.5 mi/18.5 km; 1800 ft/549 m). Beyond the point where Geoduck Creek flows into the Quinault, the trail turns north and crosses the North Fork at Sixteen Mile Camp (12.3 mi/19.8 km; 2000 ft/610 m). A large log that spanned the river here was utilized for years by hikers as a bridge, but it, too, was swept away by recent floods and has not been replaced. Consequently, the river is impassable at this point during periods of heavy rainfall, and the crossing should not be attempted at such times. (A rope stretched across the river here is helpful only when the North Fork is low, not when it is high.) The name Sixteen Mile Camp refers to the fact that this crossing is sixteen miles from the forks of the Quinault, where the trailhead was located in the 1930s.

The trail now climbs steadily through dense, gloomy stands of hemlock and silver fir as it parallels the North Fork opposite Promise Creek in a steep ascent around the base of Mount Christie. The river is a series of rapids and cascades, and its sound is always present. Mount Christie was named for the leader of the Press Expedition; Promise Creek was first called Sims River, for John W. Sims, another expedition member.

Beyond Glacier Creek (14.4 mi/23.2 km; 2800 ft/853 m), which tumbles down from a glacier on Mount Christie, the trail climbs sharply for about a half mile. At this point the terrain becomes less precipitous, and the trail crosses forest-rimmed meadowland to a junction with the **Skyline Trail** (15.9 mi/25.6 km; 3550 ft/1082 m). Mount Zindorf is visible from this point, its sharp, snow-crowned crest standing directly in the line of sight down the Quinault Valley. The path then goes through a narrow band of trees to Renegade or Low Divide Shelter (16.1 mi/25.9 km; 3560 ft/1085 m), located at the southwest edge of the big meadow at Low Divide— or Lode of Ide, to use the delightful spelling a shorthand reporter mistakenly gave it in the transcript of a congressional hearing regarding establishment of the national park. (By the same token, perhaps the High Divide could be called the Hide of Ide.)

On both sides of this flat, U-shaped saddle, which resulted from glacier carving, the forest-clad slopes rise abruptly to rugged, snowy heights—to Mount Seattle on the northwest, to Mount Christie on the southeast—but the peaks are lost to view behind spurs and buttresses. This meadow, the only bit of high country on the popular traverse across the Olympics via the Elwha and North Fork Quinault, is not truly subalpine. In fact, the thick growths of willow bordering the streams are spreading, threatening to engulf the grassy expanse, which is surrounded by stands of mountain hemlock, silver fir, and Alaska cedar.

The trail meanders over the level meadow and crosses the Quinault. Here, close to its source, the willow-fringed stream is little more than a brook. The Low Divide Ranger Station (16.4 mi/26.4 km; 3602 ft/1098 m), staffed only during the summer, stands beside a forest backdrop at the meadow's edge. Nearby are remnants of Low Divide Chalet, a lodge that catered to pack train parties. The building was destroyed many years ago by an avalanche that swept down Mount Seattle.

The Press Expedition was the first party to cross Low Divide. The explorers, who accomplished the feat in May 1890, when the pass was snowbound, were saved from starvation when they shot several bears while encamped here. Charles A. Barnes, the expedition's deputy leader, climbed almost to the top of Mount Seattle, to a point where he could see Mount Olympus and the Hoh Canyon.

Beyond the ranger station the route is known as the **Low Divide Trail**.

145 BIG CREEK TRAIL

Length 6.6 mi/10.6 km
Access North Shore Road
USGS Map Bunch Lake
Agency Olympic National Park

This route samples a variety of forest types and terrain as it takes the hiker from the lush rain forest on the Quinault River bottoms to the subalpine country of the Queets-Quinault Divide. The trailhead (500 ft/152 m) is located on the North Shore Road, 16.6 mi/26.7 km from US 101, the Olympic Highway.

On the swampy bottomlands the trail traverses typical rain forest. The undergrowth consists largely of vine maple, salmonberry, devil's club, and huckleberry, in places so thick as to be impenetrable were the way not hacked through. After about a half mile the trail follows Irely Creek to a junction with a side path (1.0 mi/1.6 km; 600 ft/183 m) that leads about 200 yards to Irely Lake. This is a popular spot with fishermen during the summer months. The lake, located in a marshy area subject to flooding, fluctuates in size from the wet to the dry season. A couple of mediocre campsites are located near the north end.

Upon leaving the river bottom, the trail climbs as it traverses above Big Creek, a tributary of the Quinault, and it now becomes somewhat rocky and rough. Here it goes through splendid stands of fir and cedar. The forest is unusually beautiful in places. The trees are tall, close together, and they tower high above an unbroken carpet of sword ferns. Eventually, the trail comes out onto slopes overlooking the canyon of Big Creek, and water is available—at least until midsummer—from numerous little streams that the trail crosses. Because of the dampness, western red cedar is predominant here, and many of the trees are large.

The trail leaves Big Creek and follows a large branch that comes in from the north, then crosses this stream to its west side (4.0 mi/6.4 km; 1330 ft/405 m) via a splendid steel bridge built by the National Park Service several years ago. Prior to construction of the bridge, hikers sometimes—particularly during periods of high water—had difficulty crossing the stream. A small but excellent campsite (capacity perhaps two tents) is hidden among the trees at the far end of the bridge and slightly downstream from it. Although brooks have been abundant so far, they disappear beyond this point, and the hiker should fill his water bottle here. The route now climbs sharply as the trail switchbacks up a steep spur toward the Queets-Quinault Divide. The forest changes until it is composed almost exclusively of western hemlock and silver fir, which prevail until approximately 3000 ft/914 m. The trail then goes through one of the finest stands of Alaska cedar in Olympic National Park. Most of the trees are big, and the trail goes by the largest-known example of this species—a giant 12 feet in diameter at its buttressed base.

The trail then ascends at a gentler grade and crosses little streams—the first sources of water beyond the branch of Big Creek. The first openings in the forest now occur—mostly little glades and meadows surrounded by subalpine trees. One of them is especially interesting because it is flat and about the size and shape of a football field. The trail levels out just beyond it and intersects the **Skyline Trail** (6.6 mi/10.6 km; 3200 ft/975 m) near the largest of the Three Lakes. Several campsites are located in this vicinity, and running water can be obtained by going about 50 yards north on the Skyline Trail.

The grass-rimmed lakes are located in a swampy meadow, where pale violets bloom among the grasses. This region is a mix of meadowland and subalpine forest. The trail goes by the largest lake, which is bordered by and half-filled with sphagnum moss. This growth is gradually converting the tarn into a bog. Another, much smaller lake lies just to the south on the same level. The third lake, a little tarn, is located on a slightly higher bench. Water lilies grow in all the lakes, blooming in midsummer, when their yellow blossoms accent the somber greens of the conifers.

One of the amenities the camper enjoys at Three Lakes is the delightful concert given by the frogs every evening. Thousands of the little fellows blend their voices in a nocturnal serenade, which is usually interrupted at intervals. The chorus sings for a few minutes, then stops abruptly, only to resume the concert, with the final curtain drawn about 9:00 P.M. Lulled to sleep by the croaking, the hiker will awaken the next morning to ultra-quiet—silence broken only by the twitter of birds, or perhaps the humming of bees gathering nectar from the flowers. After mid-August one usually does not hear this "frog music"—perhaps because the nights are too cold for the creatures to assert themselves.

Wildflowers are abundant at Three Lakes—particularly beargrass and elephant's head, which is found along the shores of the larger lake. When the dwarf huckleberries ripen (usually mid-August through early September), the hiker can spend hours gorging on the delectable fruit.

Beyond the lakes the trail climbs steeply, through stands of Alaska cedar, to a tiny but picturesque meadow just below the divide. When the lupine and beargrass bloom, the slopes above are splashed with patches of blue and white.

On the Queets-Quinault Divide (7.1 mi/11.4 km; 3600 ft/1097 m) the route becomes the **Tshletshy Creek Trail**. Another path, a remnant of the original Skyline Trail, leads south from this point. On the divide the breezes murmur in the mountain hemlocks, and one can see an array of timbered ridges and mountain spurs. Glimpses of peaks to the north, toward Olympus, lure the wanderer to the Skyline Trail.

146 FINLEY PEAK TRAIL

Fragment of abandoned trail, no longer maintained
Length 0.6 mi/0.8 km
Access Big Creek Trail
USGS Map Bunch Lake
Agency Olympic National Park

Only a remnant remains of the old Finley Peak Trail, which was part of the original Queets Skyline or Knife Edge Trail. The trail began northeast of Lake Quinault on the North Shore Road, approximately on the county line, and paralleled Finley Creek as it followed the ridge to Finley Peak (3419 ft/1042 m), then traversed north along the Queets-Quinault Divide. After construction of the Big Creek Trail, the section of the Skyline Trail from the Quinault River to the divide above Three Lakes was abandoned and, with the passage of time, has been largely obliterated. All that can be readily followed is a short stretch that goes south from the junction (3600 ft/1097 m) of the **Big Creek Trail** and the **Tshletshy Creek Trail**.

The path follows the ridge through a scattering of mountain hemlocks. The view looks both ways—east to the Quinault, west to the head of Tshletshy Creek. The ground is covered by masses of dwarf huckleberry, and the fruits ripen to a delicious sweetness from mid-August to mid-September. The peak time of ripening varies, depending upon the season. Though berries here can be abundant, the park now imposes a one-liter per-person limit on berry-pickers.

Beyond the meadows the trail goes into the deep forest, where it climbs steeply.

The path remains on the ridge, then ends abruptly where the terrain levels out (0.5 mi/ 0.8 km; 3900 ft/1189 m).

The hiker who is willing to struggle through dense forest and undergrowth on steep slopes can follow the ridge to Finley Peak, now and then finding bits of the old trail. Finley Peak was the site of Finley Creek Lookout, the first fire lookout built in the Olympic National Forest. The square log cabin, with its steep, pyramid-style roof, was constructed in 1915. The National Park Service removed it in 1947, 9 years after the creation of Olympic National Park.

147 RUSTLER CREEK TRAIL

Abandoned trail, no longer maintained
Length 2.5 mi/4.0 km
Access North Fork Quinault Trail
USGS Maps Mount Hoquiam, Mount Christie
Agency Olympic National Park

Rustler Creek, a major tributary of the North Fork Quinault River, has its source in the subalpine country of the Burke Range, not far from Bretherton Pass. The deep gash through which it flows, one of the wildest in the Olympics, is about 10 miles in length, the bulk of it free of trails other than those made by deer and elk. The creek is also known as The Rusher, a romantic appellation that perhaps better symbolizes the stream's frenetic dash down to the Quinault, leaving behind as it does so the secrets of its remote canyons and seldom-visited headwaters. This clear, sparkling stream courses over big boulders and has many cascades and pools of green water.

The Rustler Creek Trail follows the lower part of the isolated valley. Here, during the fall, one is likely to hear elk whistling, see the animals on occasion, and note that the gravel bars are marked with their tracks.

The trail begins on the **North Fork Quinault Trail,** slightly more than a mile beyond Wolf Bar, but the intersection (750 ft/229 m), located just past a puncheon bridge, is no longer marked. The path makes a switchback or two as it descends to the Quinault opposite the point where Rustler Creek flows into the river.

One must then wade the Quinault, which can be safely forded in late summer and fall. The trail begins again on the alder flats south of Rustler Creek, near a pile of rubble that was once a cabin. Little tread is left of the old trail, and about the only concrete evidence that remains to indicate this was a man-made path are ancient cut logs—mouldering, moss-covered, and rotten. In fact, the trail has disappeared to the extent that following the route is largely cross-country travel, and in order to keep oriented the hiker should always stay within sound, if not sight, of Rustler Creek. Moreover, the going is easier along the creek than it is on the steep, muddy hillside. At times one loses all semblance of trail—only to stumble upon it again—because the fragments are not linked together.

At first the trail goes through rain forest on broad, level bottomland, where the scattered trees consist largely of alder, with hemlock and spruce intermixed. The ground beneath them is grassy, and the rocks are covered with moss. After about a half mile, however, the trail angles obliquely upward and away from Rustler Creek, which above this point flows through almost continuous canyon. Here it is easy to confuse the path with numerous elk trails that lace the wet, swampy mountainside, but the trail makes several switchbacks that are crisscrossed with fallen logs. One can avoid the obstructions by using an excellent elk trail that connects the path below to the upper switchback, a gain of about 100 feet in elevation. Beyond the switchbacks, however, the hiker often has to clamber over huge windfalls—many logs are 6 to 8 feet in diameter—and struggle through ankle-deep mud that has the consistency and appearance of chocolate pudding. Under such circumstances one finds it difficult to understand how men built a trail in such unlikely terrain.

Rewards await the diligent, however, because the trail now goes through splendid stands of big firs and cedars, mixed together with smaller hemlocks; but spruce, the typical rain forest tree, is almost entirely lacking. The firs are magnificent and include some of the finest specimens of this tree preserved in the national park. They are 7 to 9 feet in diameter, straight as arrows, approach 300 feet in height, and rise without limbs for 120 to 150 feet. Many large western red cedars are also present.

As the trail meanders up the canyon, the sound of Rustler Creek is always present, and the stream is often visible. The trail then crosses Rhodes Creek, a side stream which flows down a precipitous ravine. Because the footbridge that once spanned the defile has long since disappeared, the trail descends sharply about 15 feet, and the hiker needs a bit of rope in order to get up and down one side. The path then goes by a forge and the remains of a cabin at an abandoned mine. Less than a mile beyond this point, the trail ends in an alder flat at the head of the canyon (ca. 2.5 mi/4.0 km; ca. 1500 ft/457 m).

Above the flat the Rustler flows in its lonely course for miles through gentler canyons—less steep and wall-like than the lower canyon, which is traversed by the trail. Here, in the dense, gloomy forest, the babbling stream rushes along merrily, in keeping with its alternate name.

148 ELIP CREEK TRAIL

Length 4.6 mi/7.4 km
Access North Fork Quinault Trail; Skyline Trail
USGS Map Kimta Peak
Agency Olympic National Park

This route links the **North Fork Quinault Trail** with the **Skyline Trail**, thus making a 21-mile loop trip possible, via four trails—Big Creek, Skyline, Elip Creek, and North Fork Quinault. The trail begins (1060 ft/323 m) on the North Fork Quinault Trail between Elip Creek and Three Prune Creek and climbs directly up the steep spur between them to the Queets-Quinault Divide.

At first the trail traverses Douglas-fir and hemlock forest, where it switchbacks through a series of bad windfalls for about a mile and a half. Many trees have been blown down in this area, and where they fell across the trail the logs have been cut out. The wind toppled almost every tree in several places, and they lie tangled like jackstraws, pointing in every direction, at times piled on top of one another.

Above the windfalls the forest changes to silver fir, with a little red cedar. The steep switchbacks end, and the trail now follows the narrow ridge. Here one can look in both directions—north into the deep canyon of Three Prune Creek, south into the gorge of Elip Creek. Both are heavily forested, and from the depths rise the muffled sounds of running water. The northern slope, falling away to Three Prune Creek, is the more impressive because it is exceedingly precipitous—incredibly steep for a forested slope.

As it ascends higher, the trail leaves the dense forest and enters the Subalpine Zone with its alternation of meadowland and isolated groves of trees. The higher one goes, the more open the country becomes, and little streams cross the meadows at frequent intervals. The brooks are the only source of water along this trail; none is found in the forest below.

One Tent Camp (4.5 mi/7.2 km; 3750 ft/1143 m) is located near the head of the South Fork of Three Prune Creek. As the name implies, this spot by the trail has sufficient space to pitch one tent. The trail then intersects with the Skyline Trail (4.6 mi/7.4 km; 3800 ft/1158 m) on the Queets-Quinault Divide.

149 SKYLINE TRAIL

Way trail, not maintained
Length 20.5 mi/33.0 km
Access Big Creek Trail; North Fork Quinault Trail
USGS Maps Bunch Lake; Mount Christie; Kimta Peak
Agency Olympic National Park

Originally called the Knife Edge Trail, then the Queets Skyline Trail, this route was constructed in segments until it followed the full length of the Queets-Quinault Divide. The first section, built in 1913, began approximately where the North Shore Road crossed into Jefferson County. This trail extended to Finley Peak and Three Lakes. As an accommodation to The Mountaineers, the Forest Service built a trail in 1920 from the North Fork Quinault up Promise Creek and down the divide to Three Lakes, thus extending the Skyline Trail. The last stretch, from the head of Promise Creek to Low Divide, via Lake Beauty and Seattle Creek Basin, was constructed later.

Although the path is in fairly good condition as far north as Kimta Peak and again near the end as it approaches Low Divide, the midsection, both before and after Lake Beauty, may present route-finding difficulties due to the multitude of game trails that lead off in various directions, tending to mislead hikers. As a consequence, the National Park Service has abandoned the entire Skyline Trail, and it is now considered by that agency to be a route only. No one except hikers skilled in cross-country travel should attempt the route.

Hikers planning to walk the Skyline Trail from south to north and return to the North Shore Road via the **North Fork Quinault Trail** should keep in mind that the river crossing at Sixteen Mile Camp on the North Fork may be impassable, depending upon the weather at the time, therefore they should not rely upon using the North Fork Quinault Trail as an escape exit. If upon reaching the crossing at

Mount Olympus from Skyline Trail

Sixteen Mile Camp the party is unable to cross the river, they will be forced to return the way they came or exit via the Elwha Trail. Each of these escape exits would increase by more than 20 miles the trip's total mileage.

This is a highly scenic but strenuous route. Between Three Lakes and Kimta Peak, the trail shifts back and forth, first on one side of the divide, then the other, occasionally following the ridge top but usually contouring just below. Beyond Kimta Creek the ridge is higher, with wide expanses of country above timberline. This primitive region is as wild and beautiful as any part of the Olympics. Because the winter snowfall is heavy, the route is usually blocked until late summer. The trail is a regular pathway for wildlife. Every hiker will see the tracks of elk, deer, bear, and wildcat; more fortunate ones may glimpse the animals themselves on occasion. Elk congregate in the high meadows in late summer; bears roam the slopes when the huckleberries ripen.

Beginning at Three Lakes (3200 ft/975 m) on the **Big Creek Trail**, the route crosses a meadow, then traverses northward, alternating between forest-rimmed meadows and stands of large silver fir, western and mountain hemlock, and Alaska cedar. After descending to a little meadow and pond, the trail climbs to a saddle, where Reflection Lake can be glimpsed through the forest. The lake is located in a marshy area to the right of the trail, where wildflowers are abundant. They include the avalanche lily, Jeffrey's shooting star, elephant's head, and western anemone.

The trail now climbs through meadows at the head of Elip Creek, where masses of red mountain-heather carpet the hillsides. When the plants are in blossom, bees work industriously to extract the nectar. This is wild, lonely country, with splendid views up the Quinault to snow-capped Mount Seattle and Mount Christie. The trail goes by Oval Lake (2.0 mi/3.2 km; 3850 ft/1173 m), which forms an almost perfect oval, then another lake of about the same size but irregular in form. Beyond these lakes the landscape is dotted with tiny, scenic tarns that mirror the country. Heather, buttercups, and violets border the clear, sparkling brooks, which meander from pool to pool.

After climbing over a low ridge, the trail descends to a junction with the **Elip Creek Trail** (2.9 mi/4.7 km; 3800 ft/1158 m), then contours to a point that overlooks the lush, green meadows of Three Prune Basin. On the far side, Three Prune Camp (4.3 mi/6.9 km; 3600 ft/1097 m) is located in a clump of trees. Between this camp and Kimta Peak, water may not be available after mid-August, but one need only descend a bit into one of the basins to find it.

Beyond Three Prune Basin the trail climbs through dense forest, then rounds a spur and crosses the meadows in Stalding Creek Basin, where the black mountain huckleberry grows profusely. The large berries are sweeter than the fruit of the tall blue huckleberry; consequently, when they ripen in late August, the hiker is not inclined to travel rapidly at this point. The route stays just below the divide, crisscrossing from one side to the other, and the slopes overlooking the Queets are precipitous, falling abruptly to Alta Creek. The trail then traverses above South Kimta Basin.

Whenever the trail follows the ridge top, the hiker can look both ways through trees bearded with lichen—toward the Queets or the Quinault, as choice dictates. The country gradually becomes more subalpine in character, and the trail traverses broad meadows that overlook the timbered valleys of Alta Creek and the Queets, as well as a spur of the Mount Olympus Range. At the head of North Kimta Basin, the path curves around meadowland that is often a tangle of elk-tracked snowfields. The route is marked by blazes and orange-colored markers tacked to the trees. The trail keeps high, just beneath the ridge, and hikers should be alert so as not to be misled by game trails. The path can be lost easily near Kimta Peak, where the sharp ridges and spurs are confusing.

The trail then skirts just below Kimta Peak (9.3 mi/15.0 km). On clear days the scramble to the summit (5399 ft/1646 m) is worthwhile because a glorious panorama is revealed. Far below, the Queets River meanders through virgin rain forests, and the ridges are clothed with thick stands of hemlock. Mount Olympus, only 7 miles distant, dominates the northern scene, its southern face streaked with snowfields and glaciers. Not only is the whole sweep of the Mount Olympus Range visible but also the deep, U-shaped Queets Valley, bordered by timbered ridges that extend to the horizon. Queets Basin lies to the northeast, with the Bailey Range peaks beyond. To the south and east many mountains are visible in the distance.

The region beyond Kimta Creek is one of the wildest parts of the Olympics accessible by trail. This is a country of wide horizons, of far-flung vistas to distant peaks, of quiet solitude, where one can hear the sounds of nature—the piercing whistles of marmots; the deep purring of the creeks below; the wind sighing in the subalpine firs on the ridges, and the bugling of elk in cul-de-sacs unvisited by man.

Beneath Kimta Peak the trail traverses eastward through heather meadows at about the 5000-ft/1524-m level. The view looks down Kimta Creek to cragged peaks on the skyline. As it descends, the route reenters the forest, and the path crosses many little streams. The trail is in poor condition here because the soil tends to be soft and boggy.

After losing considerable elevation, the trail climbs again, via steep switchbacks, and breaks over the divide at Promise Creek Pass (11.0 mi/17.7 km; 4980 ft/ 1518 m). The view is stunning: a large snow bowl occupies the foreground, bordered by Mount Zindorf on its eastern flank. Other peaks—Seattle, Christie, Noyes, and Meany—are visible in the distance, but Low Divide is hidden behind a spur. (The Promise Creek section of the old Queets Skyline Trail led down from this point to Cold Springs Camp, then descended through the damp and gloomy canyon to the North Fork Quinault.)

The trail now becomes more a way than a well-beaten path. Marked by cairns, the route goes left over fields of snow and heather near the basin's western rim. Rock outcrops are everywhere, the strata turned on end or at high angles, and stunted mountain hemlocks sprawl along the ridge. The views are unobstructed: rugged, snowy peaks in every direction, including Mount Olympus and the peaks surrounding Elwha Basin. One also has a good panorama of the eastern Olympics.

The sunrises and sunsets are spectacular viewed from High Camp (11.5 mi/ 18.5 km; 5300 ft/1615 m), which is located above the trail and just below the ridge. This is an excellent vantage point (especially at night when the moon is full) to watch the fog rise up from the Queets Valley, roll over Kimta Peak, and settle into North Kimta Basin. Also visible from here, directly in front of Mount Olympus, is the Queets Burn—an area north of the Queets, opposite Hee Haw Creek, that was devastated by fire in 1962.

Beyond this camp the route descends to avoid a buttress. The trail is virtually nonexistent, but the way—mostly over snowfields, heather-covered slopes, and glacier-polished rocks—is marked by cairns. After crossing a narrow ravine, the route climbs toward the divide, descends again in order to round a spur, climbs up and contours cliffs, only to descend a third time. Here it comes out onto meadows dotted with mountain hemlock, crosses three ravines, and climbs to Hee Haw Pass (12.5 mi/20.1 km; 4500 ft/1372 m), where one has a good view of Mount Tom. The trail crosses the grass-covered saddle to the west side, where the poorly marked path may be confused with a multitude of game trails, but the route climbs through forest and meadow and goes beneath a big slide.

Aptly named Lake Beauty (13.5 mi/21.7 km; 4700 ft/1433 m) lies cupped in a deep pocket, and chunks of ice often float in its waters until late summer. A campsite is located near the lake's western end. Mount Noyes and Mount Meany rise to the northeast, beyond the upper basin of Saghalie Creek; Mount Olympus and Mount Tom stand to the northwest. The stillness is unbroken save for the croaking of ravens and the murmur of the wind. The sunsets here are colorful—particularly in midsummer, when the sun disappears behind the jagged silhouette of the Valhallas in the Mount Olympus Range.

East of the lake the route crosses Beauty Pass (14.0 mi/22.5 km; 5000 ft/1524 m), where the remarkable view includes the entire width of the national park. One looks westward through a gap in the Mount Olympus Range to the distant Pacific; on the eastern horizon the Sawtooth Range marks the park boundary.

Beyond the pass the trail goes beneath rock cliffs studded with penstemons, then contours toward Mount Noyes through meadows and subalpine forest. Mount Zindorf, a broad peak with many snowfields and crags, stands across the valley of Promise Creek. After rounding a bend, the path overlooks Seattle Creek Basin. At its head, Mount Seattle rises above a wide meadow. Mount Christie and Mount Noyes are also in full view, and the tip of Mount Meany shows through a gap.

The trail traverses meadows, switchbacks down through the trees, and crosses two little gorges before it enters Seattle Creek Basin. Here the route contours beneath Mount Noyes and Mount Seattle. Elk and bear roam this country, where gentle breezes riffle the avalanche lilies and beargrass plumes, and the only sound one hears is the chatter of Seattle Creek (16.5 mi/26.6 km; 4200 ft/1280 m). After contouring the rolling, rock-strewn meadows on the southwest side of Mount Seattle, the trail goes around the south buttress and descends into stands of mountain hemlock. On hot afternoons walking from the sun-drenched meadows into the shaded coolness of the forest is almost like entering an air-conditioned home in the desert.

The trail loses elevation rapidly in the forest, ending at an intersection with the North Fork Quinault Trail (20.5 mi/33.0 km; 3550 ft/1082 m) just south of Low Divide.

QUEETS

The Queets River flows from the Olympics to the Pacific Ocean through a valley that is narrow near the river's headwaters but broadens considerably in its middle course. A large part of the watershed is drained by three tributaries that flow parallel to each other and enter the river from the southeast: Matheny Creek, Sams River, and Tshletshy Creek. They, in turn, are paralleled by three ridges—Matheny, Sams, and Tshletshy—that separate them from each other and from the Queets River. The Queets-Quinault Divide, lying between the Queets and Quinault, marks the eastern and southern limits of the valley in the mountains; the Mount Olympus Range and Kloochman Ridge define the northern and western boundaries.

The glaciers and snowfields that encircle the wild, subalpine Queets Basin are the source of the Queets River. Meltwater from three glaciers (the Queets on Mount Queets, and the Humes and Jeffers on Mount Olympus), together with that contributed by the snowfields below Dodwell-Rixon Pass, combine to form the river, one of the largest on the peninsula.

The Queets Valley has the typical U shape that results from glaciation. However, where the river exits from the Queets Basin, it has cut a narrow canyon, 100 to 200 feet deep, in the black sandstone. Below the canyon, the valley floor is broad and level. As in the Hoh Valley, the bottomlands are covered with spruce-hemlock rain forest, and the mountainsides on either side rise steeply upward, heavy with western hemlock and silver fir.

The Queets is famous as a steelhead stream, but equally renowned for salmon as well as cutthroat and rainbow trout. Consequently, anglers come from near and far to try their luck. Yet that part of the valley accessible by the Queets Trail is essentially wilderness. Because hikers must wade the Queets River in order to reach the trail, plus the fact the path goes little more than half way from the road's end to the Queets Basin, visitors are fewer here than in most Olympic valleys. Accordingly, one is more likely to experience solitude. In fact, it is the policy of the National Park Service to keep this valley wild, as one place where the adventurous can face the challenge of primitive country. Consequently, it is more or less reserved for the experienced backpacker, in contrast to the Hoh and Quinault Valleys, which are readily accessible.

The Queets Valley was first explored in 1890, when the party Lieutenant Joseph O'Neil sent to Mount Olympus followed the river from that peak to the sea.

ROADS

Queets River Road. All trails in the Queets Valley are reached via the Queets River Road, which begins on the Olympic Highway, US 101, 18.0 mi/29.0 km west of Lake Quinault, 7.0 mi/11.3 km east of Queets, a village on the Quinault Indian Reservation. The road follows the river through the Queets Corridor of Olympic National Park. Throughout its length the road is in the bottomlands.

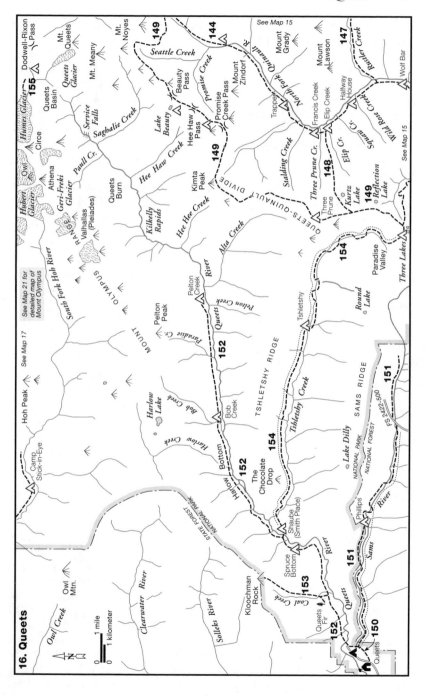

16. Queets

See Map 21 for detailed map of Mount Olympus

See Map 17

See Map 15

See Map 15

Owl Creek

N

0   1 mile
0   1 kilometer

Clearwater River

Solleks River

Owl Mtn.

Hoh Peak

Camp Stick-in-Eye

South Fork Hob River

MOUNT   OLYMPUS

RANGE

Valhallas (Pleiades)

Geri-Freki Glacier

Athena

Owl

Hubert Glacier

Humes Glacier

Dodwell-Rixon Pass

Mt. Queets

Queets Glacier

Queets Basin

155

Circe

Service Falls

Saghalie Creek

Paull Cr.

Mt. Meany

Mt. Noyes

149

144

Seattle Creek

Beauty Pass

Promise Creek

Mount Zindorf

Promise Creek Pass

Lake Beauty

Hee Haw Creek

Hee Haw Pass

149

Kimta Peak

Queets Burn

Kilkelly Rapids

Hee Hee Creek

Alta Creek

Queets   River

Pelton Creek

Pelton Peak

Paradise Cr.

152

Harlow Lake

Bob Creek

Bob Creek

152

Harlow   Bottom

Harlow Creek

152

The Chocolate Drop

154

Shaube (Smith Place)

Spruce Bottom

River

153

Coal Creek

Queets Fir

152

Kloochman Rock

STATE FOREST

NATIONAL PARK

QUEETS-QUINAULT   DIVIDE

North   Fork   Quinault   R.

Mount Grady

Mount Lawson

147

Rustler Creek

Wolf Bar

Trapper Cr.

Francis Creek

Elip Creek

Halfway House

Stalding Creek

Three Prune Cr.

148

Elip Cr.

Shunung Cr.

Wild Rose Cr.

Three Prune

Kurtz Lake

149

Reflection Lake

Tshletshy

154

Paradise Valley

Three Lakes

Round Lake

TSHLETSHY RIDGE

Tshletshy Creek

Lake Dilly

Phillips

SAMS   RIDGE

NATIONAL PARK

NATIONAL FOREST

FS 2422-500

151

151

Sams   River

Queets

150

Queets

151

Queets

Upon entering the national park (0.5 mi/0.8 km), the road goes through luxuriant rain forest. The Queets Valley was settled in the 1890s, and fifty years ago several stump ranches existed along this stretch of the river. After Olympic National Park was created in 1938, the government condemned a strip of land on both sides of the river, then added it to the park in 1953 as the Queets Corridor. The idea behind this action was to preserve one river valley on the peninsula from the mountains to the sea, but the forced removal of the people from the land created much bitterness, which has filtered down to some extent in succeeding generations.

At one point, where the road edges the river's banks (2.1 mi/3.4 km), the motorist has a good view, looking upstream, of snow-clad Mount Olympus, almost 30 miles distant.

Information can be obtained at the Queets Ranger Station (12.4 mi/20.0 km), which is staffed only during the summer. Queets Campground (13.4 mi/21.6 km), located in a stand of giant spruce, has the usual accommodations, with excellent sites adjacent to the river. The largest trees in the campground exceed 10 feet in diameter.

A particularly fine example of Sitka spruce stands about 60 feet south of the Queets River Road, just beyond the second entrance to the campground. The tree is almost 14 feet in diameter at the height of a man's chest and is quite tall, with a beautiful, vigorous crown.

The road ends at a small parking area just below the point where Sams River flows into the Queets (13.6 mi/21.9 km; 290 ft/88 m).

150 QUEETS CAMPGROUND LOOP TRAIL

Length 3.0 mi/4.8 km
Access Queets River Road
USGS Map Salmon River East
Agency Olympic National Park

The only trail in the Queets Corridor, this loop begins about 100 yards west of the entrance to the Queets Campground (290 ft/88 m), on the north side of the road. The path goes through a mix of scenes: stands of virgin timber, second-growth forest, and old fields that years ago were pioneer homesteads. During weekdays one can hear logging trucks operating in the distance.

The trail meanders back and forth in the narrow strip between road and river. At first it goes through stands of spruce, hemlock, and fir, then crosses, in succession, a field, a bottom overgrown with alder and evergreens, and another meadow. The Queets Ranger Station (1.2 mi/1.9 km; 270 ft/82 m) is located just beyond the second meadow.

At this point the trail crosses the road, and it then heads back toward the campground, alternating between forest and field. The trees are now all second growth, mostly hemlock and spruce, with big stumps of the old trees standing like specters among them. Lined by alders, the path next follows an old roadbed across the river bottom and enters a large field, where gnarled apple and cherry trees remind one that this was once the site of a pioneer family's orchard.

Queets River in Queets Corridor

Beyond this field the hiker finds the trail's most interesting feature—clumps of vine maple that, looking like huge lilac bushes, arch their limbs over the trail to create a tunnel effect. They are followed by a stand of large alders. The trees are tall for this species, their white-barked trunks curving upward like coconut palms. The whiteness is due to the presence of lichen. A conelike knoll covered with hemlocks rises to the right.

The trail goes through a stand of spruce, then intersects the unmarked **Sams River Trail** (2.7 mi/4.3 km; 300 ft/91 m), which is almost obliterated by brush and forest debris. The balance of the loop (actually the first part of the Sams River Trail) goes through typical rain forest near Sams River, where it is bordered by salmonberry bushes higher than one's head. Here the hiker can see Kloochman Rock squatting atop the ridge and looking out over the valley like the taciturn Indian wife from which it takes its name.

The trail terminates at the end of the Queets River Road (3.0 mi/4.8 km; 290 ft/88 m).

151   SAMS RIVER TRAIL

Abandoned trail, no longer maintained
Length 12.0 mi/19.3 km
Access Queets River Road
USGS Maps Salmon River East; Matheny Ridge; Kloochman Rock; Finley Creek
Agencies Olympic National Park and Olympic National Forest

The boundary between the national park and the national forest follows Sams River from its confluence with the Queets River to a point about 5 miles upstream. The boundary then leaves the river and extends along the crest of Sams Ridge between Sams River and Tshletshy Creek. Once a good trout fishing stream, the Sams has been badly damaged by silt because the land has been disturbed by extensive logging and a forest fire in the Olympic National Forest.

The Sams River Trail alternately traverses national park and national forest lands as it crosses back and forth from one side of the river to the other. Consequently, neither agency desires to undertake its maintenance, and it has become more or less an orphan, abandoned and suffering from neglect. No work has been done on it for several decades, and the path is virtually nonexistent today in many places. This is especially true in rain forest glades and where the path has been obliterated by logging. However, several remaining fragments of the trail are in fair condition.

The beginning of the trail, at the end of the Queets River Road (290 ft/88 m), coincides with part of the **Queets Campground Loop Trail.** This section goes through luxuriant rain forest, then comes out onto the banks of Sams River, where one can see Kloochman Rock across the Queets. The trail then forks (0.3 mi/0.5 km; 300 ft/92 m), but the division point is not marked. The obvious path leading right is a continuation of the loop trail; the Sams River Trail goes left, but it is very faint—in fact, easily overlooked. Bushes and the limbs of young trees encroach on both sides and obscure the ground.

Keeping close to Sams River, the route goes first on one side of the stream, then the other, to take advantage of the alder bottoms and glades. Here the trail has largely disappeared, but the observant hiker will see a cut log now and then. Because the bits of path lack continuity, it is easier to ignore them and strike out cross-country as far as the mouth of the First Canyon (3.0 mi/4.8 km; 500 ft/152 m).

At this point the trail crosses to the river's north side, which is in the national park. The canyon itself, which is about a mile long, is not negotiable except during low water because the swift, rushing stream extends to the rock walls on either side. Within the gorge, just above its mouth, anglers will find a deep, beautiful pool where steelhead can sometimes be observed lurking in the shadows.

The trail makes a gradual, ascending traverse above the canyon. Were it not for the occasional cut logs, and a switchback or two, one would not suspect that the path was man-made, because the route is blocked by countless windfalls, rotten logs, and thick brush. Nevertheless, it penetrates a magnificent stand of giant Douglas-firs, great trees that make an indelible imprint upon the mind.

Near the head of the canyon the national park boundary leaves the river. At this point (4.5 mi/7.2 km; 650 ft/198 m) the trail goes back into the national forest and does not again enter the national park. Here it meanders across beautiful rain forest glades, and one can look across the Sams and note that the timber has been logged right down to the stream's banks, a forestry practice that is frowned upon today.

(On the river's south side, opposite the trail and somewhat downstream, the hiker will find an elk hunters' camp near the remains of a trapper's cabin. The hunters once had a cable-and-bucket spanning the Sams at this point, which they used to transport elk killed illegally in the national park, north of the river. A good trail leads steeply down to the camp from a logging road about a third of a mile distant to the south.)

On the river's north bank, Camp Phillips occupies the site of the old Sams River Shelter (5.0 mi/8.0 km; 600 ft/183 m). At one time a makeshift structure—probably fashioned from the remnants of the shelter—was located here beneath a leaning cedar tree, but nothing remains today.

Beyond this camp the trail approaches a steep slide and waterfall, and in order to avoid the barrier the path crosses to the river's south bank, where it remains, briefly, until it approaches the mouth of the Second Canyon. Here it returns to the river's north side and continues to alder bottoms above the Second Canyon, then crosses again to the river's south bank and follows that side.

The trail then intersects FS Road 2422–500, which bridges the river just above the Third Canyon (8.0 mi/12.9 km; 900 ft/274 m). Beyond the road the trail has been obliterated for about 2 miles by fire, which occurred in conjunction with logging. Near the far end of the burned area, the route again crosses to the river's north bank (which now is in the national forest). The new Sams River Shelter which stood here (10.0 mi/16.1 km; 1000 ft/305 m) was destroyed by the fire.

At the lower end of the Fourth Canyon, about a half mile beyond this site, the trail leaves the logged and burned area and enters the virgin forest. Here the path parallels the north bank of the Sams. The box canyon extends approximately a mile, and at its head a 20-foot waterfall drops vertically. The trail then ends abruptly on the side of a bank (ca. 12.0 mi/19.3 km; 1400 ft/427 m) near the national park boundary. The original plan called for extending the trail to a junction with the old Finley Peak Trail, another 3 or 4 miles, intersecting with that route near Lilly Lake.

The huge pool at the base of the waterfall cannot be reached by going up the canyon. One must climb out of the gorge, traverse upriver several hundred feet, then descend the steep wall while clinging to a rope tied to a tree. The falls are a barrier to the upward migration of fish, and at times the pool contains large numbers of them.

152 QUEETS TRAIL

Length 15.4 mi/24.8 km
Access Queets River Road
USGS Maps Stequaleho; Salmon River East; Kloochman Rock; Bob Creek
Agency Olympic National Park

This valley trail was originally a path used by the Indians when they traveled up the Queets River to hunt elk. After George Shaube took a claim on the upper Queets in the early 1920s, he improved and maintained the trail for the Forest Service. The trail follows the Queets River about half way to its headwaters. The Queets Basin, at the valley's head, can be reached by traveling cross-country beyond the trail's end, but it is approached more easily from other directions.

The trail begins on the river's north bank, opposite the end of the Queets River Road (280 ft/85 m). Consequently, in order to reach the trail one must ford the Queets (and sometimes the Sams as well, because the best place to cross varies from year to year). The river can be forded safely in late summer or autumn, after the snows have melted and before the fall rains have begun; but at other times it is deep and treacherous. The hiker should carry a couple of stout poles (one in each hand, to brace against the current) and wear boots or tennis shoes with rough soles because the current is swift and strong, the water cold, and the bottom covered with slippery rocks.

The almost level trail meanders through splendid rain forests where giant spruce, hemlock, and bigleaf maples garlanded with mosses tower above a jungle of vine maple. Elk frequent the valley, grazing in the forest glades, and often the hiker can hear the bugling of the bulls. The trail crosses a field overgrown with bracken fern and thistle, where a large barn (1.6 mi/2.6 km; 375 ft/114 m) stood for many years, but finally succumbed to the elements. This was the John Andrews ranch, originally the Hunter homestead. Kloochman Rock is visible from the field, appearing as a dark knob perched atop a steep, timbered mountain. The trail then winds among bell-bottomed spruces to a junction with the **Kloochman Rock Trail** at Coal Creek (2.3 mi/3.7 km; 350 ft/ 107 m).

At the Lower Tshletshy Ford (3.9 mi/6.3 km; 400 ft/122 m), the river may be crossed, but the **Tshletshy Creek Trail** is still more than a mile distant. The Queets Trail now turns north and traverses dense forest to Spruce Bottom (4.9 mi/7.9 km; 426 ft/130 m), a camp located among big spruce trees. This is a popular spot with backpackers, and dedicated fishermen have been known to catch large steelhead in the deep pools. Although the distance from the road is not great, the place is isolated because many people are afraid to ford the river. The quiet is unbroken save for the mesmeric roar of the Queets.

The trail then follows a slope high above the Queets, only to return to the bottomland and a junction with the Tshletshy Creek Trail (5.6 mi/9.0 km; 480 ft/ 146 m), which leads to the Upper Tshletshy Ford.

Fording the Queets

After climbing up and down as it crosses spurs at the base of Kloochman Rock, the trail closely follows the Queets River and once again traverses level bottomland. Here the path meanders among grotesque bigleaf maples festooned with mosses.

The trail crosses Bear Creek, skirts the gravel bars opposite Tshletshy Creek, then enters Harlow Bottom (7.5 mi/12.1 km; 500 ft/152 m), which was named for two Indians, Frank and Ben Harlow. This flat, embracing perhaps 1200 acres, extends along the river about 3 miles, almost to Bob Creek, and has a maximum width approaching a mile. Harlow Creek, one of the larger streams entering the Queets from the north, flows across the middle. The bottom has splendid stands of Sitka spruce (perhaps the finest on the peninsula today), as well as large Douglas-fir and red cedar. The trees rise above an understory of alder and maple (both vine and bigleaf) cloaked with heavy growths of selaginella, ferns, and mosses. Most of the conifers are 6 to 9 feet in diameter, with heights that approach 300 feet. The largest ones are about 13 feet in diameter.

The trail leaves Harlow Bottom after crossing Camp Creek. At Bob Creek Camp (11.0 mi/17.7 km; 580 ft/177 m), the shelter built in 1929 by Wilbur Northup and George Shaube was destroyed by snow in the late 1970s. The floodplain on the river's north side narrows above this camp, and the trail cuts along the face of a bluff, then switchbacks down to the stream, only to climb another bluff. The river washes against its base, where deposits of glacial outwash are exposed. The bottomland widens again in the vicinity of Paradise Creek, and the trail ends at Pelton Creek Shelter (15.4 mi/24.8 km; 800 ft/244 m), which stands opposite the point where Pelton Creek flows into the Queets from the south.

One can, of course, proceed beyond the trail's end. This is an exciting route to approach Mount Olympus, but it should be attempted only by experienced, well-equipped backpackers adept at cross-country travel.

153 KLOOCHMAN ROCK TRAIL

Abandoned trail, no longer maintained
Length 3.4 mi/5.5 km
Access Queets Trail
USGS Map Kloochman Rock
Agency Olympic National Park; Department of Natural Resources, State of Washington

Kloochman Rock rises more than a half mile above the Queets River bottomlands and provides an outstanding vista of the surrounding country. The peak is heavily timbered except for the outcrop of black sandstone that caps the summit like a cupola. The word Kloochman means "wife" or "woman" in the language of the coast Indians. The peak is called Boulder Hill on old maps.

The trail from the Queets River to Kloochman Rock, used for years by fire lookouts, was abandoned in the mid-1970s and is no longer maintained. Hikers frequently report that they cannot find evidence of the old trail, despite the fact that abandoned paths usually take longer than two decades to disappear, even in the Olympic rain forest. Nevertheless, Kloochman Rock is considered to be inaccessible from the Queets Trail today. Only the toughest and most determined, most dedicated cross-country travelers are equal to the task of following the original route. The old trail is of sufficient historic interest, however, to justify its description here—in the present tense, in order to give hikers a feel for the route as it once was.

The trail to the rock begins on the valley floor (350 ft/107 m), branching left from the **Queets Trail** at Coal Creek. Near the trail's beginning, a side path leads left to the Queets Fir, the largest known Douglas-fir. This tree is believed to be at least a thousand years old, double the age of most trees in the valley. The massive trunk is more than 14 feet thick at chest height. The original height is unknown because the top is broken off more than 200 feet above the ground. Apparently this tree is the lone survivor of an ancient stand of fir that has been replaced by hemlock in the natural succession of species.

The Queets Fir was the center of a friendly controversy between Oregon and Washington in 1962, when Oregon officials contended that the Clatsop Fir, near Seaside, was larger. An impartial panel of foresters measured the trees. Final figures gave the Queets tree the greater bulk (14,065 cubic feet of wood to 10,095) and height (202 feet to 200.5 feet), but the Oregon tree had the greater diameter (15.5 feet compared to 14.5 feet). Less than three months later a storm toppled the Clatsop Fir.

Unwilling to give up the crown, Oregon found a new contender in 1975—Finnegan's Fir, near Coos Bay—which turned out to be 302 feet tall and slightly over 13 feet in diameter. Less than six months after it was declared the new champion, Finnegan's Fir was shattered by violent winds. Surely, it seems, the gods on Olympus protect their own.

Winding through hemlock forest, the trail crosses Coal Creek, the last place where water can be obtained. Huckleberries are abundant at various points along the trail. Beyond the creek the path switchbacks up the mountain, a seemingly endless climb through forests of western hemlock and silver fir. Eventually, however, one reaches the base of the rocky summit, and after a brief scramble attains the top (3.4 mi/5.5 km; 3356 ft/1023 m). Here a wooden helicopter platform has replaced the fire lookout cabin that stood atop the peak for many years.

Lookout cabins have gone the way of the great auk because airplanes are now used to spot forest fires. The helicopter pad was built by the Department of Natural Resources, with the approval of the National Park Service, in connection with its logging operations on state lands adjoining the national park. The structure has no place in a national park and should be removed; it is an intrusion on the natural scene.

Until the late 1960s, about thirty years after the national park was created, the vista from Kloochman Rock was probably unrivaled in the United States for virgin forests untouched by either forest fires or logging operations. One looked out upon an unbroken panorama of hemlock-covered mountains. But this is no longer true. Although the fires never came, the loggers did, and the visitor who knew Kloochman as it once was cannot but be saddened by the change. The country visible from the rock does not encompass a true circle but an irregular area due to intervening ridges and peaks that block the view in certain directions. Of the approximately 400,000 acres visible from the peak, at least 75 percent lie outside the national park, and in the 1960s logging operations began to invade this region—on national forest lands to the south, on state lands to the north and west. Now dozens of clearcuts are visible where formerly one saw an untouched sea of virgin forest.

Nonetheless, the view is spectacular because the area within the national park is still unspoiled. The bottomlands along the Queets, 3000 feet below, are clothed with virgin fir and spruce, and the braided channels of the meandering river flow through the forest like intertwined silver ribbons. Mount Olympus and Mount Tom, and the snowy peaks adjacent to Queets Basin, 20 miles distant, loom above the timbered foothills. The whole sweep of the Queets Valley east of Kloochman Rock is an unbroken expanse of beautiful forest.

To reach Kloochman Rock today, drive to Clearwater, Washington, then to Yahoo Lake in State Sustained Yield Forest No. 1, also known as the Bert Cole Forest. The roads beyond the lake are closed, therefore one is obliged to walk about 4 miles (via FS Roads C3100 and C3180, the latter being a spur). A so-called way trail begins at the end of C3180, but it is more like a scrambler's route. The ascent takes from forty minutes to an hour, and one must watch carefully for blazes marking the route. Ropes dangle down in difficult places, put there to assist climbers, but they are old and weathered and should not be trusted.

154 TSHLETSHY CREEK TRAIL

Abandoned trail, no longer maintained
Length 16.2 mi/26.1 km
Access Queets Trail
USGS Maps Bunch Lake; Kimta Peak; Bob Creek; Kloochman Rock
Agency Olympic National Park

This trail has been abandoned by the National Park Service and has not been maintained for years, thus it is overgrown with brush and often blocked by windfalls, making it difficult to follow. Therefore it is truly a wilderness route, one that should not be attempted by anyone who is not experienced at cross-country travel.

The trail was built in the 1920s for the Forest Service by George Shaube, with a six-man crew. The route branches right from the **Queets Trail** 5.6 mi/9.0 km above the Queets River Road and follows Tshletshy Creek—a steelhead and salmon stream—to the Queets-Quinault Divide, crossing the stream eleven times. The route traverses splendid stands of old-growth forest, and it is a good place to see wildlife. Elk and bear frequent this remote, seldom-visited valley, and the hiker will also see lesser denizens of the forest. Bird life is varied, and the harlequin ducks that nest along the stream are so unaccustomed to seeing people that one can approach them closely.

Leaving the Queets Trail (480 ft/146 m), the path winds among big spruce trees to the Upper Tshletshy Ford, where the route crosses the Queets River, which at this point is broad and comparatively shallow. Nevertheless, the crossing requires caution, and one should not attempt it when the river is high. During late summer and fall, the greatest depth is normally about thirty inches. One should carry a couple of poles and lean against the current.

A small cabin stands in the meadow on the far side. This is the Smith Place

The Queets Fir, the largest known Douglas-fir

(0.2 mi/0.3 km; 460 ft/140 m). More properly, it should be called the Shaube Place, because it was homesteaded by George Shaube in 1923. The cabin he built consisted of what is now the kitchen; the living room was added later. About 1932 Shaube sold the claim to Oscar Smith, who used the cabin as a hunting lodge rather than a permanent residence. Eventually, the cabin became known as Smith Place.

Beyond the cabin the trail enters what might well be called the forest primeval. For the next half mile, between the clearing and Tshletshy Creek, the trail penetrates what is unquestionably one of the finest stands of old-growth Douglas-fir and western red cedar in the Olympics. The colossal firs, many 7 to 9 feet in diameter, rise to great heights, possibly 300 feet or more.

The path is difficult to find as it approaches Tshletshy Creek (0.8 mi/1.3 km; 480 ft/146 m), where the trail makes the first of eleven crossings. (The others are miles beyond this point, and the creek is not visible between this crossing and the next.) The creek bed is choked with boulders, logs, and debris from winter floods. Unless one can find a log across, it is a case of wade, although the stream is usually not deep after July.

The forests along Tshletshy Creek consist of stands of Douglas-fir, Sitka spruce, red cedar, and western hemlock. Beneath the big trees, little hemlocks and sharp-needled spruces grow in such thick stands that the trail is often hidden. The hiker has to force a passage through, and when the trees and brush are wet one receives a shower bath with every step. But the real barrier to progress is not the overgrown trail but the countless windfalls that have occurred over the years at various points along the trail. The logs are large and have not been cut out, making them difficult to climb over and under.

After crossing Tshletshy Creek, the trail leaves the river bottom and climbs on terraces, where the route parallels the creek as it goes between a spur of Sams Ridge and The Chocolate Drop, a conelike hill (1754 ft/535 m) that rises from the Queets bottoms. Then, after traversing the edge of another terrace or big flat, the trail enters the canyon and contours the base of Tshletshy Ridge. The creek roars mightily in the depths of the narrow gorge, which lies between Tshletshy Ridge and Sams Ridge.

As it traverses the canyon's side, the trail climbs gradually and crosses numerous side streams. The forest is impressive—many big cedars, firs, and spruces are mixed among the ubiquitous hemlock. Gradually, however, the cedar and fir become less dominant, the hemlock and spruce more abundant.

The trail descends to campsites at Tshletshy Creek (9.2 mi/14.8 km; 1360 ft/ 415 m), where it recrosses the stream. At this point one does not have to wade because the creek is spanned by a large spruce log.

Beyond this crossing the trail deteriorates and is difficult to follow. This is not a route for the novice, and the experienced backpacker will have to do a good deal of scouting. As a consequence one does well to travel a mile an hour through this section. This crossing is the first place Tshletshy Creek has been approached or has been visible since the first crossing more than 8 miles downstream, but the route now makes up for this indiscretion. During the next 5 miles the path crosses the creek ten times in order to take advantage of favorable terrain. In fact, at times the route uses the creek bed because windfalls make travel away from the gravel bars difficult. The creek bed is broad, evidencing the fact that great floods rage through here during the winter. One should watch for orange tags tacked to the trees and follow the easiest course.

After traversing opposite a landslide that extends down to the creek from near the top of the ridge, the trail makes the final crossing (14.4 mi/23.2 km; 2275 ft/ 696 m)—and it is unique. During the summer and fall, the crossing is dry, although the stream flows just above and below.

At this point the trail leaves Tshletshy Creek and improves but steepens as it climbs toward the divide through stands of western hemlock and silver fir. Because this area—known as Paradise Valley—is isolated and seldom disturbed by man, it is much frequented by elk, and one should be alert for a glimpse of the animals. At Lily Pad Lake, a small tarn with water lilies, the forest becomes subalpine, broken by small openings. Here one can look down and see the big meadow in Paradise Valley. The trail then goes by Delta Tarn, a little triangular lake surrounded by meadows. This is not a good camping place, however, because it is swampy and infested with countless mosquitoes.

Above Paradise Valley the trail climbs sharply to the divide through stands of Alaska cedar and mountain hemlock. The path is lined by huckleberry bushes, often heavy with fruit. The trail then tops the Queets-Quinault Divide (16.2 mi/26.1 km; 3600 ft/1097 m), where it becomes the **Big Creek Trail.**

155   QUEETS BASIN WAY TRAIL

Not maintained
Length 0.3 mi/0.5 km
Access None by other trails (connects meadowland of Queets Basin with moraine of Humes Glacier)
USGS Map Mount Queets
Agency Olympic National Park

The importance of this little fragment of trail is inversely proportional to its length. Queets Basin lies on the route of a popular traverse of Mount Olympus and the Bailey Range. When going between the basin and Humes Glacier, one must keep high in order to avoid the Queets Canyon. At the western edge of the basin, this way trail climbs over a timbered spur and makes a precipitous descent to the point where two creeks come together below the glacier (ca. 0.3 mi/0.5 km). The trail ends here, but the route then ascends the loose rubble on the moraine to the glacier.

Although it is difficult to carry a heavy pack over this trail—particularly when going from the glacier to the basin, thus climbing the steep western part—the task is much easier than traveling cross-country across this rough terrain.

Plutos Gulch in Queets Basin

HOH

The Hoh River flows westward to the Pacific Ocean, and its valley extends deep into the mountains at low altitude—to the foot of Mount Olympus itself. During the Ice Age a glacier that came down the valley all the way to the ocean had much to do with shaping the present-day topography. Within the mountains the long and narrow valley, with the characteristic U shape that results from glacial action, is bordered by steep, timbered mountains. In fact, less than a mile from the river the ridges rise more than 3000 feet.

The name Hoh derives from an Indian word meaning "fast-moving water." This is an apt description because the glaciers on Mount Olympus are the river's source, and the stream receives fully 80 percent of the peak's drainage—the meltwater from six glaciers (Hoh, Blue, White, Black, Hubert, and Ice River). Consequently, the river is swift and milky due to the presence of glacial silt.

The river is already a large stream when it emerges from the terminus of the Hoh Glacier, but as it flows down the mountain it collects the water of many small streams, including Ice River. Throughout its upper course, where it sweeps half way around Mount Olympus, the Hoh flows in a deep canyon paralleled by the Bailey Range. Glacier Creek joins the Hoh at the northern base of Olympus. This stream, sustained by several glaciers (the Blue, White, and Black) is as large as the Hoh itself at this point. The enlarged river then flows westward toward the sea, its braided channels meandering on the level valley floor.

Numerous tributaries add to the river's volume. Mount Tom Creek and the South Fork Hoh are the largest ones. The valley of the South Fork is narrower than that of the main Hoh, and the bottomland disappears in its upper course, where steep slopes rise directly from the river's banks. The source of the South Fork is the Hubert Glacier on Mount Olympus. This glacier was named for Anna Hubert, the first woman to climb the mountain.

Below its junction with the South Fork, the Hoh flows through low, broken country to the Pacific.

Beyond the Bailey Range, which bounds the Hoh at its head, lies the Elwha Valley. West of Mount Olympus, timbered spurs rise between the Hoh and the South Fork. The Mount Olympus Range, which includes the sandstone peaks known as the Valhallas, forms the divide between the South Fork Hoh and the Queets River. North of the Hoh a high ridge extending west from the Bailey Range lies between the Hoh and the Soleduck and Bogachiel Valleys. The eastern part of this ridge is known as the High Divide.

ROADS

Hoh River Road. With the exception of the South Fork Hoh Trail, all trails in this district are reached via the Hoh River Road, which parallels the river from US

101, the Olympic Highway, to the Hoh Ranger Station. Outside the national park, the road goes by stump ranches and traverses cutover lands and stands of second growth. A patch of virgin forest now and then gives the motorist a hint of what lies ahead.

The Willoughby Creek Campground (3.6 mi/5.8 km) and the Minnie Peterson Camp and Picnic Area (4.7 mi/7.6 km), maintained by the Department of Natural Resources, are located in bits of rain forest similar to that found in the national park. The second camp honors a lady who took pack trains into the Olympics for half a century. Westward Hoh (5.6 mi/9.0 km) is the sole supply point in the valley. Gasoline and groceries are available here.

Beyond the Lewis Ranch, the last settlement in the valley, the road enters Olympic National Park (11.9 mi/19.2 km; 440 ft/134 m), where it traverses stands of old growth, the giant firs and spruces rising above an understory of moss-laden vine maple. Many of the conifers exceed 250 feet in height, have diameters of 6 to 10 feet, and are more than five hundred years old. One of the largest, the Preston P. Macy Tree (15.4 mi/24.8 km), honors the first superintendent of Olympic National Park. This Sitka spruce is 270 feet tall, almost 13 feet in diameter, and probably seven hundred years old. The large wildlife in the valley includes elk, deer, coyote, and an occasional black bear; among the smaller mammals are chipmunks, squirrels, snowshoe hares, beavers, otters, muskrats, and raccoons. Birds are numerous: often heard are the winter wren and the raven; highly visible are the flocks of gray jays. During the winter, sports fishermen come from near and far to match wits with the wily steelhead.

The road ends at a paved parking area (formerly a meadow) adjacent to the Hoh Ranger Station and Visitor Center (18.0 mi/29.0 km; 578 ft/176 m). Nearby, a commodious campground, located in groves of black cottonwood, spruce, and alder, has numerous sites. Directly across the river, along the lower course of Jackson Creek, the stands of large, old-growth Douglas-fir constitute some of the finest examples of this species in the national park.

The South Fork Hoh trail is reached via two roads in the Bert Cole Forest, 127,000 acres of state-owned land west of the national park. They are the Honor Camp Road and Department of Natural Resources Road 1000.

Honor Camp Road. This road leaves the Olympic Highway 0.7 mi/1.1 km south of the Hoh River. Beyond the junction with DNR Road 1000 (6.8 mi/ 10.9 km), the road continues to the Clearwater Honor Camp. The hiker headed for the South Fork Hoh should take DNR Road 1000.

DNR Road 1000. This road traverses country that has been devastated by logging. Beyond Owl Creek, where the pavement ends, the road turns sharply left and climbs to a high bench, where it overlooks and parallels the Hoh River for several miles. The road then descends to and crosses the South Fork Hoh (7.6 mi/12.2 km). The river shows white water here as it flows rapidly over large boulders that constrict the channel. A small campground is located on the east side.

Beyond the crossing the road climbs recently logged slopes. Several spur roads lead into the woods, but the main road always keeps to the right; ending at a small parking area (10.3 mi/16.6 km), where the South Fork Trail begins.

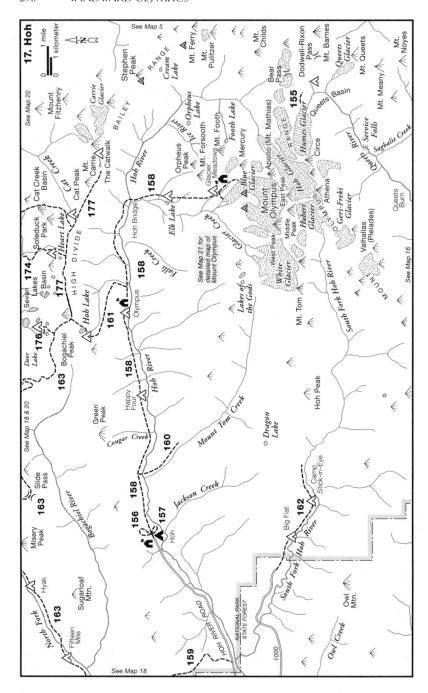

17. Hoh

0   1 mile
0   1 kilometer

See Map 5

See Map 20

See Map 18 & 20

See Map 18

See Map 16

Stephen Peak

Mount Fitzhenry

Carrie Glacier

BAILEY RANGE

Cream Lake

Mt. Ferry

Mt. Pulitzer

Mt. Childs

Dodwell-Rixon Pass

Mt. Barnes

Queets Glacier

Mt. Queets

Mt. Noyes

Bear Glacier

Queets Basin

155

Mt. Meany

Cat Creek Basin

Cat Peak

Mt. Carrie

The Catwalk

Mt. Mathias

Hoh River

Orpheus Lake

Orpheus Peak

Mt. Forsooth

Mt. Meadows

Mt. Footh

Foot Lake

Mt. Mercury

Blue Glacier

Apollo (Mt. Mathias)

OLYMPUS RANGE

Humes Glacier

Service Falls

Saghalie Creek

Queets River

Queets Burn

177

Cat Creek

HIGH DIVIDE

Soleduck Park

Heart Lake

Sevan Lakes

Basin

174

177

Hob Lake

Hob Bridge

158

Elk Lake

Glacier

East Peak

Mount Olympus

Middle Peak

Hubert Glacier

Athena

Geri-Freki Glacier

Circe

Hob Glacier

158

Falls Creek

Olympus

161

Deer Lake

Bogachiel Peak

176

Hob River

163

Lakes of the Gods

West Peak

White Glacier

MOUNTS

Valhallas (Pleiades)

Glacier Creek

See Map 21 for detailed map of Mount Olympus

Happy Four

158

Green Peak

Cougar Creek

160

Mount Tom Creek

Mt. Tom

South Fork Hob River

Hob Peak

Dragon Lake

Slide Pass

163

Misery Peak

Hyak

Sugarloaf Mtn.

North Fork

163

Fifteen Mile

Bogachiel River

Jackson Creek

158

156

157

Hoh

Big Flat

Camp Stick-in-Eye

162

South Fork Hob River

Owl Mtn.

Owl Creek

HOH RIVER ROAD

NATIONAL PARK

STATE FOREST

1000

159

156   HALL OF MOSSES NATURE TRAIL

Length 0.7 mi/1.1 km
Access Hoh River Road
USGS Map Owl Mountain
Agency Olympic National Park

One of two nature trails near the Hoh Ranger Station and Visitor Center at the end of the Hoh River Road, this route makes a loop north of the Hoh River Trail. The elevation is low—about 600 ft/183 m above sea level. Interpretive markers are posted at various points along the trail.

The path crosses Taft Creek, climbs up to a bench covered with stately Douglas-firs, then meanders through stands of hemlock and spruce to the cathedral-like Hall of Mosses. This is a colonnade of bigleaf maples, and the trees are heavily garlanded with luxuriant growths of selaginella, ferns, and mosses. When this glen was discovered by Grant Sharpe in 1954, the forest floor was carpeted with moss six inches thick, and the bigleaf and vine maples were clothed from the ground up with mosses and ferns. But popularity has taken its toll—intentionally or otherwise, visitors have destroyed the moss as high as a man can reach, and the ground cover has been trampled into oblivion. Although the Hall of Mosses is still an outstanding attraction, it is not nearly so beautiful today as it was before the trail was built.

The trail then circles around, winding among large spruce trees, whose bases are almost hidden by dense growths of vine maple, and returns to its point of origin (0.7 mi/1.1 km).

157   SPRUCE NATURE TRAIL

Length 1.2 mi/1.9 km
Access Hoh River Road
USGS Map Owl Mountain
Agency Olympic National Park

This nature trail lies between the Hoh Trail and the Hoh River and begins near the Hoh Trail Visitor Center on the Hoh River Road. The path first traverses a river terrace covered with a magnificent stand of large Sitka spruce intermixed with hemlock, Douglas-fir, and western red cedar. The trail then descends to a lower level that is periodically flooded by the river. This area, composed mostly of glacial silt, is covered with alder and maple because the floods prevent conifers from establishing a foothold. The grassy bottoms are frequented by elk because they provide good forage.

The trail comes out to the river bank, then returns to the upper terrace and crosses Taft Creek (which issues from a spring within the confines of the trail loop) and returns to its starting point on the Hoh Trail (1.2 mi/1.9 km).

158 HOH TRAIL

Length 17.0 mi/27.4 km
Access Hoh River Road
USGS Maps Mount Olympus; Mount Tom; Owl Mountain; Mount Carrie
Agency Olympic National Park

The main route to Mount Olympus, this trail traverses the river bottoms to the mountain's base, then climbs steeply to the Blue Glacier, about half way up the peak. Beyond the glacial moraine the route to the top of Olympus lies over fields of ice and snow. The trail is popular during the summer, when one is never far from company, but the hiker who goes into the upper Hoh in November is not likely to see anyone else. The weather can then change quickly from benign Indian summer to a fierce winter gale, and when storms sweep up the valley, the wind whooshes through the trees. But this is the time to see the valley's wildlife—elk and deer, bear, raccoon, and snowshoe rabbit.

The trail begins at the Hoh Ranger Station and Visitor Center (578 ft/176 m) at the end of the Hoh River Road. After crossing tranquil Taft Creek, it meanders at a level grade through the multistoried rain forest. The ground is carpeted with ferns, mosses, lichens, liverworts, and thick growths of vine maple, huckleberry, red elder, and salmonberry. Above this jungle rise the hemlocks, spruces, firs, and cedars. On the ground the fallen logs are padded with cushions of moss and millions of baby trees. At intervals the gloomy stands of conifers are broken by patches of alders or by glades where bigleaf maples and vine maples, heavily bearded with selaginella and ferns, stand in grotesque postures. As one travels up the valley, the forest changes gradually until Douglas-fir becomes the dominant species, but spruce is common as far as Lewis Meadow.

Unlike the mountain trails, this river-bottom path is smooth and flat, not stony and rough. Little wayside camps, each with its own individual attractions, are located at various points along the route. Beyond a viewpoint where Mount Tom is visible (1.5 mi/2.4 km), the trail descends to the Hoh, then climbs a bit because the river washes against a bluff opposite Mount Tom Creek. Here the trail crosses two streams that tumble down the slope, and just beyond them the **Mount Tom Creek Trail** (2.8 mi/4.5 km; 660 ft/201 m) leads to the right. The trail then crosses Five Mile Slough, a side channel of the river, and traverses grassy alder bottoms, only to recross the slough and return to the evergreen forest, which is now largely Douglas-fir.

Happy Four Shelter (5.6 mi/9.0 km; 800 ft/244 m), surrounded by large firs, stands on a bench above the river. Excellent campsites are located near the stream. Beyond this point, the trail provides periodic views of the Hoh River, at times going through bowers of vine maple that are attractive in the fall after the leaves have fallen. On sunny days, the moss formations, dripping from the recent rains, are illuminated and appear to be translucent.

The trail then descends and crosses Eight Mile Slough, another side channel of the river. Slough Camp (7.9 mi/12.7 km; 900 ft/274 m), to the right of the trail,

Large Sitka spruce in Hoh Valley

is a good place for a small party to stay. The trail recrosses the slough, then climbs over a spur blackened by the 1978 Hoh Lake fire, which swept down to the river from the ridge above. Occasionally, when walking in this area, the hiker will hear rocks clatter down the cliffs to the north, where the protective vegetation was destroyed. Most of the trees in the burned area were killed, and the devastation contrasts markedly with the adjacent greenery.

Leaving this scarred district, the trail returns to the river bottoms. The Olympus Ranger Station (9.0 mi/14.5 km; 948 ft/289 m) and a trail shelter stand at the edge of a grass-covered meadow bordered by large spruce and cottonwood trees. Behind the rustic cabin, a clear, sparkling brook provides the camp with drinking water. The river flows by the meadow's south side, and from the gravel bars south of the trail one can look up the valley and see the Bailey Range as well as much of the area burned by the Hoh Lake fire.

Douglas-fir is dominant beyond the ranger station, but spruce, hemlock, and cedar are still present. Here the trail winds through a stand of ancient firs. Many of the trees are 8 to 10 feet in diameter, and the average height is about 275 feet. Occasionally, larger specimens are found—trees that approach 12 feet in diameter and sometimes exceed 300 feet in height. The great shafts, with their ribbed bark, rise without limbs for 100 feet or more, like classic Doric columns, and breezes murmur softly in the crowns.

The route intersects the **Hoh Lake Trail** (9.5 mi/15.3 km; 1000 ft/305 m) and crosses Lake Creek, which usually flows underground at this point—at least during the summer. The route then skirts Lewis Meadow (10.3 mi/16.6 km; 1000 ft/305 m), where an old cabin once stood. This is a good campsite, but water must be obtained from the river. One can see the Bailey Range from the meadow.

The trail reaches the end of the flat bottomland at Stove Hill Camp (12.0 mi/19.3 km; 1080 ft/329 m), so called because many years ago a weary packer dumped a large woodstove beside the trail. The path formerly went directly up the steep hill, but it has since been rerouted and now switchbacks up, then crosses a couple of streams before descending to Hoh Bridge (13.0 mi/20.9 km; 1357 ft/414 m), which spans the river just above its confluence with Glacier Creek. Here the Hoh surges through a rock-walled gorge 150 feet deep, and turbulent Glacier Creek flows through a similar canyon. The slots were cut in the black sandstone of a glacial step. This is the third bridge at this site. The first one, built by Henry Huelsdonk about 1923, was replaced in the 1940s, and the present one dates from 1971. Delicious huckleberries grow in the vicinity, and hikers often stop here to have lunch. A tiny camp located beside a little stream about 200 yards beyond the bridge has two tent sites.

The trail now climbs the northern slopes of Mount Olympus via switchbacks that alternate with long, ascending traverses. The forest consists chiefly of stands of large Douglas-fir, with an undergrowth of vine maple and a ground cover of vanilla leaf and ferns, primarily sword and maidenhair. Queencup bead lilies nestle amidst the greenery on the forest floor, their blue berries contrasting with the bright greens of the other plants. At Drip Rock, a huge monolith beside the trail, water drips from an overhanging cliff until midsummer.

Upon approaching Martins Creek, where the stream plunges over an escarpment, the trail crosses above the falls. The grade eases beyond this point, the trail

Elk Lake on the Hoh Trail

rounds a bend, and Elk Lake comes into view (14.6 mi/23.5 km; 2558 ft/780 m). The shelter here is often occupied, but good campsites are located in the timber above the trail. The lake is comparatively warm, and swimmers paddle among the lily pads. As late as 1935 the lake had no fish, never having been stocked, but trout are present today. The lake marks the approximate upper limit of the Douglas-fir forest. Above it the slopes are covered with Alaska cedar, silver fir, and mountain hemlock.

The trail now climbs sharply through dense forest, crosses a few open glades—avalanche zones overgrown with slide alder and salmonberry thickets—where one can see the High Divide and Mount Carrie, then traverses around a cliff that overlooks Glacier Creek. The stream is 1400 feet below, and vantage points here provide views of the Snow Dome on Olympus, the White Glacier, and Glacier Creek. The former extent of the glacier is clearly indicated by the distinct boundary between the neighboring conifer forest and the deciduous growth that flourishes upon the old glacial bed. On hot days, when the ice melts rapidly, the creek clatters like a freight train.

After crossing a deep, rocky ravine, which is often filled with avalanched snow and where the rocks are unstable, the trail meanders to Glacier Meadows (17.0 mi/ 27.4 km; 4200 ft/1280 m). The dense forest ends here, but subalpine trees are scattered up the mountainside and on the rocky moraine above. Two shelters are located near the lower edge of the meadows, and the standard, maintained trail ends at this point.

Beyond Glacier Meadows a way trail continues up to the Blue Glacier. This primitive path, which is not maintained, goes by the summer ranger's tent, winds briefly through dense groves of subalpine fir and mountain hemlock, and again enters open country. The trail then forks (17.1 mi/27.5 km). Both paths lead to the glacier.

The right branch of the way trail climbs through brush and over large, rough boulders to a notch in the moraine just above the glacier's terminus, then ascends Indian Rock (17.5 mi/28.2 km; 4700 ft/1433 m). This point overlooks the glacier, which is broken by numerous crevasses, but the peaks of Olympus are hidden by the Snow Dome. One can camp here, but water must be carried up from below. Early in the season one can, of course, find snow to melt.

The left branch of the trail is much longer—perhaps a mile or more. After crossing meadowland (where wildflowers grow profusely), it follows a ravine that is snow-filled until late summer. The moraine abuts a steep mountainside (18.0 mi/ 29.0 km; 5000 ft/1524 m). The terrain is deceiving, the distance farther than it appears. The transition here is abrupt. After having walked for miles through luxuriant rain forests, then a fringe of meadowland, one looks out upon a scene from the Ice Age—a world of snow, ice, and barren rock. The moraine, a ridge of loosely consolidated boulders and dirt, rises abruptly from the glacier's edge, and the view is one of the finest in the Olympics. Below is the sweep of the glacier; beyond are the peaks of Olympus, the Snow Dome, Glacier Pass, and the Blue Glacier icefall. Several primitive campsites are located adjacent to the moraine and are frequently used by hikers who wish to see the alpenglow at sunrise and sunset, or by climbers intent on getting an early start to scale the peak.

Although hikers not trained and experienced in the art of mountaineering will be sorely tempted to do so, they should refrain from venturing upon the glacier or attempting to climb Mount Olympus. The ascent is a glorious experience, but over the years a number of people have lost their lives on the peak—primarily due to inexperience and lack of proper equipment.

159 SOUTH SNIDER/JACKSON TRAIL

Abandoned trail, no longer maintained
Length 10.0 mi/16.1 km
Access Hoh River Road
USGS Maps Spruce Mountain; Hunger Mountain
Agency Olympic National Park

This route was originally part of the old Forest Service trail that extended from Snider Guard Station on the Soleduck River to Jackson Guard Station (now Hoh Ranger Station) on the Hoh.

The trailhead (436 ft/133 m) is located on the Hoh River Road 0.5 mi/0.8 km inside the national park, opposite the mouth of the South Fork Hoh. The path climbs to a north–south ridge—a jog in the divide between the Hoh and Bogachiel Rivers—and follows this ridge northward, then descends to the Bogachiel along a spur that parallels Tumwata Creek. Hikers should carry water because it is not available until one reaches the Bogachiel bottoms.

Leaving the Hoh River Road, the trail climbs to a level bench, where it meanders through dark stands of spruce and hemlock. Here the path is often cut up by elk and deer tracks. This bench is part of the valley floor, and its north edge touches the base of the steep ridge that divides the Hoh and Bogachiel. At this point the trail angles up the mountain through stands of hemlock mixed with remnants of an ancient Douglas-fir forest. The largest trees are 10 feet in diameter, their gnarled crowns weather-beaten by hundreds of winter storms. The Hoh River, glimmering like molten silver in the morning sunlight, is glimpsed through the trees. As the trail gains elevation, the slopes drop sharply—on the right to the upper Hoh, inside the national park; on the left to the lower Hoh, outside the park.

Higher up the Douglas-firs disappear and the route climbs through forests of western hemlock and silver fir to the south end of the north–south ridge (3.0 mi/ 4.8 km; 2900 ft/884 m). The trail then follows this narrow divide, traversing above the head of Tumwata Creek. The ridge is forested but one can look through the trees and see Mount Olympus from a couple of points.

At the ridge's north end (5.0 mi/8.1 km; 3200 ft/975 m), the trail angles sharply westward along a spur that parallels Tumwata Creek, then begins its descent into the Bogachiel Valley. The upper part of this spur is covered with stands of silver fir so dense the forest floor is barren due to lack of sunlight. The trees are tall and slender, limbless to great heights, with compact, bushy tops. This young forest is then replaced, where the trail dips to the shaded north side of the ridge, by mature stands of silver fir, and the ground is carpeted with oxalis. As the trail loses altitude, the forest becomes almost exclusively western hemlock. The undergrowth of ferns and oxalis is luxuriant.

Upon reaching the foot of the spur (10.0 mi/16.1 km; 1000 ft/305 m), the trail forks. Both branches cross bottomland through typical spruce-hemlock rain forest to the Bogachiel River. The right branch leads to a point opposite Flapjack Camp (10.9 mi/17.5 km; 580 ft/177 m); the left branch to a ford farther downstream (11.5 mi/18.5 km; 550 ft/168 m). The river must be forded at either crossing in order for one to reach the **Bogachiel Trail.**

160 MOUNT TOM CREEK TRAIL

Mostly abandoned, no longer maintained
Length 1.2 mi/1.9 km
Access Hoh Trail
USGS Maps Mount Tom; Owl Mountain
Agency Olympic National Park

This trail has not been maintained for years, and it is now virtually nonexistent except for the little bit north of the river. The necessity of fording the Hoh deters many visitors from attempting to explore the south side of the river.

The route, used mostly by fishermen, begins at a junction with the **Hoh River Trail** 2.8 mi/4.5 km above the Hoh River Road. The trail goes down through an alder and maple flat to a campsite on the river, above the confluence of Mount Tom Creek.

The river must be crossed in order to reach what is left of the old trail on the

south side. At this point the stream is divided into braided channels, and one must wade—or, if lucky, find a log spanning the main channel. The river can be safely forded only in late summer and fall.

The old trail followed the east side of Mount Tom Creek, then crossed over to the Mount Tom Creek Shelter (1.2 mi/1.9 km; 800 ft/244 m), but this structure has been removed by the National Park Service. The route goes through dense rain forest on the river bottom, and many windfalls that have not been cut out lie across the fragments of the path that are discernible.

Mount Tom Creek is the largest tributary of the Hoh between the South Fork and Glacier Creek. The stream has its source on Mount Tom, and climbers sometimes approach the peak by following Mount Tom Creek, although the ascent is easier by way of Mount Olympus.

161   HOH LAKE TRAIL

Length 6.5 mi/10.5 km
Access Hoh Trail; High Divide Trail; Bogachiel Trail
USGS Map Bogachiel Peak
Agency Olympic National Park

Hoh Lake is a gem in the Olympic high country, but the trail leading to it requires a bit of strenuous hiking. The path begins 0.5 mi/0.8 km east of Olympus Ranger Station where it intersects the **Hoh Trail** at 1000 ft/305 m above sea level. The trail ascends a steep, forested spur to the lake, then traverses high, open slopes to Bogachiel Peak. The trail has thirty-three switchbacks in all—twenty-nine of them below the lake. In 1978 the largest forest fire in the history of the national park blackened about a thousand acres of virgin timber near Hoh Lake, including much of that in the switchback section of this trail. Most of the trees were killed, but some survived on the perimeter of the burn. The fire was caused by a lightning strike.

On the Hoh bottomlands the trail has a gentle grade as it meanders among big firs and the vine maple to Lake Creek (0.6 mi/1.0 km), which chatters madly as it rushes down toward its rendezvous with the Hoh. After paralleling the stream briefly, the trail climbs via long switchbacks shaded by dense stands of tall hemlock. At the fourth switchback it enters the devastated area (1.0 mi/1.6 km; 1500 ft/457 m), where the scene is appalling. The forest on this slope was primarily large, old-growth western hemlock with some Douglas-fir. Between this point and the twenty-second switchback on Broomstick Ridge, the trail switchbacks in and out of the burned area, and the contrast is striking. But already nature has started to heal the wounds—in many places tiny conifers two or three inches high are springing up from the burned soil. On Broomstick Ridge the thick stands of small, slender trees were also killed, and the trail now goes through a ghost forest, the bark having sloughed off many trees. Mount Tom is visible through the fire-killed timber.

Upon attaining the crest of the spur (3.5 mi/5.6 km; 3500 ft/1067 m), the grade eases, the burned district is left behind, and the trail climbs through stands of

Glacier Vista near White Glacier, Hoh Trail

Hoh Valley filled with morning fog

tall silver fir. The path then leaves the ridge and crosses several streams as it goes through a wet area. The country now becomes a mix of meadows and groves of subalpine trees—primarily silver fir, mountain hemlock, and Alaska cedar—and the slopes above and to the west of Hoh Lake come into view. Here islands of burned trees are mingled with the living ones. This was not the main area swept by the fire, but close to the perimeter, and the patches have created strikingly beautiful silver forests of fire-killed trees.

The path then comes out into a meadow that has the odd name C. B. Flats (4.8 mi/7.7 km; 4050 ft/1234 m). This grassy area is surrounded by subalpine forest and strewn with sandstone boulders. Mount Olympus is visible from this point, and at the meadow's far edge Lake Creek thunders down the mountainside. The trail crosses the stream below two waterfalls, then switchbacks up to Hoh Lake, the creek's source (5.3 mi/8.5 km; 4500 ft/1372 m).

This deep, orbicular lake occupies a dish-shaped glacial cirque. The slopes are covered with heather and clusters of subalpine firs, and herds of elk are often observed here. Mount Olympus and Mount Tom loom high above the Hoh Valley to the south. The lake contains Eastern brook and rainbow trout, but it often remains frozen until mid-July, and sometimes well into August. When the snow melts, rolling meadows appear, crisscrossed with elk trails and colorful with beargrass and lupine. On the northern, shaded sides of the ridges, the snowdrifts remain until late in the season, long after the south-facing slopes are covered with mountain flowers.

Sunrises and sunsets are memorable when viewed from Hoh Lake. Mount Olympus takes on a soft, velvet white in the morning, but it is more colorful at sunset when the alpenglow reflects various tones of pink, gold, and purple. After the sun has disappeared behind the western ridges, the summit snows are still bathed in bright sunlight, but the hemlocks near the lake form dark silhouettes. Fog settles heavily here, and it is often misty and cold—especially when the lake is still frozen.

Camping at Hoh Lake and C. B. Flats is available by reservation. Contact the Wilderness Information Center. Although the only places burned near the lake were two knolls covered with subalpine fir, the heavy use by backpackers over the years, aggravated by the effects of the firefighters' camps, has severely damaged the subalpine plant life. Alternate sites for camping are available on the High Divide.

Beyond Hoh Lake the trail climbs toward the High Divide, switchbacking up through subalpine country to a promontory on the eastern rim of the cirque. Here the view of the upper Hoh Valley, the Bailey Range, and Mount Olympus is spectacular. When the mountains are still blanketed with heavy snow in early summer, the contrast with the dark green forests and the river is marked.

The trail then contours steep slopes overlooking the Hoh and ends just below the summit of Bogachiel Peak, where it intersects the **High Divide Trail** and the **Bogachiel Trail** (6.5 mi/10.5 km; 5200 ft/1585 m).

162 SOUTH FORK HOH TRAIL

Length 3.3 mi/5.3 km
Access DNR Road 1000
USGS Maps Owl Mountain; Mount Tom
Agency Olympic National Park

The South Fork Hoh Trail begins on state land at the end of DNR Road 1000. The trail leads into an area of Olympic National Park that is off the beaten track, a splendid rain forest frequented by herds of elk. This valley is a botanist's and zoologist's paradise, but the trail is shunned by most hikers because it is remote and does not lead to the high country. However, fishermen are attracted by the runs of salmon and steelhead. The bottomlands where the trail meanders are bordered by steep, heavily forested slopes without trails; thus in effect the area is a cul-de-sac.

The trail descends steeply from the parking area (800 ft/244 m) to a lower level, where it traverses rocky flats, logged during World War II, that are covered with alder and second-growth spruce. At the boundary of Olympic National Park (0.4 mi/ 0.6 km; 750 ft/229 m), the trail enters the virgin forest, which is mostly Sitka spruce and western hemlock, with a scattering of Douglas-fir.

Within the park the trail meanders, with many little ups and downs, through lush, junglelike rain forest. At one point the path goes by a splendid example of Douglas-fir. This tree is eleven feet in diameter, possibly 300 feet tall, and its trunk, free of limbs for about 150 feet, rises straight as an arrow, with little taper.

The trail crosses a small creek, then a larger one that flows in a rocky channel, before descending to Big Flat (1.3 mi/2.1 km; 732 ft/223 m). This level bottomland is aptly named; it consists of open, grassy stretches bordered by giant spruces and groves of bigleaf and vine maple. At one time a shelter stood beside the trail where the path enters the flat but a falling tree demolished the structure. However, the hiker can find good campsites close by the river, at the far edge of the flat. Here one can well imagine, in this fairyland rain forest setting, that goblins and elves lurk in the hidden recesses.

Because Big Flat is located near the park boundary, the sounds of logging on adjoining state land disturb the wilderness solitude on weekdays. One can hear the crash of falling trees, the noise of logging trucks, the whirring of chain saws. The park's boundaries were not drawn logically here. The entire watershed of this stream should have been included within the park. Logically, the boundary should have followed the ridge from Owl Mountain to a point directly south of the confluence of the South Fork and the Hoh, then should have gone straight north. This would have protected the lower South Fork, as well as the integrity of the visual approach when one goes into the park via the Hoh River Road. Now visitors to the Hoh rain forest see an ugly clearcut on the apex of the divide lying between the South Fork and the Hoh.

Beyond Big Flat the trail goes through luxuriant rain forest, including groves of mammoth spruces, to an attractive riverside camp, then crosses a swale (2.5 mi/4.0 km). No sign or side path is present here to indicate that Camp Stick-in-Eye (750 ft/229 m) is located in the woods to the right, on the north bank of the South Fork, hidden from view by a screen of large conifers. The camp, which can accommodate a large party, received its name when John E. Stout poked a stick in his eye while camping here in 1978. This is a calm, peaceful place. No artificial lights mar the beauty of the night, when the trees form dark silhouettes, the stars shine brilliantly, and the tired hiker can drift into slumber while listening to the murmur of the river.

Beyond Camp Stick-in-Eye the trail deteriorates, but the route goes through beautiful glades and stands of large spruce. Many logs lie across the trail, which in places disappears entirely. Although fragments can be noted farther upstream, the trail can be said to end at the base of a big boulder about 40 feet high, where the bluff comes down to the river (3.3 mi/5.3 km; 800 ft/244 m).

At one time the trail went about 5 miles beyond this point, ending at the base of Hoh Peak, where the bottomland is pinched out by slopes that rise directly from the river's banks. However, the experienced hiker does not really need a trail here but can wander at will across the flats—through the maple groves, the stands of giant fir and spruce, the vine maple thickets—to what apparently was an elk forage study plot (ca. 4.0 mi/6.4 km). At this point a good camp is located on the opposite side of the river. The visitor who listens attentively will hear elk bugling, kingfishers shrieking, ravens croaking—and may be lucky and see a bald eagle feasting on a spawned salmon.

Above the base of Hoh Peak, the river flows through a wild, rugged canyon which is visited mostly by mountain climbers headed for the Valhallas. Although this route requires extensive cross-country travel, it is the most convenient approach to the western part of the Mount Olympus Range.

The cluster of peaks southwest of Mount Olympus, constituting part of the Mount Olympus Range, was unnamed for many years. Eventually, the peaks were christened The Pleiades, for the seven daughters of Atlas and Pleione, in keeping with the theme of using names from Greek mythology for geographic features in the Mount Olympus Range. The name was not publicized, however, and did not come into general use. Neither did names such as Hee Hee Peak and Hee Haw Peak, given by the first climbers in the area in 1966. Then, in the early 1970s, Harold Pinsch, a Bremerton climber, called the peaks the Valhallas, thus introducing Norse mythology, and this name has become well established. Since then, climbers have given the names of Norse gods and goddesses to the various peaks, pinnacles, and glaciers.

BOGACHIEL-CALAWAH

Because the Bogachiel and Calawah Rivers lie largely on the outer slopes of the Olympics, the foothills and ridges that border the streams are comparatively low. Except for meadowland near the head of the Bogachiel, the watersheds are covered entirely by virgin forests.

With an elevation 5474 ft/1668 m above sea level, Bogachiel Peak is not one of the higher peaks of the Olympics, yet it forms the divide between the valleys of the Bogachiel, Soleduck, and Hoh Rivers. The Bogachiel has its source in the snowfields on the steep western side of the peak, which is too low to have glaciers; consequently, the stream is clear, despite its Indian name, which means "muddy water." Thus the Bogachiel contrasts markedly with the Hoh, a river that is milky from glacial silt. The Bogachiel is well known for its runs of steelhead and cutthroat trout.

Timbered ridges divide the Bogachiel from the Hoh on the south, and from the Calawah and Soleduck on the north. As the river emerges from the mountains, the bottomland widens, although it is not as level as that along the Hoh and Queets. The North Fork, a major tributary, joins the river at the base of Sugarloaf Mountain, but the Calawah River is the Bogachiel's largest tributary. The valley of the South Fork Calawah above the confluence of Sitkum River lies within the national park. The South Fork Calawah parallels the Bogachiel, and the trail over Indian Pass provides access between the two valleys. The Sitkum and North Fork Calawah are in the national forest. In 1951 a large forest fire devastated most of the North Fork Calawah watershed.

When Olympic National Park was created, the Bogachiel was considered the best-preserved wilderness on the Olympic Peninsula, and this valley still retains its primitive landscape, almost unmarked by the activities of man. Within the national park, superlative rain forest is found on the Bogachiel and Calawah. Although both valleys lie on the edge of the park, they are undeveloped and isolated, and these qualities give to them a special appeal. The Rugged Ridge Trail and the Indian Pass Trail are the only routes that enter the Calawah Valley. The bottomlands along both rivers are the winter range of the elk herds that roam during the summer and fall on the uplands of the High Divide, Seven Lakes Basin, and the upper Bogachiel.

ROADS

Bogachiel River Road (FS Road 2932). This road leaves the Olympic Highway, US 101, at Bogachiel State Park, just north of the Bogachiel River, and parallels the stream 4.3 mi/6.9 km to the point where the Bogachiel Trail begins. Little of interest can be observed along the road, bordered as it is by stump ranches, stands of second-growth timber, and cutover land. The road formerly extended another 2.0 mi/3.2 km to the national park boundary, but this part is no longer usable and it is now part of the Bogachiel Trail.

The Rugged Ridge Trail can be reached by driving on two Forest Service roads—29 and 2900–070.

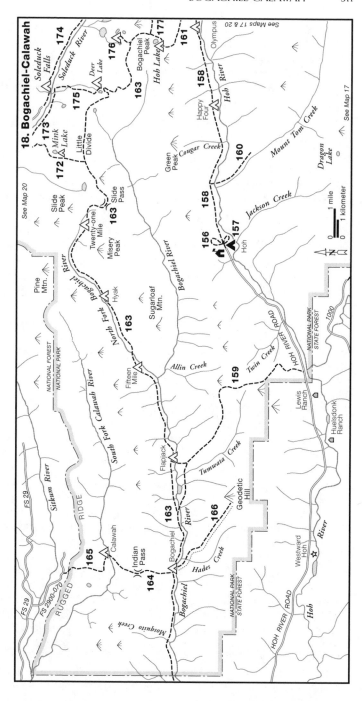

FS Road 29. This road leaves US 101 just north of the LaPush Road, near the Forks Ranger Station. The road is paved for the first 6 miles, then graveled. Klahanie Campground is located at 5.2 mi/8.4 km.

FS Road 2900–070. This road branches to the right from FS Road 29 at 10.8 mi/17.4 km, then crosses the Sitkum River. The parking area for the Rugged Ridge Trail is located on this road at 2.2 mi/3.5 km.

163 BOGACHIEL TRAIL

Length 32.7 mi/52.6 km
Access Bogachiel River Road (FS Road 2932)
USGS Maps Bogachiel Peak; Slide Peak; Hunger Mountain; Indian Pass
Agency Olympic National Park

The Bogachiel Trail traverses the northwestern slope of the Olympics, where the hiker can expect quiet, undisturbed solitude. The trail parallels the Bogachiel River to the base of Sugarloaf Mountain, then follows the North Fork Bogachiel to its headwaters and climbs to Slide Pass and Little Divide. Beyond this point the route meanders along the Soleduck-Bogachiel Divide to Bogachiel Peak, at the head of the Bogachiel.

The trailhead, relocated in recent years, is 5.0 mi/8.0 km from US 101, after one turns south on Undi Road, which later becomes FS Road 2932. (Undi Road is found on the opposite side of 101 near the entrance to Bogachiel State Park.) About 0.25 mi/0.4 km from the trailhead is a junction with an interpretive trail. This short path (700 ft/213 m) goes left and leads into the small but attractive wetlands nearby. The main trail skirts the bottom of the wetland, passing ferns, large maple and alder trees. Near the first crossing of Morganroth Creek, the trail passes a grove of large spruce trees. The trail then enters the virgin forest and shortly afterward crosses into the national park (2.0 mi/3.2 km; 350 ft/107 m). Within the park it traverses luxuriant bottomland and a cutover area where decaying stumps remind one that big spruce trees once grew here. The trail soon returns to the virgin forest, however, and penetrates typical stands of spruce-hemlock having a dense undergrowth of moss-draped vine maple. The terrain is uneven, the trail rising and dipping slightly.

At the junction of the **Indian Pass Trail** (6.1 mi/9.8 km; 450 ft/137 m), is Bogachiel Camp, formerly the site of a ranger station and trail shelter, located in the midst of bell-bottomed spruce trees. The rain forest now becomes increasingly luxuriant and, so far as the Bogachiel is concerned, reaches its optimum development in this section. Splendid stands of Douglas-fir cover the slopes north of the river; spruce and western hemlock occupy the bottomlands, where elk roam during the winter and spring. The largest known silver fir, almost 7 feet in diameter, is located on the south side of the river, about 2.5 mi/4.0 km above the Bogachiel Camp. Beyond the junction with the **South Snider/Jackson Trail** (8.2 mi/13.2 km; 500 ft/152 m), the route meanders to Flapjack Camp (10.3 mi/16.6 km; 650 ft/ 198 m); then at the base of Sugarloaf Mountain it leaves the Bogachiel and follows the North Fork. This stream flows into the main river from the northeast.

Fifteen Mile Shelter (14.4 mi/23.2 km; 1000 ft/305 m), surrounded by giant Douglas-firs, stands on a bench above the North Fork, near a falls and rapids. At

The Bogachiel Trail winds through natural flower gardens

the point where the trail crosses the stream, the river has cut a gorge in thick beds of sandstone. Beyond this crossing, the trail climbs high above the chattering stream, which is visible below, then returns to the river bottom.

Hyak Shelter (17.4 mi/28.0 km; 1400 ft/427 m) is located near the river at the edge of a meadow encircled by big trees. Here one can see the ridges to the north and south. The trail then traverses just above the North Fork, and for several miles the forest appears to have been manicured. The tall, straight trees—mostly hemlock, but also Douglas-fir, cedar, and silver fir—lift their crowns above masses of oxalis, vanilla leaf, and ferns. The parklike appearance is enhanced by the lack of brushy undergrowth and fallen trees.

At Twenty-one Mile Camp (20.6 mi/33.2 km; 2214 ft/675 m), where a trail shelter collapsed in 1999, the trail begins to climb to the head of the North Fork Bogachiel, switchbacking through forests of western hemlock. Near Slide Pass (22.1 mi/35.6 km; 3600 ft/1097 m), where the trail crosses over from the North Fork to the Bogachiel, the forest is chiefly silver fir although it includes both western and mountain hemlock.

As it follows the Soleduck-Bogachiel Divide, the trail climbs, first on one side of the ridge, then the other, and the hiker can glimpse the ridges across the Bogachiel Valley. The ridge then widens, and the trail breaks out into a meadow having sweeping views across the upper Bogachiel to Mount Olympus and the Bailey Range. On the north slope, Blackwood Lake, encircled by forest, lies cupped in a bowl a thousand feet below, and Slide Peak rises to the northwest. The lake contains Eastern brook trout. Looking down Blackwood Creek, beyond the lake, one sees a series of forested ridges that extend almost to the Strait of Juan de Fuca.

Mountain hemlocks are scattered in the meadows, and the ground is covered with a variety of bushes and plants—juniper, huckleberry, bracken fern, heather, strawberries, Columbia lilies, stonecrop, and mountain azalea. A benchmark gives the elevation as 4304 ft/1312 m. The trail then follows the ridge to a junction with the **Mink Lake Trail** at Little Divide (24.8 mi/39.9 km; 4130 ft/1259 m), where a tiny meadow provides a good view of several peaks—Olympus, Tom, Hoh, and Bogachiel.

The route contours through dense forest above Bogachiel Lake, which lies at the foot of a steep slope, then crosses a notch to the Soleduck side and descends to a junction with the **Canyon Creek Trail** in a swampy meadow at the upper end of Deer Lake (28.4 mi/45.7 km; 3550 ft/1082 m).

The path now climbs back toward the Soleduck-Bogachiel Divide, meandering through a district known as The Potholes. Here it goes by a half dozen small lakes, where beargrass makes showy displays in late July. Numerous campsites are located among the tarns, but the area is inclined to be marshy; consequently, gnats and mosquitoes are likely to be annoying.

As the trail gains altitude, the forest becomes thinner, giving way to meadows and clumps of mountain hemlock, with vistas of softly outlined ridges to the north and east. Deer Lake looks like a blue disk in the forest below. This is beautiful high country—rolling terrain with knolls topped by mountain hemlocks. Heather, lupine, and huckleberry are abundant.

After going by The Snake Pit, a clump of mountain hemlocks contorted and coiled like so many boa constrictors, the trail crosses the divide and breaks out into Bogachiel Basin. Here it climbs at a moderate grade as it traverses a steep mountainside, and Bogachiel Peak looms ahead. The rock gardens, slides, and grassy slopes are colorful with an array of wildflowers: glacier and avalanche lilies bloom in early summer, often pushing up through the receding snow; lupine, daisies, and mountain buckwheat blossom later. The rock outcrops are decorated with phlox, lomatium, harebell, penstemon, tufted saxifrage, paintbrush, violet, and stonecrop. Wildlife is also abundant. Bears visit this area to feast on huckleberries, and when they appear the shrill whistles of marmots pierce the air. The elk herds that range the Bogachiel and Hoh bottoms during the winter move up to this high country in the summer. They are often in sight here, either grazing in the meadows or resting on the snowfields during the afternoon heat.

Near Bogachiel Peak the terrain becomes more rugged, and the trail follows a razorback ridge where both red and white mountain-heather and stunted subalpine trees grow among blocks of sandstone. The trail intersects the **Seven Lakes Basin Trail** at a boulder-strewn notch in the ridge (31.8 mi/51.2 km; 4900 ft/1494 m). This vantage point overlooks the Seven Lakes Basin.

Between this junction and Bogachiel Peak, the hiker walks the "magic mile," one of the most beautiful and interesting paths in the Olympics. The trail crosses rock slides, makes seven short switchbacks as it ascends a steep slope, then curves like a slalom skier as it follows the ridge, going through meadows and scattered stands of subalpine trees, mountain ash, and juniper. The snow lies in deep drifts here well into summer, but after it disappears the wildflowers come into their own: false hellebore, elephant's head, arnica, phlox, thistle, Columbia lily, penstemon, anemone, bistort, spiraea, paintbrush, and stonecrop. The trail climbs among rough sandstone boulders to a saddle overlooking the snowfields on the north side of Bogachiel Peak, then contours the western slope to a U-shaped pass on the south side, where it intersects the **Hoh Lake Trail** and the **High Divide–Bailey Range Trail** (32.7 mi/52.6 km; 5200 ft/1585 m). The view from this point of the upper Hoh Valley, the Bailey Range, and Mount Olympus is outstanding.

164   INDIAN PASS TRAIL

Length 3.4 mi/5.5 km
Access Bogachiel Trail
USGS Map Indian Pass
Agency Olympic National Park

The route over Indian Pass goes north from the Bogachiel River to the South Fork Calawah, where it becomes the **Rugged Ridge Trail.** Before creation of Olympic National Park, both paths were part of the old Snider-Jackson Trail, which extended from the Soleduck to the Hoh.

Beginning at an intersection with the Bogachiel Trail near Bogachiel Camp (450 ft/ 137 m), the trail crosses the river bottom through stands of large spruce, then climbs to a level bench covered with hemlock forest so dense the gloom is perpetual. The trees are not large, but they are tall and close together.

As the trail approaches Indian Pass, the hemlock is replaced by silver fir, interspersed here and there with a big spruce or Douglas-fir. The pass (1.8 mi/ 2.9 km; 1041 ft/317 m) marks the divide between the Bogachiel and Calawah watersheds. The forest at this point is almost exclusively silver fir.

According to geologist Rowland W. Tabor, the South Fork Calawah may once have drained to the Bogachiel via Indian Pass, but was later diverted by the glacier to the Calawah. The elevation of the pass is about the same as the gravel terraces along the Bogachiel.

Beyond the pass the trail descends at a moderate grade to the South Fork Calawah (3.4 mi/5.5 km; 745 ft/227 m). The stream is not bridged, but in late summer one can, with care, boulder-hop from one side to the other without getting wet. The Rugged Ridge Trail can be found on the north bank.

165 RUGGED RIDGE TRAIL

Length 3.0 mi/4.8 km
Access FS Road 2900–070
USGS Map Indian Pass
Agencies Olympic National Forest and Olympic National Park

This is another fragment of the old Snider-Jackson Trail of Forest Service days. The trailhead (1000 ft/305 m) is located in the national forest on FS Road 2900–070, 2.2 mi/3.5 km beyond its intersection with FS Road 29.

Rugged Ridge, the divide between the Sitkum River and the South Fork Calawah, forms the national park boundary in this area. Higher in the east, where its elevation exceeds 3000 ft/914 m, the ridge peters out near the confluence of the two streams.

The trail begins in western hemlock forest and crosses Rugged Ridge almost at once, where it enters the national park (0.2 mi/0.3 km; 1200 ft/366 m). Here it goes through stands of slim Douglas-firs as it traverses a spur that extends from Rugged Ridge toward the South Fork Calawah. The trail crosses a half dozen little streams between the park boundary and the spur's crest, the forest changing until it becomes mostly silver fir and western hemlock. The growth of sword ferns and moss

Bogachiel Saddle, where three major trails come together

is luxuriant; salmonberry and devil's club form thickets by the streams. The trail is not steep, but it goes up and down to cross the creeks, with intervening level sections. At the fourth stream, waterfalls are present both above and below the trail. Upon rounding the end of the spur (1.6 mi/2.6 km; 1350 ft/411 m), the trail attains its high point. Here it turns eastward and makes a steep descent to the South Fork Calawah, crossing three streams along the way. The third one is picturesque—a stone wall on the far side is covered with various kinds of ferns. Above the trail are Seven Step Falls, a multiple cascade, and another wall shingled with ferns. Trilliums bloom here in May.

The South Fork Calawah River (3.0 mi/4.8 km; 745 ft/227 m) is not bridged, but one can cross easily in late summer or fall, either by wading or stepping from one boulder to another. During the winter or spring, when the water is high, the stream is dangerous, and one must find a log spanning the channel.

The route beyond this crossing, known as the **Indian Pass Trail**, leads to the **Bogachiel Trail**.

166 GEODETIC HILL TRAIL

Abandoned trail, no longer maintained
Length 4.0 mi/6.4 km
Access Bogachiel Trail
USGS Maps Indian Pass; Winfield Creek; Spruce Mountain
Agency Olympic National Park

The trail to Geodetic Hill, also known as Spruce Mountain, was built during World War II to provide access to an airplane spotter station. The trail has not been maintained since the war and has become so overgrown with little trees and obstructed by windfalls that it is now virtually nonexistent. Accordingly, the hike is not only strenuous but also largely a matter of route-finding.

The path begins on the south bank of the river (500 ft/152 m), about a half mile above the Bogachiel Camp and climbs the spur east of Hades Creek, which was probably named for the rank growth of devil's club. Most of the way the route traverses stands of large hemlock and silver fir. At the higher elevations, the forest is almost exclusively silver fir, including some of the largest known examples of this species. About halfway to the summit, the trail goes by several huge Douglas-firs that have been scarred by lightning. The trail then follows the ridge, where the ground is often matted with club moss.

When the lookout cabin was built on Geodetic Hill (4.0 mi/6.4 km; 3044 ft/ 928 m), the trees on the summit were cut down, but young ones have grown up since then and now obscure the view.

SOLEDUCK

One of the largest rivers on the peninsula, the Soleduck has its source in the northwestern Olympics. Near the Pacific Ocean this stream combines with the Bogachiel to form the Quillayute. Most of the Soleduck drainage basin lies outside the mountains, and this stream does not penetrate the loftier Olympics. Mount Appleton (6000 ft/1829 m) is the highest peak. The upper valley, within the national park, is bordered by ridges about a mile high. Three ridges—Aurora, Happy Lake, and Boulder—rise to the north and east, and a long, sinuous divide to the south stands between the Soleduck and Bogachiel. The High Divide and Cat Creek Ridge border the headwaters. Beyond them are the Hoh and Elwha Valleys.

Technically, the Soleduck has its source in a basin on Cat Creek Ridge north of Haigs Lake, but Bridge Creek, the first major tributary, is equally large. This creek receives the flow of numerous streams that tumble down from the snowfields in Soleduck Park, a rolling meadowland on the northern slopes of the High Divide. Lined by dense evergreen forests, the creek rushes down the steep slopes to its rendezvous with the Soleduck.

Never quiet in the mountains, the Soleduck is a tumultuous stream, dashing through rocky canyons, leaping and tumbling over boulders shaded by low-hanging limbs of maple, fir, and hemlock. Below Canyon Creek the river is more tranquil, and the valley floor—heavily forested with Douglas-fir and hemlock—broadens considerably. Numerous tributary creeks now flow into the Soleduck, and the river is further enlarged by the addition of two major branches, the North Fork Soleduck and the South Fork Soleduck. The Soleduck abounds in cutthroat and rainbow trout and during the winter is often fished for steelhead. Soleduck (also spelled Sol Duc) is an Indian word meaning "sparkling water," and the river's clarity justifies the name.

Although the Soleduck terrain is rugged, it is a region of soft outlines. The high country is primarily meadowland dotted with dozens of subalpine lakes, the majority of them located in Seven Lakes Basin. Lying at the northern base of Bogachiel Peak, this basin contains some of the largest mountain lakes in the Olympics. Because the elevation is comparatively low, glaciers are nonexistent in the Soleduck.

The Sol Duc Hot Springs, accessible via the Soleduck River Road, are one of two places in the Olympics where thermal springs exist. The origin of the hot water is not known, but chemically it resembles surface water. Unlike the Olympic Hot Springs, which are located on the Elwha, the Sol Duc Hot Springs do not lie on a fault.

The springs of "fire chuck" (i.e., hot water) were known to the Indians, who visited them to take advantage of their curative effects. According to Indian legend, the Sol Duc and Olympic Hot Springs were the tears of two dragons who fought a duel on one of the peaks. The combat ended with neither creature victorious, whereupon the dragons crawled into their caves and wept from mortification.

Theodore Moritz, believed to be the first white man to see them, was taken to the place in the early 1880s by an Indian whom he had befriended. (Theodore Dugas and C. L. Willoughby were also purported to have viewed the springs in 1884 while on a hunting trip.) Later Moritz built a cabin at the site and filed a claim on the land. Michael Earles, a wealthy timberman, purchased the springs in 1910, built a wagon road from Lake Crescent, and constructed an imposing hotel, but it was destroyed by fire in 1916.

ROADS

The Olympic Highway, US 101, together with US 410 from Grays Harbor to Olympia, encircles the Olympic Mountains. Yet only four trails, each described in this chapter, begin virtually at the border of the highway itself. Trail 167, the Pioneers Path Nature Trail, is accessed at the Forest Service's Klahowya Campground adjacent to Snider Ranger Station, 9.0 mi/14.5 km west of Fairholm, the supply point located at the extreme western end of Lake Crescent. The North Point Trail (no. 168) is accessed 8.0 mi/12.9 km west of Fairholm; the Bigler Mountain Trail (no. 169) is accessed 9.0 mi/14.5 km west of Fairholm; and the Mount Muller Trail (no. 170) is accessed 5.0 mi/8.1 km west of Fairholm.

Soleduck River Road. The road leaves the Olympic Highway, US 101, 1.9 mi/ 3.1 km west of Lake Crescent, and follows the national park boundary around the western end of Aurora Ridge. Here it goes through thick stands of second-growth fir on land that was logged prior to creation of the park.

Beyond the Aurora Ridge Trail (2.5 mi/4.0 km), where the park boundary jogs west to the Soleduck, the road follows the river, which now forms the boundary for about 5 miles. At this point the road enters the virgin forest, largely old-growth Douglas-fir, and about a mile beyond crosses the North Fork Soleduck.

At the picturesque Salmon Cascades (7.0 mi/11.3 km), where the Soleduck River tumbles over large boulders, one can watch salmon fight their way through the white water rapids during the spawning season.

Backcountry permits may be obtained at the Soleduck Ranger Station (11.8 mi/ 19.0 km; 1679 ft/512 m). Across the river, the Sol Duc Hot Springs development consists of a store, cabins, and swimming pool. The chemicals present in the mineralized water range from such common elements as iron and aluminum to rarer ones like strontium and barium.

The road then leads to a large campground on the Soleduck (12.2 mi/19.6 km). Located in a stand of big firs, this is a popular place and during the summer months it is often filled to capacity, especially on weekends. Camping quotas are in effect May 1 to September 30 for the entire Soleduck drainage, excluding the North Fork. Contact the Wilderness Information Center for details.

Ample parking is provided at the end of the road (13.8 mi/22.2 km; 2000 ft/ 610 m), where the Soleduck Trail begins.

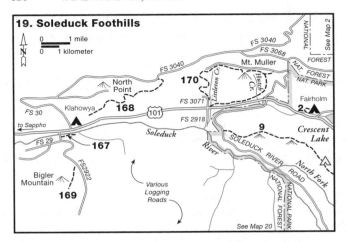

167 PIONEERS PATH NATURE TRAIL

Length 0.3 mi/0.5 km
Access US 101
USGS Map Pysht
Agency Olympic National Forest

This trail begins adjacent to Klahowya Campground, just off US 101. The road leading into the campground from the highway forms a figure eight. The elevation is about 750 ft/229 m above sea level.

Pioneers Path is a nature trail marked by square signs—each sign a block of wood with a maple leaf carved on it, and a footprint on the leaf. The path makes a circle south of the western loop of the figure eight. The trail comes out to the Soleduck River, follows the stream a short distance, then loops back to its starting point (0.3 mi/0.5 km). Signs tell visitors to Follow the Footsteps of the Pioneers, but to have reproduced the early day scene more realistically, the Forest Service could have established the trail in a stand of virgin timber remote from the sounds of modern civilization—certainly not in second growth adjacent to a busy highway, where one hears the noise of motor vehicles.

The signboard at the trailhead states: "Though quiet and serene today, this area was once a storm of activity. Pioneers carved homesteads in the forest, and the high-pitched scream of loggers' steam whistles echoed through the valley. Loggers, using long steel saws and lots of muscle, felled trees which were hauled to mills by steam locomotives. Since then a new forest has grown up, covering all but the memories."

The trail goes through second-growth stands, mostly hemlock with some fir. Along the trail one sees the last vestiges of the virgin forest—old rotted logs lying among decayed stumps that have springboard slots. When they felled the big trees, the loggers stood upon steel-tipped boards inserted in notches chopped in the bases of the trees. The undergrowth is largely vine maple, salmonberry, western hemlock seedlings on nurse logs, oxalis, sword ferns, and red huckleberry. Oxalis grows in the dense shade; red huckleberry on the stumps.

168 KLOSHE NANITCH TRAIL

Length 3.5 mi/5.6 km
Access US 101
USGS Map Snider Peak; Deadmans Hill
Agency Olympic National Forest

The Kloshe Nanitch Lookout Cabin sits atop one of the higher elevations of Snider Ridge, on an outcrop that bears the same name. The name comes from the Chinook language and means "good view" or "look out." Nearby is a separate knob known as North Point, which served as a lookout site until 1979, but is now blocked by a locked gate and occupied by a private building. Kloshe Nanitch overlooks the Soleduck Valley from the north. It can be reached by either a primitive 8.0-mile-long road or a 3.5-mile uphill trail. The trailhead is located at the end of West Snider Road, which begins east of Milepost 211 on U.S. 101, about 20 miles from Fork. Visitors can drive to the end of West Snider Road and park in a large lot located on land owned by the Department of Natural Resources. Elevation is 1000 ft/305 m. Note: West Snider Road does not connect with East Snider Road, which is where hikers formerly parked to access this trail.

The trail begins with a gentle ascent for the first mile (1.6 km), then climbs steeply once it crosses a stream. Switchbacks are numerous, the path zigzagging upward through a mixed forest that gives way to spruce and fir at the higher elevations. Near the summit, the Kloshe Nanitch trail junctions with the Lookout Loop Trail. Bear left to visit the lookout cabin. To the right, the Lookout Loop leads to a junction with the Snider Ridge Trail. From that junction, it is a 4.0 mi/6.4 km hike to a connection with the Mount Muller Trail.

As an alternative to walking this steep trail, one can drive on a primitive road to an upper trailhead, with a small parking area and a vault toilet. From West Snider Road, take FS Road 3040 near the Snider Work Center (formerly a ranger station) and climb in a west-northwest direction about 2.5 mi/4.0 km. Here, at 2000 ft/610 m, it makes a sharp switchback and now runs in an easterly direction below the crest of Snider Ridge. At 5.0 mi/8.1 km, this rough road traverses below Snider Peak, which has an elevation of 3000 ft/914 m. At a Y in the road at 6.0 mi/9.7 km, bear right and follow FS Road 3040-595 to reach the upper Kloshe Nanitch trailhead (3160 ft/963 m).

169 BIGLER MOUNTAIN TRAIL

Abandoned trail, not maintained
Length 3.5 mi/5.6 km
Access US 101
USGS Map Snider Peak
Agency Olympic National Forest

Bigler Mountain is an isolated, conelike foothill which much resembles The Chocolate Drop, a similar geographic feature in the Queets River bottoms.

The trail, such as it is, is hardly worth mentioning, and has little to offer the hiker. It is definitely not maintained, has succumbed to reclaiming-the-land attacks of Mother Nature, and is rapidly traveling the road to nonexistence.

The path can be reached from Highway 101 near the Snider Ranger Station, which is 9 miles west of Fairholm. First cross the bridge spanning the Soleduck River, then drive south on the Cooper Ranch Road for a half mile to its intersection with FS Road 29. Now follow the latter for 1 mile, which brings you to a junction with FS Road 2922. Drive 1.5 miles on FS Road 2922.

The trail has a rather obscure beginning. No marker of any kind is present to indicate that a trailhead is located here. Actually, the trailhead is just a wide spot in a very straight road, with room to park one or two vehicles, and no more. Here one will find a long-abandoned, overgrown logging road with a trail down the middle. This road and trail combination gets progressively poorer as one proceeds (on foot) and it ends after 3.5 mi/5.6 km on the side of Bigler Mountain, never attaining the top of the peak.

The trees and dense vegetation obscure whatever view would be present otherwise. Lower down, alders grow in thick stands that make attractive displays. About halfway up the mountain the forest growth changes to Douglas-fir. This is largely second-growth because the virgin timber on Bigler Mountain has long since been logged.

170 MOUNT MULLER TRAIL

Length 13.0 mi/20.9 km
Access US 101
USGS Map Mount Muller; Snider Peak
Agency Olympic National Forest

This is a new trail, built in the 1990s. The trail was constructed by the Forest Service on national forest and state land, with the assistance of several organizations—the Washington Conservation Corps, ITT Rayonier, and the Port Angeles Backcountry Horsemen. The trail builders incorporated in the new trail the few fragments that remained of the old CCC-built trail of the 1930s, which has largely disappeared over the years. Mountain bikes, horseback riders, and hikers are all permitted on the new trail.

The trailhead, which is the staging area for equestrians, is located on FS Road 3071, a half mile north of US 101, at Milepost 216, 4 miles east of Klahowya Campground. One should carry water because it is available only from Littleton Creek (at the trailhead) and at Hutch Creek (10.0 mi/16.1 km), near the end of the loop made by the trail.

The slopes of Mount Muller and Snider Ridge have been badly scarred in the past by both logging and fire, but with protection the land is gradually recovering. The trail begins (1000 ft/305 m) in a stand of large second-growth forest and climbs steadily, making a steep ascent. Switchbacks are numerous, but at times the trail goes more or less straight. At Grouse Meadows (2.5 mi/4.0 km), the path enters open country.

The route then turns eastward at Jims Junction (3.0 mi/4.8 km; 3200 ft/975 m) and follows Snider Ridge, alternately traversing stands of trees and open areas where wildflowers make showy displays. Good views are had from the meadows. To the north one can see Vancouver Island and the Strait of Juan de Fuca; to the southeast, Mount Olympus rises above the foothills of the western Olympics. Also visible are Lake Crescent to the east and the Soleduck Valley to the south and west. The trail then emerges into the meadows that surround the upper levels of Mount Muller and Panorama Point. Both viewpoints can be reached by following short spur trails—first, northward to the summit of Mount Muller (5.5 mi/8.9 km; 3748 ft/1142 m), the highest point on Snider Ridge, from which unobstructed views await in all directions; secondly, southward to Panorama Point (5.3 mi/8.5 km; circa 3500 ft/1067 m), which commands splendid views to the south and west.

Beyond Mount Muller, the ridge trail continues going east, again alternately crossing stands of forest and open meadows. At Mosley Gap (7.1 mi/11.4 km; 2800 ft/ 853 m) the path begins its descent from the ridge through forests and rock formations. At 8.7 mi/14 km, a spur trail perhaps 300 yards long leads to what is known as Fout's Rock House. This is a pile of giant boulders standing on end. Below this interesting formation, the trail continues its descent to the Soleduck Valley. On the floor of the valley, the trail parallels US 101, going through stands of trees that are being managed by the Forest Service according to the latest silvicultural methods, including thinning the stands in order to give them the semblance of an old-growth forest. The trail then returns to its starting point at Littleton Creek (13.0 mi/20.9 km).

171   NORTH FORK SOLEDUCK TRAIL

Last 4 miles not maintained
Length 10.0 mi/16.1 km
Access Soleduck River Road
USGS Maps Mount Muller; Lake Crescent; Bogachiel Peak
Agency Olympic National Park

The trailhead (1450 ft/442 m) is located on the Soleduck River Road, 8.1 mi/13.0 km from US 101. The route follows the North Fork Soleduck River almost to its headwaters, then climbs toward Happy Lake Ridge. Although the route was surveyed to the ridge more than forty years ago, the trail was never completed to link up with the Happy Lake Ridge Trail, but ends about 1.5 mi/2.4 km northwest of Boulder Lake. Numerous brooks cross the trail; thus the hiker need not carry water. Because the route traverses a primitive forest where elk are likely to be observed, one should keep alert, because viewing the animals adds still another dimension to the splendors of this path.

The trail first climbs over a low ridge (1750 ft/533 m) through large second-growth western hemlock and Douglas-fir. The trees are perhaps 150 years old. Apparently, fire swept these slopes about the time the pioneers were arriving in the Pacific Northwest. On the north slope, survivors of an old stand of fir are scattered through the forest. The towering, fire-scarred giants make the hemlocks look like pygmies. Here the trail descends to the North Fork Soleduck, where a ford is required (1.0 mi/1.6 km; 1500 ft/457 m).

Meandering through bottomland, the route comes out to the river bank, where it follows ledges in the rock. The stream is beautiful—perfectly clear, cascading over stone barriers that create deep pools in the river. The trail then returns to the bottomland.

Although generally climbing, the trail goes up and down, at times penetrating stands of Douglas-fir, on other occasions crossing flats overgrown with salmonberry bushes, where the trail is just a narrow, obscure lane. Riverside Camp (2.9 mi/4.7 km) is located just beyond a large boulder about 4 feet high that stands beside the trail. A beautiful place by the North Fork, this camp has room for several tents. Beyond Fryingpan Camp (3.0 mi/4.8 km), a smaller but comfortable spot, the trail switchbacks up through stands of western hemlock, and the river roars madly in its canyon. The forest here appears to be in transition from Douglas-fir to hemlock.

After crossing two large creeks, the path goes through an almost pure stand of virgin Douglas-fir. The trees are not unusually large, generally 4 to 5 feet in diameter and perhaps 250 feet tall, but the forest is nonetheless impressive—one big fir after another, to the almost total exclusion of other species. One who hikes through this stand can readily understand why the timbermen would like to turn their loggers loose in Olympic National Park.

The trail then leaves the North Fork Soleduck (ca. 5.5 mi/8.9 km) and follows a major tributary. The route climbs a bit, and this branch of the river can be heard surging through its canyon. The path descends to the stream and crosses to the south side (6.0 mi/9.7 km; 2100 ft/640 m). Here the river is a combination of deep pools and rapids. This is the first of ten crossings where one must either wade, step from boulder to boulder, or search for a tree that has fallen across the river. The forest changes—the Douglas-firs disappear, replaced by western hemlock and silver fir.

Beyond this point the route has not been maintained for many years. One must not only struggle through the windfalls and brush but also contend with the numerous river crossings during the next 2 miles, the trail shifting back and forth, first on one side of the river, then the other. The crossings are mandatory; to attempt to stay on one side would be folly. As one hiker stated succinctly, this section of the route is not a high-speed trail.

The North Fork Soleduck Shelter (9.0 mi/14.5 km; 3000 ft/914 m) stands on the east bank of the river, which at this point flows north. The dense forest is composed of western hemlock and silver fir, with some Douglas-fir. Beyond the shelter the trail ascends the mountainside about a mile toward Happy Lake Ridge, but, never having been completed, it comes to a dead end on a forested spur (ca. 10.0 mi/16.1 km; 4500 ft/1372 m). One can, however, travel cross-country to the ridge. The terrain is moderately steep, the forest floor comparatively open.

172 MINK LAKE TRAIL

Length 4.3 mi/6.0 km
Access Soleduck River Road
USGS Map Bogachiel Peak
Agency Olympic National Park

This route begins at Sol Duc Hot Springs (1679 ft/512 m) on the Soleduck River Road and climbs past Mink Lake to Little Divide, the watershed between the Soleduck and Bogachiel Rivers. This ridge is lower than the High

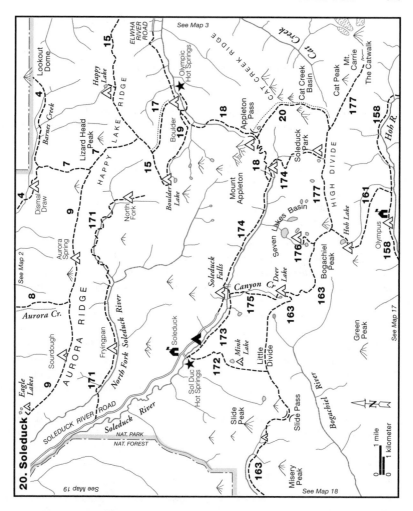

Divide, which lies between the Soleduck and the Hoh. At times it is erroneously called Low Divide, the name of the pass between the Elwha and the Quinault. One should carry water because it is not available between the hot springs and Mink Lake.

The first half mile traverses second-growth fir and hemlock growing on land logged during development of the hot springs. The path then enters the virgin forest. As the trail climbs higher, the Douglas-firs disappear and hemlock becomes the dominant species. The undergrowth is largely huckleberry.

Mink Lake (2.5 mi/4.0 km; 3080 ft/939 m) is a good example of a lake that is slowly destroying itself. Bordered by forest and half-choked with vegetation, it is in the late stages of lacustrine evolution. The lake contains Eastern brook and rainbow trout. Bird life is abundant, and the camper who stays here is likely to be awakened before dawn by the weird call of the loon.

Above Mink Lake the trail goes by a marsh known as Intermittent Lake, which is slightly larger than Mink Lake. The trail then climbs into the Subalpine Zone, where it crosses several brooks as it traverses forests of hemlock and silver fir, and a dense understory of huckleberry. During the last mile the route switchbacks up through stands of mountain hemlock broken by patches of meadowland.

The trail ends where it intersects the **Bogachiel Trail** at Little Divide (4.3 mi/ 6.9 km; 4130 ft/1259 m). The tiny meadow here, overgrown with bracken fern, lupine, and wild strawberries, has a good view of several peaks. On warm summer days, when the meadow is bright with lupine, bumblebees buzz from bush to bush.

173 LOVERS LANE

Length 2.8 mi/4.5 km
Access Soleduck River Road
USGS Map Bogachiel Peak
Agency Olympic National Park

How this trail received its name can be inferred—the level path is suitable for casual strolling, particularly in the moonlight on a warm evening. The trail parallels the Soleduck River from the Sol Duc Hot Springs to the **Canyon Creek Trail** near Soleduck Falls.

The trail begins near the swimming pool at the hot springs (1679 ft/512 m) and for about a half mile goes through second-growth forest, where logging occurred years ago, then enters stands of virgin Douglas-fir. Here it crosses three streams spanned by logs provided with handrails. The first stream is Mink Lake Creek, beyond which the path winds among big firs and through luxuriant glades to Hidden Lake Creek. This stream is often dry, particularly in late summer and fall. The third stream, Canyon Creek, is the largest of the trio.

The forest now becomes mostly western hemlock, but Douglas-fir is still present. Near the trail's end the hiker has not only beautiful views of the river but also of a waterfall where a tributary stream plunges over a cliff.

The trail intersects the Canyon Creek Trail near Soleduck Falls (2.8 mi/4.5 km; 1930 ft/588 m).

174 SOLEDUCK TRAIL

Length 8.5 mi/13.7 km
Access Soleduck River Road
USGS Map Bogachiel Peak
Agency Olympic National Park

The Soleduck Trail parallels the river to Bridge Creek, then follows that stream to Soleduck Park and the High Divide, where the path joins the High Divide–Bailey Range Trail.

This route has two trailheads. The principal one is located at the end of the Soleduck River Road (2000 ft/610 m); the alternate one, at the eastern edge of the Soleduck Campground (1700 ft/518 m). The alternate path more or less parallels the river, traversing glades and stands of old-growth Douglas fir until it joins the main trail (1.0 mi/1.6 km from the campground; 200 yards from the main trailhead at road's end.)

The broad, smooth trail meanders through Douglas-fir forest to a junction with the **Canyon Creek Trail** at Soleduck Falls (0.7 mi/1.1 km; 2000 ft/610 m). At this point the river plunges over a sandstone barrier, then flows through a deep, narrow canyon. The rock beds stand vertical, and the river parallels the bedding.

Above the falls the route climbs gradually. The forest chiefly comprises stands of tall Douglas-fir and western hemlock, but as the trail penetrates deeper into the mountains, hemlock becomes predominant and silver fir replaces Douglas-fir. Because the forest is more or less even-aged, the trees are relatively uniform in size—a somewhat unusual phenomenon in the Olympics. Luxuriant glades and fern glens are found in the wetter places. After crossing two creeks, the trail becomes rocky as it climbs steadily, and the river rushes noisily by as it tumbles down in a series of cascades.

The route intersects the **Appleton Pass Trail** (5.0 mi/8.1 km; 3100 ft/ 945 m) in a stand of Douglas-fir and hemlock so dense that almost nothing grows upon the forest floor. The trail then climbs to Upper Soleduck Camp (5.3 mi/8.5 km; 3150 ft/960 m). At this point one should not be misled by a path that leads down to the river's edge. A trail shelter formerly stood upon the opposite bank, but both the shelter and the bridge have long since disappeared. The trail does not cross the Soleduck here but veers left and goes uphill, climbing above the river as it traverses through forests of Alaska cedar and silver fir. The trail then crosses the Soleduck, and it is a matter of wading because winter floods destroyed the high log that formerly served as a bridge below the confluence of the river and Bridge Creek (5.5 mi/ 8.9 km; 3300 ft/1006 m). At this point the path leaves the river, turns south and follows Bridge Creek, then crosses the stream (6.5 mi/10.5 km; 3800 ft/1158 m). The route now leaves the dense forest and enters subalpine country. After climbing a bit, the trail enters the high, open country of Soleduck Park, where rolling meadowland sweeps above a silver forest to the High Divide. Bridge Creek Camp (7.7 mi/12.4 km; 4500 ft/1372 m) was formerly the site of Heart Lake Shelter.

With each upward step the hiker's view of the Soleduck Valley becomes more impressive. Heart Lake (8.1 mi/13.0 km; 4750 ft/1448 m), a little tarn shaped like a valentine, lies on a bench in the upper part of Soleduck Park, where it mirrors the meadows and subalpine trees. The greenish lake is the source of Bridge Creek. Above the lake the trail ascends to the High Divide and a junction with the **High Divide–Bailey Range Trail** (8.5 mi/13.7 km; 5050 ft/1539 m).

Soleduck Park lies on the northern slope of the High Divide between Seven Lakes Basin and Cat Creek Basin. The southern or Hoh River side of the divide is timbered to the ridge top, but the shaded northern slopes that make up Soleduck Park are open country because snowdrifts last until late summer and thus keep the timberline about a thousand feet lower. One of the finest examples of subalpine country in the Olympics, this area makes an excellent base camp for trips to the nearby Bailey Range. During the winter Soleduck Park is covered by deep snow.

On clear days, when haze is not pronounced, the distant Pacific is visible as a bluish band above scattered trees that fade away on the slopes to the northwest. Cat

Creek Ridge looms over Soleduck Park on the east; Mount Olympus and the Bailey Range rise to the south and east, with the Hoh Valley lying between Olympus and the High Divide.

Many years ago, advocates of winter sports proposed the development of a ski resort in Soleduck Park, complete with lodge and mechanical lifts, as well as extension of the road up the valley. Such development would have destroyed the superlative wilderness character of this part of the Olympics. However, the death knell was given the project by a combination of factors—bad winter weather, poor snow for skiing, and lack of population within reasonable distance. Moreover, it would have been incompatible with the preservation of an unimpaired landscape in a national park.

175 CANYON CREEK TRAIL

Length 3.1 mi/5.0 km
Access Soleduck Trail
USGS Map Bogachiel Peak
Agency Olympic National Park

The trail begins at Soleduck Falls (2000 ft/610 m), where it branches from the **Soleduck Trail.** Here the river plunges over a sandstone barrier, then surges through a deep, close-walled canyon lined with ferns. Mist sprays over the wooden footbridge that spans the river just below the falls. The bridge dates from 1939.

On the south side the trail intersects **Lovers Lane** (0.1 mi/0.2 km; 1930 ft/

Deer Lake, Canyon Creek Trail

588 m). The path then follows aptly named Canyon Creek, which has carved a deep gorge between Deer Lake and the river. The forest is mostly western hemlock and Douglas-fir; the plant growth is luxuriant. Bunchberry forms dense mats, devil's club grows rank in moist clefts, and huckleberry flourishes almost everywhere. The well-kept trail crosses Canyon Creek via a bridge built over a waterfall (1.0 mi/1.6 km; 2378 ft/725 m), then climbs, rather sharply at times, to Deer Lake (2.9 mi/4.7 km; 3525 ft/1074 m), crossing the creek again at the lake's outlet. Often a stiff breeze is present at this point, sweeping across the surface of the lake. (Technically, one should refer to the Deer Lakes, because they are two in number. The trail goes by the larger one; the smaller lake, less than one-seventh as large, lies just west of the main one at the same elevation.)

Typical of many subalpine tarns in the Olympics, Deer Lake is nearly encircled by forests broken by little patches of meadow that are covered with luxuriant grasses. The plumes of beargrass are conspicuous along the shore in July, and shooting stars, elephant's head, marsh marigold, and other wildflowers grow profusely on the marsh at the head of the lake. Frogs and orange-bellied newts are abundant in the marshy edge of the lake, where dippers flit about. Fish include Eastern brook and rainbow trout.

The lake is in a heavily used area, and the National Park Service has restricted camping near it in order to restore vegetation on the trampled spots. Hikers should stay on the trail, not walk on the fragile heather, and camp only in designated areas.

Near the upper end of Deer Lake the trail merges with the **Bogachiel Trail** (3.1 mi/5.0 km; 3550 ft/1082 m).

176 SEVEN LAKES BASIN TRAIL

Length 1.1 mi/1.8 km
Access Bogachiel Trail
USGS Map Bogachiel Peak
Agency Olympic National Park

The access trail leading to Seven Lakes Basin begins at a gap (4900 ft/1494 m) in the Soleduck–Bogachiel Divide, west of Bogachiel Peak, where it branches from the **Bogachiel Trail**, 3.4 mi/5.5 km beyond Deer Lake.

The trail climbs a bit through sandstone boulders, where it is often partly covered with snow. (Hikers should not be misled by what appears to be a trail leading up a chute to the right. This is a false lead; an abrupt cliff is on the other side.) The path ascends to a notch in the ridge that overlooks Seven Lakes Basin, then descends into the basin itself, first to Lunch Lake (0.9 mi/1.4 km; 4400 ft/1341 m), then to Round Lake (1.1 mi/1.8 km; 4300 ft/1311 m). The ranger station is located on a knoll above Lunch Lake.

Seven Lakes Basin is irregular in shape, about two and a half miles long by a mile wide, covering approximately 1600 acres, and surrounded by rocky peaks. The basin contains more lakes than most areas in the Olympics, and it is underlain by thick beds of sandstone. The altitude ranges from 3700 to 4600 ft (1128 to 1402 m). Because the basin receives heavy snowfall during the winter, the lakes do not thaw until late in the season—usually in July, sometimes in August. This is a popular area, and people have wandered from lake to lake; thus they have created a multitude of way paths in the basin.

Chris Morgenroth named the basin about the turn of the century. He was a pioneer settler on the peninsula who served as a ranger during the early years of the Olympic National Forest. When he viewed the glacier-scoured basin from a distance, he counted seven glittering lakes. Actually, they number about a dozen, not counting pools and ponds, and range in size from little potholes up to lakes about 400 yards long. They are known for Eastern brook, cutthroat, and rainbow trout.

Soleduck Lake, at 31 acres, is the largest. Other named ones include Morgenroth, Long, Clear, Number Eight, Lunch, Round, and No Name. Three small tams are located in the upper basin, at the base of Bogachiel Peak, but none contains fish. Two were named in the early 1970s by Mark Wilder, the backcountry ranger at that time. He called the western one Mirror Lake because it reflects the surrounding ridges; the eastern one, Question Mark Lake because it always assumes that form when the ice melts. The pool in the middle is known as Chuck's Hole, in honor of Charles N. Connor of Port Townsend. Mirror Lake is also called Y Lake.

177 HIGH DIVIDE–BAILEY RANGE TRAIL

Length 6.2 mi/10.0 km
Access Bogachiel Trail; Hoh Lake Trail; Soleduck Trail
USGS Maps Mount Carrie; Bogachiel Peak
Agency Olympic National Park

This trail provides the hiker with vistas that are among the best in the Olympics. The route is noted for its succession of spectacular views of Mount Olympus, the Bailey Range, and the valleys of the Bogachiel, Hoh, and Soleduck. The sunrises and sunsets observed from vantage points along the way are often outstanding. During the night fog frequently forms in the valleys, and sometimes it cloaks the ridges and peaks in heavy mist. The trail is popular and regularly traveled. During the summer people are constantly coming and going in both directions, especially on the High Divide section. But in late fall, or when the weather is stormy, the hiker can experience solitude.

The route follows the High Divide, then skirts the Bailey Range at the 5000-ft/ 1524-m level, ending abruptly on the south side of Cat Peak. The High Divide forms the watershed between the Hoh and Soleduck; the Bailey Range, that between the Hoh and Elwha. The ridge forming the High Divide extends from Bogachiel Peak to the head of Cat Creek, a tributary of the Elwha, and the elevation averages about 5000 ft/1524 m. Snow piles up to great depths here during the winter, particularly on the northern slopes, which extend down into Seven Lakes Basin and Soleduck Park. The snowfall on the Bailey Range is probably greater still.

The trail begins on the south side of Bogachiel Peak at an intersection (5200 ft/ 1585 m) with the **Hoh Lake Trail** and the **Bogachiel Trail**. This point overlooks the Hoh Valley, Mount Olympus, and the Bailey Range. One can also look down the upper Bogachiel from this gap in the ridge. The path then traverses the sidehill below the summit to a junction with a spur (0.2 mi/0.3 km) that climbs about

200 yards to the top of Bogachiel Peak, where a fire lookout cabin once stood (5474 ft/1668 m).

The side trip to the summit is a must for every hiker. The panorama includes virtually the entire northwest corner of the peninsula. The Bogachiel River winds westward in sweeping curves toward the foothills. The distant valley, clothed with virgin forest, fades into a purplish haze, but on clear days the Pacific Ocean is sometimes discernible as a band of blue. The view to the north includes Seven Lakes Basin, while directly east are the slopes of the High Divide and, beyond them, the Bailey Range. Southward, across the deep Hoh Valley, stands Mount Olympus, a massive pile of rock, snow, and ice.

Beyond Bogachiel Peak the trail goes up and down as it follows the High Divide, often utilizing the gentle swales and humps of ridge-top depressions. The slopes fall away steeply on the timbered south side to the Hoh, which contrasts markedly with the meadowland on the north side facing the Soleduck. Olympus and the Bailey Range are almost always in full view—the latter a long, curving chain of peaks that parallels the upper Hoh. The glacier-scoured Seven Lakes Basin lies north of the divide, and one looks down upon its many lakes—patches of deep blue, varied in shape, in a pastel landscape. Elk frequent this region during the summer and autumn, often congregating near the pools or on the snowfields. Occasionally bears are observed. Wildflowers are everywhere—avalanche lilies, lupine, common bistort, bluebells, columbine, monkey flowers, daisies, gentians, beargrass, and both red and white mountain-heather.

A small campsite is located in the broad, grassy saddle (0.9 mi/1.4 km; 5000 ft/ 1524 m) at the eastern base of Bogachiel Peak, but one must go down into the basin to obtain water.

Beyond this point the trail climbs up and down as it follows the divide, passing scree slopes and meadows on the left, stands of subalpine fir and mountain hemlock on the right. The path then crosses the southern end of an abutting ridge that extends northward between Seven Lakes Basin and Soleduck Park and descends to a junction with the **Soleduck Trail** (2.1 mi/3.4 km; 5050 ft/ 1539 m) above Heart Lake. The trail now overlooks the beautiful uplands of Soleduck Park, the meadow country at the head of the Soleduck River, then climbs over the south end of Cat Creek Ridge (3.0 mi/4.8 km; 5100 ft/1554 m) where the ridge abuts the High Divide. Here one can see Mount Appleton and Appleton Pass.

Upon leaving the High Divide, the trail descends through meadows and stands of subalpine fir and mountain hemlock to the head of Cat Creek. The view of Mount Olympus from points along here includes the Blue Glacier. An excellent campsite is located by Ocarina Lake, a small tarn below the trail (3.4 mi/5.5 km; 4900 ft/1494 m). Beyond the lake the trail descends to a junction with the **Cat Creek Way Trail** (4.0 mi/6.4 km; 4500 ft/1372 m).

The trail reaches its low point in the saddle at the head of Cat Creek (4390 ft/ 1338 m), where it goes through dense stands of subalpine trees. The shade is welcome, particularly on hot days, and refreshing breezes are often present. The path is smooth, almost like walking on a carpet, and it goes by several black pools and crosses a heather-and-huckleberry slope that overlooks Cat Creek Valley. The trail then traverses above jumbled piles of boulders and comes out into a meadow at the foot of Bear Grass Hill (5.1 mi/8.2 km; 4800 ft/1463 m) on the flanks of Cat Peak.

A sign here indicates this is the end of the maintained trail and that the route beyond is unsafe for horses.

As the name implies, the slopes of Bear Grass Hill are covered with an abundance of beargrass—and huckleberry bushes. Exposed to long hours of sunshine, the berries ripen to a delicious sweetness. When the beargrass is in blossom, it blankets the hillside meadows like fields of cotton. Mount Olympus looms directly ahead, across the Hoh Valley.

The trail now contours high above the Hoh along the steep slopes of the Bailey Range. Here one has an unobstructed view up and down the river, and the 1978 Hoh Lake burn is visible. The path, blasted from solid rock, traverses mountainsides cut by gullies and avalanche paths. At one such crossing, a little stream trickles from the rocks about 50 feet below the trail (5.5 mi/8.9 km). This is the only source of water along this part of the route.

The path ends abruptly, and the hiker is confronted by a cliff (6.2 mi/10.0 km; 5000 ft/1524 m). This point is about 300 feet below the western end of The Catwalk, the narrow arête linking Cat Peak with Mount Carrie. When the trail builders reached this point, the National Park Service ran out of funds with which to complete the project. This was about the time the United States became involved in World War II, when trail-building operations were suspended. The trail had been projected to connect with the Long Ridge Trail near Ludden Peak.

The popular Bailey Range Traverse (see Appendix 1) begins where the trail ends, but it should not be attempted by the hiker who is inexperienced at cross-country travel.

Hoh Valley from the Bailey Range

APPENDIX 1

BEYOND THE TRAILS: CROSS-COUNTRY TRAVEL

The network of trails in the Olympic Mountains, just a bit shy of 900 miles in combined length, makes it possible for hikers and backpackers to experience firsthand almost every variety of terrain, topography, vegetation, and wildlife that occurs in these mountains—from the swift rivers and big trees of the lowlands, with their elk herds and prowling cougars, to the meadows, snowfields, and glaciers of the subalpine high country.

This book is primarily a trail guide, but in order to give hikers and backpackers a reasonable glimpse of what lies beyond the maintained paths, this appendix has been included. It describes one major cross-country route (the Bailey Range traverse), followed by a step-by-step description of the ascent of Mount Olympus.

Backpackers who are adept at cross-country travel and technical mountaineering can venture farther than one who is limited to maintained trails. The loftier goals now come within reach—the grand traverses and the climbs of the higher, more rugged peaks.

"Cross-country" means just that: traverses across the country without benefit of man-made trails—or, perish the thought, roads and highways. The high traverse and the climb described here offer just a brief sampling of the possibilities. Numerous other traverses, requiring equal or greater skill or stamina to negotiate, are possible, as well as climbs of peaks which vary greatly in difficulty.

Hikers, climbers, and backpackers seeking more detailed information about these activities should consult the *Climber's Guide to the Olympic Mountains*, prepared by Olympic Mountain Rescue and published by The Mountaineers. Hikers and backpackers who lack the necessary expertise to engage in these rewarding pursuits can qualify themselves by attending classes in alpine travel and basic mountaineering taught by The Mountaineers or by other outdoor clubs in the Pacific Northwest.

BAILEY RANGE TRAVERSE
(NATIONAL PARK ROUTE)

Length 15.0 mi/24.1 km

Access North—High Divide–Bailey Range Trail via Soleduck Trail or Cat
Creek Way Trail
South—Elwha Trail and Dodwell-Rixon Pass
East—Elwha Trail; Long Ridge Trail
West—Mount Olympus traverse (ropes required)
USGS Maps Mount Carrie; Hurricane Hill; Mount Queets; Mount Olympus

The Bailey Range Traverse, in the heart of the national park, is perhaps
the finest high-country route in the Olympics. Although the range is remote, the
number of persons making the trek has increased greatly in recent years. This has
been due in part to the showing on television of motion pictures about the Bailey
Range.

The route begins at the end of the **High Divide–Bailey Range Trail**, where a
steep path climbs the side of Cat Peak to the western end of The Catwalk (0.1 mi/
0.2 km; 5300 ft/1615 m). This narrow spine of broken rock is overgrown with contorted subalpine trees that have been gnarled and twisted by the prevailing winds.
High on both ends, with its low point in the middle, the arête widens somewhat at
Boston Charlie's Camp (0.4 mi/0.6 km; 5200 ft/1585 m). Here, at the Mount
Carrie end, the backpacker may rest after struggling over the sharp, angular rocks
and squeezing through the thick-branched trees. The camp, supposedly named for
an early-day mountain man, is a level place beside a pool of stagnant water and,
early in the season, a snowbank. The flat spots may be utilized as tent sites, but
most people prefer to camp on the meadows ahead, where water may or may not
be available.

Beyond Boston Charlie's Camp, the way trail climbs steeply, then breaks out
into the grassy meadows on the flanks of Mount Carrie, where wildflowers bloom
profusely. The rare white lupine is one of the plants found here.

At this point the path divides (0.6 mi/1.0 km; 5500 ft/1676 m). A crude way
trail to Mount Carrie goes up; another primitive path contours along the side of
the Bailey Range. (Neither trail existed until the late 1970s, when the Bailey Range
Traverse became popular. As more and more people made the trek, they created way
paths of sorts along various parts of the range.)

One can leave the traverse at this point and follow the upper trail to the peak.
The ascent requires about an hour, the rough path leading almost to the top (1.6
mi/2.6 km; 6995 ft/2132 m). Mount Carrie's upper slopes consist of snowfields,
shale slides, and bands of broken, razor-sharp slate set on edge and streaked with
veins of quartz. The vista from this peak is remarkable. One can see, in a single,
sweeping glance, the U-shaped Hoh Valley from Mount Olympus to the national
park boundary. The valley is clothed with primeval forest as far as the eye can see.
On the level bottomlands the river's channels look like braided strands of molten
silver. No sign of civilization is visible in the rain forest below. The panorama also
includes the Hoh Canyon, nearly enclosed by the Bailey Range and Mount

A climber takes a break on the way to the summit

Olympus. The Carrie Glacier is close at hand; in the distance one can see the Bear Pass icefields and a number of snow-clad peaks.

Beyond the fork in the trail, the traverse route follows a way path along the side of Mount Carrie at approximately the 5500-ft/1676-m level to Eleven Bull Basin (ca. 5.0 mi/8.0 km; 5000 ft/1524 m) west of Stephen Peak. This is the most difficult part of the traverse—the slope is steep, and one must use care because the footing is precarious. At Eleven Bull Basin the hiker has a choice: keep low beneath Stephen Peak, more or less contouring to Cream Lake, or climb up and over the peak (perhaps descending to Stephen Lake to camp). Cream Lake is located at the lower end of Ferry Basin, and the terrain now becomes much easier to negotiate. The route climbs up through the basin past Lake Billy Everett (ca. 8.0 mi/12.9 km; 4800 ft/1463 m) to the stagnant glacier between Mount Ferry and Mount Pulitzer. Except when the fog rolls in, making routefinding difficult, the way beyond this point is obvious—almost due south, along the top of the range, crossing the east shoulder of Mount Pulitzer to Pulitzer Pass (ca. 10.5 mi/16.9 km; 5600 ft/1707 m). Here a lone tree, all its limbs pointing to the leeward, marks the pass. This is a good place to camp, despite the wind, because it is level and water is available.

Beyond Pulitzer Pass the route follows the crest of the range, skirting Mount Childs, then topping Bear Mountain (ca. 13.5 mi/21.7 km; 5819 ft/ 1774 m) near Bear Pass. The way then descends heather slopes to Dodwell-Rixon Pass, where the traverse ends (ca. 15.0 mi/24.1 km; 4750 ft/1448 m). One can exit by traveling down the Elwha Snowfinger to the Elwha Basin and the **Elwha Trail**—or, for more exciting adventure, descend into Queets Basin, then cross the glaciers of Mount Olympus to the **Hoh Trail** at Glacier Meadows. No one should attempt the last route except persons who are not only properly equipped with ropes and ice axes but also have the knowledge of how to use them correctly.

The attractions of the Bailey Range are varied, and they lure and seduce the dedicated backpacker. The mountains are quiet and peaceful, the stillness broken infrequently by the wind, the whistles of marmots, or the barking of coyotes. At times the peaks are awash in brilliant sunshine; more often, however, fog drifts across the ridges to create eerie patterns among the peaks and crags. Rock, snow, and ice dominate near the crest, but lower down the meadows shelter cold, blue lakes and brooks that flow from sun-cupped snowfields. Bees buzz in the heather, hawks soar overhead, and elk and bear roam the upland.

This is the backbone of the wilderness Olympics, where from high vantage points the mountains appear to circle upon themselves, ridges and canyons extending for miles in every direction.

ASCENT OF MOUNT OLYMPUS (NATIONAL PARK ROUTE)

Length 3.5 mi/5.6 km
Approach Hoh Trail
Length of Approach 17.0 mi/27.4 km

Because it was named Mount Olympus by a mariner who spotted it while sailing along the western coast of North America in 1788, the highest peak on the Olympic Peninsula has become the legendary home of the New World's gods, the lodestone or Rome to which all trails on the peninsula lead, the ultimate goal

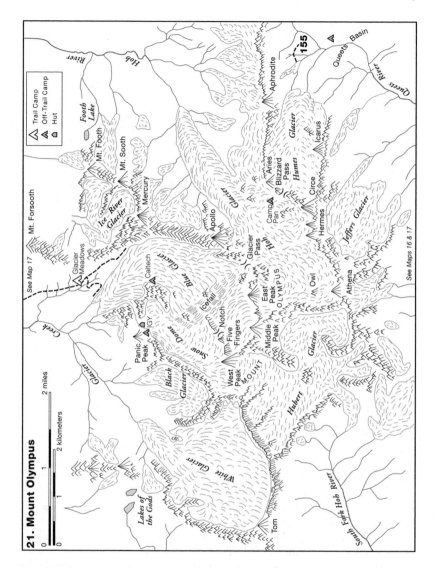

21. Mount Olympus

of the mountaineer. When considered in this sense, Olympus becomes not only the focal point on the peninsula but also a symbol of high mountains everywhere. Not everyone who attempts the climb is successful, with the weather generally the deciding factor.

Unlike most high peaks on the peninsula, Olympus is largely devoid of meadowland—where the forest ends, the ice begins. Excluding the mountains in Alaska, Olympus is exceeded in the extent of its glaciers by only two peaks in the United States—Mount Rainier and Mount Baker, both in the Cascade Range. The largest glaciers are the Hoh, White, and Blue. The latter was named in 1912 by Edward

Allen. Accompanied by Charles M. Farrer and Earl Rice, he scouted the north side of Olympus to determine the suitability of routing the 1913 summer outing of The Mountaineers via the Hoh River. The men viewed the glacier from the ridge north of Mount Tom.

Hikers and backpackers should bear in mind that the ascent of Olympus is a climb, not a hike, despite the fact that much of the route to the top involves walking. But walking on slippery glacial ice and packed snow (usually frozen icy hard in the morning) is a far cry from simply strolling up a mountain path. No one who has not been properly trained and equipped should attempt to scale the peak, deceptively easy though the climb appears to be.

One feature that climbers sometimes find dismaying: In order to get near enough to the mountain to climb it, one must first backpack 17 miles via the Hoh Trail to Glacier Meadows. Most climbers take two days to negotiate the 17 miles. The first day they backpack 9 miles from the Hoh Ranger Station to Olympus Shelter, at the foot of the mountain. The second day they travel to Glacier Meadows. The first day's 9 miles are almost level; the second day's 8 miles are mostly uphill.

Upon arriving at Glacier Meadows, climbers can camp at the meadows and go to bed with the sun, then rise at the ghastly hour of 3:00 A.M. to begin the ascent. If they are awake at sunrise and/or sunset (some have been known to get in their clothes and climbing gear while half asleep), they can enjoy viewing the mountain bathed in alpenglow. They also have another option: If they have the necessary stamina, they can backpack on the second day all the way to Caltech Moraine, across the Blue Glacier. This puts them in a position to attain the summit at an early hour, but more than one climbing party has elected to abort the climb and really sleep late the next morning.

The purpose in starting early is to gain the summit before clouds close about the peaks in the afternoon. During good weather the climb is not difficult, but it is hazardous, especially when the crags are shrouded in fog and routefinding becomes a nightmare. The mountain is deceptive, the glaciers heavily crevassed. On a hot, clear day, the snowfields are like an oven, but when the weather is stormy, the climber—bundled in several layers of warm clothing—has to contend with the elements. The climb may start in fair weather, under blue skies, with the summit attained in wind, rain, fog, sleet, or snow—and no view other than perhaps a brief glimpse through the clouds. But on clear days the scene is glorious.

At the glacier's edge the climbers rope up while admiring the alpenglow on the upper slopes. The snow is hard and firm, but softens rapidly under the warm sunlight. The glacier's appearance varies from one year to the next, depending on the amount of winter snowfall and summer warmth. By August the lower part is normally free of snow, and the ice revealed—dense, crystalline, deep blue, glowing intensely in the depths of the crevasses. The cold air chills the climbers, making warm clothing a necessity, but now and then warm air from the valley sweeps across the ice.

The glacier, broken by crescentic crevasses, has a gentle grade, and the climbers progress rapidly to Caltech Moraine, located at the base of the Snow Dome. Here they apply sunburn cream and put on dark glasses. Parties planning to ascend the various peaks in this area often camp on the moraine, thus avoiding the trek up

Looking down the Snow Dome

and down the glacier each day. This site, used by the California Institute of Technology as a base camp when studying the glacier, has a splendid view, plenty of running water, and is free of insects. However, the camp is usually not clear of snow until mid-July, sometimes later.

The climb steepens at this point, but rock outcrops provide roosts along the way where one can rest while gazing at the icefall, and perhaps observing an avalanche. This wall of jumbled ice blocks is a thousand feet high and a mile wide, extending from the Snow Dome to Glacier Pass. The peaks of Olympus rise above the cirque at its head.

The route then makes a steep ascent of the Snow Dome, and the panorama of the Olympics widens with each upward step. The dome is a mile long by a half mile wide, and when outlined against the blue sky it is immaculate. The configuration is believed to be due to the underlying rock structure and sculpturing by the wind. On the rocks at the dome's north end, slightly away from the climbing route, stands a hut used by scientists during the International Geophysical Year (IGY) in 1957–58. Not intended to be permanent, it was supposed to have been removed at the conclusion of the studies, eighteen months later, thus leaving the mountain unmarred by man-made structures. However, the research has been extended year after year, and it now appears unlikely that this intrusion on the wilderness will ever be removed. A climbers' high camp is located north of the cabin, at the base of Panic Peak, the rock mass that overlooks the Black Glacier.

Beyond the Snow Dome's crest (6850 ft/2088 m), the route zigzags to avoid crevasses and ascends to a notch (7200 ft/2195 m) in the ridge leading down from West Peak. Here a bergschrund sometimes makes the approach difficult. This break in the snow varies from year to year and may range from 10 to 30 feet in width, more than 100 feet deep. Usually, however, it can be crossed via a snow bridge.

The route now goes across the upper cirque above the icefall. East Peak and Middle Peak are straight ahead; beyond them, countless snow peaks on the horizon, with Mount Rainier shining above the distant haze. Middle Peak can be ascended from this point by crossing the cirque to the peak's west side and climbing directly to the summit. The route to West Peak swings right beneath Five Fingers Peak (7880 ft/2402 m). One can scramble to the top of this false summit, where the view is splendid, but the scene to the west is blocked by West Peak, a wedgelike mass of rock rising above the highest snowfield. The route goes left, avoiding the false summit, and traverses ledges of rotten rock to Crevasse Pass, the notch between the two peaks. A steep snow slope, the loftiest in the Olympics, leads to a ledge on the side of West Peak, or one can rock climb directly from Crevasse Pass. The route follows the ledge across the east face to a vertical chimney in a wall about 15 feet high. This is the last obstacle. After climbing this wall, one follows a knife-edge ridge of broken rock to the summit, the highest point on the Olympic Peninsula (7980 ft/2431 m).

Here the climber finds himself in the midst of a sweeping, 360-degree view of the Olympic Mountains. Hundreds of peaks and ridges, streaked with snow, encircle this vantage point. Many have razor-edged crests, others are rounded, but all are splotched with snowfields or glaciers. The lower slopes are heavily timbered. Canyons and valleys, often filled with fog, wind away in all directions through the tangle of peaks. One looks out over unspoiled wilderness—with the sole exception of the IGY hut, no houses, roads, or other signs of civilization are visible.

The slopes of West Peak fall away vertically on every side: north to the Snow Dome, west to the White Glacier, south to the Hubert Glacier, and east down the route just ascended to Crevasse Pass. Across the broad upper cirque tower East Peak and Middle Peak; beyond them are the Cascades, topped by Mount Rainier and Mount Baker; across the South Fork of the Hoh, the Valhallas are prominent, then the Mount Olympus Range dwindles into forested foothills; on the far side of the White Glacier the bulk of Mount Tom is outlined against timbered ridges that stretch endlessly toward the Pacific—a band of misty blue. This is, in fact, one of the few points where one can stand and see both the ocean and Mount Rainier.

Having arrived at the top of this pinnacle, the alpinist should relax and spend some time, not only to savor the view but also to let the imagination have free rein, recalling that this was the sacred abode of an Indian god, the Thunderbird, a realm where no warrior dared to go. The climber can also picture the seafarers who sailed along this coast two hundred years ago, or—more recently—the joy of the climbers from The Mountaineers who made the first ascent in 1907. Looking at the splendor all around, one can appreciate why that crusty old mariner, John Meares, named the peak Olympus because he deemed it a worthy home for the New World's gods.

The descent to Glacier Meadows takes perhaps half as long as the climb. After carefully climbing down West Peak, which is no place to foozle, one can indulge in

The final snow slope leading to the crest of Mount Olympus

a brief but swift glissade on the snow to Crevasse Pass. This is followed by a much longer one down the Snow Dome to Blue Glacier. But progress is slow on the glacier, where the snow becomes soft during the hot afternoon. Here the sun creates rivulets that flow over the ice in constantly changing patterns, and deep within the glacier unseen streams roar ominously. Many hollows, pools, and crevasses reflect brilliant shades of blue, as do the moulins, vertical "wells" which extend to great depths. Millions of tiny ice worms, looking like inch-long snippets of black thread, wriggle on the snow. After heavy rains, short-lived glacial fountains sometimes appear, playing like miniature geysers.

The East Peak (7780 ft/2371 m) is climbed by using the same approach to the glacier, but instead of ascending the Snow Dome the climbers go directly to Glacier Pass (6100 ft/1859 m), the U-shaped notch between the Blue Glacier and the Hoh Glacier. The route then traverses beneath an icewall on East Peak, where climbers should move rapidly because the ice may avalanche. Better yet, they should descend 600 feet onto the Hoh Glacier to avoid the hazard. The route then ascends the steep slopes of the glacier. East Peak was first climbed in 1899 by Jack McGlone, a member of the Dodwell-Rixon survey party.

Bob Wood's camera captures climbers atop West Peak of Mount Olympus, the highest point on the Olympic Peninsula, August 4, 1955.

Because it is located between the other two, Middle Peak (7930 ft/2417 m) can be climbed by either route. The west side is a rock climb; the eastern approach is via steep snow almost to the summit. The first ascent of Middle Peak occurred in 1907, when members of the Explorers Club and their guides climbed it by way of the Queets Basin.

West Peak is the goal of every climber who visits the mountain, principally because it is the highest point. However, the supreme Olympic experience is not the climb itself but spending a night on Five Fingers Peak, the flat-topped crag adjacent to West Peak. The climber who sets up camp on this platform at midday need not melt snow for water; while the sun is still high, enough water for cooking and drinking can be collected from the dripping snowbanks along the edges of the level area.

As the evening progresses, the changing vistas are incredibly beautiful. When the sun disappears over the Pacific, the alpenglow is striking. The snowy peaks change quickly from white to rosy pink, then red, and finally lavender and purple as the shadows creep up from the deep canyons. With the coming of darkness the stars appear, the lights of Victoria, B.C., flicker faintly, and one can see the beacon lights along the coast. The nights are usually not cold during July and August, but they are inclined to be a little windy. Occasionally a cold breeze blows from the north all night, and the snow is frozen hard in the morning. The day breaks bright, clear, and cold, with fog in the low valleys, clouds in the distance.

APPENDIX 2

AGENCY CONTACT INFORMATION

Wilderness Information Center (WIC)
3002 Mount Angeles Road
Port Angeles, WA 98362
(360) 565-3100
www.nps.gov/olym/wic

Olympic National Park
600 East Park Avenue
Port Angeles, WA 98362-6798
(360) 565-3130 (visitor information)
(360) 565-3131 (recorded visitor
information)
(800) 833-6388 (visitor information:
TTY)
(360) 565-3015 (fax)
www.nps.gov/olym

Web cams
The park offers views of Lake
Crescent and Hurricane Ridge (plus
weather statistics), as well as links to
other cameras in the area:
www.nps.gov/olym/cams/index.htm

Department of Natural Resources
1111 Washington Street SE
P.O. Box 47000
Olympia, WA 98504
(360) 902-1000
(360) 902-1125 (TYY)
www.dnr.wa.gov

Olympic National Forest Headquarters
1835 Black Lake Boulevard SW
Olympia, WA 98512-5623
(360) 956-2402
(360) 956-2401 (TDD)
www.fs.fed.us.r6/olympic

Hood Canal Ranger District
295142 Highway 101 S.
P.O. Box 280
Quilcene, WA 98376
(360) 765-2200
(360) 765-2200 (TDD)

Pacific Ranger District
North Office
437 Tillicum Lane
Forks, WA 98331
(360) 374-6522
(360) 374-6522 (TDD)

South Office
353 South Shore Road
P.O. Box 9
Quinault, WA 98575
(360) 288-2525
(360) 288-2525 (TDD)

Note: The former Hoodsport office is
now a Shelton/Mason County
Chamber of Commerce visitor's
center, staffed by volunteers. Some
park and forest materials are available
here. Northwest Forest Pass parking
permits can be purchased here.

APPENDIX 3

REGULATIONS

Fees: Olympic National Park has entrance fees, which are valid for seven days or by annual pass. Other 12-month passes available are a National Parks Pass, Golden Eagle Passport, Washington and Oregon Recreation Pass, and a Golden Age Passport for permanent U.S. residents age 62 and older. Wilderness camping permits are required for overnight wilderness camping within Olympic National Park and can be obtained at the Wilderness Information Center (WIC) in Port Angeles, the Quinault WIC (South Shore Lake Quinault USFS Ranger Station) or the Forks WIC in Forks, WA. A Frequent Hiker Pass is available that covers wilderness fees for 1 year from date of purchase. There are also daily or annual Olympic National Forest trailhead parking permit fees at selected trailheads within the forest. For a list of trailheads where permits are required (numbering 20 in 2005), visit the ONF website, click on "Passes and Permits," then click on "Trailheads Needing Pass."

Volunteer Passes: In Pacific Northwest national forests, a pass can be earned by contributing to a work project on national forest land. Participating on one work party earns a free one-day Northwest Forest Pass. Participating on two work projects earns a second one-day pass. Two one-day volunteer passes can be redeemed for a 12-month volunteer pass. The passes cover parking on National Forest Service land only. The Washington Trails Association is one of several groups that coordinate volunteer trail-maintenance projects within the state. Contact information for the WTA: (206) 625-1367, www.wta.org. The volunteer program at Olympic National Park was undergoing revision at the time of this book's printing. For the latest information on opportunities and recognition, contact the Park's volunteer coordinator at (360) 565-3141.

Food Storage Regulations: Olympic National Park is home to an active black bear population, and secure food storage is a topic of elevated interest among the park's wilderness rangers. Olympic's black bears are not as notorious as the marauding bruins of California's central Sierra, and by promoting conscientious food storage within Olympic National Park, rangers hope to keep it that way. Their goal is to keep bears gathering food in natural bear fashion rather than pilfering available human food. Doing so reduces the chances of food-induced bear-human conflict.

So be aware: For overnight backcountry trips, the park requires that all food, garbage, and scented items (including toothpaste, deodorant, sunscreen, lip balm, and toiletries) must be either 1) stored in animal-resistant containers, 2) hung from park bear wires, or 3) hung at least 12 feet high and 10 feet out from the nearest tree trunk 24 hours a day.

Use of bear canisters, which typically weigh two-plus pounds when empty, is mandatory in areas without bear wire and where food cannot be hung at the prescribed height and distance. That likely could involve just about any trip that includes a high-elevation campsite (loosely defined as any site higher than 4,500 feet). Lighter, soft-sided food bags, such as the Ursack, have not been approved for use in Olympic National Park.

If you don't own a canister, the Wilderness Information Center in Port Angeles has a pretty good supply of them, from a variety of makers, available for loan. The park suggests a $3 donation for using one. Keep in mind: On busy weekends the WIC may run out of canisters. The park's Web site offers a list of area locations where canisters can be rented or purchased.

Bear wires, which use a simple pulley system to hoist food bags up to a secure height, are found in some of the park's most popular backcountry campsites. They're a wonderful creation. Claim a hook early in the day on busy weekends.

Quotas and Reservations: Within Olympic National Park, overnight quotas are in effect between May 1 and September 30 for high-use wilderness camp areas. The park does this to help minimize impact and negate overcrowding, in an effort to preserve a wilderness ambience. Reservations between these dates cannot be made more than 30 days in advance of your departure date. Permits for quota areas must be picked up at the WIC or a staffed ranger station during business hours.

Quota areas, subject to change, are Royal Basin/Royal Lake, Flapjack Lakes, Sol Duc/Seven Lakes Basin/Mink Lake area, Hoh Lake and C.B. Flats, Grand Valley, and Lake Constantine. Within quota areas, camping is permitted only in designated sites. Campsites are not individually assigned; they are available to permit-holders on a first-come, first-served basis. Deviating from a permit's itinerary within a quota area is not allowed, except in an emergency.

Permits are not available at Hurricane Ridge. Permits for Grand Valley, Badger Valley, and all Hurricane Ridge area trips must be obtained through the WIC in Port Angeles.

APPENDIX 4

SELECTED READING LIST

Danner, Wilbert R. *Geology of Olympic National Park*. Seattle: University of Washington Press, 1955.

Dodwell, Arthur, and Rixon, Theodore F. *Forest Conditions in the Olympic Forest Reserve, Washington*. Washington, D.C.: United States Geological Survey, U.S. Government Printing Office, 1902.

Fagerlund, Gunnar O. *Olympic National Park, Washington*. Washington, D.C.: National Park Service, U.S. Government Printing Office, 1954.

Kirk, Ruth. *Exploring the Olympic Peninsula*. Seattle: University of Washington Press, 1964.

Kitchin, E. A. *Birds of the Olympic Peninsula.* Port Angeles, Washington: Olympic Stationers, 1949.

Lyons, C. P. *Trees, Shrubs and Flowers to Know in Washington.* Toronto, Canada: J. M. Dent & Sons, Limited, 1956.

Newman, Coleman C. *Roosevelt Elk of Olympic National Park.* Port Angeles, Washington: Olympic Natural History Association, 1958.

Olympic Mountain Rescue Council. *Climber's Guide to the Olympic Mountains,* 3rd ed. Seattle: The Mountaineers, 1988.

Sharp, Robert P. *Glaciers.* Eugene, Oregon: University of Oregon Books, 1960.

Sharpe, Grant, and Sharpe, Wenonah. *101 Wildflowers of Olympic National Park.* Seattle: University of Washington Press, 1954.

Spring, Ira, and Fish, Byron. *Lookouts: Firewatchers of the Cascades and Olympics.* Seattle: The Mountaineers, 1981.

Stewart, Charles. *Wildflowers of the Olympics.* San Francisco: Nature Education Enterprises, 1972.

Tabor, Rowland W. *Guide to the Geology of Olympic National Park.* Seattle: University of Washington Press, 1975.

Webster, E. B. *Fishing in the Olympics.* Port Angeles, Washington: The Evening News, 1923.

———. *The Ferns of the Olympics.* Port Angeles, Washington: Smith and Webster, Inc., 1918.

———. *The Friendly Mountain,* 2nd ed. Port Angeles, Washington: The Evening News, 1921.

Whitney, Stephen R. *A Field Guide to the Cascades and Olympics.* Seattle: The Mountaineers, 1983.

Wilhelm, Eugene J., Jr. *Common Birds of Olympic National Park.* Port Angeles, Washington: Olympic Natural History Association, 1961.

Wood, Robert L. *Across the Olympic Mountains: The Press Expedition, 1889–90,* 2nd ed. Seattle: The Mountaineers, 1976.

———. *Men, Mules and Mountains: Lieutenant O'Neil's Olympic Expeditions.* Seattle: The Mountaineers, 1976.

———. *Trail Country: Olympic National Park.* Seattle: The Mountaineers, 1968.

———. *The Land That Slept Late: The Olympic Mountains in Legend and History.* Seattle: The Mountaineers, 1995.

INDEX

TRAILS

ABOUT THE AUTHOR

Photo by Peter L. Hemp

Robert L. Wood first saw the Olympics in 1946. Since then, he spent literally thousands of days exploring them, hiking the valleys, climbing the peaks, probing the wilderness. When weather forced him down from the hills, he turned to researching the history of the Olympics. He became their literary explorer by writing books such as *Across the Olympic Mountains: The Press Expedition, 1889–90*; *Men, Mules and Mountains: Lieutenant O'Neil's Olympic Expeditions*; *Trail Country: Olympic National Park*, and *The Land That Slept Late: The Olympic Mountains in Legend and History*.

THE MOUNTAINEERS, founded in 1906, is a nonprofit outdoor activity and conservation club, whose mission is "to explore, study, preserve, and enjoy the natural beauty of the outdoors. . . . " Based in Seattle, Washington, the club is now the third-largest such organization in the United States, with 14,000 members and seven branches throughout Washington State.

The Mountaineers sponsors both classes and year-round outdoor activities in the Pacific Northwest, which include hiking, mountain climbing, ski-touring, snowshoeing, bicycling, camping, kayaking and canoeing, nature study, sailing, and adventure travel. The club's conservation division supports environmental causes through educational activities, sponsoring legislation, and presenting informational programs. All club activities are led by skilled, experienced volunteers, who are dedicated to promoting safe and responsible enjoyment and preservation of the outdoors.

If you would like to participate in these organized outdoor activities or the club's programs, consider a membership in The Mountaineers. For information and an application, write or call The Mountaineers, Club Headquarters, 300 Third Avenue West, Seattle, Washington 98119; (206) 284-6310.

The Mountaineers Books, an active, nonprofit publishing program of the club, produces guidebooks, instructional texts, historical works, natural history guides, and works on environmental conservation. All books produced by The Mountaineers are aimed at fulfilling the club's mission.

Send or call for our catalog of more than 450 outdoor titles

The Mountaineers Books
1001 SW Klickitat Way, Suite 201
Seattle, WA 98134
800-553-4453
mbooks@mountaineers.org
www.mountaineersbooks.org

Other titles you may enjoy from The Mountaineers Books:

100 HIKES IN™ SERIES: Best-selling guidebooks with detailed information on every trail including access, mileage, elevation, hiking time, and the best season to go.

50 HIKES IN™ MOUNT RAINIER NATIONAL PARK, 4th Edition,
Ira Spring & Harvey Manning
**100 HIKES IN™ WASHINGTON'S NORTH CASCADES NATIONAL
PARK REGION,** 3rd Edition, Ira Spring & Harvey Manning
100 HIKES IN™ WASHINGTON'S ALPINE LAKES, 3rd Edition,
Vicky Spring, Ira Spring & Harvey Manning
100 HIKES IN™ WASHINGTON'S SOUTH CASCADES & OLYMPICS,
3rd Edition, Ira Spring & Harvey Manning

**100 CLASSIC BACKCOUNTRY SKI AND SNOWBOARD ROUTES
IN WASHINGTON, Rainer Burgdorfer**
The best, most challenging descents in Washington. Descriptions include access, starting elevation and high point, tour length and time, skill level required, best times to go and permit information.

**EXPLORING WASHINGTON'S WILD AREAS: A Guide for Hikers, Back-
packers, Climbers, X-C Skiers & Paddlers,** 2nd Edition, Marge & Ted Mueller
A guide to the undisturbed trails of Washington's federally preserved backcountry, featuring 55 wildernesses and roadless areas and over 1000 mapped trails.

BACKPACKER'S EVERYDAY WISDOM: 1001 Expert Tips for Hikers,
Karen Berger
Expert tips and tricks for hikers and backpackers selected from one of the most popular *BACKPACKER* magazine columns. Problem-solving techniques and brilliant improvisations show hikers how to make their way, and make do in the backcountry.

**WILDERNESS NAVIGATION: Finding Your Way Using Map, Compass,
Altimeter & GPS,** 2nd Edition, Bob Burns & Mike Burns
Backed by more than 60 years of field research, it includes the most reliable and easy-to-learn methods of navigation yet devised.

**CONDITIONING FOR OUTDOOR FITNESS: A Comprehensive
Training Guide,** 2nd Edition, David Musnick, M.D. & Mark Pierce, A.T.C.
The most comprehensive guide to conditioning, fitness, and training for all outdoor activities, written by a team of sports fitness experts. Offers "whole body" training programs for hiking, biking, skiing, climbing, paddling, and more.

100 CLASSIC HIKES IN™ WASHINGTON, Ira Spring & Harvey Manning
A full-color guide to Washington's finest trails by the respected authors of more than thirty Washington guides, written with a conservation ethic and a sense of humor, and featuring the best hikes in the state.